# WINNING
# OFFICE
# POLITICS

## DuBRIN'S GUIDE
## FOR THE '90s

Andrew J. DuBrin

**PRENTICE HALL**
Englewood Cliffs, New Jersey 07632

Prentice-Hall International (UK) Limited, *London*
Prentice-Hall of Australia Pty. Limited, *Sydney*
Prentice-Hall Canada, Inc., *Toronto*
Prentice-Hall Hispanoamericana, S.A., *Mexico*
Prentice-Hall of India Private Limited, *New Delhi*
Prentice-Hall of Japan, Inc., *Tokyo*
Simon & Schuster Asia Pte. Ltd., *Singapore*
Editora Prentice-Hall do Brasil, Ltda., *Rio de Janeiro*

© 1990 by

PRENTICE-HALL, Inc.

Englewood Cliffs, NJ

10 9 8 7 6 5 4 3

**Library of Congress Cataloging-in-Publication Data**

DuBrin, Andrew J.
  Winning office politics: DuBrin's guide for the '90s / by
Andrew J. DuBrin.

    p.  cm.
  Includes bibliographical references.
  ISBN 0-13-964958-1
  1. Office politics.   2. Success.   3. Organizational behavior.
I. Title.
HF5386.5.D83   1990                                    90-7274
650.1—dc20                                             CIP

ISBN 0-13-964958-1

**PRENTICE HALL**
**Englewood Cliffs, New Jersey 07632**

PRINTED IN THE UNITED STATES OF AMERICA

To Carol, the Total Woman

# INTRODUCTION

Office politics have been out of the closet for over a decade. A number of writers about general interest business topics—including myself—have been exposing the previously hush-hush tactics people use to gain advantage in all areas of work. The topic of gaining power on the job is now included in most textbooks about human behavior on the job. Furthermore, a number of leading business schools, including Cornell and Harvard, offer courses in power and politics.

*Winning Office Politics: DuBrin's Guide for the '90s* is an extensive updating and expansion of my 1978 book which has been read by an estimated one-half million people, and continues to serve as manual for job success. The book has also been used as supplementary reading in many business courses. A new *Winning Office Politics* has been made necessary by several realities. One is that much more knowledge has accumulated about organizational politics. The 1990s career person needs an updated kit of political tactics to compete effectively on the job.

Not only are office politics tougher today, but the stakes are at their highest. In an era of corporate takeovers, downsizings, restructurings, and shakeouts, deft use of political tactics is needed for survival. A related problem is that too many baby boomers in the 1990s are vying for a limited number of positions in both private and public organizations. At the same time, the number of middle management positions has been substantially reduced by most employers. Companies are trimming down to reduce costs incurred in takeovers and also to compete successfully in a global marketplace.

To ignore office politics is to ignore those underlying forces that account for the differences in success between equally talented people. People who understand and use office politics to their advantage are much more likely to succeed than their politically naive counterparts. Because more people than ever are at least aware of office politics, to gain a competitive edge you need more political skill and knowledge than previously.

Despite the increasing awareness of political forces in the workplace, most books about management still concentrate on what *should* be done rather than what *is* done on the job. A recently published handbook of management contains over 2300 pages of documented facts and expert opinion. Yet a person who applies only those ideas, techniques, and strategies to his or her job probably never will receive more than one promotion. Unless you practice some form of sensible office politics, you are doomed to a lifelong purgatory of entry-level assignments. As a 55-year old office mail room clerk said when he was forced into early retirement (because the personnel department spotted that he was overpaid for the job): "I can proudly say I never played politics one day in my career."

At one time it was thought that office politics were played primarily by middle managers in business who were attempting to climb the ladder, and executives who were either still climbing or trying to hold on to their positions. We know now that people at all job levels, in both private and public organizations, use politics to gain competitive advantage or just survive. *Winning Office Politics* is a modern unisex guide for practicing sensible and ethical politics at every job level—no matter what the organization.

Although the art and practice of office politics have become somewhat public, it is still a topic surrounded by secrecy and denial. Many executives still insist that most decisions about people in their organizations are based on merit, and that decisions about money, material, and equipment are based on objective facts (rather than attempts to please certain people). When interviewed for this book, many executives contended that "very little office politics takes place in our company." Yet virtually every person at lower levels in the organization could point to instances of political favoritism.

The reader might be concerned about following the suggestions and advice in this book because other people, including your boss, might be privy to the same information. You might be thinking, "If others know what I'm up to, my methods won't work." Such concerns are ill-founded for three important reasons: First, if other people read this or similar information, you will need to be knowledgeable about office politics as a defensive tactic. Being naive will merely place you at a severe disadvantage. Second, only a few people who read valid information about self-improvement or career management actually apply the information. They either think the information is not really helpful or they are too lazy to change their habits. (About one-fourth of the U.S. and Canadian population still smoke cigarettes despite all the information about its negative consequences.) Third, even if one-half million people buy this book (a fantasy I share with my publisher) and another one-half million people borrow and read their copies, less than one percent of the workforce will have read this book. Why not join the ranks of that small minority who win at office politics rather than become its victim?

*Andrew J. DuBrin*
*Rochester, New York*

# ACKNOWLEDGMENTS

The many hundreds of employed (or formerly employed) adults I have spoken to directly, or have been interviewed by my students and research assistants, receive my primary thanks on this project. Many of these students who are career people themselves have provided me insights about the machinations taking place within their companies. Those younger and less job experienced have been particularly helpful in exposing the operation of office politics at the bottom of organizations.

A large number of managerial and professional people receive my gratitude for their indirect contribution to this project. These are the people I have unobtrusively observed practicing either ethical or unethical politics. Included in this group are several individuals who used political tricks to disparage or discredit me. The small number of people who have used positive political tactics to gain my approval also receive my thanks.

Because of the comprehensive nature of this book, some of my ideas are borrowed from other writers and researchers, many of whom are included in the references. It would be impossible to accurately trace the origin of every nonoriginal idea contained in the following pages. Many strategies and tactics are hundreds—if not thousands—of years old.

The media people and researchers who have welcomed my commentary on organizational politics also receive my accolades because they have encouraged me to keep exploring the topic of this book.

My editor, Tom Power, who responded so positively to the idea of a modern guide to office politics, deserves special appreciation. Thanks also to my three children (who are no longer children), Drew, Douglas, and Melanie for their continuing interest in my writing.

# CONTENTS

Introduction **v**

CHAPTER 1 The Inevitability of Office Politics **1**

CHAPTER 2 Measuring Your Political Tendencies **19**

CHAPTER 3 Planning Your Political Campaign **33**

CHAPTER 4 Getting the Boss on Your Side **53**

CHAPTER 5 Impressing the Higher-Ups **71**

CHAPTER 6 Gaining the Support of Co-Workers **89**

CHAPTER 7 Gaining the Support of Lower-Ranking People **109**

CHAPTER 8 Basic Power-Grabbing Tactics **123**

CHAPTER 9 Advanced Power-Grabbing Tactics **141**

CHAPTER 10 Boosting Your Career **159**

CHAPTER 11 Making Political Use of Information **181**

CHAPTER 12 Devious Political Tactics **195**

CHAPTER 13 Political Blunders **215**

CHAPTER 14 Outwitting Difficult People **233**

CHAPTER 15 Bouncing Back from Career Adversity **255**

CHAPTER 16 Surviving a Corporate Takeover **277**

**CHAPTER 17**   Defending Yourself Against Unfair Politics **295**
**CHAPTER 18**   Stemming the Tide of Office Politics **313**
                 References **323**
                 Index **331**

# CHAPTER 1

# THE INEVITABILITY OF OFFICE POLITICS

In an ideal world, everybody would receive salary increases, get promoted, and receive a fair share of desirable and undesirable assignments, and, in general, receive other goodies strictly on the basis of merit. Nobody would need to curry favor, laugh at the boss's unfunny jokes, cultivate obscure people just to obtain their cooperation, purchase stock in the company even though it's a bad investment, write notes of appreciation to an executive who might be eliminating his or her job, or send a St. Patrick's Day card to a boss named Clancy O'Leary. People would be assigned work and rewarded strictly on the basis of merit. And business decisions would be based almost entirely on such considerations as return on investment and cost-effectiveness. To be successful in business, all you would need is talent, hard work, good job performance, and a share of good breaks.

As the world is in the 1990s, and has always been constituted, you need one more vital ingredient to get your share of organizational goodies: political savvy or the ability to practice sensible and ethical office politics. To some, the term office politics connotes deceit, deception, and self-interest. In this book, office (or organizational) politics is the subtle and informal methods of gaining any type of power or advantage. Politics are played to obtain power—the ability to control people or resources, or to get others to do things you want done.

Office politics are ubiquitous. Many a low-ranking manager has joined a golf club with the hope of worming into a foursome with a key company executive, or a sales associate has purchased an expensive

1

dress in her own store in order to impress the store manager. Many an executive has scheduled a lunch with the chief executive officer of a predator company to establish a favorable climate in case of a takeover.

Office politics is omnipresent for 12 fundamental reasons.[1] Knowing these reasons will help alert you to when politicking is called for, or equally important when it is likely that others will be using political tactics to win your favor or discredit you.

## SCARCITY OF RESOURCES

Resources such as money, material, and people are limited in every organization. No matter how large and prosperous the organization, not everybody can have all the budget or subordinates he or she wants. People squabble over such resource decisions as who deserves more secretarial help, or who should receive full-time use of a personal computer. Limited resources lead people to political means to corral as many resources as they think they need or deserve. With declining resources, such as when an organization is trimming down, the in-fighting becomes more intense. As the reader may be painfully aware, many organizations of the 1990s are trimming down.

Another important way in which resources are limited is the pyramidal shape of most organizations. The scarcity of powerful positions leads to politicking to obtain these positions. At the bottom of the hierarchy are loads of relatively powerless positions. As the top of the pyramid is approached, their power is concentrated with several people at the top controlling most of the power. Even during a budget crunch, the chief executive officer (CEO) can find the money to attend a business conference held at a vacation spot. During the same budget tightening, a first-level supervisor might lack the authority to order fresh-cut flowers for the reception area.

Peggy, a computer analyst, was a near victim of the political ploys used by a manager who was fighting the battle of declining resources. The company had ordered a hiring freeze on most categories of workers. This meant that people who left the department could not be replaced. Jason, the boss, was concerned that his empire was crumbling. Rumor had it that his entire department would be merged with another within one year. Shortly after learning of this rumor, Jason received a request from Peggy for a departmental transfer which offered her a more challenging position. Jason declined her request, knowing that if Peggy left she would not be replaced, thus shrinking his department by one less person. The smaller a department, the more likely it would be engulfed by a larger department.

Jason knew that by staying with his department, Peggy might be without a job within one year. Yet his struggle to hold on to whatever human resources he had compelled him to deny Peggy's request. Peggy then launched a countermaneuver by encouraging her potential new boss to explain the problem to the vice-president of human resources. The countermaneuver worked; Peggy did receive the transfer, and Jason's department was collapsed into another within four months—an event that took place earlier than scheduled because of the suspicions aroused by Jason's attempt to hang on to Peggy.

## A COMPETITIVE WORK ENVIRONMENT

Forces in the organization that breed competitiveness also foster politicking. For instance, when a company hires a large number of ambitious people, these individuals attempt to outperform each other in order to achieve recognition and advancement. During job cutbacks employees compete for the remaining positions. Whatever reason people feel compelled to compete with one another, they often resort to office politics to improve their competitive edge.

People who would ordinarily choose not to engage in office politics may be forced to when placed in a firm with highly ambitious co-workers. Sterling, an investment banker, describes his experiences: "My parents were very genuine people. Both had worked their way up from entry-level to supervisory positions. They believed in the traditional work ethic that hard work is its own reward, and that diligence would be ultimately rewarded. During my history of part-time and temporary jobs, I had always practiced their philosophy. Keep plugging away at your job, and you will be noticed by the company. Their philosophy worked until I joined an investment banking firm shortly after receiving my MBA from Northwestern University.

"It became apparent to me one month after I was hired that I was thrown into competition with a glory-seeking crew. Everybody was looking to make megabucks. In order to do this they had to be assigned good clients by the partners in the firm. Or they had to do whatever was necessary to develop some good clients of their own. My colleagues would never miss an opportunity to impress the partners. At meetings they would sit on the edge of their chairs and nod with approval at almost anything a principal said.

"They would compete with each other to see who could stay latest at the office. Of course, they would all exit quickly as soon as the last partner left the office. The girlfriends, boyfriends, and spouses of these young investment bankers said they were lousy partners because they were so unreliable about showing up for dates or coming home.

"Another political tactic widely used in our firm was sending informational memos and electronic messages to important people. Quite often these memos and messages were nothing more than unsubstantiated gossip about supposed business developments in client firms. The intent of these communications was to impress the principals that the investment banker in question was on top of new developments.

"To develop new clients, my colleagues would gear their recreation toward activities that would lead to valuable contacts. If an investment banker heard that wealthy people jogged, he or she would rush out and purchase a pair of jogging shoes. Most of them would only spend time at bars where exchanging business cards had a remote chance of leading to a substantial new account.

"Soon I was playing the same political games as my colleagues. I felt I had to in order to survive. My earnings were quite satisfactory to me, but I was worried about becoming an unknown because everybody else was bucking so hard to get noticed."

## SUBJECTIVE PERFORMANCE STANDARDS

People often resort to job politics because they feel that the organization does not fairly judge their suitability for promotion. Similarly, when management has no objective way of differentiating effective from less effective employees, they will resort to favoritism. The adage, "It's not what you know but who you know," applies accurately to organizations that lack clear-cut standards of performance.

The story of Melissa, a public affairs coordinator at a hospital, illustrates how subjective ways of measuring job performance contribute to politicking. Her job description reads, in part, "The public affairs coordinator will foster constructive relationships with influential groups in the community. The coordinator will ensure that the appropriate agencies and individuals recognize the function of Riverview Hospital and appreciate the score of services it offers."

Melissa contends that in practice she is the linking pin between the hospital and the community. Her boss Fred, the chief hospital administrator, believes her job is to publicize the hospital so that Riverview gets its share of patients and donations. However, Fred recognizes that it is difficult to measure the extent to which Melissa is achieving the desired results.

Melissa also recognizes that it is difficult to measure her contribution to the hospital. As one antidote to her dilemma, Melissa sends a monthly activity report to Fred, which in turn can be sent to other hospital officials who care to know what the public affairs coordinator is conducting. One month's activity report included this entry:

> May 3: Had lunch with Theresa Birdwhistle, local president of the Junior League. It is apparent that the Junior League is seeking to lend their support to another worthwhile community service activity. I think we have established a climate quite favorable for Birdwhistle and her friends to seriously entertain the possibility of taking on a project of mutual benefit to both Riverview Hospital and the Junior League. Since we are currently overcommitted with volunteers, the exact nature of their contribution will have to be determined at a later date.

Melissa has found supplementary ways to cultivate her boss, recognizing that her activity report does not always speak for itself. It is difficult to translate such activities into hospital beds filled or financial donations. Asked what special things she does to foster a good working relationship with her boss, Melissa was quite specific:

> I would never do anything unprofessional or unethical to help me get along well with Fred. I have enough common sense to realize that there are limits to what I would do to get my boss on my side. My approach to pleasing my boss is not too different from my approach to pleasing people in the community served by the hospital. I try to establish a favorable climate between my boss and myself. In this way, Fred will view my work with a positive frame of mind. If your boss is neutral or negative toward you as a person, he may fail to appreciate the full extent of your contribution.

> One tactic I use is to help Fred with vexing personal problems that might spill over to the job. Through casual conversation, I learned that Fred and his wife are planning a big weekend trip to New York. Their babysitter changed her mind at the last minute about taking care of Fred's two children for the weekend. I quickly got in touch with my younger sister who said she would enjoy a weekend babysitting assignment. I then told Fred of my sister's availability. He was delighted.

> Fred and his wife had a wonderful weekend and their children were well taken care of for the time they were gone. Fred was very appreciative of my efforts. It seemed to add something to our working relationship.

> My most constructive approach to winning Fred over to my side was to appeal directly to his professional ego. As part of my regular duties, I meet with representatives of the Rotary, Lions, and Elks clubs. At one time I was introduced to the program chairperson of our downtown Rotary club. I recommended Fred as a potential luncheon speaker. The program coordinator did contact Fred, who was flattered by the opportunity to make a presentation. Fred performed admirably and was very appreciative that I had recommended him for such an honor.

Melissa's tactics are not really devious; she did what was necessary to be seen favorably when her contribution was difficult to measure. Because her job results did not speak for themselves, she was placed in the position of trying to convince her boss that she was doing a good job. A better approach for Melissa would have been to supplement her politicking by coming to an agreement with Fred as to her specific job duties. For instance, one such objective might have been to increase the number of donations to the hospital from business and industry. Her performance could then have been measured against that standard.

## UNCLEAR JOB DEFINITIONS

Closely related to subjective standards of performance is the problem of unclear job definitions. People whose jobs are not clearly defined have much more time available to get involved in office politics. Instead of following a tight work plan, they are free to poke around for ways to increase their status or engage in office gossip. Such people are referred to as "office wanderers." They flit around the office, store, factory, mill, laboratory, or hospital, schmoozing with anybody available for quasi-business interaction.

If asked why he or she spent one hour visiting other departments on a given morning, the wanderer might reply, "Part of my job is to keep informed of the pulse of the company. Unless I keep in touch with people from different departments, I will lose out on what is really happening. You lose the human touch when you stay in your office poring over reports." Such a defense is valid *if* the person's job did require understanding the pulse of the organization. However, a person with an unclear job definition is often at a loss to find constructive work to perform.

## IMITATING POWER HOLDERS

Lower-ranking employees sometimes engage in office politics because key players perched at the top of the pyramid are politicos. One such person is Les, a true survivalist. He models those behaviors and attitudes he believes will impress the power-holders in his company. Les is talented and works hard but he believes that copying certain accepted actions by the company's executives prevents him from drawing unfavorable attention to himself.

Michelle, the company recruiter for professional and technical personnel, uncovered an interesting manifestation of Les's political ploys. Part of Michelle's job was to recruit into the corporation young college-trained accountants, many of whom were targeted for Les's department. Les rejected two consecutive candidates Michelle submitted for his approval. Concerned, Michelle invited Les to lunch to discuss the situation. Before they finished the first glass of wine, Les confided to Michelle:

"You've worked very hard on behalf of my department, and I like you as an individual. So I'll be honest with you, Michelle. You are sending me the wrong type of job candidates. I have no doubt that the last two candidates you sent me could perform the job. They seemed bright enough and I am sure they can get along with people."

"Then what are your objections to them? Has it anything to do with their lifestyles? Do they have any annoying habits or mannerisms?"

"Not at all, Michelle. It's just that I want to recruit into my department the same type of people the people in power around here are seeking. The president believes that only people with MBA degrees from the top 20 business schools should be invited into our company in beginning professional jobs. One of the candidates lacked an MBA and the other came from a school in Pennsylvania that I had never heard of."

A person who meets Les for the first time might be perplexed by his appearance. Les wears expensive Italian-style suits with broad, upturned shoulders and Italian-style shoes to match, accompanied by flamboyant silk ties. Les's attire would be stunning if worn by a well-built man. Yet on roly-poly Les this high-fashion clothing is wasted. Out of curiosity, I asked Les how long he had been wearing his present style of clothing. Nondefensively, he said:

> Ever since I became the director of financial services. I don't care much for these suits myself and my wife says I look much better in more traditional suits. However, if you'll notice, every male executive in this company wears Italian- or French-styled suits. I wouldn't enter the office in an inexpensive suit. Why wear clothing that contrasts sharply to the style favored by our executive team?

Les is playing politics by imitating what he sees happening in the executive suite. He is playing it safe by attempting to recruit only those people who would have been recruited by his superiors. Instead of blindly modeling after his superiors, Les might have asked a few key executives if they had any particular hiring policies and preferences for young professionals. These executives might have welcomed a questioning of their informal policies.

Les's attempt to dress in a manner similar to his superiors was a sensible strategy, poorly implemented. He was dressing expensively, but not appropriately since the clothing did not fit his physique. A workable compromise for Les would have been to *modify* his clothing in the direction of the style worn by superiors.

## WIN–LOSE ORGANIZATIONAL PHILOSOPHY ━━━━━━━

As management writer Stephen P. Robbins observes, the more an organization's culture emphasizes a win–lose approach to giving out rewards, the more employees will engage in politicking.[2] Under a win–lose philosophy, the reward pie is fixed so that any gain one person or group achieves is at the expense of another person or group. If $20,000 in annual salary raises is to be distributed among five employees, then any employee who gets more than $4000 takes money away from one or more of the others. Such a practice results in people going out of their way to be noticed, and taking active steps to discredit others.

Jayne, one of four sales managers for an office supply company, found out that the owner intended to eliminate two of the sales manager positions in order to reduce overhead. The two displaced sales managers would be offered sales positions with the company. In effect, there would be two winners and two losers after the consolidation. Desperately not wanting to be demoted, Jayne launched her campaign strategy. She requested and received a private meeting with the owner.

Jayne's pitch was that only she among the four sales managers had truly met the company's sales objectives during the last two years. Puzzled, the boss asked for more details. Jayne explained that a major objective of the company was to open up new accounts. Although the total new business her sales group achieved was slightly lower than the other three groups, Jayne noted that it was "legitimate new business."

Jayne reasoned that the new business generated by the other three sales managers was really the culmination of potential accounts the company had been trying to cultivate for years. The accounts opened up by Jayne and her group, in contrast, were based on entirely new leads who had not already had previous discussions with representatives of the company. After investigating the merits of Jayne's arguments, the owner appointed Jayne as one of the two sales managers of the consolidated groups.

Jayne's behavior was undoubtedly self-protective, but not particularly unethical. She presented the owner a clear analysis of how her group was truly achieving the objectives desired by the company. However, should the other three sales managers learn of her political ploy, Jayne will have created several enemies. Under a win–lose situation, collecting enemies is almost inevitable.

## CRAVINGS FOR POWER

The lust for power is a normal human need, with executives craving more power than most people. To obtain this power they seek, many executives and potential executives engage in high-level office politics. Derek, a 45-year old sales manager for a tire manufacturer, has a thirst for power that expresses itself in many subtle and some not-so-subtle ways.

A visitor to his office can immediately sense Derek's almost immature desire to appear powerful and important. In a company where most managers conduct their work in shirt sleeves, Derek wears a vest and jacket even during the summer. His shirts are French-cuffed; his boots have three-inch heels. Derek's office is uniformly furnished in leather, chrome, and glass.

Derek's guests have no choice but to sit in chairs set at a level six inches lower than the two chairs Derek uses. Several photos and plaques adorn Derek's wall. One photo shows him wearing a captain's cap seated at the helm of a large speedboat; another shaking hands with the mayor of Cleveland; a third depicts him standing while his wife and two children are seated. One plaque attests to the extraordinary number of miles he has traveled on one commercial airline. Another plaque gives Derek the accolade, "Outstanding Alumnus Award," based on both his community activities and his contribution to his college alumni fund.

In the three years that Derek has been in charge of sales for his company, his total number of subordinates has grown from less than 50 to over 100. As Gloria, the personnel manager explains it, much of the growth of Derek's empire is for legitimate business reasons.

> Derek might be accused of being an empire builder, but you cannot justifiably say he is feather-bedding. The marketing and sales department is very efficient. It seems that everybody has a worthwhile function to perform. We get no complaints in the personnel department that people in Derek's area are being underutilized. It's just that Derek keeps on picking up activities and functions that perhaps should be reporting somewhere else.
>
> A case in point is the advertising department. We used to make extensive use of advertising agencies and their facilities. Now we do a good part of our advertising with in-house people. We use agencies more for special promotions and innovative campaigns. Before Derek took over, we had three people in the advertising department. We now have ten. In Derek's defense, our total expenditure for advertising is less than before we revamped our approach to advertising.

A presentation Derek made to the president and board of directors of his company further illustrates his mode of operation. Accompanied by his assistant and a neatly organized set of flip charts, Derek tried this gambit:

> Good afternoon. I wouldn't have requested a meeting unless I thought I had a plan for reorganization that would pay enormous dividends to Superior Tire. As you may know, I have been a student of organization planning for many years. The reason I have not asked the other vice-presidents to attend this meeting is that some will be personally affected by the proposed changes. Therefore, they would lack the objectivity necessary to judge my proposal. Self-interest and subjectivity can destroy any sound business proposal.
>
> Everybody in this room realizes what a problem it is to be held accountable for something over which you have too little control. How can you hold a vice-president of marketing responsible for the whims of the distribution department? My salesforce might outsell another brand of tires in a given month, but if we can't get them delivered to where they are needed, when they are needed, our good efforts are nullified. Cancellations because of late delivery are disastrous to our business.
>
> One logical way to prevent this lack of coordination between sales and distribution is for my department to control distribution. They should report to marketing. When the distribution people boggle a shipment, I want to personally lay them out on the carpet. To make our business run smoothly, they must report to me. Distribution should be working for us. As things now stand, they sometimes try to tell us how much to sell and when to sell it. Ladies and gentlemen, let's put some realism back into the tire business.

Malcom Bardwell, Chairman of the Board, was the first to speak: "Please Derek, let's hear your next proposal before we comment on the first one. We need the total picture of what you are proposing before we comment on each proposal separately." Derek then launched into the other half of his plan:

> My second proposal is again in the interests of business efficiency. Admittedly, it will increase the stature of marketing, but this is a secondary consideration. As marketing prospers, so does the entire corporation. Remember, we're in business to sell tires and related products to the public. No sales, no company.
>
> From what I gather, the deal has almost been consummated to acquire a small battery manufacturer. We have all agreed that they have a good product that could gain its share of the market and turn in a profit for Superior Tire. My analysis is that they have limped along for several years with a good product, but badly lack sales support. The tentative plan we have agreed upon is for our tire sales representatives to also sell batteries once the acquisition is complete. Because Superior will not be altering the battery company except to add sales support, let's make the logical organizational move. I propose that the new subsidiary, Atco Battery, report to the marketing division of our company.

Derek did get board approval for his first proposal. What is significant for our purposes is that Derek made a large-scale political maneuver designed to enlarge his sphere of influence. He was playing office politics at the highest level. It is precisely this drive for power that is responsible for so much of the politicking that takes place in most organizations. Derek attempted to increase his power by taking control of another important part of the business—distribution. Recognizing that only so many resources exist at his company, Derek cleverly tried to gain control of a new resource, Atco Battery.

## MACHIAVELLIAN TENDENCIES OF PEOPLE

Another fundamental reason people engage in political behavior is that they possess a desire to manipulate other people, referred to as Machiavellian tendencies. People with Machiavellian tendencies often have the ability to shape the attitudes and desires of others so that it turns out for personal advantage. We have conducted surveys which suggest that both men and women manipulate others but that men are even more manipulative.[3]

Manipulation in the sense used here refers to such things as getting people to do what you want them to do by making misleading or false promises. For example, suppose you want a vice-president to accompany you to a trade show because you want co-workers to think that you are important enough for the vice-president to accompany you on such a trip. You obtain the vice-president's consent by implying to that person that many important customers and prospective customers will be attending the show. In reality, you have no knowledge that these people will be attending the show.

Extreme Machiavellians will also do such things as setting up rivals to fail or be embarrassed. Frank, an industrial engineering manager, explains what happened to him: "My boss, Roger, was about my age and I sensed he felt competitive with me. He rarely gave me full credit for ideas that I had submitted to him. One day, he called me into his office to inform me that I had been promoted to supervisor of a small industrial engineering unit that would report to him. The mission of this group was to build a system for measuring the productivity of customer service specialists in a chain of hotels owned by the parent company. I was told that the key factor in evaluating my performance would be the creative output of our group.

"The mission sounded quite important because the new thrust of industrial engineering is to improve the productivity of service workers. Within one month after I began my assignment, it was apparent that Roger had staffed my department with the company's least innovative, and most burned out industrial engineers. It was very difficult to get them to think beyond their usual way of doing things. We tried brainstorming, but that wasn't too successful. When I presented them a creative idea to explore, the group doomed it from the outset by focusing on its flaws.

"As you would expect, my performance appraisal at the end of the year was poor. Our group had made very little progress toward developing a method to measure the productivity of customer service specialists. The group was ultimately disbanded, and I took a position in another company. My career is proceeding fine now, but Roger got what he wanted. He set me up to fail and succeeded."

Frank ultimately landed on his feet, but he would have saved himself a possible career setback by confronting the situation sooner. He should have met with the engineers in the group before accepting the assignment. Once he realized that his group lacked innovative talent, he should have requested permission to change its composition.

## EMOTIONAL INSECURITY OF PEOPLE

Being insecure and lacking self-confidence prompts many people to politick. Olaf, a middle manager in a large corporation, is worried that he is not a big enough contributor to be considered valuable. He thinks he could be squeezed out in the next company retrenchment. Olaf's reasoning is not totally unfounded. He is far from being considered a fast tracker. Instead his superiors and co-workers rate him as an average performer. He makes few major mistakes but does not come forth with creative contributions.

Olaf has had a lifelong pattern of worrying about whether he is performing well. As a youngster, while playing Little League baseball, he would often glance at the coach for a sign of approval that he had made the right play. In college, Olaf frequently asked his professors if he might submit a preliminary draft of a paper to determine if he understood the assignment correctly.

As manager of spare parts, Olaf looks for opportunities to gain approval from as many higher-ranking managers as he can. His most irksome ploy is to ask persons, "What did you think of my report? Was it the information that you needed?"

Olaf's job insecurities are best revealed through his use of body language in his contacts with his boss and higher-ranking managers. During a staff meeting, Olaf nods approval and smiles whenever his boss speaks. To Olaf, the boss is always right. A co-worker commented that Olaf would nod more vigorously and smile wider in proportion to the importance and power of the person speaking. In contrast, he usually remained expressionless when a peer or lower-ranking employee spoke.

Olaf's immediate boss, soon annoyed with his insincere smiles and nods, asked Olaf why he nodded with approval at almost everything a manager said. Olaf's smile converted to a worrisome expression. He explained, "I don't think I give approval to everything. But it certainly is a good policy to agree with management. If your own subordinates don't agree with you, who will? I'm here to back you up, not tear you down. And one way I can prove that is by showing my appreciation for your words of wisdom. When you or your manager says something that I think is unsound, you'll hear from me. Do you understand my reasoning?"

In truth, Olaf never would express disagreement with a boss. He is too insecure to be anything but a yes-person. Olaf's form of office politics has become almost a reflex action. When he spots a person of higher rank, his brain sends a message to his body to express approval. Until Olaf becomes a more confident person, he will probably continue to practice his naive form of office politics.

In the long-run, his attempts at ingratiation will be self-defeating. His unwillingness to approve co-workers' ideas is in sharp contrast to his approval of the words of those above him. Because of this Janus-like tactic, Olaf is on the way to losing the support of his co-workers—a fatal mistake in any team effort.

## BELIEF IN EXTERNAL FORCES

Another way of being insecure is to believe that one's fate is in the hand of external forces. People who have such an "external locus of control" do not think that they have the major control over their own destiny. Consciously or unconsciously such individuals reason that because their own talent and reputation cannot get them far, they must get others to champion their cause. (To some extent these people are right; talent and hard work are not sufficient for success. Yet people with an external locus of control believe too little in their own capabilities.)

People with an external locus of control are the first to blame politics for their personal failures. To protect themselves against future failures, they are likely to engage in politicking to the point of appearing insincere. Sandra, a store manager, was blatantly political in her dealings with higher management. When a regional manager visited the store Sandra would rush to open doors for them, or set a revolving door in motion. Also, she readily agreed with any criticism a regional manager made of her store, and smiled incessantly during their visits.

When asked by a sales associate in the store why she fawned over the regional manager, Sandra replied: "You don't fool around with power. A regional manager is the person who decides whether or not a store manager is doing a good job."

Sandra was certainly not wrong in behaving politically toward the regional manager. However, she underestimated the contribution of the store's performance in determining whether or not she would be perceived as doing a good job. She thus placed too much faith in external forces rather than her internally controlled performance as a store manager.

## HUNGER FOR ACCEPTANCE

The simple desire to be accepted by others is a major motive behind some instances of political maneuvering. Tom is a case in point. In his early years, Tom was a mediocre person with few friends and admirers. Intuitively, he recognized that he was never going to be accepted for his business accomplishments. Tom needed other ways of being appreciated and accepted.

How he chose to gain acceptance is evident at the office. Over a 12-year time span, Tom has worked his way up from office messenger to supervisor of central duplicating. A machine operator in Tom's department calls him the Candy Man. She explains:

> I don't know who gave Tom this nickname, but it fits. The guy is lovable. Who can refuse a Candy Man, especially when his candy is free? Every Friday afternoon Tom comes back from lunch with bags of candy. He keeps some on his desk, just lying there for freeloaders. He also flits around to all the desks in our department and hands out candy. Even if you half ignore the guy, you're likely to wind up with a piece of candy on your desk.

> Randy, one of the two supervisors reporting to Tom, calls him the Yankee Clipper. I asked Randy why somebody would call a person in charge of the duplicating department the same name as that given to Joe DiMaggio, an all-time great baseball player. Randy replied, "It's kind of a nice little joke. A Yankee is supposed to be frugal. A clipper could be someone who clips things. Well, Tom clips coupons to save money. He doesn't cash in these coupons himself. Instead, he provides this coupon-clipping service for others in the office who are interested in cashing these coupons. The people who use these coupons think Tom is very kind. By rotating the most valuable coupons among different women, Tom avoids being accused of favoritism."

> The name Yankee Clipper has another important connotation in reference to Tom. He also clips magazine and newspaper articles that he thinks might be of interest to key people in the company. I suppose it's kind of a valuable service. Assume Tom learns that our company is thinking of opening a

branch in Dusseldorf, West Germany. The executive in charge of the project will soon find in his office mail—neatly mounted on a sheet of paper—several timely articles about West Germany. Tom isn't pushy about the matter. He makes a notation that the clipping is just for the reader's potential interest.

An acceptance-hungry person such as Tom is an easy target for castigation. Yet is Tom practicing senseless office politics? Tom's approach to gaining acceptance from others is naive, but harmless. Passing out candy and coupons on company time may not be in the best interests of company efficiency. Nevertheless, it is doubtful that he wastes more time than others during the work day. His news clipping service may serve the corporate good.

Recognizing that Tom will never be an executive, his approach to gaining favor is suited to his lifestyle. Psychologically, Tom is a little person. His political strategies for gaining favor and approach to office politics are suited to him. All he wants from the office is a decent job, a regular paycheck, and the acceptance of his co-workers.

## SELF-INTEREST

Looking out for number one is a major contributor to office politics. Many people engage in politics because they place their own welfare before that of their employer. Vince, a middle-aged plant manager, is one such self-interested person. His judgment in selecting an assistant manager illustrates his politically motivated behavior. During an expansion phase of the business, his company had landed a big contract. Vince's boss suggested to him that the plant was busy enough to warrant having an assistant plant manager. After some hesitation, Vince agreed that his workload had increased to the point where he could use some assistance.

Vince was told that the company reserved assistant plant manager positions for people who seemed to have high potential for becoming executives of the future. Vince was therefore given a choice of hiring Larry or Norm, two current employees, as his assistant manager. Vince told his boss that he would need 30 days to reach a final decision. Both men were industrial engineers with supervisory experience. Vince had some interaction with the two men and had been favorably impressed by both. In his usual systematic approach, Vince began to collect information about the capabilities of the two candidates for the new position.

When Vince checked with another manager about Larry and Norm, he was told that Larry was the much stronger person. Although Norm made a better appearance and was more articulate, the manager said he wasn't a person of great substance. Norm was known to back down in disputes with a union steward. He also was seen as not being able to establish good working relationships with the supervisors.

Three weeks later Vince announced that Norm was the new assistant plant manager. Vince's reasoning appeared to be that the assistant plant manager usually had a good shot at becoming plant manager. Once placed in the position of assistant manager, a strong person like Larry might quickly become as capable as his boss. Larry posed a threat to Vince, while Norm did not. As things worked out, Norm became more of a flunkie than a true assistant plant manager.

An incident involving the manager of quality control, Pete, further illustrates Vince's self-interested behavior. Pete was a highly professional quality control manager who called problems as he saw them. At one time, Pete was arguing for tighter quality standards on the motors the company was manufacturing. Pete's demands were indirectly a criticism of Vince who had been responsible for setting the quality standards of the plant in the previous job. Therefore, it was in Vince's best interests not to agree that the plant's quality standards were low.

Vince began his anti-Pete campaign softly. During a luncheon meeting at which Pete was present, Vince said smilingly, "If Pete gets his way, we'll be building motors that will last for 50 years in washing machines built to last five years. Our junkyards will be filled with perfect little motors."

Vince's innuendoes about Pete became more vitriolic. In a phone conversation with the division general manager Vince said that Pete was losing perspective—that he was becoming an unrealistic nit-picker just to make a name for himself. Vince's comments had some impact. The final set of quality standards was a compromise between what existed and the new standards suggested by Pete.

Vincent's quest for self-glory finally gave him a corporate black eye that may have leveled off his career for good. The division general manager announced that a new company policy was to take up the slack in any unused manufacturing capability by performing subcontract work for other manufacturers. In a meeting, the division general manager asked Vince how interested he would be in taking on some subcontract work.

Without realizing the implications of what he was saying, Vince replied, "That's not exactly the type of activity I prefer for my plant. We could do it in an emergency, but I prefer to be associated with something a little more glamorous. You can't develop a reputation as a top-flight plant manager by taking on subcontract work." You could see the disdain on the division manager's face from across the room.

Vince's self-interest led him to play office politics. Unfortunately for him, the political strategies he chose were ill-advised. Vince might have fared better if he had chosen a strong assistant plant manager. When the new manager performed well, Vince might have recommended that he or she was ready to manage another plant. Bad-mouthing Pete, the quality control manager, was immature. A more effective political strategy would have been to admit that times have changed and that tighter quality standards were in vogue. Making a show of adapting to the times is good office politics. Finally, Vince should have grabbed the subcontract assignment. Pleasing your boss is a much surer path to glory than accepting only assignments you think are glamorous.

## DESIRE TO GOOF OFF

Although office politics is usually played to gain power, some employees politick simply to avoid hard work. By performing favors for the boss, or showing the boss approval in a variety of ways, the poorly motivated employee escapes undesirable assignments. For example, a warehouse employee admitted to one of my researchers that he was allowed to take naps in the storeroom because he ran personal errands for the boss. In his words, "Taking the boss's car in for a lube and oil change is worth at least three undisturbed naps."

People in higher-level jobs than a warehouse attendant also use politics to avoid undesirable assignments. Many middle managers and professionals scheme to avoid transfers to locations that would disrupt their lifestyles. For example, a transfer to New York or Los Angeles is often considered undesirable because of the high living expenses, poor air quality, and long commutes found in these two cities. To avoid such a transfer, some people have launched a campaign to convince their boss of how valuable they are in their present assignment. In essence, these players are using politics to *not* get ahead.

The people described so far all practice office politics for different reasons and use somewhat different tactics. Each achieves slightly different results. Some overemphasize the use of politics. A person with a reasonable degree of insight into people can learn to be an effective office politician with about ten minutes per month of intelligent planning. In addition, an equal amount of time is devoted to carrying out the planned maneuvers. For example, a 12-second compliment to the right person might pay large dividends.

Before beginning to acquire some new political tactics, it might be time for you to take a candid look at your own proclivities toward office politics. Self-examination in this area could heighten your chances of winning at office politics.

# CHAPTER 2

# MEASURING YOUR POLITICAL TENDENCIES

A predisposition to play office politics and seek power can best be measured in degrees. Some people are totally political. Everything they do on the job has the ulterior motive of making them look good or advancing their cause. At the other extreme are completely ingenuous, nonpolitical individuals whose primary concern is getting the job done. Most people fall somewhere between these two extremes. I have constructed a 100-item questionnaire to help you measure your tendencies toward politicking and power seeking.

Every question contained in the Political Orientation Questionnaire relates to some important facet of office politics.[1] An earlier version of this questionnaire has been tried out with thousands of working people in many types of jobs, representing a wide range of employers in both private and public organizations. (Average scores and interpretations will be presented later.) The present version is adapted to the needs of the 1990s. The more candid you are in filling out this form, the more accurately you will be able to measure your tendencies toward being a power seeker or office politician.

## POLITICAL ORIENTATION QUESTIONNAIRE

### Directions

Answer each of the following statements mostly true or mostly false. In some instances "mostly true" refers to "mostly agree" and "mostly false" refers to "mostly disagree." We are looking for general tendencies; there-fore, do not be concerned if you are uncertain as to the most accurate answer for a given question. In answering the questions, assume that you are taking this questionnaire with the intent of learning something about yourself. Obviously only you will see the results. *Do not* assume the mental set that you are taking this questionnaire as part of the screening process for a job you want.

|  | Mostly True | Mostly False |
|---|---|---|
| 1. The boss is always right. | ✓ | |
| 2. It is wise to flatter important people. | ✓ | |
| 3. Power for its own sake is one of life's most precious commodities. | | ✓ |
| 4. If you are even one-eighth Native American, mention it on your resume (assuming you believed it would help you get the job you wanted). | | ✓ |
| 5. I would ask my boss's opinion on personal matters even if I didn't need the advice, just to show I respected his or her judgment. | | ✓ |
| 6. If I had the skills, I would help an executive in my firm with a household chore on a Sunday afternoon. | ✓ | |
| 7. Dressing for success is a sham. Wear clothing to work that you find to be the most comfortable. | | ✓ |
| 8. If I were aware that an executive in my company was stealing money, I would use that information against him or her in asking for favors. | | ✓ |
| 9. I would invite my boss to a party in my home even if I didn't like that person. | | ✓ |
| 10. A person shouldn't flirt with key people in the company just to gain advantage. | ✓ | |

| *Continued* | Mostly True | Mostly False |
|---|---|---|
| 11. It is a good idea to figure out why a co-worker might be befriending you. | | ✓ |
| 12. If my boss were a prominent person, I would voluntarily start a scrapbook about him or her. | | ✓ |
| 13. Given a choice, take on only those assignments that will make you look good. | | ✓ |
| 14. I would never share with my boss negative feedback about him or her, unless I was trying to get somebody else in trouble. | | ✓ |
| 15. If someone higher up than you in the organizational hierarchy offends you, let that person know about it. | ✓ | |
| 16. I like the idea of keeping a "blunder (error) file" about a company rival for future use. | | ✓ |
| 17. I would have an affair with a top executive's spouse if I were attracted to that person. | | ✓ |
| 18. Never waste lunch time by having lunch with somebody who can't help you solve a problem or gain advantage. | | ✓ |
| 19. One should tell the truth or not, depending on how much good it will do you. | | ✓ |
| 20. Honesty is the best policy in practically all cases. | ✓ | |
| 21. Don't tell anybody anything at work that he or she could conceivably use against you in the future. | ✓ | |
| 22. One should personally select the subordinates on whom one's success greatly depends. | ✓ | |

| *Continued* | Mostly True | Mostly False |
|---|---|---|
| 23. If you have to punish somebody severely, do it quickly, and then get that person transferred because he or she might undermine you in the future. | _____ | ✓ _____ |
| 24. Act and look cool even when you don't feel that way. | _____ | _____ |
| 25. If you don't know the correct answer to a question asked by your boss, bluff your way out of it. | _____ | _____ |
| 26. If I worked for a clothing manufacturer, I would never wear a competitive brand of clothing to the office. | _____ | _____ |
| 27. If you disagreed with a major action taken by your boss, it would be a good tactic to complain to a good friend of yours who was a member of the board of directors. | _____ | _____ |
| 28. I would go out of my way to develop an interest in a hobby I knew that my boss preferred. | _____ | _____ |
| 29. Why go out of your way to be nice to any employee in the company who can't help you now or in the future? | _____ | _____ |
| 30. Before taking any important action at work, I think how it might be interpreted by key people. | _____ | _____ |
| 31. I try to be as nice as possible to all other employees in my organization, even if I don't like a particular person. | _____ | _____ |
| 32. I would attend a company picnic just to be seen, even if I had something more important to do that day. | _____ | _____ |
| 33. If necessary, I would say rotten things about a rival in order to attain a promotion. | _____ | _____ |

| *Continued* | Mostly True | Mostly False |
|---|---|---|
| 34. If a customer was very pleased with the way I handled his or her account, I would ask the customer to write a complimentary note to my boss. | _____ | _____ |
| 35. I would very much like to have my name on an office tower, the way Donald Trump does. | _____ | _____ |
| 36. It is necessary to lie once in a while in business in order to look good. | _____ | _____ |
| 37. If you have important confidential information, release it to your advantage. | _____ | _____ |
| 38. Accept advice willingly; don't obscure the issue by questioning why you are being given the advice. | _____ | _____ |
| 39. The best way to impress people is to tell them what they want to hear. | _____ | _____ |
| 40. It is important to have lunch with the right people regularly. | _____ | _____ |
| 41. Looking good when accomplishing something is as important as the accomplishment itself. | _____ | _____ |
| 42. Don't simply wound an enemy. Shoot to kill. | _____ | _____ |
| 43. If your rival for promotion is making a blooper, why tell that person? | _____ | _____ |
| 44. Hard work and good job performance are usually sufficient for career success. | _____ | _____ |
| 45. If I wanted to show someone up, I would be willing to write memos documenting that person's mistakes. | _____ | _____ |
| 46. If I had a legitimate gripe against my employer, I would air my views publicly (such as writing a letter to the editor of a local newspaper). | _____ | _____ |

| *Continued* | Mostly True | Mostly False |
|---|---|---|
| 47. Before you write a final report to your boss, find out what conclusions the boss really wants to see in the report. | _____ | _____ |
| 48. I would be willing to say nice things about a rival with the intent of getting him or her transferred. | _____ | _____ |
| 49. I would stay late in the office just to impress my boss. | _____ | _____ |
| 50. Why teach your subordinates everything you know about your job? One of them could then replace you. | _____ | _____ |
| 51. All in all, it is better to be humble and honest than to be important and dishonest. | _____ | _____ |
| 52. Do not enter in a cooperative venture if you perceive the other person to be somewhat of a loser. | _____ | _____ |
| 53. I have no interest in using gossip to personal advantage. | _____ | _____ |
| 54. While on vacation, it's a smart idea to pick up a small gift for your boss. | _____ | _____ |
| 55. Don't be a complainer. It may be held against you. | _____ | _____ |
| 56. Past promises should be broken if they stand in the way of one's personal gain. | _____ | _____ |
| 57. It is necessary to keep some people in place by making them afraid of you. | _____ | _____ |
| 58. Be extra careful about ever making a critical comment about your firm, even if it is justified. | _____ | _____ |
| 59. I would spend a social evening with my boss doing something I disliked (such as bowling or watching an opera) if it would help me get promoted. | _____ | _____ |

| *Continued* | Mostly True | Mostly False |
|---|---|---|
| 60. Reading about office politics is as much fun as reading a good novel. | _____ | _____ |
| 61. Jack wants to be a hero, so he creates a crisis for his company and then resolves it. His tactic is worth a try. | _____ | _____ |
| 62. I would go out of my way to cultivate friendships with powerful people. | _____ | _____ |
| 63. I would never raise questions about the capabilities of my competition. Let his or her record speak for itself. | _____ | _____ |
| 64. Keep a few secrets in your head. It is a bad idea to put controversial topics in writing. | _____ | _____ |
| 65. If I needed to, I would backdate a memo to pretend that I warned the company of a forthcoming crisis. | _____ | _____ |
| 66. If I were a tournament level golfer and my boss were a duffer, I would gladly team with him or her in a club match. | _____ | _____ |
| 67. I would have an affair with a powerful person in my company, even if I didn't like him or her. | _____ | _____ |
| 68. I am unwilling to take credit for someone else's work. | _____ | _____ |
| 69. If someone compliments you for a task that is another's accomplishment, smile and say thank you. | _____ | _____ |
| 70. If I discovered that a co-worker was looking for a job, I would inform my boss. | _____ | _____ |
| 71. Even if I made only a minor contribution to an important project, I would get my name listed as being associated with that project. | _____ | _____ |
| 72. It is only necessary to play office politics if you are an incompetent. | _____ | _____ |

| *Continued* | Mostly True | Mostly False |
|---|---|---|
| 73. If you have angered a rival, get him or her removed from your department, if possible. | ——— | ——— |
| 74. There is nothing wrong with tooting your own horn. | ——— | ——— |
| 75. It's a good idea to use the same jargon as your boss, even though you dislike jargon. | ——— | ——— |
| 76. An office should be cluttered with personal mementos such as pencil holders and decorations made by my friends or family. | ——— | ——— |
| 77. Once you have offended someone, never trust him or her with something important. | ——— | ——— |
| 78. One should take action only when sure that it is ethically correct. | ——— | ——— |
| 79. Only a fool would publicly correct mistakes made by the boss. | ——— | ——— |
| 80. I would purchase stock in my company even though it might not be a good financial investment. | ——— | ——— |
| 81. I would never use personal influence to gain a promotion. | ——— | ——— |
| 82. If I wanted something done by a co-worker, I would be willing to say, "If you don't get this done, our boss might be very unhappy." | ——— | ——— |
| 83. Even if I thought it would help my career, I would refuse a hatchet-man assignment. | ——— | ——— |
| 84. It is better to be feared than loved by your subordinates. | ——— | ——— |
| 85. If others in the office were poking fun at the boss, I would decline to join in. | ——— | ——— |

| *Continued* | Mostly True | Mostly False |
|---|---|---|
| 86. In order to get ahead, it is necessary to keep self-interests above the interests of the organization. | _____ | _____ |
| 87. It may be necessary at time to present some false financial figures to help sell one's proposal to management. | _____ | _____ |
| 88. Once you become the boss, it is a good idea to transfer from your department anyone whom you suspect dislikes you. | _____ | _____ |
| 89. If you happen to dislike a person who receives a big promotion in your firm, don't bother sending him or her a note of congratulation. | _____ | _____ |
| 90. I laugh heartily at my boss's jokes even when I think they are not funny. | _____ | _____ |
| 91. It is difficult to get ahead without discrediting others here and there. | _____ | _____ |
| 92. I would learn first of my boss's political preferences before discussing politics with him or her. | _____ | _____ |
| 93. If you do somebody a favor, remember to cash in on it at a later date. | _____ | _____ |
| 94. I would be careful not to hire a subordinate who might outshine me. | _____ | _____ |
| 95. Never tell anybody the real reason you do something unless it is to your advantage to do so. | _____ | _____ |
| 96. A wise strategy is to keep on good terms with everybody in your office even if you don't like everybody. | _____ | _____ |
| 97. I would never openly criticize a powerful executive in my organization. | _____ | _____ |

| Continued | Mostly True | Mostly False |
|---|---|---|
| 98. All forms of office politics boil down to kissing people's rear ends. | ———— | ———— |
| 99. If servile flattery toward key people helps me get ahead, I'll do it. | ———— | ———— |
| 100. My primary job is to please my boss. | ———— | ———— |
| Score | ———— | ———— |

## SCORING YOUR ANSWERS

Give yourself a plus one for each answer you gave in agreement with the keyed answer. Note that we did not use the term *correct* answer. Whether an answer is correct is a question of personal values and ethics. Each question that receives a score of plus one shows a tendency toward playing office politics or grabbing power. The scoring key is as follows:

| Question Number | Political Answer | Question Number | Political Answer |
|---|---|---|---|
| 1. | Mostly True | 20. | Mostly False |
| 2. | Mostly True | 21. | Mostly True |
| 3. | Mostly True | 22. | Mostly True |
| 4. | Mostly True | 23. | Mostly True |
| 5. | Mostly True | 24. | Mostly True |
| 6. | Mostly True | 25. | Mostly True |
| 7. | Mostly False | 26. | Mostly True |
| 8. | Mostly True | 27. | Mostly True |
| 9. | Mostly True | 28. | Mostly True |
| 10. | Mostly False | 29. | Mostly True |
| 11. | Mostly True | 30. | Mostly True |
| 12. | Mostly True | 31. | Mostly True |
| 13. | Mostly True | 32. | Mostly True |
| 14. | Mostly True | 33. | Mostly True |
| 15. | Mostly False | 34. | Mostly True |
| 16. | Mostly True | 35. | Mostly True |
| 17. | Mostly False | 36. | Mostly True |
| 18. | Mostly True | 37. | Mostly True |
| 19. | Mostly True | 38. | Mostly False |

| Question Number | Political Answer | Question Number | Political Answer |
|---|---|---|---|
| 39. | Mostly True | 70. | Mostly True |
| 40. | Mostly True | 71. | Mostly True |
| 41. | Mostly True | 72. | Mostly False |
| 42. | Mostly True | 73. | Mostly True |
| 43. | Mostly True | 74. | Mostly True |
| 44. | Mostly False | 75. | Mostly True |
| 45. | Mostly True | 76. | Mostly False |
| 46. | Mostly False | 77. | Mostly True |
| 47. | Mostly True | 78. | Mostly False |
| 48. | Mostly True | 79. | Mostly True |
| 49. | Mostly True | 80. | Mostly True |
| 50. | Mostly True | 81. | Mostly False |
| 51. | Mostly False | 82. | Mostly True |
| 52. | Mostly True | 83. | Mostly False |
| 53. | Mostly False | 84. | Mostly True |
| 54. | Mostly True | 85. | Mostly True |
| 55. | Mostly True | 86. | Mostly True |
| 56. | Mostly True | 87. | Mostly True |
| 57. | Mostly True | 88. | Mostly True |
| 58. | Mostly True | 89. | Mostly False |
| 59. | Mostly True | 90. | Mostly True |
| 60. | Mostly True | 91. | Mostly True |
| 61. | Mostly True | 92. | Mostly True |
| 62. | Mostly True | 93. | Mostly True |
| 63. | Mostly False | 94. | Mostly True |
| 64. | Mostly True | 95. | Mostly True |
| 65. | Mostly False | 96. | Mostly True |
| 66. | Mostly True | 97. | Mostly True |
| 67. | Mostly True | 98. | Mostly False |
| 68. | Mostly False | 99. | Mostly True |
| 69. | Mostly True | 100. | Mostly True |

## INTERPRETING YOUR SCORE

Your total score on the Political Orientation Questionnaire provides a rough index of your overall tendencies toward craving for power and being an office politician. The higher your score, the more political you are likely to be in your dealings at work. The lower your score, the less you are inclined toward politicking.

Based on a group of over 500 managers, professionals, technicians, sales representatives, and administrative assistants, the average score for both men and women is 21. Keeping this figure in mind will give you a quick estimate of whether you are above or below average with respect to behaving politically on the job. A more informative method of interpreting your score is to place it in one of five political categories: Machiavellian, Company Politician, Survivalist, Straight Arrow, or Innocent Lamb.

### Machiavellian

If you scored 76 or more points on the questionnaire, you have a voracious craving for power, and an almost uncontrollable tendency for doing things for political reasons. A Machiavellian is a power-hungry, power-grabbing individual. People who fall into this category are often perceived by others as being ruthless, devious, and power-crazed. It would not be out of character for a Machiavellian to use electronic surveillance devices to gain advantage over rivals. Machiavellians will try to succeed in their careers at almost any cost to others. A few Machiavellians, however, are obsessed with power but not particularly devious. Donald Trump could be classified as a Machiavellian who is power-crazed without being unusually devious.

A Machiavellian is often a sycophant during his or her climb to power. If it appears to be advantageous, a Machiavellian will fawn over a superior whom he or she dislikes. A person with a strong lust for power will voluntarily discredit the rival of a boss. One such sycophant hired a detective to uncover derogatory information about a new company manager who posed a threat to his boss.

A person falling into the top category of our questionnaire lives in constant peril. He or she usually has created a number of enemies on the way to the top. If you are a Machiavellian, there are probably people right now who are plotting revenge. As a Machiavellian begins to slip from power, people lurk in the background to give that person a last definitive shove.

A score of 100 on the Political Orientation Questionnaire would indicate an obsession with power and politics so overwhelming that it would be crippling. It would be difficult for you to get your legitimate tasks accomplished because of your preoccupation with weighing the political consequences of your every action. Unless you established an elaborate record-keeping system, you would soon forget what self-serving lie you told to whom.

### Company Politician

If you scored between 56 and 75 points, you are a Company Politician—a shrewd maneuverer and politico: someone who, typically, lands on both feet when deposed from a particular situation. Many successful executives fall into this category. A Company Politician is much like a Machiavellian, except that the former has a better developed sense of morality and ethics.

A Company Politician's lust for power is not an all-consuming preoccupation. Many Company Politicians will do whatever they can to advance their cause except to deliberately defame or injure another individual. You have to be insightful to be a Company Politician. Before utilizing a political strategy such as keeping a blunder file on others, you would have to determine if the organization would tolerate such shenanigans.

### Survivalist

A person with a score of from 36 to 55 falls into the Survivalist category. Those placed here probably practice enough office politics to take advantage of good opportunities. You are concerned about making any obvious political blunders such as upstaging your boss in an interdepartmental meeting. You smile frequently at your boss when salary review time rolls around. If your boss invited you to a church breakfast, you would not say, "No thanks, I'm an atheist."

As a Survivalist, you probably practice enough office politics to keep you out of trouble with your boss and other people of higher rank. A Survivalist would send a gift to a boss's newborn baby even if he or she did not care for babies. Many ambitious, career-oriented people who still want to lead a balanced life are Survivalists. We have also noticed that many people in their late twenties and early thirties who have MBA degrees fall into this category of office politician. Most Survivalists aspire toward executive positions.

### Straight Arrow

A score of 16 to 35 places you in the Straight Arrow category. Such an individual would not be perceived by others as being an office politician. Nor would he or she be seen as a person intent on committing political suicide. A Straight Arrow believes fundamentally that most people are honest, hard-working, and trustworthy. A Straight Arrow's favorite career advancement strategy is to display job competence. In the process, people who fit into this category may neglect other important career advancement tactics such as cultivating key people.

### Innocent Lamb

Scores of less than 15 place you in the bottom category of desire for playing politics and seizing power. An Innocent Lamb believes all organizations to be meritocracies—that good people are rewarded for their efforts and thus rise to the top. Their only political strategy is "By their works ye shall know them." Thus Lambs keep their eyes focused clearly on the task at hand, hoping that someday their hard work will be rewarded.

Innocent Lambs with an abundance of talent occasionally do make it to the top. (Outstanding inventors, artists, novelists, and athletes are sometimes Innocent Lambs.) Unless you happen to have an extraordinary aptitude it is difficult to advance in your career by practicing the Innocent Lamb philosophy of life.

The middle-aged office messenger referred to in the Preface to this book was an Innocent Lamb. Forced into retirement at age 55, he boasted of never once having practiced office politics. A person who scored zero on the Political Orientation Questionnaire is best suited for work that is 100 percent technical, involving almost no attempts to influence other people. A geological engineer who makes only one or two yearly visits with the boss might fit this description.

Few readers of this book are likely to be Innocent Lambs. If you were, the very subject of office politics might be so repugnant that, instead of this book, you would choose one about business ethics or how to be an effective leader.

An Innocent Lamb should read this book for self-protection, while a Straight Arrow, Survivalist, or Company Politician might want to read it to become even more knowledgeable about winning (and losing) tactics of office politics. A Machiavellian would finish this book to find out if there is any strategy someone else is using that he or she missed.

To climb the organizational ladder rapidly, the best chances are for those low to moderate Company Politicians or high Survivalists—scorers in the 50 to 65 range. People falling into this range are usually shrewd, but they are not in strong danger of tripping over their own ruthlessness.

# CHAPTER 3

## PLANNING
## YOUR POLITICAL
## CAMPAIGN

A political campaign conducted in the office is much like an election campaign—planning increases both of their chances for success. Planning your campaign involves knowing what you want to achieve, and how you are going to achieve it. Before jumping head first into choosing political tactics, it is also imperative to size up your environment. In one company it might be considered wise political strategy to purchase a house in the same neighborhood as the chief executive officer. In another company the same tactic might be considered pushy and offensive. In the former situation, you have improved your chances for success; in the latter, you have decreased them.

Planning your political campaign is more important today in the turbulent business environment of the 1990s. Many of these plans have to be implemented in the short-range because the political climate changes so rapidly as companies juggle around the people in power. You also may be forced to formulate new plans rapidly to suit the whims of the new power holders.

Establishing goals and sizing up the political climate to determine what types of political strategies are likely to work best are both important. Yet to be a first-rate office politician you also have to execute your tactics with sensitivity and tact. Suppose you discover that your boss is receptive to feedback about the attitudes of other members of the department toward her. It would be inadvisable to provide her a five-page document about how she is perceived by other people in the department. Your best chances for capitalizing on this tactic would be if you used offhand spoken comments rather than written reports. A cagey manager would not want written evidence to exist that he or she engages in this kind of intrigue.

## ESTABLISH GOALS YOUR POLITICKING
## CAN HELP YOU ACHIEVE

Office politics is rarely worth playing for its own sake. Political behavior should be geared toward important goals such as getting promoted, receiving a raise, or escaping from a boss who is retarding your career progress. First you specify the goal, and then choose a political tactic or strategy to help you achieve it. A good time to select tactics and strategies is after reading this entire book.

A goal, of course, is anything you want to achieve. Your political goals should ordinarily represent a mixture of short-, intermediate-, and long-range goals. Progress toward reaching your long-term goals (such as taking control of the company) can be achieved by attaining a series of shorter-range goals (such as ingratiating yourself to one executive secretary this week). To achieve your short-term goal of ingratiating yourself to one executive secretary this week, you might establish a daily goal of helping a particular secretary learn a new computer software package being used by the company.

Here is an example of a worksheet, establishing a political goal, and a tactic to help attain that goal. Gerard, a financial analyst, established the goal of getting out from under his boss, whom he thought was preventing him from getting deserved recognition. His specific political goal was, "Leave my department for a lateral transfer or promotion within six months." To accomplish this goal, Gerard's tactic was "market yourself to other executives in the company." Using his network of contacts, Gerard identified two managers whose departments were expanding to justify adding at least one more financial analyst.

Gerard met with both managers and explained tactfully and constructively how he needed more recognition in order to make a bigger contribution to the corporation. The gambit worked. One of the managers Gerard cultivated was receptive to his pitch and worked through the personnel department to get Gerard transferred. His parting comments to his former boss were, "I have mixed emotions about leaving you, but here is an opportunity to achieve the visibility I need to make the kind of impact I want around here."

## EVALUATE THE COST EFFECTIVENESS
## OF YOUR CAMPAIGN

Gerard's political campaign was decidedly worthwhile. There was relatively little time and effort involved in first identifying and then meeting with two managers who could help him. Also, the risks associated with tactfully discussing career opportunities with two in-company managers were slight. If Gerard's plans were discovered, his boss might be miffed which would put him in no worse position than he was before he began his campaign. The potential gain of achieving recognition for his ideas far outweighed the risk involved.

Management writer, Steven Robbins, supports the analysis just presented and recommends that before you select a political strategy, assess any potential costs of using it against its potential benefits. Many instances exist in which the costs of influencing others exceed the benefits derived from exerting the influence. A common mistake is that although the benefits of power are obvious, the cost is often overlooked. Power is effective when your amount of power is not counterbalanced by somebody else's power used against you.[1]

The person against whom you exert power will often retaliate in an attempt to fix the power imbalance. This attempt to regain power often results in an act of revenge. Similarly, political tactics that cause resentment usually are not cost-effective. The resentful person will wait for the right opportunity to seek revenge—often at a time you can least afford it.

> Administrative assistant Lorraine resented it when a co-worker, Helen, suggested to their boss that she (Lorraine) would soon be asking for parental leave and would therefore probably not be interested in a transfer to a supervisory position. The boss accepted the co-worker's judgment without corroborating the facts with Lorraine. In reality Lorraine was interested in becoming a supervisor despite her plans to accept a two-month maternity leave. One year later, the boss resigned from the company, and recommended Lorraine—who had returned from parental leave —to be her successor. Upon leaving the company, the supervisor apologized for listening to hearsay from Helen that Lorraine was not interested in becoming a supervisor.

> Shortly after Lorraine took over as supervisor, the company consolidated several departments. Helen's department was combined with Lorraine's, and Helen was reassigned as an administrative assistant reporting to Lorraine. Without any compunction, Lorraine went out of her way to keep Helen busy with the most arduous assignments in the department, and gave the most stringent performance evaluations her conscience would allow.

Risk assessment is an important part of the cost–benefit equation. In Gerard's case, the risks involved in speaking to other managers in the company seemed minimal. At other times, the risks associated with tricky political maneuvers may be substantial. The politically naive will often resort to going over their boss's head with a complaint about the boss. Although this tactic may be effective in some situations—such as the overthrow of Steve Jobs of Apple Computer by the man he hired into the company as president—it is very risky.

Unless the boss has already been the butt of complaints from many others, the person who listens to your complaint will immediately review your discussion with your boss. Upper management usually sides with the boss, and you will be left working for an angry boss. The result could be nit-picking performance evaluations, modest salary increases, some undesirable work assignments, no recommendations for promotion, and very little recognition.

## GET INFORMATION FROM SECRETARIES AND ADMINISTRATIVE ASSISTANTS

Secretaries and administrative assistants can be an excellent source of information for planning a political campaign. "Assistants" (the term that replaced secretary in most organizations) are an important information hub. They are often aware of pending organizational changes that could lead to demotions or promotions; they can identify the powerful people in the organization; and they know who their immediate boss likes and dislikes. Assistants who think positively of you will often share their perceptions with powerful people. Correspondingly, assistants will often make negative comments to their bosses about people they dislike.

The most effective way to obtain specific information from secretaries, says Marilyn Moats Kennedy, is to treat them with respect. "They are professionals with needs and ambitions of their own. Treat the relationships you build with them as trading relationships between equals."[2]

One way to treat assistants with respect is to ask for their input on problems, but do not ask them to compromise their ethics by filling you in on confidential information. For example, you might say to the administrative assistant to the chief information officer, "I'm doing some career planning. Do you think information systems managers in this company will have a better future in the field or here in headquarters?" This approach is much better than blatantly asking, "What have you heard lately about transferring most information systems operations out to the field?"

## IDENTIFY THE TRUE POWER

To properly plan a political campaign, it is necessary to identify the true powerholders in your organization. These are the people you must impress, in addition to your boss, in order to gain advantage. Use subtlety and tact in making your power analysis; otherwise you will be branded by others as a brash office politician. As mentioned above, administrative assistants can be a good source of information for identifying powerful figures. Four other techniques for identifying the true power are also recommended. Several of these techniques could incorporate information from administrative assistants.

### Ask Innocent-Appearing Questions

An unwise question to ask, particularly if you are a newcomer to the organization, is "Who are the most influential and powerful people around here?" You are better advised to ask innocent-sounding questions. Make it appear you are merely interested in accomplishing your work. Bernie, a newly recruited management trainee who was intent on becoming an executive knew he had to impress key executives to reach this objective. Bernie developed a workable plan to get through to the executive vice-president.

He noticed that a distinguished looking older gentleman was nicknamed "Mr. Secretary." This same person was often seen at lunch with either the president or the executive vice-president. When Bernie saw Mr. Secretary in the parking lot one day, he introduced himself and queried Mr. Secretary as to his position. "I'm the president's chief administrative assistant. I take care of correspondence and arrange travel for Mr. Goldfarb, our president."

"How interesting," answered Bernie. "That job must keep you pretty busy. I look forward to seeing you again." Bernie made a mental note to learn more about the situation.

The next day, Bernie asked the same question of three people. "As you may know, I'm new here and am trying to understand the company as best I can. I'm trying to learn who does what. Could you please tell me what that kindly gentleman, Mr. Secretary, does? I'm not familiar with that job title." Phil, the man in charge of the elevators, gave Bernie the most complete and useful answer.

"Be nice to that guy. He may look harmless enough but he about runs this place. The president trusts him as much as he would his lawyer. They tell me the old fellow approves all the recommendations for promotion. Mr. Goldfarb usually endorses what he says. Get on Mr. Secretary's bad list and you might as well quit."

Bernie then proceeded to cultivate Mr. Secretary by making enthusiastic comments about the company and his job whenever they met. Before long, Mr. Secretary had put Bernie on the promotable list in his secret dossier of lower-ranking managers.

## Check Out the Organization Chart

Whatever the nature of your organization, it will probably serve you well to study the most fundamental document about the political structure of your firm—the organization chart. An up-to-date chart gives you a graphic description of who reports to whom and the relative rank of each person named. You will also learn which departments rank higher than others and, therefore, most likely to contain a larger number of powerful people. An organization chart will never reveal things such as the amount of influence held by a person such as Mr. Secretary, but you will learn how things are *supposed* to work.

Unless you have valid information to the contrary, it is best to take heed of the pecking order as revealed by the organization chart. Jeff, a prolific memo writer, was newly arrived on the scene as an audit manager in a state agency. Three months into the job, Jeff thought it time he began sending memos to appropriate parties, advising them of his suggestions for the improvement of state auditing procedures. Jeff's memos were concise, well written, and factually based. Unfortunately, their lack of political astuteness led to their rejections. Jeff explains his mistake:

> I was sending out about five copies of each memo. I was naive enough to rank the recipients according to those I thought could use the information the most. In this way, I sometimes placed a lower-ranking official's name above that of a higher-ranking one. In another instance, I implied that a person of lower rank should take exception to the audit procedures of a person of higher rank.

> If I had checked out the organization chart, I could not have made those errors. Now I'll have to wait for people's ruffled feathers to become unruffled before I try to correct my mistakes. You simply cannot violate protocol in our agency if you want to get something important accomplished.

## Talk to Oldtimers

The worst person to approach for information to give you political advantage would be a person who sees you as a potential rival for a promotion. An older person in the company who is comfortably placed on a plateau is unlikely to be threatened by a person snooping around for information about the informal power structure. A long-term employee might be willing to answer such questions as:

- What kinds of programs are likely to get funded these days?
- Which types of community activities does top management really think are worthwhile?

- Are managers and professionals really expected to use all of their vacation time?
- How important is it to show up in the office on Saturday mornings?
- Are we really supposed to be using the personal computers on our desks?
- How many years should I wait for a promotion before concluding that I'm not considered promotable?

## Ask Your Boss an Indirect Question

Your boss is a logical source of information about the power structure of the company or your department. Asking your boss an indirect question about the right people could pay dividends. A direct question such as "Who are the powerful people around here that I should try to impress?" is tacky. A better approach is to ask your boss which executive in the company is the most interested in your department's output, or makes the best use of the reports your department generates.

Charlie, an industrial engineer, is a case in point. He and his colleagues in the operations research department conducted studies about how to make the organization run more smoothly. Wanting his hard work to increase his visibility, Charlie said to his boss, "I note that ten executives receive copies of our research reports. But who at the top really cares about our work?" His boss answered, "Ed Boswell, the senior vice-president of planning."

Charlie had the hubris to write a handwritten note to Boswell stating how glad he was that the planning vice-president was interested in operations research. Charlie soon became assistant to the general manager—a promotion that may have come about because a senior executive became aware of Charlie's presence in the organization.

## Decide Whether You Fit in with the Powerful People

After you have taken the time and trouble to identify the powerful people in your organization, it is important to evaluate how you fit in with them. If your personal style or background characteristics differ radically, it is highly probable you will not be invited to join in the power elite.[3] How well you fit in can be attributable to a wide range of factors including age, education, race, sex, ethnic background, major personality characteristics, personal style, lifestyle, or your area of expertise.

It is often more important to determine if you have a *disqualifying* rather than a *qualifying* characteristic. The former frequently are more well defined than the latter. In some technically oriented companies, for example, it is difficult to rise to the top unless you have a laboratory or engineering background. The qualifying characteristics, aside from the proper technical background, are less tangible and difficult to measure—for example, good problem-solving ability and the capacity to work under pressure.

### Conduct a Power Analysis

After you have identified the powerful players in the organization, and decided how well you fit, you are ready to conduct a power analysis. A "power analysis" tells you how much clout a manager really possesses. The informal power possessed by an executive can be quite different than his or her formal power as indicated by the organization chart. The steps taken to identify the power players will have given much of the information you need to conduct a power analysis. Going through the steps described next, however, will give you more refined answers. Marilyn Moats Kennedy urges you to find accurate answers to ten questions about the key people to conduct a power analysis:[4]

1. *To whom does this person report? What is that person's position?* The higher a person reports in the hierarchy, the more power the person possesses. A vice-president who reports to a president is more powerful than one who reports to another vice-president.

2. *What is this person's management style?* Is this person very authoritarian, or will he or she consult with other team members about important issues? It is much easier to cultivate a manager who will welcome your input on major decisions.

3. *Who reviews this person's decisions, and are those decisions often vetoed?* A powerful manager can make many decisions without having to confer with a superior. If the power player you have identified has many decisions vetoed by the next level of management, that individual may not really be so powerful.

4. *How much impact do these persons' decisions have on the organization?* A powerful executive is one whose decisions relate to the overall profitability or budget of the firm. Executives involved with the major thrust or purpose of the organization (line managers) make decisions of high impact. In contrast, executives involved with the secondary purposes of the organization (staff managers), or who provide support and advice to others, are less powerful. In a bank, a vice-president of consumer loans would have more power than the vice-president of data processing.

5. *How rapidly has this person been promoted within this company?* On balance, a person who has been promoted frequently is a more powerful person than one who has received infrequent promotions. A person who has been in one position for many years may be considered unpromotable and may have relatively little power. An exception to this principle is the individual who rose rapidly in the organization to the point that few promotions are possible. A 38-year-old vice president of finance may be quite powerful but cannot be promoted unless he or she becomes president.

6. *How many people report to this person and what kind of work do they perform?* Executive power is measured to some extent by the number of people reporting directly and indirectly to that person. Another important consideration, however, is the job level of employees in his or her empire. A data processing manager with 250 data entry specialists under him might be less influential than a manager of financial analysis with 35 people reporting to her.

7. *How many people of equal rank consult with this person on his or her decisions?* An unequivocal sign of power is the person who is consulted by co-workers for advice. This is true because such advice is not required and carries no penalty for noncompliance. In a Washington, D. C., think tank, one senior analyst was consulted by almost any other analyst who was applying for a major grant. Junior analysts who became the protege of this senior analyst discovered that they were treated with considerable respect—and respect is a form of power!

8. *With whom does this person have business meals?* A powerful person has business breakfasts, lunches, and dinners with people doing different types of work and from different departments. A variety of contacts helps the person get plugged into many different information networks. A person who lunches with the same few people everyday may be isolated from the larger organization.

9. *How liked or disliked is this person?* A person who is widely liked has a better chance of remaining powerful than one who is widely disliked. It is also politically unwise to be closely linked to a despised executive. Others may begin to perceive you as that person's flunky, and you may be ousted from power when that person is overthrown.

10. *What is this person's educational and socioeconomic background and heritage?* However unfair, a wealthy, well-educated person with excellent family connections may have more power than people with less prestigious backgrounds. Knowing a person's

background can therefore give you more insight into his or her potential power.

## SIZE UP YOUR BOSS ════════════════════════════

Office politics begins with making a favorable impression on your boss, once you have determined what impresses that person. If you work for a boss long enough you will usually learn what pleases him or her, but long enough may be too long. It is better early in your relationship to find answers to ten significant questions about your boss. Answers can be found through direct observation, gentle questioning of your boss, or by asking the questions of co-workers and the boss's assistant. If you intend to win at office politics, find answers to these questions soon.

1. *What mission is my boss trying to accomplish?* The key to creating a favorable impression on your boss is to help him or her accomplish the most important task facing the department. In some fields the answer to this question is straightforward. If your boss were a restaurant owner, it would be safe to assume that your boss was trying to increase patronage and profits. In other situations, your boss's true mission may be less obvious. In some bureaucracies your boss may want to run an inefficient department because efficiency might lead to a cutback in funding and headcount.

2. *What practices by subordinates usually irritate my boss?* Avoid annoying someone you are trying to impress. If your boss prefers telephone calls rather than memos, keep memos to the absolute minimum. If your boss believes strongly in goal setting, do not tell your boss that goals interfere with your spontaneity.

    Alison, an inexperienced reporter, landed a job with her local newspaper, the *Observer Dispatch*. She and her friends had always called the newspaper, "The O.D." Her first day, Alison noted that her boss cringed when a visitor to the office asked, "What is the circulation of the O.D.?" The boss replied, "The latest figures indicate that the *Observer Dispatch* reaches 95,000 families."

    When asked by her boss how she enjoyed her first full day working for the newspaper, Alison replied without a wince, "So far, it looks as though I'm going to enjoy being a reporter for the *Observer Dispatch*." Her boss smiled and Alison had started her journalism career on a positive note.

3. *Does your boss accept compliments graciously?* Virtually all people enjoy receiving compliments. But "virtually all" does not mean everybody. It is to your political advantage to observe how your

boss receives compliments before praising his or her ordinary actions. It is not unknown for a boss to sometimes be rebuffed by a compliment. As one gruff boss said to a subordinate who complimented his post-vacation tan, "Stop kissing my ass and get on with your work."

4. *Who are your boss's enemies?* An astute office politician learns early not to make favorable comments about the boss's enemies. Assuming you are on good terms with your boss's assistant, ask that person who the boss likes the least outside the department. Or, ask your boss which departments cooperate least with your department. "Lack of cooperation" usually means that your boss is involved in a continuing conflict with that department head.

Tim, an account executive, noted that his boss, Janis, and Alan, another account supervisor, clashed. Hoping to foster a good relationship with his boss, Tim asked Janis if she had a moment to talk.

Said Janis, "What's up, Tim?"

"You may not have heard this yet," said Tim, "but just in case you didn't, I thought you might get a charge out of it. Alan's department seems to have gone off the deep end. I think they want to either set back advertising ten years or put us out of business. Maybe both.

"Alan is proposing that our agency set up a product-testing laboratory at our expense. We would then subject each product we advertise, or propose to advertise, to extensive product testing. We would then advertise only those products that passed our scrutiny. I wonder if Alan thinks we are the Consumer Protection Agency instead of an advertising agency."

"This *is* a good one, Tim," said Janis. "At times I wonder about Alan myself. If he keeps thinking like that, I may have to talk to our president about him. Any other tidbits?"

5. *What is the most vexing problem facing my boss?* Give top job priority to those problems of biggest concern to the boss. It makes both political and common sense to tackle these problems. If you find a solution, you will be highly valued by your boss. If you find no solution, you will still be perceived positively for having tried providing you do not exacerbate the problem. When your boss fails to tell you his or her biggest problem, it's up to you to find out.

> Ed, a manager in a government agency, asked his boss Jim, "What should I be doing to help the agency run more smoothly?" "Truthfully," replied Jim, "we are facing a rather bizarre problem that can be best described as an embarrassment of riches. We have a $15,000 surplus in our budget. If I turn it in at the end of the fiscal year—which is two months from now—our budget for next year will

probably be shot down by that amount. Of course, we can't do anything frivolous with the surplus such as purchasing an elaborate
piece of furniture or painting for the office."

"Give me 24 hours," responded Ed, "I may have an honorable solution to our problem." Ed then made a phone call to an acquaintance
whose agency faced a similar problem. The next morning Ed reported back to Jim with his findings. His recommendation: Spend
the $15,000 for a consulting study of the effectiveness of Ed's de-
partment in carrying out its mission. The money in the budget would
then be used in an acceptable way that had considerable precedent
in government. Jim accepted Ed's idea, and it worked. The consultants made their study, the department used up its budget almost to
the dollar, the results of the study were useful, and Ed received a
superior rating on the next performance review.

6. *What does my boss regard as good performance?* A serious practitioner
of office politics finds a good answer to this question early in a
relationship with the boss. The answer may not always be as obvious
as it sounds. Your analysis of what constitutes good performance
does not always coincide with that of your boss. Subjective judgment is called for in evaluating many types of higher-level jobs.

The importance of understanding what constitutes good job
performance is underscored by the situation of an attorney named
Mandi. After graduating from law school she accepted a position in
a small legal department with a large business firm. After one
month on the job, Mandi swung into action. She began to cultivate
clients throughout the corporation, extolling the capabilities of the
company legal department. She sent clippings from professional
journals and newspapers that illustrated the legal implications of
business decisions to various executives.

Within three months, business was booming in the company
legal department. Executives were asking questions such as "Are
there any legal consequences to offering price reductions for customers who receive shipments from our factory?" and "Is it legal for
the company not to list a gay marriage in the section of the company newspaper that lists employee marriages?" In addition, managers throughout the company were now asking questions, such as
"Can I write off part of my summer cottage as a business expense if
I use it to demonstrate our line of motor boats to customers?"

Pleased with her performance, Mandi asked her boss, "How
do you like the results I have been achieving? It's obvious from the
activity of our department that our executive team is becoming
much more sensitive to legal problems."

Her boss replied, "Please, Mandi, stop your public relations
campaign right now. We have a small department that is supposed

to work on only a handful of intricate legal questions faced by the corporation. Certainly we are not a company-sponsored legal clinic. If you don't slow down your public relations activity, we'll soon have a waiting room full of employees wanting to discuss their pending divorces with us."

7. *What forms of office politics does my boss practice?* A cautious guideline is to assume that the type of office politics practiced by your boss is the type of office politics the boss would consider acceptable for a subordinate to use. Smart politics should include those practices condoned by your boss. He or she may use a particular political strategy, probably considering it good human relations rather than office politics. The experiences of human resource specialist Ray illustrate this point.

Ray was responsible for conducting company attitude surveys to uncover morale problems within the organization. His department would then alert top management to these problems with the intent of remedying the most pressing concerns. Ray excitedly told Gary, his boss, about a new type of attitude survey he planned to conduct: one that was elaborate and scientifically developed.

Gary said, "Not a bad idea, Ray. Run your survey if it pleases you. But remember, the best way of finding out what's disquieting our people is to increase your bar bill."

"I don't understand. How can increasing a bar bill help uncover morale problems?"

"Simple," explained Ray. "I systematically invite a large number of managers, one at a time, for a beverage after work. I do this about three late afternoons per week. The results of the survey can then be used to verify the problems I have uncovered in the bar. Besides, I cultivate a lot of supporters for our programs this way."

Ray joined the fun without sacrificing his professional scruples. He did conduct his scientific-type surveys. Ray's new wrinkle was to flesh out the results of his survey with the alcohol-facilitated comments made by managers who joined him regularly for after-work cocktails. When Ray and Gary were finished with their respective informal interviews, they would frequently confer with each other before heading home to the suburbs.

8. *Does my boss welcome conferring with subordinates?* The modern manager is supposed to consult with team members before making a decision. Nevertheless, managers vary widely in the amount of time they are willing to spend in conference with subordinates. Some managers feel busy and productive when placed in one-to-one relationships with the people they supervise. Others enjoy

calling frequent brief meetings about both important and trivial problems. Still other managers believe that mature and competent team members spend most of their time working independently.

It is to your advantage to learn your boss's stated and unstated position on this important aspect of managing. For example, too much conferring with a boss can make you appear ineffective, annoying, or both. Mike, a second-rate office politician, was apprehensive about the arrival of Dave, the new vice-president of manufacturing to whom he would report. "I had better get a relationship going with him right away before the barracudas in my department get to him first," Mike told his domestic partner.

A barracuda himself without realizing it, Mike began his campaign to cultivate a good relationship with Dave. He made two trips a day to his new boss's office. Once, the excuse was to hand deliver an important message to Dave's assistant. Twice the excuse was "Dave, I just happened to be in your area. Do you have a moment to chat?"

After 15 minutes of conferring with Mike about Mike's perception of the problems within the manufacturing division, Dave forthrightly noted that he had another appointment. After Mike left, Dave said to his assistant, "Who is this pest and why is he bothering me?" Mike unwittingly had put one foot in the company bucket and it would take him many months to extricate himself. If Mike had been patiently observant, he would have discovered by Dave's actions that he only wanted to confer with subordinates when he initiated the conference.

9. *What are important personal facts about my boss?* The smaller your boss's mind, the more important it is to remember personal facts about that person such as birthdate, names of family members and household pets, favorite sports, hobbies, personal gifts, and colors. You have to tread lightly in capitalizing on this information; otherwise, you will appear to be a servile flatterer.

   The recommended way of using such information is to allude to personal facts about your boss in the midst of casual conversation. For instance, just before business gets underway at a meeting you might comment to your boss, "How is Mitzy's (the boss's pet dog) pregnancy going?" or "Did you ever get that barometer you were hoping to get for your birthday?" Without knowing such facts about your boss, you would not be able to capitalize on such relationship-building comments.

10. *What are my boss's mood cycles?* Part of planning your political campaign is to know the right time to approach your boss with requests.

Ask your boss's assistant about the best time to discuss controversial matters (such as asking for a bigger budget) with him or her. Most executives are the most approachable after they have had time to sort through the major problems facing them for that particular day. Monday and Tuesday afternoon are generally good times to gain a boss's favorable attention on work-related matters. Monday morning is the worst time to approach most busy managers because they are preoccupied with staff meetings or planning for the week.

If your boss looks terrible, it may be because of a natural downturn in his or her mood cycle. Stay away, except for emergencies. If your boss is mired in a personal problem, wait until things are under control before making your thrust. Karen, a public relations specialist, had a wonderful idea (she thought) about how her company could win more favor in the community. In an optimistic mood, Karen asked for an appointment to confer with Ned, the president.

"Ned, I know that you've been out sick for three days, and that your entire family has also been ill, but this won't take more than a few minutes of your time. Why not have the company donate a machine shop to the state prison about 40 miles north of here? By doing it, we would endear ourselves to the community groups who believe that prisons aren't doing a proper job of rehabilitating prisoners. We could then hire the first few graduates of the program as soon as they were released."

"Good God, Karen," snapped Ned, "I have enough problems facing me without you telling me how we can spend another $50,000 on public relations. Who should we lay off to hire those ex-cons? We don't have enough for our present employees to do. Why don't you stick to speech writing for a while?"

Karen's poor timing did no good for herself, the company, or the prisoners who might have benefitted from her progressive thinking.

## FIGURE OUT WHAT TYPE OF POLITICS ARE PLAYED AT THE TOP

Top-level politicking often serves as an appropriate model for lower-level politics. It is reasonable to conclude that if key people in the organization favor a limited number of tactics for holding them in good stead with the company, these tactics are worth considering. In some organizations that are less than political jungles, the top executives still engage in some politicking. Such ethical and tame political tactics include involvement in prestigious community activities or active support of the right political party. Club memberships often fit into this same category.

Observation of what is going on at the top of the organization, can help you avoid political tactics that might backfire. For example, top management might underplay their power by such means as dressing casually or having the minimum amount of assistants. If you emphasize looking and acting powerful by dressing formally and requesting two personal assistants, you could fall into immediate disfavor.

## INVESTIGATE THE EXTENT OF NEPOTISM

The best time to size up the political climate of an organization, and to begin planning your political campaign, is before you become a member. If your aspirations are high, determine if nonfamily members have an equal chance for success.

Believers in a meritocracy think that only small family businesses and the governments of tiny municipalities still practice nepotism. They wonder how could large organizations find enough family members to fill their key jobs. The answer is that the ranks of blood relatives and those through marriage are combed to find reasonably competent people for important positions. Often a distant relative is recruited into the fold if that person's special talents are needed by the organization.

Tony's situation illustrates the importance of digging for details about possible nepotism. He was offered a position as a sales representative with Farnsworth Metal Fabricating Company. Tony thought it was the opportunity he had been waiting for. Farnsworth was a medium-size company specializing in low-priced foreign steel. The company was expanding into new markets in both the mid-western and eastern United States, and Ontario, Canada.

Tony expected to become a sales manager within a few years. However, before he accepted an offer he attempted to check out if anybody but a Farnsworth could get ahead in the company. To conduct his analysis, Tony perused a company telephone directory. He reported back to his wife:

"Honey, I think I've found the right company. I could locate only three employees named Farnsworth. One person is Byron Farnsworth, the president, whom they tell me is 66 and wants to retire. The second is Elton Farnsworth, the manager of manufacturing. He is 45, but because he works in manufacturing and not sales, he is not a potential competitor for future openings in the sales department.

"Gail is the third Farnsworth. She is a kindly, white-haired woman in charge of the company books. I doubt that, at her age with her experience, she will be in line for key jobs in the future of the company."

After three months on the job, Tony discovered some good news and bad news. The good news was that he correctly sized up Farnsworth Metal Fabricating as an aggressive company with a bright future. A new $6 million facility was planned for Ontario within the next year. Business was booming. The bad news was that three senior people in the company would be retiring within a year. Replacements for all three executives were announced. Each replacement was married to a Farnsworth offspring.

Tony's analysis was too superficial. He neglected to inquire about the number of family members through marriage who worked for the company. Old Mr. Farnsworth had two sons and daughters, one of whom was a college senior and interested in business. Either he, or any person he might marry, could conceivably block opportunities for outsiders. Tony relied exclusively on a telephone directory as a source of information about the company.

Before he joined the company, Tony should have questioned several employees or suppliers about the extent to which it was a family company. Tony's career was not doomed, but he lost precious time in his quest to become an executive.

## ANALYZE THE POLITICS BELOW YOU

Part of planning your political campaign involves determining what types of politics your subordinates are using. The better you understand the nature of politicking below you, the more effectively you will be able to guard against being the victim.

Many maneuvers designed to please you are harmless; some are not so harmless. No sure-fire procedure exists for uncovering the types of office politics your subordinates are using, but it helps to speculate on the answers to a few probing questions. The answers to these questions may suggest countermaneuvers on your part.

*Why is this person telling me this?* A team member may bring information about other people to your attention for work-related reasons. At other times, the information may have the political motive of attempting to unfairly discredit another person. A subordinate might casually mention, "We're all rooting for Jason. It seems as though he's made great strides in overcoming his marital and financial problems." You then have to ask yourself whether Jason really has a problem or the information is merely designed to remove Jason from consideration as a serious contender for promotion.

*What methods are they using to depose me?* Without becoming paranoid, it is worth analyzing whether people in your department are formulating devious schemes to have you removed from your position. A bizarre case of character defamation occurred in a bank when a graffiti buff wrote the following message on the executive laboratory wall: "Brad Jones makes Margaret Thatcher seem like a pussycat."

Brad's reaction was first shock; the second, laughter. His third reaction was self-protective. During their next scheduled meeting, Brad commented to his boss, "I think I am becoming an important person in the bank. People are now writing nasty things about me on lavatory walls. It's nice to know that I'm being noticed."

*Is politics being used to cover up a lack of results?* Many forms of office politics are used for the sole purpose of bringing favorable attention to a person who is doing a satisfactory or better job. At other times, politics are played to cover up poor performance. As the boss, you have to recognize the difference because you are held accountable for the performance of your total department.

Buck passing is a commonly used form to cover up poor results. One subordinate complained to his boss, "I would have gotten my report out on time except for those inexcusable delays in the information systems department." When the boss investigated, she discovered that the information systems department had detailed logs indicating that no report had been sent back late to information systems users in the previous three months. She then knew precisely where the blame lay for the late report.

*What methods are being used to impress me?* Part of your job as a boss is to sort out authentic from faked good job performance. When a document passes your desk relating to the productivity of a subordinate, it behooves you to ask, "Is this document a reflection of good performance or is it an exercise in puffery?" Dale, a faithful civil servant, found out the difference quite by accident. He recounts:

One morning I received a memo from another department praising the work of Cindy, one of my team members. The other department pointed out what an important contribution Cindy had made while she was on loan to their department. I was pleased that one of my people had performed so well in a special assignment. I made a copy of the note and placed it in Cindy's permanent personnel file.

Three days later, I was having lunch with Sam, the head of the department in which Cindy carried out her temporary assignment. I commented about the complimentary memo. He, in turn, told me about a remarkable coincidence. Maggie, a specialist who was on loan to my department, had received an almost identical note from my department praising her accomplishments while on temporary assignment. Undoubtedly, the two women had been writing "heroine" notes about each other. I simply destroyed the memo and forgot the matter.

## CHECK OUT THE INFORMAL
## STATUS SYMBOLS ━━━━━━━━━━━━━━━━━━━━━━━━━━━━━━━━━

A superficial way of impressing other people on the job is to use the status symbols associated with successful people. The most impressive status symbols—the *formal* ones—are conferred on people by the organization. Using them is tantamount to stealing. Thus you cannot put a sterling silver or gold-plated thermos decanter in your office if these accouterments are handed out only to vice-presidents and above. Nor can you give yourself the job title, "vice-president of communications" when you are the mailroom supervisor.

What you can do is make judicious use of *informal* status symbols. At best, such symbols will help you attract followers who are impressed by your status, thus enhancing your power. Identifying these symbols is thus part of planning your campaign. Before such a strategy can be implemented, however, you must shrewdly observe what constitutes an informal status symbol in your firm. A good place to start is to learn what status symbols are in vogue with the company fast trackers. Older executives who have reached their plateau are usually less concerned about status symbols.

A disconcerting characteristic of company status symbols is that they are not universal. What gives you status in one company might be considered in poor taste at another. Status symbols are also subject to flux. At one time carrying an attache case was impressive; now they are carried by most professionals and managers.

In one company we investigated, carrying the *Wall Street Journal* is no longer an effective status symbol. Too many lower-ranking people now carry the *Journal*. It is still important to read that paper, but carrying something more esoteric like *Success* suggests that you are an entrepreneurial thinker, or at least customer-minded.

Rare plants have become widely used status symbols. The company gives the tallest and most exotic plants to the highest-ranking executives. To give the impression of being powerful, some lower-ranking managers bring their own plants to the office. Generally this practice is not restricted. In one company, however, a middle manager brought a five-foot fig plant to the office. It was so impressive that the company president ordered it removed.

The ultimate informal status symbol in many companies is for an executive to walk into a meeting without an attache case or memo pad.

It's as though you are beyond carrying papers. The less important people practically back-pack into a meeting.

## AVOID FIGHTING OTHER PEOPLE'S WARS

A final suggestion for planning your political campaign is use politics to help you or your group rather than to fight other people's wars. Avoid sacrificing your own position in a way that will help neither you nor the victims. An exception is when you are so disturbed by unethical behavior that you feel compelled to engage in a political battle even if it jeopardizes your position.[5] For example, it might bother you that your boss is using idea's from your co-worker Sarah, without giving her any credit. She feels defenseless and unable to handle the matter. You therefore intervene by confronting your boss about her unethical practice. Your boss is now angry with you and Sarah, but you feel ethically pure.

A better approach for you would have been to advise Sarah on how to handle the situation, but insist that she keep your name out of any negotiations with the boss. (You might have told Sarah to explain to the boss that she needed more recognition for her ideas in order to achieve her career goals.)

Another problem in fighting a power struggle with your boss over a third party is that you will probably lose unless you enlist the support of a powerful third party. If you have evidence that your boss has given an inadequate salary increase to a co-worker, you would need the help of a top executive to help you fight this battle.

The general point of planning your political campaign is to map out political actions that not only will enhance your position but also be worth the effort in terms of return on your invested time and energy. Fighting other people's battles or engaging in other actions that will be self-defeating are ways of losing at office politics.

# CHAPTER 4

## GETTING
## THE BOSS ON
## YOUR SIDE

Impressing your boss is the most basic strategy of office politics. If you cannot gain favor with your boss it will be difficult to advance in your present firm. Should you clash with one particular boss, you can sometimes be gracefully transferred to another department or find a job in another firm. Both these moves are contingent on your boss not giving you a harsh reference. After finding a new position you will have one more shot at impressing the person who evaluates your work performance, helps decide on your salary increase, and recommends you for promotion and special assignments.

To help you in your quest to cultivate your boss, there are a number of strategies and tactics. Some, like "help your boss succeed," represent an all-encompassing philosophy of winning at office politics. Others, such as "teach your boss a new skill," are minor and specific, yet still an important part of your political game plan.

Pick and choose from the political maneuvers presented in this chapter. Decide which tactics are best suited to your skills and style—and your boss's style. If your favorite strategy or tactic is missing, it is conceivable that you will find it somewhere else in the book, including the chapter on devious types of office politics. Keep in mind that you may have to make frequent use of tactics to impress your boss. In the turbulent environment of the 1990s you will have many new bosses.

## CHECK OUT THE CHEMISTRY
## BETWEEN YOU AND YOUR BOSS ━━━━━━━━━━━━━━━━━━

As a starting point in developing a good superior–subordinate relationship, check out the chemistry between you and your boss. If the two of you are a poor natural fit, you will always be handicapped in your relationship with your boss. One tip-off to positive chemistry is when your boss typically laughs at your attempts at humor. Another is when he or she is excited about most of your ideas and suggestions. Positive chemistry is also most likely present when your boss is impressed with your work.

Correspondingly, negative chemistry may be present when your boss remains stone-faced at your attempts at humor, is indifferent to your ideas and suggestions, and remains unimpressed by your actions. One method of dealing with negative chemistry is to get away from your boss's jurisdiction at the earliest opportunity. If this is not feasible, work extra hard at all the suggestions given in this chapter.

## UNDERSTAND YOUR BOSS ━━━━━━━━━━━━━━━━━━━━━━

One of the most important steps in managing your boss, according to Christopher Hegarty, is to understand him or her. Too often subordinates make the wrong assumption about their boss. A good starting point is to figure out if your boss has a need to be liked, a need to be disliked, or a need to be needed.[1]

Such judgments can often be made on the basis of a boss's actions. If your boss is happiest when you show appreciation, continue to show appreciation whenever feasible. A boss who has a need to be disliked is relatively rare, so don't overemphasize this approach. A boss who needs to be needed is happiest when asked for advice and emotional support. Oblige such a boss by capitalizing on appropriate opportunities to get his or her input on your thinking.

### Find Out Your Boss's True Objectives

Another way of understanding your boss is to know what that person is trying to achieve. If you help your boss reach his or her objectives, you will be on your way to cultivating a good superior–subordinate relationship. This task would be simplified if managers routinely and explicitly explained what they are trying to accomplish. More often you have to dig for a clear statement of what the boss is really trying to accomplish. Reggie, a sales representative for a textile company, discovered the importance of getting a true picture of his boss's objectives.

Reggie was proud of his sales performance in his competitive, lower Manhattan territory. Reggie would excitedly explain to his boss how hard he had worked to convince a clothing manufacturer to buy goods from his company. Sarah, his boss, would nod with faint approval.

After two more ungracious compliments from Sarah in regard to having opened new accounts, Reggie confronted her: "Why am I beating my head against the wall? Aren't we in the business to sell textiles to clothing manufacturers? Don't you like my customers? Are we trying to lose money in order to avoid taxes?

"No," said Sarah. "I've hinted at it before Reggie. Our company is no longer interested in the little customer. Your specialty is the small manufacturer who costs us too much to supply. I think we actually lost money on your last two sales. Forget the little operator and concentrate on big enchiladas who can order 3000 yards at a time."

Reggie got the message and also a few extra dollars in his pocket. Now he turns over the customers his company does not want to a jobber who welcomes sales of any size. Reggie gets a small commission. More importantly, he is helping Sarah reach her objective of cultivating major customers.

## Figure Out if Your Boss Is a Reader or a Listener

Another worthwhile aspect of understanding your boss is recognizing if he or she prefers written or oral reports on important topics. Some bosses feel the most comfortable with written information backed by documentation. The details in a written report give many bosses a sense of control. Other superiors may prefer an oral summary, partially because they are too impatient to read. The political advantage of delivering information in the right mode is you may be perceived as doing a good job.[2]

A staff assistant comments on how she capitalized on knowing whether her boss was a reader or a listener. "To Pam, serious information had to be transmitted in person, and usually over lunch or drinks. She only wanted to receive memos to record routine information or to document important information we had previously discussed. I think better use of written reports would have saved us a lot of time, but I was in no position to challenge her preferred way of receiving information."

## Understand Boss Language

Managers in bureaucracies frequently attempt to be polite by softening the language in their demands. It is important, however, not to misinterpret this softness. Keep in mind that "If it's not too much trouble" means "Do it . . . and the sooner the better." "If I may make a small suggestion . . ." means "Do it this way." "I don't want to rush you," means "Hurry up."[3]

## SUPPORT YOUR BOSS

Supporting your boss is fundamental to being liked by that person. Although support can take many forms, it follows the same general principle of defending your boss in time of need. Similar to any relationship between two people, who needs an antagonist for a partner?

### Listen to Your Boss's Problems and Suggestions

A remarkably simple method of supporting your boss is to be a patient listener. Active listening to your boss can take a number of forms: listening to personal problems, asking for suggestions and then following them, nodding with enthusiasm and smiling when the boss speaks, or taking notes during a meeting.

Tom, a mechanical engineer, facilitated a good employee–boss relationship by demonstrating that he listened carefully to his boss's suggestions. On one occasion, Alex, his boss, commented when he stopped by Tom's work area, "Say, that looks like an interesting way to reinforce a valve. Where did you learn about that?"

Tom responded, "Indirectly, the credit must go to you. Remember, one day over coffee we were talking about the strength of valves. You mentioned that a researcher named Schwartz had written the most comprehensive paper on valves. I sent for a reprint and found the exact information I needed. Did I forget to thank you for that suggestion?"

### Cover Your Boss's Blooper

Why try to show up your boss's blooper? Instead capitalize on the occasional blooper to display a supportive attitude. Your relationship might be all the better for your act of self-interested kindness. Ram, an assistant to the vice-president of international marketing, showed support for his boss by catching and correcting a blooper. Ram's hurried assignment on Thursday afternoon was to prepare some flip charts based on his boss's notes. The Friday presentation would focus on the international outlook for the firm's products.

As Ram dutifully prepared the charts, he noticed a key line Jose had written for one of the charts: "As the U. S. dollar strengthens, exports will increase naturally." Ram noticed immediately that the converse of this statement was true: A strong U. S. dollar means greater difficulty in exporting because American goods become more expensive relative to other currencies.

Ram notified Jose immediately that he had caught an *unintended* error, and was taking the liberty of changing it to avoid any confusion in the presentation. Muttering to himself that he usually gets the implications of changes in exchange rates confused, Jose thanked Ram profusely for catching this slip. Friday's presentation went without a glitch, and Ram's timely efforts were much appreciated by his boss.

## Be Deferent

Most bosses appreciate a show of respect for their positions. By being appropriately deferent you might be able to show support for your boss and thus improve your relationship. Here are a few deferent statements that might appeal to a boss's sense of authority without making you appear obsequious:

> "Yes sir (or ma'am), that sounds like a good idea."
> "Okay coach, what do I do now?"
> "That suits me fine. You're the boss."
> "From your vantage point as a manager, how do you see this problem?"

## Respect Deadlines

Many deadlines are legitimate in the sense that they reflect true organizational needs. By respecting deadlines imposed by your boss, you are giving substantial support. Much of anybody's reputation in an organization is based on their dependability in getting tasks accomplished by the time promised. When you respect deadlines you enhance your reputation, and help the boss meet his or her deadlines. One executive told us, "The kind of back up I need is a dependable subordinate. Flashes of genius are fine, but in my operation, I need the support of dependable people."

## Take Criticism Cheerfully

Except for a minority of tyrants, most managers feel uncomfortable criticizing group members, and therefore prefer to reserve criticism for when it is urgently needed. A subordinate who rebels against criticism makes the boss's job all the more difficult. Accepting valid criticism is thus another way of showing support for your boss. A marketing director commented: "I dread performance reviews with people who won't learn from them. I'm telling them what doesn't work, and they sit there defending their actions instead of taking heart."[4]

## HELP YOUR BOSS SUCCEED ═══════════════════════════════

When you are caught up in the pressures of pursuing your own ambitions, it is easy to forget the primary reason you were hired: Your prospective boss thought you could help accomplish the department's objectives. Even if nepotism helped you get your job, the person who accepted you into the department believed you would contribute directly or indirectly to his or her success. Most of your job activities should be directed toward this vital success strategy—help your boss succeed.

The emphasis in helping your boss succeed is going beyond the ordinary requirements of your job, as illustrated by the deft maneuvering of Beth, an assistant store manager within a chain of appliance stores. She and her boss, Monica, agreed that although they now operated one of the most successful stores in their region, more success would be forthcoming if only headquarters would cooperate.

The two women ardently believed that by doubling the physical capacity of their store, business would also double. So far, Monica had not convinced management that expansion would pay a suitable return on investment. Too often in the past, store managers had wanted a larger store more for appearance than for legitimate business reasons.

At the next regional meeting of managers, a home office executive asked Beth how she liked her job: "Terrific," answered Beth, "In these uncertain economic times, it's nice to be working for a store that is on the upswing. Another thing I like about my job is Monica's attitude. Most managers would grumble about having to squeeze all the merchandise and all those customers into such little space.

"Last week we were practically selling TVs off the manufacturer's truck. If we had more room, many of those customers might have browsed around the store some more. But so be it. We do the best with what we have."

Within three weeks, preliminary plans had been formulated to put an additional wing on the appliance store managed by Beth and Monica. Before six months had passed, the store had enlarged 40 percent. Sales had increased one-third, and Beth had been recommended by her boss to participate in profit sharing. Beth gave considerable credit for her success to Monica, and rewarded her with an outstanding performance evaluation.

Another way to help your boss succeed is to perform well on crucial tasks—make-or-break factors in the job.[5] Such factors commonly include helping your boss increase profits, cut costs, attain affirmative action goals for hiring women and minorities, and preparing a budget. People who help accomplish their crucial tasks are perceived as valuable team players.

"L.T.," a production assistant in a furniture company, became a crucial subordinate to his factory superintendent and boss, Ron. In so doing, L.T. took the big first step in his journey toward becoming an executive. The company was faced with a serious problem. Small bubbles were surfacing on the finish of tables and desks when they were exposed to temperatures above 80 degrees Fahrenheit. Customers by the dozens were demanding refunds or refinishes on the company products. Furniture retail stores, in turn, were demanding credit from the company and threatening to discontinue as customers unless there were guarantees that the bubbling problem was conquered.

Managers and specialists alike devoted as much time as possible to the mysterious problem that posed potentially disastrous consequences to the company. After four days of frantic searching for causes and much buck passing, no logical reason for the bubbling had been isolated.

L.T. came up with a plan. He telephoned all his acquaintances and former classmates who worked for furniture makers. He asked each of them if they ever had a seemingly unresolvable technical problem at the factory and what they did about it. One acquaintance said his factory had a similar baffling problem of laminate that became unglued. To deal with the problem, they hired a chemical engineering consultant from Atlanta who solved the problem in three days.

L.T. told his boss about the consultant. The boss hired the consultant who proceeded to detect the cause of the bubbling. Apparently, one large batch of solvent was contaminated when the wrong acid was used in preparation. L.T.'s boss was enthusiastic about the consultant's efforts, and equally enthusiastic about L.T.'s judgment in recommending him.

## MATCH YOUR STYLE TO YOUR BOSS'S STYLE

A more political method of cultivating your boss, rather than becoming a crucial subordinate, is to imitate his or her style. Industrial psychologist Robert Hecht says that you can enjoy a productive, anxiety-free working relationship if you identify and understand your supervisor's "work style." The first step toward peaceful coexistence is to identify your supervisor's work style from among these four:

- *Forecaster style.* Idea oriented, meticulous, and concerned about all the steps necessary to achieve long-range goals.
- *Associator (or feelings) style.* Attentive to the impact of ideas on workers at all levels. Managers of this type believe that appreciating and understanding workers' feelings is vital in managing others.

- *Systemizer style.* Focused on methods, logic, and written documentation. A manager with this style believes that *how* something is done determines its results.
- *Energizer style.* Concerned with results rather than ideas or goals. A manager with this style believes that if something works, it should be used. Such managers exude energy, drive, and determination. Often these managers would rather do something wrong than do nothing and be right.

After you identify your supervisor's work style, you should be able to make a complementary adjustment. If your style differs from your supervisor's, compromise and use an appropriate strategy. A manager with an energizer style doesn't want to hear, "Let's call a meeting to really thrash out this problem before taking action." Instead, explain how you are going to take immediate action. Avoid locking yourself into one style, because you will have to adapt to many managers in your career.

Hecht also advises that whatever style your manager exhibits, go along with it. It's your boss's show; if you want to move up, you must become a team player.[6]

A less complicated method of imitating your boss's style is to use your boss's favorite phrases, and to quote your boss in meetings. Michelle was the manager of a small branch of a casualty insurance company. She and the other four branch managers in her region would meet at least twice a month with regional manager Vince, to discuss plans, problems, and new business developments.

After one of these meetings, one of Michelle's cohorts said to her, "When did you start using those expressions that Vince uses ad nauseam, 'At this point in time,' and 'To me the bottom line is . . .'? Do you also intend to imitate his style of clothing?"

The not-so-good natured kidding by another manager did not daunt Michelle. She persisted—performing to the best of her ability as a branch manager and copying certain of Vince's expressions and attitudes. Four months later, a new position opened up for an industrial accounts manager. The person chosen for this position would personally handle several major accounts. The accounts manager would still function as a branch manager, but an assistant would be appointed to deal with the more routine administrative aspects of the position. Michelle, who had worked so hard to cultivate her boss, was the first industrial accounts manager for her region.

Yet another way to copy your boss's style is to imitate his or her body language. The process is called "mirroring" because you become a reflection of your boss's gestures, facial expressions, and even breathing pattern. Imitating your boss's breathing pattern when conferring with that person is the most effective technique—partially because it is so subtle. The payoff from mirroring is that you establish good rapport with the person whose body language you are imitating.

A financial analyst who agreed to try mirroring for a couple of weeks found that the technique improved his relationship with his boss. He observed, "At first I thought this would be such a flagrant way of sucking up to the boss that it would backfire. But I was wrong. As I became more adept at mirroring, my boss gave me more nods of approval. He began to accept my ideas more readily. I plan to definitely keep this technique in my bag of tricks."

## MINIMIZE OBVIOUS ATTEMPTS AT SELF-PROTECTION

An effective way of looking good to your boss is to take responsibility for the negative consequences of any bad decision you make rather than being defensive. Seth Allcorn observes that many workers find ways to protect themselves from the consequences of their decisions. Among the wimpy techniques they use are blaming others, failing to admit mistakes, blaming the mistakes on organizational procedures, or simply hoping that the problem will go away.[7]

The person who appears overly defensive to the boss is eventually seen as weak, and therefore as a poor candidate for promotion or other choice assignments. One such person is Garth, who was accused of sexual harassment by a temporary worker. She complained to Garth's boss that he invited her out for dinner and remarked twice that she had a lovely figure. The temporary worker's story was partially corroborated by another office temporary who overheard one of Garth's comments about the first woman's figure.

Garth's boss listened to the complaint, and then decided the charges were too light to qualify as a valid case of sexual harassment. As the boss viewed the event, Garth had not persisted long enough to create a hostile environment (a major criterion of sexual harassment). When his boss confronted Garth about the complaint, Garth contended bitterly that the temporary worker's assertions were vastly exaggerated. He complained that the woman was simply a troublemaker seeking revenge because he did not offer her a full-time assignment.

Garth's boss was dismayed at his self-protective behavior. He told Garth that he would have written the charges off as a minor case of less than professional behavior if Garth had admitted that he had made a pass at the temporary worker. Instead, he would now be regarded as a person with a weak moral fiber—one who denies he can be guilty of any wrongdoing.

## AVOID UPSTAGING YOUR BOSS

To upstage your boss privately or in a group meeting is a quick way to ruin a relationship. Marilyn Kennedy cautions against upstaging your boss even if that person is barely older, and, in your opinion no more competent. In most organizations it is more important to respect rank than the person holding the position.[8] Upstaging can take many forms, including:

- Your boss tells a good joke in a meeting, and you call out the punchline before the boss finishes.
- Your boss tells a good joke in a meeting, and you attempt to top the joke.
- Your boss presents some technical facts, and you publicly correct these facts.
- Your boss says, "We are task-orientated around here." You respond, "You really mean, task-oriented. But don't feel bad, most people make the same error."
- Your boss purchases a new car which he or she proudly talks about. Within one week, you purchase an even more luxurious car.
- Your boss throws a party at his or her house. One month later, you throw a much more lavish party and invite the same people, along with the company president.

## REWARD YOUR BOSS

Many managers complain that a major part of their job is giving rewards to others (such as compliments and praise), yet they receive few of these rewards themselves. Finding legitimate ways to reward your boss can therefore help satisfy an unmet need. A sincere compliment is an excellent and straightforward reward. For example, if your boss reschedules a computer training course to fit your vacation schedule, you might write a note of appreciation. Or, if your boss closes a major sale, you might remark, "I'm very impressed. I would like to learn the details of how to pull off such an important accomplishment."

A more difficult reward to administer, yet one with a big payoff, is to praise your boss to top management. Executed with aplomb, praising your boss in high places can cement a positive relationship. The benefits may be direct—your boss might recommend you for a favorable salary increase. Or they could be indirect, because as your boss prospers, so do you—providing you both have a good working relationship.

A compliment about your boss to upper management should be couched in specific terms that make sense to executives. Avoid the use of nebulous flattery such as labeling your boss, "the type of manager Harvard Business School hopes to produce," "an inspirational leader," or "an ideal model for learning about the mysteries of management."

Sean, a hospital administrator, had an excellent idea. At a hospital board meeting, Sean was asked by the administrators how he enjoyed working at Hillside General. He expounded:

> Things are going well for me at Hillside. Hospital administration is my career so it's important to me to work for a real pro. So often the chief executive officer of a hospital is a physician who has little regard for the administrative process. Such a person runs the ship as if he or she were royalty. Not Dr. Jacobs. The man knows how to manage. He keeps a careful eye on hospital productivity. He is very concerned that we keep the hospital beds filled and that we stay within budget.

> He prefers good patient care to philosophizing. But at the same time, Dr. Jacobs has concern for the feelings of people. I have seen him personally intervene in a situation where it appeared that a Mexican-American was the victim of an ethnic slur. And the person Dr. Jacobs upbraided was a resident from Cornell Medical School.

One week later, Dr. Jacobs commented casually to Sean, "It's good to know that my top administrator and I have compatible management styles. Let me know if I do anything that interferes with your performance on your job."

## SHARE YOUR ACCOMPLISHMENTS
## WITH YOUR BOSS _____

Most jobs in organizations are team efforts. If you make a contribution, it is usually a shared one. If you are an advertising copywriter and you think of a slogan that catapults your client's product to the top, it is not solely your accomplishment. It's easy to forget that the artist who prepared the layout on which to present your slogan made an important contribution. It's also easy to forget that you tried out the slogan on the office messenger whose pupils dilated when he heard your sonorous phrase. And did you forget your boss who may have pushed your thinking in the right direction to think of the prize-winning slogan, "We're Number One for a good reason"?

Kevin was creative both as a laboratory technician and an office politician. His suggestion for saving the company $10,000 per year by recycling laboratory wastes netted him a $3000 suggestion award. As the company photographer took a picture of Kevin standing between his boss and the manager of the suggestion award program, Kevin turned to his boss and said, "It's the atmosphere you set up in the lab that helps me think creatively."

## PRESENT ALTERNATIVES TO YOUR BOSS ⎯⎯⎯⎯⎯⎯⎯

An indirect way of cultivating your boss is to find ways of not being blamed for wrong decisions. In this way you can avoid your boss thinking that you made a bad decision. A technique to avoid making a bad decision—one practiced by a number of shrewd office politicians—is that of presenting your boss with alternatives when faced with a difficult decision. It works this way:

*YOU:*   We have a difficult problem facing us. A company with a bad credit rating wants to place a $10,000 order on 90-day terms. We can readily fill the order from current inventory, but it could prove very expensive if the customer doesn't pay. The way I look at it, we have three alternatives for dealing with this problem:

*One,* we could tell the customer to take out a loan and then come back to us when he has the cash.

*Two,* we could request that the customer make a substantial downpayment and give us the balance due in 90 days.

*Three,* we could demand a 30-day payment because the customer lacks a top credit rating.

*BOSS:*   I like the first alternative. Let's deal with them on a cash basis.

As Murphy's law (If anything can go wrong it will) predicted, the prospective customer does not wish to borrow money to purchase goods from your company. Irritated, the customer finds another supplier. Your boss is upset about the lost sale, but accepts most of the blame because it was he or she who chose what appeared to be the wrong alternative. Use this technique rarely and selectively, because if overdone it will make you appear indecisive to your boss. Also, make sure that your boss does not always get blamed for choosing a poor alternative solution.

## TEACH YOUR BOSS A NEW SKILL ━━━━━━━━━━━━━━━━

Even an Innocent Lamb would not object to the political tactics of culti-vating your boss by teaching that person a valuable job skill. Such skills could relate to computer usage, accounting concepts, research methods, giving presentations, interviewing, and decision making. Introducing new skills will generally help a superior–subordinate relationship.

Mitch, a management trainee interested in scientific approaches to management, noted that his boss, Ralph, was having difficulty deciding whether to make station-to-station or person-to-person calls. Mitch vol-unteered to help his boss find the best answer by use of a payoff matrix —a relatively uncomplicated mathematical way of making these types of decisions. Ralph used Mitch's results. After a six-month trial period, the amount of money paid for toll calls decreased. Mitch explains what happened:

> Ralph was really excited about my little payoff matrix. I told him the matrix could be applied to a variety of quantitative business problems. Ralph then asked me how he could go about learning this technique. I volunteered to teach him the method, figuring an informed boss is a happy boss. I could feel my stature grow in Ralph's eyes once he learned how to run a payoff matrix.

## UNCOMPLICATE YOUR BOSS'S JOB ━━━━━━━━━━━━━━

Teaching your boss a new skill can uncomplicate the boss's job in a specific way. Also keep in mind the general principle of making life less complicated for your boss. Your role is to take problems away from your boss, not add to his or her burden. As you take away minor problems from your boss, he or she has more time to work on major ones. The payoff is that your boss develops more confidence in you. Matt, a systems analyst, violated this principle. Consequently, his relationship with his boss, Ken, suffered.

Matt pleaded with Ken's assistant, "Are you sure I can't see Ken today? I've got a devil of a problem with one of the supervisors that has to be resolved before quitting time."

The assistant replied, "I suppose I could arrange it. Toward the middle of the afternoon, but only for a brief time. How about 2:45?"

At 2:45 Matt plunked himself down in Ken's office and began rat-tling off his problems. "Old Jeb won't let me into his department. He said he's not going to allow any wiseguy staff specialist snooping around.

The guy is afraid I'm going to discover that he's doing something wrong. What he doesn't realize is that we're here to help him."

Ken countered, "Right now your problems seem small to me. Top management is going through another reorganization I have to work on. Why can't you and Jeb work out your differences? Why do I have to fight your petty battles for you? Are you a systems analyst or a factory mouse?"

Matt became a better office politician after that confrontation, but he had already damaged his relationship with his boss. A better approach for Matt would have been for him to resolve his problem with Jeb and *then* inform his boss about what he accomplished.

## DO YOUR BOSS'S DIRTY WORK

"I'm sorry to have to inform you about this, but upper management has instructed me to tell you about our new rest break plans," said Sherry. "From now on, no electric percolators will be authorized in the office. Anybody who wants coffee, tea, or the like will have to use the vending machines located near the company cafeteria. Only under emergency situations are you to bring beverages back to your desk. It is preferable that you drink your coffee at the benches designated for that purpose near the vending machines. Furthermore, rest breaks are not to exceed 15 minutes."

Sherry did not relish being the bearer of bad-news assignments, but she continued to volunteer for them. Sherry knew that taking care of your boss's dirty work can help you endear yourself to that person. Many a company hatchet specialist has accelerated his or her career by a willingness to implement the decision of downsizing a company or reducing pay.

## BE LOYAL

A major strategy for cultivating a good relationship with your boss (and the organization) is to be loyal. Loyalty is expressed in many ways other than being a sycophant. One such expression is to defend the boss when he or she is under attack by people from other departments. Such a defense does not necessarily mean that you think your boss is entirely correct. It is possible to defend the merit of what your boss says without agreeing with the boss's entire position.

Brian, an educational coordinator in the evening school division of a college, was invited to a curriculum development meeting which was also attended by a number of high-ranking college officials. At one point,

Steve, a representative from another division of the college, fired a few salvos at Arden, the evening school director—and Brian's boss.

Said Steve, "It's apparent to everybody here that the evening school has been suffering from declining enrollment. I suspect that the evening school is not shifting with the times. The courses you offer are too old, too out of date. Where are your modern courses? When can the public get its appetite whetted for courses in laser technology? Or in protecting the environment? Or in consuming foods that don't cause cancer or heart disease? Arden looked solemn and concerned. Brian spoke for him:

> Hold on, Steve. I can see the merit in your argument. But let's hear the other side of the story. In my position as education coordinator, I get a careful look at the enrollment for new courses. It's been our experience in the past that so-called modern courses have a very short shelf life. By the time they are offered, the public is usually not very interested in the topic. Even if the course does run once, there may not be a sustaining interest.
>
> A few years ago we offered a computer literacy seminar for people who wanted to upgrade themselves in almost any job. We predicted that 400 people would register for the course. When it came right down to people putting their money on the line, about 25 registered. The second time we offered the seminar, only four people registered. Offering modern courses to the public is not as easy as it sounds.

A sigh of relief flashed across Arden's face. After the meeting, he commented to Brian, "I thought your comments were well taken. I wish I had said that about the computer utilization seminar. Yet coming from you, it was more convincing than if I had defended myself."

## MAINTAIN FREQUENT CONTACT WITH THE BOSS

A sensible way of cultivating your boss is to keep in frequent contact but do not become a pest. Office politicians frequently find a reason for seeing their boss even if a legitimate reason does not exist. Their tactics include bringing in telephone messages, getting the boss's reaction to a routine memo, or asking for clarification on a problem. Herb, a man who now has the top marketing job in his company, describes his approach to maintaining frequent contact with the boss:

> When I was a sales manager, I made an effort to travel with my boss. For example, if I heard he was going to St. Louis on a business trip, I would try to arrange some appointments in St. Louis. I would then casually mention to him that he and I were traveling to the same town. Inevitably, he would

invite me to sit down next to him on the plane. That's where a lot of business is conducted. My boss learned more about my hopes for the future there than he did at the office.

Once in town, we would agree to meet for dinner. There is a certain intimacy about having dinner together out of town. It's a good way to develop an edge over other rivals and to get management support of your program. I owe much of my rise to the top to talent, but talent is not enough. Unless your boss understands you as a person, you are just another worker in the department. Traveling together adds the personal touch.

## KNOW WHEN TO ENGAGE IN SMALL TALK

In the next chapter you are advised to engage in "big talk" in order to impress higher ups. Nevertheless, small talk can have its place in cultivating your immediate boss. Small talk is particularly recommended when your boss is stressed out and apparently does not want to get involved with heavy issues. Under these circumstances, preface your important conversation with a brief comment or two about the weather, traffic conditions, or leaf raking. Jumping right into meaningful conversation might add to your frazzled boss's stress.

Small talk can be consistently appropriate if your boss is small minded. A surprising number of successful executives are small minded with respect to their core interests. Recently I chastised a friend for her preoccupation with the weather when others were trying to talk about something more personally meaningful. Her response was, "My boss is the same way, and he's the general manager of our division. All he really likes to talk about is the weather."

Small talk can also be useful in enhancing your relationship with the boss when used at social gatherings. Conversely, many bosses prefer not to talk shop in a social setting. Above all, do not press for your boss's reaction to your proposal, or for a work commitment of any kind, at a company party. However, if your boss asks you a work-related question at a social function, dropping small talk is appropriate.

## HELP ALONG YOUR BOSS'S PERSONAL LIFE

Many people improve their relationships with the boss by getting involved socially. The risk involved is that you might cross a boundary that shouldn't be crossed. Nevertheless, many people do get on the good side of the boss by becoming part of his or her social life.

An indirect way of getting involved in your boss's personal life is to recognize his or her personal interests. An *extreme* use of this technique is to introduce your boss to a potential date. Other techniques include helping to repair or refinish a car, lending your boss your season pass to a team sport, or merely sending birthday and holiday cards.

Paul might be considered a Machiavellian for pulling the caper he did. Looking for a way to cultivate his boss, Paul noted that his boss had an avid interest in wine making. While at a garage sale, Paul found an ancient wine press that was still functional. It looked like a bargain at $25. Paul said to his boss the next Monday morning, "I just inherited something that might be of interest to you. An aunt of mine willed me an old wine press along with a host of much less valuable articles. I know you are interested in wine making. How would you like to buy this press from me for $5?"

Paul felt that if he offered the wine press as a gift, his boss would be hesitant. By purchasing it from Paul, the boss would not feel he was taking advantage of a subordinate's generosity or that he was being manipulated.[9]

A direct way of getting involved in your boss's personal life is to accept a social invitation from the boss for lunch, dinner, golf, and so forth. If handled correctly, these business–social occasions can help develop a stronger working relationship with the boss. Keep these suggestions in mind:[10]

1. *Take cues from your boss about mentioning work.* You may have some urgent work issues to discuss over dinner. Before getting to these, find out if your boss is interested. How does the boss react at your first attempt to mention your interest in promotion? Does the boss quickly change the topic or appear interested? If your boss doesn't feel comfortable talking about the subject, drop it for now.

2. *Consume alcohol in moderation.* These days almost nobody is viewed negatively for being a light drinker. Drinking heavily, or lighting a joint, can peg you as an office bozo. Another problem with too much alcohol is that it really does lower inhibitions and defenses, thus increasing the chances that you will be too candid. As one computer programmer said over a joint shared with his boss, "The group is willing to put up with your technical incompetence because you're such a nice guy."

3. *Avoid revealing personal problems.* A modern boss should recognize that most people have at least one troublesome problem in regard to relationships, health, or finances. In reality, many bosses regard problems as a sign of weakness. For the same reason, don't reveal any lack of confidence you might have in your professional abilities. If you want to discuss your problems, use somebody other than your boss as a confidant.

4. *Be cautious in making negative comments about co-workers.* The intimacy of an after-hours encounter with the boss makes it a temptation to discuss the foibles of other department members. If your boss digs for information, it is best to make constructive comments about how a given co-worker can be helped rather than focusing on that person's weaknesses.

5. *Keep the relationship professional if romance is in the air.* Suppose it is obvious that the boss has romantic intentions. The antidote is to parry the advances with statements about your being happily married or having an exclusive relationship, or a "significant other." As one woman said to an interested boss, "One of the reasons I was able to accept this dinner invitation with you is that my boyfriend trusts me entirely. He knows that I am 100 percent faithful."

   Nevertheless, if you are romantically inclined toward the boss, getting involved may be worth the risk. Legions of marriages and other long-term relationships stemmed from dating the boss. At some point you may want to transfer from the department, but isn't a big romance worth a job transfer?

6. *Avoid confusing your role as a subordinate with your role as a friend.* Even if your social outing with the boss leads to a personal friendship, do not lapse into role confusion. Keep firmly in mind that you are still a subordinate and should not attempt to exploit your friendship by asking for special favors. Instead, let your boss take the initiative in treating you better than your co-workers who neglected their boss's personal and social life. Isn't the purpose of your politicking to gain an edge without being too obvious?

# CHAPTER 5

# IMPRESSING THE
# HIGHER UPS

Playing smart office politics requires more than performing well and getting in good graces with your immediate boss. It is also important to cultivate powerful people in the company—from your boss's boss to conceivably, the CEO. Because top-management changes are so frequent in the 1990s, getting in good with key people is more challenging than ever.

Cultivating higher-ups is usually done for the offensive purpose of helping you find a sponsor—an influential person who will help pluck you from obscurity to organizational stardom. Yet defense is also important. Cultivating higher-ups may provide a hedge against a poor relationship with your immediate superior. If your boss is unimpressed by you or your performance, your reputation can be salvaged by a higher-up. If a high-ranking official extols your virtues, your boss's negative opinion of you might be overruled.

Whether you are cultivating influential people for offensive or defensive purposes, the strategies and tactics recommended in this chapter will apply. Keep in mind that many techniques for cultivating your boss (described in the previous chapter) can be applied at higher levels. Similarly, the tactics described in this chapter can sometimes be used with an immediate superior.

## SHINE AT MEETINGS

Meetings are the major setting for impressing higher-ranking people. At most meetings you attend, at least one person present will be a higher-up. When attempting to create a positive impression, remember that you are not trying to dominate or win control of the meeting; nor are you trying to resolve a conflict. To demonstrate good judgment and management potential, keep five impression-making tactics in mind.

1. *Appear articulate, poised, and successful.* Everybody has heard about the importance of sounding good and looking good, but not everybody realizes how important it is at meetings. Looking good at a regular staff meeting usually does not require that you appear as if you were a sales associate at Bloomingdales. Wearing jackets at an action-oriented meeting is becoming rare nowadays. However, it usually does mean that you look well rested and wear sparkling clean and neatly pressed clothing. Use correct grammar, and pepper your speech with action words such as "penetrate," "analyze," "surge," and "crunch."

2. *Ask set-up questions.* A set-up question asks an influential person a question he or she is able and eager to answer—and perhaps wishes to be asked. Bart was present at a meeting attended by John Chadwick, the chairman of the board who was actively interested in environmental protection and human rights. At midmeeting, Bart turned to John and said, "Sir, may I ask a question? Your answer may help resolve a few of the issues raised this morning."

   "Go ahead, by all means," replied Chadwick.

   "Mr. Chadwick, are we in business strictly to make a profit?"

   "So glad you asked that question, Bart. Certainly not. As a business organization, we have a social responsibility as well as profit responsibility."

3. *Allow others to talk.* People who dominate meetings often do so because they are tense or trying too hard to create a favorable impression. Unless you have called the meeting and its primary purpose is for you to give information to others, avoid overtalking. This is particularly true if you are trying to impress higher-ups. Ben's situation is not unusual.

   Ben was a compulsive talker at meetings. It was important to him that everyone be aware of his opinion on every issue raised. Despite his urge to control meetings, Ben was an effective manager. Yet his behavior in meetings excluded him from at least one key promotional opportunity. A new assistant general manager position opened up. Ben was one of the candidates suggested to the general manager. The latter commented:

   "Sorry, you'll have to do better than that," said the general manager. "I've been in meetings with Ben and I find him obnoxious. The guy won't shut up and give other people a chance to talk. How could he ever find the answer to problems I asked him to investigate if he did all the talking?"

4. *Take notes when influential people speak.* A potent form of flattery is to take notes of important messages delivered at meetings. If you take notes on everything said, others will think you are acting as the meeting scribe. It is better to be selective. Take a few notes when your boss speaks. Take copious notes when a higher-up offers information. Later on in the meeting, or at a future date, these notes can be used to advantage.

Ned attended a production meeting in which the vice-president of manufacturing was also present. He brought along his usual yellow tablet and jotted down information he perceived as being important. Toward the end of the meeting he addressed the vice-president. Pointing to his tablet, he said, "Sir you mentioned at the outset of this meeting that some of our products were becoming overpriced in comparison to the competition. We at the manufacturing engineering level would certainly agree. Could you give us some more information on that topic? It's of vital concern."

Score one for Ned. All at once, he set up the vice-president as influential, paid him a compliment (by taking notes on the information the higher-up presented), and created a good impression in the process.

5. *Avoid daydreaming.* A major problem facing many people at a meeting is how to stay fully awake. As an alternative to falling asleep, many people begin to drift into a dreamlike state. One man confessed that he dreamed about recent sexual experiences during budget review meetings. The danger in daydreaming, of course, is that you will miss out on some important information or be unable to answer a question specifically asked of you.

The executive director of a settlement house turned to a supervisor during a staff meeting and asked, "Bill, what do you think of the proposal just advanced by Clara?" Bill replied, "I'm sorry. I must have been daydreaming. What proposal?" Bill not only missed out on an opportunity to impress the executive director, he left a lasting negative impression.

## SHOW THAT YOU IDENTIFY WITH MANAGEMENT

Although it is important to get along well with co-workers, such camaraderie can be overdone. Workers who appear more identified with their work group than with top management run the risk of being passed over for promotion. To impress top management, you must act like an executive. Especially guard against creating the impression that you would feel uncomfortable if placed in an executive environment. An example of this problem took place with Steve, a sales representative who was recommended for promotion to branch manager by his immediate manager. The promotion was vetoed by the national sales manager for these reasons:

"Steve is undoubtedly a leader with respect to sales performance. But inside the sales office, he tries too hard to be one of the gang. I've seen him about five times over the past couple of years. Once I saw him matching quarters with the office assistants to decide who would buy the coffee and soft drinks.

"At a regional sales meeting, I noticed that Steve spent a good deal of time at the bar with other sales representatives. He seemed to have no interest in spending time with members of management. Maybe when he matures more, we can reconsider him. He'd never get the respect of the other sales representatives. They would see Steve as one of them. We need people with more executive stature as branch managers."

## APPEAR COOL UNDER PRESSURE

A man attending a seminar on power and politics returned from the lunchbreak with a drawing of a duck. Holding the drawing above his head, he said to the other seminar participants, "Allow me to summarize what we have learned this morning. A smart executive is much like a duck. On the surface the executive appears cool, calm, and under control. Yet underneath, the executive is paddling like all fury."

In addition to the laughter it provoked, the seminar participant's analogy contained an important message for those interested in impressing top management—appear cool under pressure. Although modern managers are supposed to express honest feelings, expressing panic generally hurts your reputation with influential people.

Bursts of emotion are generally more permissible for first-level supervisors than for executives. An exception is that some executives use exhortations effectively. The odds are in your favor, however, if you appear to be in emotional control when things around you are falling apart. Observe these examples of coolness under pressure:

- Asked how things were going in the company he was recently appointed to run, an executive said, "All the parts are in working order except for marketing. Right now we just don't have a big enough backlog of orders to keep us going. We hope to correct that situation soon."

- The manager of the data processing center in a bank was confronted by three employees who said they would resign by the end of the week unless the bank would offer them a 10 percent salary adjustment and flexible working hours. The manager replied, "Do what you think is best. If you resign now, I will recommend that you are never rehired by the bank. All three of you can readily be replaced in the short-run by a quick call to one of our temporary help agencies." The employees decided not to quit, and to discuss their demands at a later date.

## TALK BIG, SHUN TRIVIA

Small talk can keep you placed in a small job. If you have a predilection for talking about the weather, your sinuses, or grocery store coupons, save these comments for the right occasion. The right occasion is when you are spending time with people who enjoy small talk. The wrong occasion is when you are trying to impress higher-ups (and also your boss).

When you have the chance to talk to an influential person, some trivia may be necessary for an initial warm-up, but quickly shift the topic to big talk—that is, comments about important issues affecting the organization.

The following example illustrates the difference between making small and big talk over the same issue when meeting a high-ranking official from your organization. The person talking is the manager of a branch motor vehicle department. The visitor to the office is the State Commissioner of Motor Vehicles.

| | |
|---|---|
| *MANAGER (using small talk):* | Look at that rain outside. It's been like that for three days. This sure is the rainiest place I've ever lived. I guess it's fine if you're a farmer or plant. |
| *COMMISSIONER:* | Did you say something? |
| *MANAGER (using big talk):* | This rain creates an interesting problem for the Motor Vehicle Department at the branch level. Common sense would suggest that our workload decreases when it rains. My calculations and those of my staff indicate that we are extra busy on rainy days. I think a good number of people wait for a rainy day to take care of their routine business with us. I wonder if this is a national trend. |

*COMMISSIONER:*                                    You have raised an important issue about
                                                   our workload. I think the problem war-
                                                   rants further study.

Another method of thinking big is to frame your argument in terms
of the benefits it will accrue to the organization. This tactic is effective
because it softens the self-interest in your proposal.[1] If your suggestions
appear too self-serving, others will denounce you. In asking for a corner
office, a big-thinking customer service manager might say, "Although
status isn't important to me, I think the customer service manager should
have a corner office. It sends the message to our customers that the
company thinks customer service is important."

Despite the importance of talking big, there are times when small
talk works to your advantage. Small talk is useful in putting others at
ease. To set up a favorable climate among you and others is important at
the start of a meeting of two or more people and in business-social
occasions. Examples of good small-talk topics with an influential person
include:

- Is your suit custom tailored?
- How's your division doing?
- Is your family in town with you?
- Is there anything I can do to make your visit with us more comfort-
  able?

## SHOW AN INTEREST IN YOUR FIRM
## AND ITS PRODUCTS

Showing a genuine interest in your organization and in its products or
services impresses higher-ups in both profit and nonprofit firms. This
tactic works because so many workers feel no bond of identification with
their employers. Many employees are not even familiar with what their
organization is trying to accomplish. You can stand out by showing you
know and care about what your firm is doing.

### Invest in Your Firm

A wise investment in your future is to purchase company stocks and
bonds, particularly if you work for a company where such a practice is
not widespread. Few companies would demand that you invest in the

firm as a condition of employment, but it impresses the higher-ups when you show enough faith in the company to become an investor. An investment of this nature is more likely to pay off in a small company than in a mammoth corporation. In the small company, top management is more aware of who is purchasing stock.

Carol, a purchasing manager, traces her promotion to vice-president of business operations, to having extended herself to invest in her company. Carol had worked her way up from assistant buyer to purchasing manager in five years. When the company went public, Carol invested most of her savings ($6000) into company stock. Six months later she was offered a promotion to vice-president of business operations. The president informed Carol that she was given the edge over her competitor for the position because she had enough faith in the company to make a stock purchase.

Although Carol's stock has gone down slightly in price, the $6000 investment has paid extraordinary dividends. She enjoys the power and prestige of being a company officer, and her earnings have increased by $4000 per year.

## Promote Your Company's Products or Services

Find a way to promote your company's products or services and you will endear yourself to those higher in the company hierarchy. A routine application of this tactic is to purchase goods made by your company when possible. The next step is to casually mention that you are actively using the product. As a Sherwin-Williams (the paint company) engineer casually mentioned to a vice-president, "I have some field test information for you. Five years ago I painted my cottage with our top-quality latex exterior covering. Can you imagine that there is still no chipping or peeling?"

A nonroutine tactic is to promote your company's goods and services by involving other people. Linda, the payroll manager in a darkroom supply manufacturer, decided to start a camera club. Her basement contained a substantial-sized darkroom in addition to a knotty-pine recreation room, thus being a natural for club meetings. Linda organized phototaking field trips and darkroom sessions. She gently suggested that club members try darkroom supplies made by her company. Four club members started their own darkrooms because they were satisfied with the equipment displayed in Linda's basement.

Linda's club received a write-up in the company newspaper. Six months later, Linda was offered a promotion to office manager. The favorable attention she had brought to herself through her camera club had facilitated her receiving a promotion.

## CONTACT NEWLY ARRIVED
## OFFICE HOLDER

Contacting a newly arrived office holder is practiced to excess at the White House. When presidential aides are newly installed, the switchboard suffers from electronic overload. The army of well-wishers, sycophants, and some people with the good of the country in mind want to assure themselves that the new broom has not swept them away. Because this technique is used primarily in Washington, D. C., and by financial sales representatives, it probably has not been overused in your office. Send your well wishes after the dust has settled. Most of the greetings flood in during the new official's first 30 days in office.

Duane, a human resources manager in a multidivision company, learned through formal channels that Hal Winters was newly installed as the president of the corporation's largest division. Duane had worked three levels under Hal some years previously. To his knowledge, the working relationship was favorable. Duane carefully mapped out his political ploy. He mailed to the home of the newly arrived president the following hand-written note:

> Dear Hal:
>
> Count me as one of the many well-wishers who offer you congratulations on a sterling achievement. I wish you all the success you deserve in your new position.
>
> Just in case you might be staffing your organization, I have enclosed my resume. Working for you in the past was a very positive professional experience.
>
> > Best of luck,
> >
> > Duane Anderson

Six months later, Duane was interviewed for the division human resources manager position at Winter's division. He was finally edged out for the position by a more experienced candidate from the corporation. Although disappointed, Duane did not burn his bridges. One year later when the new personnel manager departed, Duane was interviewed again. Duane obtained the position this time; the opportunity probably would not have arisen if he had not written Hal a congratulatory note.

## DISPLAY BUSINESS MANNERS
## AND ETIQUETTE

The proper use of business manners and etiquette is both an offensive and defensive strategy for gaining favor with higher-ups. From the offensive standpoint, displaying manners and etiquette considered desirable by the higher-ups might help you project a favorable image. From the defensive standpoint, displaying manners and etiquette considered unacceptable by the higher-ups will prevent you from gaining favorable attention.

To observe what constitutes acceptable manners *in your particular organization*, you have to observe the fast trackers and higher-ups. If you aspired to an executive position at Apple Computer it would enhance your image to wear neatly tailored sports attire to a meeting. At an investment banking firm aspirants to executive positions would dress much more formally.

A more indirect approach to displaying the correct manners and etiquette is to rely on the advice of experts,[2] and hope that their advice will apply to your organization. The fit is usually quite good because most suggestions about proper etiquette extend from having sensitivity to people and political awareness. Pay attention to the following reminders on etiquette:

1. *Respect other people's senses.* Any assault on other people's senses—sight, sound, smell, or touch—should be avoided. Strong cologne and perfume are unwelcome, as are grotesque color combinations in your clothing, pinching co-workers, and making loud noises with chewing gum.

2. *Show class at lunch.* Business manners and etiquette are on display at lunch more vividly than at most other office occasions. Doing lunch gracefully can get you noticed, and doing it gracelessly can block your career. Iced tea has become the power beverage to replace whiskey; eating heavily is often considered taboo; ordering the most expensive item on the menu is tacky; avoid foods that require a struggle to eat neatly such as linguini with clam sauce; order coffee or hot tea only after the meal; and let the host pay regardless of the person's sex. And finally, do not talk serious business until the meal has been cleared. (This is one reason why so many marketing and sales people require two-and-one-half hour lunches.)

3. *Be diplomatic.* Diplomacy helps you say "No" to something without closing the door on it forever, or making an extremely negative statement that might boomerang immediately or later. Suppose an executive asks you if you think the new companywide program on quality awareness is working. You think the program is almost a failure. If you say the program is wonderful you might be perceived as a yes-person who is unaware of problems. However, if you are too critical you might be perceived as disloyal. A diplomatic alternative is to say, "The concept seems to be sound, yet the execution

and implementation of the program needs some work. I have a suggestion or two I would like to offer."

4. *Avoid smoking on the job unless you work for a tobacco company.* In most environments, smokers are forced to smoke in very restricted areas including smoking outside the building. You can get tagged as a permanent underling if you stand outside the building puffing away with others on a cigarette break. If smoking is very important to you, it would serve your image better to smoke in a hideaway not seen by higher-ups.

5. *Stand up only for infrequent visitors.* It is still considered polite to stand up when an infrequent visitor of either sex enters the office. However, if another worker enters your work space frequently, such as an office assistant who needs regular access to your files, standing up is not required.

6. *Remember names.* Successful office politicians remember the names of work associates, even if they are seen only occasionally. A good memory for names is also likely to impress higher-ups. The most sensible tip for remembering names is to make sure you learn it in the first place, and then jot it down.

7. *Make appointments with high-ranking people rather than dropping in.* Schmoozing with co-workers may sometimes be politically advantageous. A taboo in most firms, however, is for lower-ranking employees to casually drop in the office of an executive.

8. *Display bias-free language.* Using language that puts down any group can be considered a form of job discrimination, and is also considered poor manners. Speaking in bias-free terms will thus impress many higher-ups who themselves may be attempting to find new terms to replace biased language. Examples: Use "engineer" to replace "woman engineer," "Afro-American customers" to replace "black customers," "Asian employees," to replace "oriental employees," and "physically challenged employees" to replace "disabled employees," and "cost accountants" to replace "bean counters."

## SQUEEZE POLITICAL ADVANTAGES OUT OF LUNCH

As previously mentioned, business lunches are a good opportunity for displaying manners and etiquette thus giving you some political edge. Luncheons can also be used for obtaining much larger gains, as suggested by "power lunching." The purpose of the power lunch is to gain total control over the work associate, customer, or client.[3] In this application of the power lunch, you arrange to invite a higher-up. The first step in setting up the power lunch is for you to choose the location. It adds to your power image to select a restaurant where the hostess or host will recognize you by name.

Once you are in the right restaurant, find the right table. The right table is one with high status, usually not located adjacent to the kitchen or restrooms. Follow the lead of the higher-up in ordering a before-lunch beverage. Ordering the same drink helps build rapport. A caution about alcoholic beverages is that your power lunch could be diverted into a pleasure lunch, particularly if you are sexually inclined toward your guest.

Having set up the right atmosphere, it is time to make your pitch to impress your influential guest. Discuss your creative ideas for strengthening the organization, improving profits, or cutting costs. Perhaps even mention your professional goals. But avoid attempting to pin down your guest for a specific commitment about a promotion, special assignment, or the like. Such initiatives are likely to peg you as pushy and tactless. The goal in a power lunch with a higher-up should be to create a favorable impression that might give you a power edge in the future.

Despite the allure of power lunching, an entirely opposite approach might be more impressive to serious-minded executives. Impress key people with the idea that you are too involved with your work to engage in the frivolity of eating lunch out. Instead, eat at your work area or "graze." The grazer nibbles on food such as nuts, raisins, Chinese noodles, or carrots at frequent intervals during the day, much like a humming bird.

An executive visiting the grazer's work area will usually be impressed by his or her commitment to the cause. Tom, the head of a Long Island, New York, software consulting firm said, "In our business you can only justify business lunches when they are held to solve a client problem or prospect for new business. Taking two hours out of the work day to make small talk, takes a big bite out of productivity. A professional in our business needs to make good use of every available minute."

In short, take the lead of many powerful people who attend business lunches only out of necessity. It is certainly more impressive to be working than dining at midday.

## GET YOUR NAME IN FRONT OF INFLUENTIALS

A major strategy for cultivating influential people is to get your name in front of them. Whatever it takes, do what you can to ensure that the right people recognize your name. Photocopying machines and special projects have contributed markedly to the political technique of getting yourself known to influentials.

Now everybody but Innocent Lambs sends photocopies to influential people to keep them posted of their significant achievements. Electronic mail can be used for the same purpose, assuming the executives in your organization use the system. A typical ploy is to send a higher-up a copy of a memo that indicates how much money you saved the company by completing a particular assignment. A general approach is to send copies of information that makes you look good. Iggy, a product planner and an apparent Machiavellian, used a semidevious application of photocopy warfare. He explains how:

> My technique is based on statistical probabilities. When somebody introduces a new product idea, I write a memo pointing out some of the problems that might be associated with that product. I can always comment that consumer demand is uncertain. Only about one percent of new product ideas ever become profitable. Thus, I am almost always right. When a product idea flops, my memo is right there pointing to its potential pitfalls.
>
> So far, my technique has earned me the reputation of being a good company critic. I should be able to cash in on this reputation at a later date. My technique is not unique. Theater critics have been doing that for years. They are negative about most shows. Because few ever have long runs, the critics are right most of the time.

A potent way of impressing higher management is to be associated with special projects, major committees, and task forces. It is generally considered a feather in your career cap to be appointed to a project. Therefore, an impressionable technique is to find ways to have your name listed on as many projects as possible.

Karen, a financial analyst, used the project route to bring her name to the attention of higher-ups. She would ask the chief financial officer (CFO) on a project if she could volunteer her service to take care of an overload situation. Karen would then use her after-hours time to complete the extra-duty assignment. The only recompense Karen asked for and received was that her name be listed down at the bottom of the list of project members.

Four months later, a project director chose Karen as the financial analyst on his team, primarily because he was looking for a financial analyst with project experience. Karen's participation in the project eventually helped her land a position in the marketing department. A team member on Karen's project was an executive in the marketing department. Karen had parlayed a footnote into a first-rate assignment.

## LAUGH HEARTILY AT HIGHER-UPS JOKES ━━━━━━━

It is not necessary to laugh heartily at *all* your boss's jokes. If he or she frequently tells jokes, it will be obvious to your boss that some of the jokes are funnier than others. Higher-ups see you less frequently and therefore tell you fewer jokes. Machiavellians and Office Politicians always laugh at jokes told by higher-ups even when they have heard the joke before. Eddie, a Machiavellian, was almost caught.

*HIGHER-UP:*   Eddie, have you heard the one about the politician who visits the Native American reservation? In a speech, he tells the native-borns that if he is elected, they will all get improved medical care. The Native Americans shout, "hoya, hoya." He then tells them that if he is elected they will get a second pension from the federal government to pay for some of the wrong the white people have done to the red people. Again, shouts of "hoya, hoya."

                After the speech, the politician says to the chief: "I would like to walk across your fields and see some of your cattle."

                "Okay," says the chief. "But I hope you brought your boots. The fields are covered with hoya."

*EDDIE:*   (With a wide grin, and a burst of laughter) That's fabulous. It's the best I've heard this year. Where did you learn that joke?

*HIGHER-UP:*   Hold on Eddie, I think you told me that joke last year. That's where I heard it. What made you laugh so hard?

*EDDIE:*   A good joke is just as funny in the retelling. Besides, your delivery was fabulous.

## APPLY THE JAPANESE WORK ETHIC ━━━━━━━

Self-interest is the primary motivator behind most instances of office politics. To impress important people, it is sometimes necessary to appear more interested in the good of the work group and the organization, rather than in advancing your own cause. Such is the Japanese work ethic—the self-sacrificing corporate employee who cares more about the success of other people and the corporation than in personal success. Furthermore, the harmony-conscious Japanese middle manager will suppress desires for individual recognition in order to bring success to the work group.

You have to search out the right opportunities to act Japanese (rather than as a self-serving American). Here are a few possibilities:

- You receive a compliment from the vice-president for your sterling individual performance during the last six months. You reply: "I feel a bit uncomfortable accepting full credit for my accomplishments. It was truly a team effort. To me the most important statistic was the fact that our department turned in its best performance in four years."

- You drop the rumor that another division in the company offered you a new position carrying substantially more responsibility and pay. A person with good connections at the top asks you why you did not pursue the offer. You explain, "Yes, the offer certainly was tempting. However, the timing wasn't right. We have so much important work remaining to do in my unit. I would be letting down the team if I left now."

- Your boss asks you if you would be willing to be acting manager on Fridays for the next two years because she is enrolled in an executive MBA program that runs on Fridays. You reply, "With pleasure. What helps you helps the organization." (Silently, you are savoring the opportunity to obtain the managerial experience you need to advance your career.)

## CLIMB THE SOCIAL LADDER

A widely recognized strategy for cultivating higher-ups is to socialize with them. Many an aspirant to more power has joined a country club in order to maintain social contact with influential people. Golf remains as the most important sport for networking. No other sport is so popular with executives, and few sports other than fishing or clam digging allow so much time for conversation. Socializing with the higher-ups can be an effective way of cultivating them if you keep two basic principles in mind.

*First,* it is important to use socializing primarily to create a favorable climate of acceptance for yourself. For many a naive office politician, climbing the social ladder has backfired because the person attempted to pin down an influential politician during a social occasion. Staff specialist Jimmy provides an example of the violation of this principle.

After completing a round of golf on a hot, humid day, Jimmy headed to the showers. Under the shower next to him stood Badge, a vice-president of his firm whom Jimmy knew primarily through the golf club. Jimmy made his first influence attempt: "By the way Badge, they tell me you are looking for a new department head. I haven't had the chance to tell you this back at the office, but I've been looking for more responsibility. I think a department head position would be ideal for me. Please keep me in mind."

Taken back, Badge mumbled, "Young man, let's keep business out of the locker room. I come here to play golf and relax, not to talk shop." Badge was irritated enough by the incident to carry it one step further. The next day he wrote a memo to Jimmy's boss, recommending that the latter instruct Jimmy about the proper communication channels to be used for requesting transfers and promotions.

*Second,* it is important to adjust your social activities to the preferences of the people you are trying to cultivate. If paddle tennis rather than golf is big at the executive level in your organization, then pursue competence in that sport. On the negative side, avoid cultivating higher-ups through social activities they find uncomfortable. For example, don't invite an influential person to a party where tobacco and alcohol flow if he or she is strongly opposed to smoking and drinking. Because of the number of executives who bitterly oppose smoking and drinking, it pays to do your homework about their preferences.

Elise, a customer representative in an investment firm, explains how she avoids bloopers when entertaining influential people. "My printed invitations include a small checklist for foods liked and disliked, which I ask the potential guest to complete and send along with the RSVP. I began doing this when I realized what strong food preferences people have developed. One of the partners in my firm is convinced that all chicken contains salmonella poisoning. Another is convinced that beef causes colon cancer.

"My dinner meals for guests always offer a few choices. And I won't even sit a beef-hater next to a beef-eater. I even try to keep all the smokers clustered together at one table."

## DON'T CRITICIZE THE PRESIDENT'S PET PROJECT

The director of internal audit at an industrial firm also teaches evening students at two universities. He comments on his approach to teaching decision making:

"I use real-world illustrations to prove that nonquantifiable factors often dominate managerial decision making. When lecturing on capital budgeting, the following basic techniques are presented: payback ROI (return on investment), NPV (net present value), and PPP (president's pet project). I cite a real example of a corporate president who wanted to acquire a Lear jet for his small company.

"Based on the actual data, students invariably reject the acquisition as nonjustifiable. They have great difficulty perceiving how, after discrediting the president's pet project, their continued employment at that firm might be considered unjustifiable.

"I also introduce an example of a product-line divestiture where all of the analyses unquestionably indicate to drop the line. The only catch is that the company president started his career as brand manager for that product and still feels an affinity toward it. Again, most students still vote to eliminate the product.

"There is not much hope for such students after graduation. With such a prodigious inability to consider nonquantifiable data, they will most likely be eliminated."[4]

The morale to this professor's tale is that if you want to impress the president or any other higher-up, avoid strictly rational thinking when evaluating the merits of that executive's favorite project. Instead, emphasize whatever merits exist in the proposal. Do not lie—simply look for hidden value.

## AVOID TRUMPETING BAD NEWS

A good critic is needed in every organization, but overplaying the role can erode your power. Key people in the organization are frequently angered by the person who consistently makes a gloomy interpretation of their actions and policies. A trumpeter of bad news is not simply a person who passes along negative messages, but rather one who originates them. Martin S. Feldstein, the Harvard economist whose academic accomplishments led him to become the head of the Council of Economic Advisers, illustrates the problem.

Feldstein became involved in one scrape after another with the Reagan Administration officials because he trumpeted the dangers of big deficits. Even when it was apparent that the White House advisers preferred to downplay the deficit, Feldstein persisted with his gloomy warnings. The bad news message delivered by Feldstein was in opposition to Reagan's optimistic forecasts about the economy. At one point, the White House Chief of Staff, James A. Baker III ordered that all Feldstein speeches be approved by the White House in advance.

Before the hassle about his budget deficit warnings, Feldstein was reprimanded for being too candid in forecasting years of high unemployment and for championing a proposal to boost taxes on unemployment benefits. "Marty feels he's got to tell it as he sees it," remarked a White

House official. "He has to remember that if you're part of the team and you disagree with the President, you keep those differences to yourself."

Ultimately, Dr. Feldstein was placed under considerable pressure to resign before his two-year term expired. Despite his exemplary academic credentials, he was seen as having flunked "Politics 101."[5]

## GET YOUR HANDS DIRTY
## BEFORE THE RIGHT AUDIENCE

Showing higher-ups that you have the skill and willingness to perform manual tasks can create a good impression. Among these manual tasks are unjamming a photocopying machine, retrieving a seemingly lost file on a computer, fixing a printer, or adjusting an out-of-whack VCR. The former president of a paper company is a classic illustration of the "dirty hands" principle. A difficult mechanical problem arose in the mill. In order for the problem to be fixed, it was necessary for a person to climb into a vat of wet paper mulch and turn off a valve.

Not one of the production workers would volunteer to attempt the task. Sensing the urgency of the problem, the manager in question took off his jacket and climbed into the vat himself. He ruined his suit in the process, but upper management became aware of his act of loyalty. His career received a significant boost upward.

Performing a hazardous task is even more impressive than simply getting one's hands dirty. Such tasks present themselves infrequently but nature can sometimes play a hand in their occurrence. A payroll supervisor made himself a hero during a heavy snowstorm. At the height of the storm, all roads were closed to automobiles, and all offices and factories were shut down. The supervisor recounts his heroics:

> The way things were going, it was obvious that people were not going to get their paychecks on time. Some more work needed to be done to get the paychecks processed so they would be ready when the storm cleared— probably another 48 hours. I hopped into my snowmobile and got to the factory office about 8 A.M. By 2 P.M. I had all the checks processed. Later, I received a personal letter of gratitude from the controller. People still remember me as the man who rescued the paychecks during the big storm. I think my paychecks are a little bigger because of my stunt.

## BEFRIEND A HIGHER-UP'S CHILD

Being nice to your boss's child is an effective political strategy. Although the strategy is more difficult to implement, befriending a higher-up's child can have a big personal payoff. You may have to dig for information about appealing to that particular child. Here are three techniques that have met with good results:

- A systems analyst brought in hard-to-obtain empty beer cans for an executive to bring home to his 12-year-old son who was an avid beer-can collector. The analyst learned of the beer-can collection through a friendship with the executive's assistant.
- A Little League baseball coach was extra nice to the awkward son of the vice-president of claims in an insurance company (particularly after he checked out the boy's surname in the company telephone directory). During warm-up time and at one of the games, the grateful Little Leaguer said to his father, "Daddy, here is the nice man who has been helping me learn how to throw a sidearm pitch."
- A facilities manager in a manufacturing company heard through a friend that the 17-year-old daughter of the director of manufacturing was looking for summer work. He telephoned the vice-president and said, "Do you think you could persuade your daughter to do groundswork this summer? I have a summer job open here for a groundskeeper, and I think it's about time we hired a woman for this kind of job."

The next time you want to impress a higher-up try several of the many tactics we have presented. Begin with one that you could use comfortably. Then visualize yourself doing it with aplomb, and you will be half way toward cultivating an influential person.

# CHAPTER 6

# GAINING THE
# SUPPORT OF
# CO-WORKERS

Gaining the power edge is best played in a step-by-step, logical sequence. To eventually become powerful and influential in the organization, it is important to first gain favor with peers. Solo artists who neglect to cultivate their peers on the way to power may never get to exercise that power. A study of power in corporate life showed that individual performers received rewards for their immediate accomplishments, but did not always achieve the level of career success they sought. A frequent problem was that they had not developed the kinds of connections necessary to succeed in higher-level jobs.[1] Keep in mind also, that when a company downsizes, co-workers are sometimes asked their opinion about who are the most valuable employees.

What if you want to live a comfortable and secure life, free from the competitive pressures of a higher-level job? Cultivating peers is still important. You may need their support to help you get your job accomplished or you may need them to come to your defense when you are attacked from above. Developing friendships on the job is also important for mundane reasons such as having an office friend take care of your job properly while you are sick at home.

What about the office curmudgeon who wants to be left alone to complete tasks without having to bother others in the office? Such a person still needs to cultivate—or, at least, not totally alienate—co-workers. It is self-defeating to be bad-mouthed by co-workers or recommended as the first person to be axed in cutback times.

## BE A TEAM PLAYER ━━━━━━━━━━━━━━━━━━━━━━━━━

An essential strategy for cultivating your peers is to function as a team player within your group. Two studies recently conducted indicated that approximately 45 percent of men and women endorsed team play as important for getting work accomplished through others. Although men were perceived as using team play more frequently than women, 43 percent of our respondents thought that both sexes make equal use of teamwork.[2] To become a better team player, certain basic principles should be kept in mind.

### Be Supportive

A potent way of behaving like a team player is to support other group members. Support can take any form of showing that you believe in and are willing to help others. You can give verbal encouragement for the ideas expressed by others, listen to another person's problems, or help someone with a knotty technical problem. Karen noticed that Frank, one of her office mates, was perched in front of his personal computer. He was rubbing the back of his neck with his left hand, and had a worried frown. Although on her way out to lunch, Karen stopped to say: "Your body language tells me your stuck. I'm not an expert, but I've made about every common mistake possible on a computer. What can I do to help?"

Karen's co-worker explained that he was doing something wrong in attempting to rename a file, and that he couldn't concentrate on his work until he figured out what he was doing wrong. Karen calmly showed him that he was using the right command, but he did not specify the right computer drive. Larry's problem was solved, and Karen had developed an ally. The next time she and Larry were in a joint meeting, Larry vociferously endorsed her suggestion for the department expanding its services.

### Share Credit for Victories

"We won team, we won," said Frank excitedly to his four lunchmates. "The world's largest manufacturer of air conditioners is going to use our new electronic switch in every one of their units. I just got the good news today. Thanks to all of you for giving me so many good suggestions to explain the merits of our switch. I know that the vice-president of marketing will be pleased with our sales department."

It seems as though Frank is reliving the past glory of his basketball-playing days at college. One interpretation is that as he closes a sale he fantasizes that he has thrown the ball through the hoop in the final second of a basketball game. Possibly, but a more parsimonious explanation is in order. Frank is astute enough to recognize the importance of sharing his accomplishments with other people on the team.

When and if Frank should become the boss, the people who shared credit for his success will probably accept him as a manager who cares about the welfare of his subordinates. Equally important, the next time Frank needs help in taking care of a customer, his teammates will offer their cooperation.

## Make Use of Humor

In order to be seen as a team player, it is sometimes important to overcome the envy of co-workers when you receive a promotion. Humor can help you defuse some of the envy and resentment. Business owner I.C. (Ishwer Chhabildas) Shah did it this way when he worked for a large company and was promoted to product manager. Shah told his potentially envious co-workers that the vice-president for marketing chose him because the product had too many chiefs and not enough Indians. As a kicker, Shah told them that the initials to his name, I.C., meant "Indian Chief."

## Share Information and Give Opinions

At most of the staff meetings she attends, public relations specialist Tamara makes comments such as "Let me share with you some important information I've picked up on that topic," "I have some scuttlebutt that might be worth something," or "Let me give you my candid, but very personal reaction, to your proposal." Statements and actions like this have helped Tamara to develop her reputation as a good team player in her department. She is also seen as a person to count on when help is needed. Tamara explains why she is so open with and helpful to her co-workers:

> Before entering the public relations field, I was an account representative selling stocks, bonds, and other investments. There were about 15 of us in one large office during a period when most of the individual investors had lost interest in the market. Gradually, we began to guard our potential clients jealously. Management placed a lot of importance on generating new business.
>
> One incident proved to me that I no longer wanted to work in an office where people are only looking out for themselves. A woman walked into our office without a prior appointment, asking to make some investments. Something like that happens very rarely. She was referred to Milt, whose turn it was to get the next "over the transom" inquiry. I thought the woman looked familiar.

As the woman was leaving the office, she stopped by my desk and re-minded me that we had been classmates in college. She told me that she had recently inherited some money and decided to invest about $20,000 in blue-chip stocks. I jokingly asked her why she hadn't come over to my desk when she recognized me. She claimed that Milt had told her it's not a good idea to purchase stocks from friends because a friend can't be objective.

I felt pity for Milt, but I guess he needed the commission badly. Milt helped me learn something about myself. I could enjoy working in an atmosphere only where people cooperated with each other.

## Touch Base with Co-workers

Brett, an information systems specialist, had an idea that could conceiv-ably reduce the operating cost of his department by about $45,000 per year. According to his logic, his division really didn't need its own com-puter because the parent company—some 200 miles away—recently had installed a computer powerful enough to handle more work than the parent company needed computerized.

Brett planned to propose that his division sell its own computer and have a hookup installed to the parent company's computer. He realized that if this idea were presented in a department meeting with no prior warning it could create a furor in the department. Perhaps other people in the department (including the boss) would think that such a move would shrink their power as an information systems department.

Brett decided to presell the idea by holding private discussions with everyone above entry-level positions in the department, including the boss. It took Brett six rest-break conversations, ten luncheon conferences, and four after-hours drink sessions to gain acceptance for his idea.

When Brett presented his idea, replete with flip charts and cost figures, everybody at the meeting smiled. They agreed that, in the long run, if Brett's ideas were accepted by top management, the department would be remembered for its contribution to the corporate welfare. If Brett had surprised his co-workers and boss by presenting his ideas in a meeting without forewarning, he might not have received the support he needed. His proposal might have been shot down with a series of distor-tions and rationalizations. People don't like big surprises in meetings when the surprise might affect *them*.

## ASK ADVICE

Asking co-workers their advice about both work and nonwork problems can help you strengthen your relationships with them if done with fi-nesse. Asking too much advice can result in your being perceived as a pest or an overly dependent person. If you do ask for advice, it is important to share credit for the success of your ideas with your advisors. Seeking advice is an effective relationship builder because asking for another person's advice is a compliment. It implies implicitly that you think the other person has good judgment or possesses valid information. Here are several examples of the type of advice seeking that will tend to enhance relationships with co-workers:

- I've noticed that you're a very creative person. What do you think I should do to enhance my creativity?
- What do you think I could do to help me get my work done during normal working hours? I'm tired of bringing home work at night.
- The company has finally agreed to repaint my office. I get a choice of off-white or beige. Which color do you think best fits my personality?

Notice that the first question could be interpreted as a competitive threat to a co-worker. If you become more creative, you might outshine the person whose advice is being asked. The second two questions, however, can be answered honestly without giving someone a competitive edge. Below are a few examples of the type of advice-asking to avoid because valid answers to them could place you in an advantageous position, thus worsening your co-worker relationships. (The purpose of office politics, of course, is to obtain an advantageous position. However, co-workers do not want to think that you are gaining advantage directly at their expense.)

- I have never won a suggestion award. In what areas do you think the company is looking for good suggestions?
- What do you think I could do to be regarded as a top performer by the boss?
- What do you think I should do to become more promotable in the eyes of management?

## EXCHANGE FAVORS

*Quid pro quo* arrangements with others in the workplace are a standard way of getting things accomplished. Our research suggests that one-third of managerial, professional, and sales workers believe that exchanging favors is an effective way of getting work accomplished. At the same time, reciprocity is a good way of cultivating a network of peers. The approach is particularly effective if you do a favor for someone today without asking for something in return. Although your intent may be to cash in your I.O.U. in the future, your act of generosity will not be forgotten.

Jack, a mortgage processing manager in a bank, provides us a healthy and sensible way of exchanging favors. Patti, a sales manager in the mortgage department, and he were chatting in the company cafeteria about Patti's upcoming presentation to management. She explained that she would be trying to sell the executive group on a new program that would pay a commission to mortgage representatives for mortgages they secured for the bank. Commissions were to be paid to representatives as an incentive for encouraging realtors to place home mortgages with the bank.

Patti said that although her plan was straightforward and sensible, she needed to add some pizazz to her presentation. "Somehow, I've got to convince the executive group that my plan is financially sound. A simple flip-chart presentation with an arrow pointing toward the northeast probably won't do the trick. It's too much of a cliche."

Jack came to Patti's rescue. He volunteered to prepare a computerized spreadsheet analysis that would show management how much additional profit would be generated from different levels of commission. The facts and figures for the analysis could be derived from existing bank records, combined with a little speculation. Jack told Patti he could do the entire spreadsheet analysis at home in one evening, working with his personal computer.

Jack followed through as promised, and the results were indeed impressive. Top management was convinced that Patti had done her homework, and the new commission plan was implemented within six months (a rapid move within a bank). Jack now had bonded his relationship with a co-worker, and would certainly receive her support if needed in the future.

## EXPRESS AN INTEREST IN COLLEAGUES' WORK, FAMILY, AND HOBBIES

Almost everyone is self-centered to some extent. This basic fact about human behavior makes expressing an interest in the job activities and personal life of co-workers an effective tactic for building relationships with them. Sales representatives rely heavily on this fact in cultivating relationships with established customers. They routinely ask the customer about his or her hobbies, family members, and work activities. Index files and computer disks of the astute salesperson contain job and personal facts about customers such as major job responsibilities and hobbies.

Here is a sampling of the type of questions to ask co-workers for the purposes of getting them on your side:

- How is your work going? (highly recommended in almost all situations)
- How are things going for you? (works with everyone excluding a completely paranoid personality)
- How did you gain the knowledge necessary for your job?
- How does the company use the output from your department?
- How's your career going?
- How is your newborn doing? (works well even if the infant has a medical problem, providing you ask the question compassionately)
- How well did Crystal do in the county cat show?

A danger in asking questions about other people's work is that some questions may not be perceived as well-intentioned. There is a fine line between honest curiosity and snooping. You must stay alert to this subtle distinction. A payroll specialist once asked an administrative assistant in her department, "What did you do today?" The administrative assistant interpreted the question as intimating that administrative assistants may not have a full day's work to perform.

## STORE UP A RESERVOIR OF GOOD FEELINGS

Writer Jane Michaels correctly observes that people who are courteous, kind, cooperative and cheerful develop allies and friends in the workplace. Storing up a reservoir of good feelings involves practicing basic good manners such as being pleasant and friendly. By the simple act of being nice, you obtain some co-worker support. Every reader of this book probably is aware of this observation, just as they are aware that the oil level in a car should be checked before every trip. Nevertheless, not remembering to use such basic facts can be hazardous to your work relationships and automobile trips.

Storing up a reservoir of good feelings also involves not snooping, spreading malicious gossip, or weaseling out of group presents such as shower or retirement gifts. In addition, it is important to be available to co-workers who want your advice as well as your help in times of crisis.[3]

A solid tactic for storing up a reservoir of good feelings is to be a good listener. It is also the simplest technique of gaining the support of co-workers. One of the biggest impediments to good listening among impatient, success-oriented people, is that they are too eager to react to comments. Have you noticed how Type A people tend to interject comments before the person they are supposed to be listening to has finished his or her sentence?

Becoming an effective listener takes practice. A good way to practice becoming an effective listener is to communicate nothing except for a few nods of approval while your co-workers respond to the questions you ask them about their work and personal life.

## SHARE GOSSIP

Gossip is now being taken seriously by management scholars. In the past gossip was thought to be province of the small-minded people in the office who had nothing more constructive to do with their idle moments. Careful scrutiny of the subject, however, reveals that gossip serves several important work purposes. Gossip improves morale by adding spice and variety to the job. It may even make some highly repetitive jobs bearable. Gossip is seen as a humanizing factor in an otherwise technological and depersonalized workplace. At the same time it is a deep-well source of team spirit.[4]

Another important purpose of gossip fits directly into its use as a vehicle for building peer relationships. Gossip is considered to be a socializing force because it is a mode of intimate relationship for many workers. It also serves as the lifeblood of personal relationships on the job. If you are able to pass on juicy tidbits of information to co-workers, your stature with them will increase. Nevertheless, if you overdo your role as a source of gossip you will not be trusted; others will fear that you will soon be passing along rumors about them. You also obviously run the danger of being perceived as a "gossip."

An important consideration in passing along gossip is not to spread negative information about people unless you know it to be true, and that it will soon be public information. Suppose you heard from a very reliable source that a company executive was soon to be indicted for insider trading. A scandal of this nature always becomes public knowledge, so it would not be a discredit to you to pass along such a rumor. (A common misinterpretation is that rumors deal only with false information.)

In order to impress co-workers with your fund of gossip, you need to cultivate information sources. Usually this means trading information with other people in order to bring about an equitable exchange between passing along versus receiving gossip. If you only collect information, your sources of information will dry up quickly. Such was the case with Arnold.

Arnold, the manager of a planning department, had a staff of three plan-
ners working for him. The department was involved with collecting information that had a bearing on the future of the company—an activity that
did not keep them continuously busy. Periodically, Arnold would ask his
staff members questions such as "Okay, what's hot today?" or "What's the
scuttlebutt?" Almost never did Arnold reciprocate by furnishing his staff
with tidbits that he had collected. One day, Tom, a planner in the department, confronted Arnold. "Arnold why don't you tell *us* something for a
change?" said Tom. "You're in a position to receive a lot more inside information than we are."

Arnold persisted in his predilection for one-way communication. Soon, his
own department was no longer a source of morsels of information. He then
had to cultivate other sources of information in order to gather gossip that
he could in turn pass along to co-workers.

In gathering raw material for passing gossip along to co-workers, it
is useful to keep in mind what type of gossip is perceived to be the juiciest.
Information about job changes, including resignations, firings, demotions, transfers, and special assignments is always in demand. Information about office romances, extramarital affairs, and separations is in even
more demand. New areas of high-intensity gossip include rumors about
cross-dressing, sex-change operations, sexual threesomes or foursomes,
and the contraction of a serious sexually transmitted disease.

Information about mergers and acquisitions, hostile takeovers, and
layoffs is also of topical interest, but strictly speaking this information is
classified as rumor rather than gossip. Gossip refers more specifically to
tidbits about people.

## BE DIPLOMATIC

Despite all that has been said about the importance of openness and
honesty in building relationships, most people fail to be convinced. Their
egos are too tender to accept the raw truth when faced with disapproval
of their thoughts or actions. To foster smooth working relationships with
peers it is therefore necessary to gloss over disagreement. Diplomacy is
still an essential part of governmental and office politics. Translated into
action, diplomacy often means finding the right phrase to convey disapproval, disagreement, or discontent. Here are some delicate situations
and the diplomatic phrases to handle them:[5]

A co-worker asks, "Did you hear about the affair the boss is having
with Jason?"

(You want to say, "Why are you so small minded? The two of them
are adults and can do what they want.")

*The diplomatic answer:* "No, I don't pay attention to details about people's personal lives. But I would certainly be interested in any news you might have about work."

Another worker in the department gets a new hairstyle that makes her look like an adolescent male. She questions, "How do you like my new hairstyle? My hairstylist claims it works wonders for me."

(You want to say, "I hate it. You look just like a nephew of mine whom I detest.")

*The diplomatic answer:* "I like the clean lines of your new style. But your previous hairstyle did a much better job of emphasizing your femininity."

During a staff meeting, a co-worker suggests that the entire group schedule a weekend retreat to formulate a five-year plan for the department. The boss looks around the room to gauge the reactions of others to the proposal.

(You want to say, "What a stupid idea. Who needs to ruin an entire weekend to do something we could easily accomplish within a workday afternoon?")

*The diplomatic response:* "I've heard that retreats sometimes work. But would spending that much time on the five-year plan be cost effective? Maybe we could work on the plan during one long meeting. If we don't get the planning accomplished in that time frame, we could then reconsider the retreat."

## PUT OUT FIRES INSTEAD OF FIGHTING THEM WITH FIRE

Diplomacy is a form of smoothing over potential conflict in order to preserve relationships with another person. Another form of resolving conflict is to find a solution to a conflict with a co-worker rather than retaliating for an unsavory deed. Nancy, a registered nurse, resented Cathy's carelessness about checking supplies. She repeatedly asked Cathy to be more careful, but without success.

Nancy decided to retaliate by not checking the supplies when it was her responsibility. Unfortunately this time the supervisor found out about the checking errors. Both nurses came close to receiving official reprimands on their records. A better approach for Nancy would have been to offer to check supplies for Cathy. In return Cathy might perform a task that Nancy disliked. In this way, Nancy could establish a good working relationship with Cathy. Constantly nagging Cathy to do a better job of checking supplies could only injure their relationship.[6]

## USE APPROPRIATE COMPLIMENTS ━━━━━━━━━━━

An effective way of cultivating your co-workers (or 99 percent of other human beings) is to compliment their work or something with which they are closely identified such as their children or hobbies. Compliments to co-workers are less fraught with misinterpretations of your intent than are compliments to your boss or higher-ups. People of higher-rank may interpret your compliments as politically motivated, so extra sincerity and finesse are required. Three important points about compliments should be kept in mind, as they could make the difference between getting the results you want with compliments versus wasting time with misdirected flattery.

### Compliment Concrete Accomplishment

Cora, a real estate broker in a large office learned in a human relations course that it is more effective to compliment a person's actions than a person's traits and characteristics. People generally find it more meaningful for you to point out what a good job they have done than to state what fine people they are. Besides, complimenting a person's characteristics may sometimes make that person feel self-conscious.

Cora found a number of ways to implement this technique in her real estate office. The payoff to Cora is that the other realtors in the office gave her a helping hand when it was needed. One such instance took place when an out-of-town client wanted to be shown a few homes in the $300,000 range. Unfortunately, the day he chose was the very day Cora's daughter was graduating from high school. Despite his envy, a co-worker of Cora's gave the man a tour of the more expensive neighborhoods in town. Here are two of Cora's most effective compliments:

Jack received a handwritten message from Cora stating:

> Congrats, Jack on giving us a lesson on the art of overcoming difficult odds. We all thought it would be impossible to sell a retired couple a home in a suburban neighborhood densely populated with children. Your sales pitch that the young children would give the couple a new interest in life was certainly an ideal display of sales acumen—particularly because it proved to be true.

> Henry, the office handyperson and "gopher," was told in front of the president of the firm, "Hooray for Henry. We're the only real estate firm in the area whose FOR SALE signs didn't blow down during the last storm. And because ours was the only FOR SALE sign standing in the Chestnut Street neighborhood, I received calls from three prospective buyers."

## Individualize Your Compliments

A powerful way of using compliments is to individualize them rather than using the same compliment for everybody. Your co-workers will perceive you to be insincere if they all hear the same compliment from you. Tony, a high-school teacher, kept a written record of the compliments he had paid to other teachers. He wanted to ensure that he would not be seen as the type of person who dispenses insincere flattery. During a high-school open house, he heard complimentary comments about two other faculty members made by parents.

Rather than accept these compliments at face value, Tony asked the parents for clarification. He asked both parents specifically how the teacher in question was helpful to their children. Armed with specifics, Tony was able to pass on two penetrating compliments. To Fred, he said, "I heard something very positive about you last night at the open house. Mrs. Gonzalez said that because of you her oldest son is no longer afraid of math." To Doris, he said, "I heard something at the open house last night that might be of interest to you. Mrs. Austin said that you are one of the few teachers who has been able to understand the eccentricities of her son. I know her son, and he surely is difficult to understand."

## Find Something to Compliment

Another important point to consider when complimenting co-workers is that some people have few praiseworthy actions. Nevertheless, it is still worthwhile to find *something* to praise about every one of your co-workers. People remember compliments for a long time, and even your least competent co-worker occasionally does something that warrants attention. Marsha, a social worker in a community agency, found a way of complimenting each one of her peers although she had to stretch her imagination at times. Two examples:

> Clyde, a cynical and hostile old-timer, in recent years processed more cases than any other counselor in the unit. He was able to process so many because of the abrupt treatment he gave to most of his clients. His opening statement to most people seeking his help was, "Okay, what are you trying to get from me?" To compliment Clyde, Marsha said, "You certainly seem to do a good job of chasing away the people who have no legitimate need for our help."

> Priscilla, a marriage counselor in the agency, was the opposite of Clyde. She tended to cling on to clients, which resulted in her seeing less than her share of clients. In thinking up an authentic compliment for Priscilla, Marsha said, "Priscilla, could you help me develop skill in making clients depend on me for advice and support? I notice that your clients take their relationship with you very seriously."

## BECOME A CENTER FOR PROVISIONS ════════════

Political players for small stakes sometimes cultivate peers by providing them with emergency supplies, snacks, and physical remedies. They become distributors of legal substances to co-workers who want to be taken care of by others.

### Manipulate Office Services and Supplies

Some people systematically cultivate peers by the very nature of their formal authority to hand out supplies—particularly when funds are limited. To capitalize on such a position, you have to treat people *un*equally. In a system where everybody gets a share of supplies based strictly on need, there is no particular advantage to playing the role of the office supplier. Good-natured Monica, describes how her job as the office supplier has improved her lot:

> I have two jobs in my office. I'm in charge of the word-processing center; I'm also in charge of handing out office supplies. When I want a special favor from a person, I can be very generous with word-processing services and office supplies. If somebody is nice to me, or if I figure I may need help from that person later on, I make sure the word processing gets done promptly.
>
> Manipulating office supplies works even better. The company has a series of requisition forms people have to fill out to obtain supplies such as yellow pads, paper clips, rubber bands, and staples. If I'm trying to be nice to somebody, I might throw in an extra lined pad or whatever. It's not stealing because the supplies are used on company premises. If somebody gives me a hard time, or I'm not interested in that person doing me a favor later on, I pull the strict company policy routine. I might even make a comment that the person is using too many of a particular item in comparison to others in the office. If I want to be mean, I make sure that there is a written justification for every supply request.

### Maintain a Goodie Drawer or Desk-Top Dish

Another way to gain favor from co-workers is to supply them with an assortment of candies or other treats. A goodie drawer or desk-top dish might contain items such as gum drops, chocolate candy, sticks of gum, or raisins and nuts. The people you cultivate with this approach tend to be office moochers, but even a moocher may someday be of help to you. Charlie, the keeper of the goodie drawer in his office, illustrates the potential value of such an arrangement:

> Accuse me of going out of my way to please people if you will, but friendships are important to me. I keep fresh candies on my desk and in my

drawer. Because of it, people often pay me a visit. It is a small token to pay for making friends. Your friendship may be returned when you need it the most. Like the time my mother phoned me one morning at work to tell me that my cat had just died.

I was just too upset to work, yet I felt foolish asking the boss if I could go home to make funeral arrangements for my cat. I brought my problem to Jane, a woman who had made many a trip to my desk for an afternoon sweet. I explained my problem. Jane was so sympathetic that she offered to have my calls transferred to her desk and to explain to callers that I was tied up on some important project. By the next day, I felt better able to cope with my job despite the loss of my cat. It also made me feel good to know that Jane cared enough about me to help out in a pinch.

### Serve as the Office Paramedic

"Rachel, I have a terrible headache. I don't have time now to make a trip to the drug store for some aspirin. Could you help me out?"

"Say, Rachel, I burned my left hand this morning. Like a fool, I tried to catch the coffee percolator when it slipped from my hand. Do you have any soothing ointment in your kit?"

Rachel is neither a physician, nurse, physician's assistant, nor a nurse's aide. She is a friendly billing specialist who keeps one drawer in her desk loaded with first-aid supplies. It is said that the only emergency she cannot properly handle is a snakebite. Rachel is genuine in her desire to serve other people. She glories in the role of office paramedic. But Rachel also has an ulterior motive. She explains it unashamedly:

"Helping other people in the office with their ailments has endeared me to them. I think I have more friends in the office than anyone else. Work would be a lonely place if I didn't have any friends. People have come to count on me, and that's pretty good for a billing specialist. If it weren't for my first-aid station, I think I would be just another clerk in the office."

Being the office paramedic can also pay dividends beyond those sought by Rachel. The paramedic can be a communications hub. He or she can pick up valuable tidbits about new developments in the office. A paramedic in one office learned of a new opening while handing out a headache tablet. She was the first to apply for the position and was selected. The new job represented a $3000 per-year salary increase for the friendly paramedic who could now upgrade the location of her office first-aid station.

## MAKE A GOOD SHOWING AT
## THE OFFICE PARTY OR PICNIC

We have all heard about the importance of acting sober, refined, and professional at the office party or picnic in order to impress top management.

The guidelines, however, are slightly different when you are trying to cultivate co-workers. Your emphasis should be on doing and saying things that will help form a bond between you and others at your level.

A starting point is to set political goals. Think in advance about which people you want to cultivate. Don't neglect the opportunity to compliment a co-worker's home or possessions, or comment on his or her charming spouse or "significant other." Complimenting a person's spouse or special friend, however, must be done softly to avoid arousing threats of envy. Roxanne, for example, alienated a co-worker by mentioning at a picnic, "Your boyfriend is so cute. Let me know when you grow tired of each other."

Avoid talking shop excessively. Because work is a shared experience for those at the party or picnic, there is a natural tendency for many people to talk about happenings in the office, factory, or store. Talking shop at office parties and picnics may make you appear shallow and narrowminded. Instead, build your image by discussing sports, hobbies, current events, or other areas of shared interest.[7] Prior to leaving for the party or picnic, invest twenty minutes reading the newspaper or receiving news from television or radio. You can then bring up tidbits of news that are relevant to the situation, thus appearing well-informed.

One of the most important informal rules for conducting yourself at the office party or picnic is to look like you're having fun. Move about the party or picnic area rather than standing or sitting in one place. Chat with many people and smile frequently. Being the "life of the party" is a tired cliche, but appearing relaxed and happy is a good way of building relationships with your office mates. If you dread parties and picnics, practice smiling in the mirror before attending. Also, use relaxation techniques such as consciously inhaling or exhaling periodically, and relaxing your muscles.

At the office picnic, engage in sports in a noncompetitive, friendly way. Even if you are an advanced player in volleyball, softball, or pitching horseshoes, don't offer advice unless asked. Avoid spiking a ball into a co-worker's face just to impress. If you win at an individual sport, win by a very close margin. If you are a neophyte at whatever sport is being played, join in anyway and laugh heartily at your own ineptitude.

Finally, if you are unattached and can arrange it, invite a sexy, charming person to accompany you to the picnic or office party. Even if you have to rent one, bring a beauty queen or hunk to the party and have that person flaunt his or her good looks. Encourage the person to flirt with your co-workers. At a picnic ask the person to wear a tank top or similar shirt that reveals the outline of his or her contours. Such garb is particularly titillating, and is not really outrageous enough to suggest that you are in poor taste. Remember, your guest is the sexy one, not you.

The downside to the charming-companion technique is that you may engender the envy of co-workers and superiors. Nevertheless, the net effect is likely to be positive. John, a financial analyst, puts it this way: "I had only been with the firm for a few months, when a big holiday bash was scheduled. I had met this truly gorgeous administrative assistant when I was taking my company physical. I phoned Meg (the administrative assistant) and explained who I was, and asked her if she would be willing to be my escort to the company party. She told me that she liked the idea of attending as my escort rather than as a date. Since she already had a regular boyfriend, being my date was out of the question.

"Meg turned in a beautiful performance. She wore a black strapless gown, three-inch heels, and a string of pearls. Co-workers were coming over to talk to us like crazy. During the next week in the office, four people, including one of the gals, complimented me on my good taste.

"And the story has a very happy ending. Meg and her boyfriend broke up in early February. She called me to tell me she was now available. We have been seeing each other regularly ever since."

## IMPROVE THEIR SOCIAL LIFE

Under the right circumstances, improving the social life of one of your office mates is an effective way of cultivating that person. The "right circumstances" means that the person you are trying to fix up wants to be fixed up. Otherwise, you probably will create an enemy rather than an ally. A recommended initial gambit is, "I think a friend of mine would be interested in meeting you. Would you be interested in meeting this person?" Doug is a case history of a successful application of this approach to cultivating your co-workers. He describes his winning tactic:

> I'm an attorney in a large law office. A new attorney named Gary joined us as a corporate tax specialist. He was also new to town, and had been divorced for a number of years. The guy seemed so lonely that I befriended him. I realized from my own bachelor days that the last thing a single man wants is to spend his evenings having dinner with a married couple. So I got right to the heart of the matter.
>
> I asked Gary if he were interested in meeting unattached women. He said definitely, yes. I then made up a list of all the unattached women I knew—those I would like to date if I had the opportunity. My list contained six names. I turned over this list along with their phone numbers to *him*. Gary was appreciative of my friendly gesture. He became doubly appreciative when the third lead developed into a solid relationship. One payoff was that I felt wonderful for having helped out a newcomer to town. Another was that Gary came to my rescue at a meeting of the professional staff. I

proposed that the partners give us more options on selecting a retirement plan. Gary was the first to second the motion, concurring with my proposal. After Gary spoke, several others also expressed their agreement.

Being a matchmaker for co-workers may not always be the best way to help them with their social life. Instead, help them develop skill in meeting people for themselves. A widespread method of developing leads for social life is to place an ad in the personal section of the local newspaper. Many unattached people are hesitant to place an ad, so you may have to encourage your lonely co-worker to place an ad. Taking your generosity one step further, you might help your friend compose an appealing ad.

You can develop skill in writing ads yourself by studying the personal ads and looking for good models, including key phrases. For example, a person 50 percent overweight is described as "full bodied," and a "professional" is any employed person who is not an entry-level worker. Study a book about personal ads to gain additional insight into and skill in preparing such an ad.

Sue, a licensed practical nurse, took an aggressive approach to helping a co-worker rebuild her social life through a personal ad. She learned that Becky, another nurse on the floor, was in the process of breaking up with her boyfriend. Without asking Becky's permission, she placed an ad describing Becky (the ads are anonymous). Sue had the responses mailed to her, and brought the most promising ones to Becky as a surprise. Reluctantly, Becky did telephone one of the men who answered the ad. An immediate romance developed, and Sue had created a permanent ally in Becky. Beware, however, that many people would become upset if somebody else placed a personal ad on their behalf.

## AVOID BEING DESPISED AND HATED

Niccolo Machiavelli noted approximately 490 years ago that a prince should take steps to ensure that he is not despised and hated.[8] Machiavelli believed that so long as you did not deprive other men of their property and women, you would not be despised and hated. In today's work environment, you can be despised and hated for much less. To avoid encouraging their wrath, be careful not to:

1. Use their desk when they are out of the office, and leave the desk strewn with your belongings.
2. Sit on their desks.

3. Try to sell them life insurance, mutual funds, or tax shelters.
4. Win a $2000 suggestion award using an idea you obtained in conversation with one of them.
5. Correct their mistakes in public.
6. Sneeze over their lunches.
7. Ask to borrow money.
8. Borrow money and then do not pay it back.
9. Always have your work completed on time.
10. Smugly mention that you forgot it was payday, so you will pick up your paycheck next week.

## ACT LIKE AN INNOCENT LAMB

Being nonpolitical can be a winning political strategy. If you develop the reputation among your co-workers of being an Innocent Lamb, they will trust you and support you when you need support. To develop such a reputation, you will need to avoid all devious political tactics and, in general, appear more interested in the welfare of the firm than in your personal welfare. Steve, an industrial engineer, pulled one of the most clever ploys my research has uncovered. His tactic made an immediate and lasting impression on his boss and co-workers. Steve describes his coup:

As an industrial engineer, my job is to save the company money. The cost savings I suggest should far exceed my salary and benefits. If I don't provide a good return on investment for my services, I am a liability to the company, not an asset. One assignment I had two years ago was to design a system for decreasing the cost of paperwork in the company. I spent about three months studying the forms we used for internal purposes.

After completing the study, I made my recommendations to our boss and his boss. They were both impressed by the annualized cost savings of $25,000. It looked as though my proposal had a good chance of being implemented.

In the meantime, I had shown my report to Sybil, one of the less experienced engineers in the department. She had a particular interest in the flow of paperwork. She told me she liked my report very much. So much so that I sparked her thinking to piggyback on to some of my ideas. Her calculations revealed that her method would save the company about $50,000 per year. Her analysis looked accurate to me.

I requested an appointment for us to meet with my boss. I said my plan for the redesign of the paperwork flow in our company should be discarded.

In its place, I proposed that we use Sybil's ideas which would save the company an *additional* $25,000 per year. My boss said, "Sounds great to me. But don't you realize that Sybil will now get the primary credit for this important system?"

I told my boss, it isn't important who gets the credit. The important issue is that our department does its very best for the good of the company. He looked at me as a father does when he has just learned that the son has received an outstanding citizenship award. Sybil, too, was smiling. I knew I had set a good relationship for myself with two people whom I thought were well worth cultivating.

# CHAPTER 7

# GAINING THE
# SUPPORT OF
# LOWER-RANKING
# PEOPLE

Mutiny is the fate of the irrational and irascible ship commander. If you fail to cultivate your subordinates and others of lower rank, you too may be subject to sabotage, backstabbing, stiletto throwing, bad mouthing, and lack of support. To cultivate lower-ranking people, three sensible general strategies are fundamental.

1. Use the tactics recommended earlier for cultivating your boss, higher-ups, and co-workers and turn them in the direction of the people below you. Most people below you on the organizational ladder would enjoy being treated as if they outranked you or were your peer.

2. Read any management book about human relations or motivation and apply the principles contained therein to dealing with people below you in the hierarchy. Principles of effective human relationships on the job are well known; the problem is that they are not widely used.

3. Treat everybody of lower rank than yourself as if he or she were a customer. Smile at them, resolve their conflicts with you with diplomacy and tact, be appreciative of everything they do for you, and say "Ya'll come back" after they visit your office. Imagine how happy you would be if your boss treated you as if you were a big customer.

This chapter deals with a number of tactics and strategies that have particular relevance for gaining the support and respect of people below you. By featuring these suggestions we do not imply that other elements of office politics or human relations are unimportant. We merely have focused on a group of political realities that ladder-climbers often neglect in their haste to achieve success. To repeat, in the 1990s, you need the support of every person you can find to help solidify your stature in the organization.

## SOLICIT OPINIONS BEFORE TAKING ACTION

The management buzz word of the 1980s and 1990s is participative management. The participative manager consults with team members and receives their input before making a decision and taking action. At the extreme, the participative manager gets everybody's approval before acting. Whether you merely consult with people of lower rank or get their full approval before taking action the result is similar—people will be pleased that they were included in the decision-making process. The result will usually be better support for you and an interest in helping you implement the decision.

An important caution about participative management is that some people prefer to provide input in the manager's decision making, while others do not. A consultant visited a plant in which a Japanese-style manager (highly participative) was placed in charge. Interviews with key people revealed different perceptions of Taduschi Kamato's (the new manager) effectiveness.

The plant engineering manager made this evaluation: "So far the new leadership at this plant is very good. A big improvement over my experience in working for American-owned companies. Our boss is trying his hardest to create a democratic climate around here. Instead of making all the big decisions on his own, Kamato carefully consults with us. He will not make any major decision until we have reached consensus. This makes me feel that I'm helping to run the plant.

"I'm consulted not just on engineering decisions. Kamato consults me and the other managers reporting to him on all decisions. He encourages us to do the same with the people reporting to us. In this way, every worker in the plant provides some input to decision making."

The plant financial manager saw things differently. "We suffer from weak leadership in the plant. Taduschi backs away from the important demands of his job. He expects his staff to make all the tough decisions. Right now he's asking my advice on developing a strategic plan for the company's manufacturing activities in this country. He loves to pass assignments down the line. He's always pestering me and others for our opinion on everything. I think he should allow us more time to do our own work. I sometimes think he uses Japanese-style management as a cop out. Instead of doing any demanding work, he gets us to do it."

## FIGHT FOR THEIR DEMANDS

An axiom of effective management is for the supervisor to bring forth the demands of group members to top management, and then fight for these demands. Carrying out this principle enhances your stature among group members, and helps you win their support. Peggy recaps how her boss fought for her group's demands:

> As a group of direct mail specialists, there was no valid reason for us all to have to work in the office everyday. As long as we had a computer-hookup to the company, we could do some of our work at home. The problem was that the company did not have a work-at-home-program. We explained to Bob, our manager, how convenient and efficient working at home would be. He seemed sold on the idea, but he said it would have to be cleared with top management.
>
> He came back and told us that management scoffed at the idea. Sensing our disappointment, Bob told us that if we would present him with more documentation about the benefits of working at home, he would pursue the matter again. We did our homework, and Bob took up the battle again. Two months later, he received approval for us to begin the telecommuting program. Since that event, Bob became our hero.

## ACT PROMPTLY ON ADMINISTRATIVE MATTERS FACING SUBORDINATES

One day I was playing in a club tennis tournament against Allan, a highly placed bank executive. Dusk was settling in as we finished our match, which had been delayed because of a last-minute meeting called by my opponent's boss. As we walked off the court toward the locker room, I noticed a forlorn-looking young man seated at a table courtside. He glanced at Allan with an air of expectation. Because his face was unfamiliar, I assumed he was my opponent's friend or relative who had come to watch him play. In the locker room, Allan revealed to me the man's true identity. He told me:

"I'm sorry again about being late for our match. It's been one of those crazy, mixed-up days. Would you believe it, I even have a performance appraisal scheduled for this evening? I'm late for that too. That fellow we saw seated at the table works for me. His performance evaluation is two weeks overdue. He's leaving on vacation tomorrow. I told him the only way we could get together today was for him to meet me here at the club, after the match. Too bad he has been forced to wait more than an hour. I hope he's not too miffed."

Bosses who neglect or procrastinate about taking care of miscellaneous administrative matters of group members are a source of annoyance to their people. In contrast, those bosses who respond promptly to the administrative matters facing subordinates receive high marks and support. Here are some of the paperwork demands group members want taken care of relatively quickly:

- Performance appraisals and salary reviews
- Requests for personal days off
- Requests for transfers or early retirement
- Travel advances
- Requests for tuition reimbursement
- Authorization for parental leave
- Filing of grievances against the company
- Processing of charges of sexual harassment (if *you* are the person being charged, the paperwork will be handled by somebody else)
- Approval of expense account vouchers

Prompt handling of such paperwork can give you extra stature as a leader that will compensate for not being highly charismatic. In fact, a frequent problem with emotional and flamboyant leaders is that they neglect paperwork. And a subordinate who needs reimbursement for a business trip wants cash more than inspiration.

## GIVE OUT RECOGNITION

The least expensive method—in terms of money and time—of cultivating people below you is to sprinkle them with any appropriate form of recognition. "Show people how important you think they are," contends every primer on supervision. Similar to the omnipresent DON'T DRINK AND DRIVE signs, many more people understand the concept than apply it to their own situations. Yet investing a small amount of time in recognizing a person of lower rank than yourself can pay large dividends in terms of cultivating a loyal follower. The recognition in question usually involves making public the accomplishments of a worker. Two case histories of creative approaches to giving recognition follow.

Rosemary Sherman, charge nurse in a geriatric ward, called a floor meeting. "Ladies and gentlemen," she began, "the subject of today's meeting is a question of life, death, and teamwork. Our ward, and our very hospital, has averted disaster through the initiative and spirit displayed by one of the members of this hospital. Who performed this important act? No, it was not the chief of surgery. No, it was not the chief of medical services. No, it was not the head nurse. It was custodial worker Flora Barnes who suspected that the carafes on the patients' nightstands were contaminated.

"Miss Barnes was correct. Our laboratory results proved that staphylococci were present in the carafes. Who knows how many of our patients would have become terminally ill if this unsanitary condition had not been caught in time? Flora could you please tell us about your heroic act?"

Blushingly, Flora said, "Thank you for making such a fuss over me. I was just doing my job. I noticed those carafes were awfully dirty. I figured somebody should be told about it. Thanks again Nurse Sherman. I'm proud to be working for such a fine woman who appreciates me."

Murray, the manager of financial services, was scheduled to make a presentation to top management about the financial feasibility of launching a new product. Two days before the meeting, he said to Scott, a financial analyst in his department, "Why don't you come along to the meeting with me? You collected most of the important information we needed to make the revenue and cost projections on this new product. It would make sense to me if you made at least part of the presentation. It will be a good opportunity for you."

Scott was flattered that he was asked to contribute to a presentation to the company higher-ups. Scott and Murray performed admirably in the meeting. Their projections for a good profit for the proposed product were convincing and the product proved to be a winner. Scott's reputation as a young analyst with potential was instantly established.

Shortly thereafter, Scott received a one-step promotion to the position of senior financial analyst at another division of the company. He bade farewell to Murray and thanked him for his contribution to his professional growth. Scott did not forget Murray, as the latter explains:

> It seems that Scott appreciated my efforts on his behalf much more than I realized. The controller in Scott's division resigned to take a position with another company shortly after Scott arrived on the scene. This immediately created an opening at the top of the financial organization—one for which Scott was not qualified. He is a rational enough person to realize that you don't jump from junior financial analyst to division controller in two steps.

Instead of putting his hat in the ring for the job, Scott recommended me for the position. He spoke glowingly about how effective I was in developing younger people and how smoothly my department ran. Being a member of the corporation gave me an added edge over company outsiders. I was promoted to the controller's position.

Scott was now working for me again. Over lunch one day, I asked Scott what was the determining factor in his nominating me as a contender for the controller's slot. He pointed specifically to the incident about my bringing him along to the meeting with top management so he too could achieve some recognition.

## LISTEN TO PEOPLE'S PROBLEMS AND SUGGESTIONS

Listening is the essential tool of the participative manager. It is also an excellent way of cultivating people of lower rank, as well as anybody else in the organization. When asked about the attributes of a good boss, many employees will include "One who listens to me." Being a good listener, however, is not sufficient to earn you credits for being one. You also have to be *perceived* as a good listener. Consider these gestures and words to enhance your appearance of being an effective listener:

- Lean forward in your chair when the person says something that appears to be the main point of his or her concern or argument.
- During the speaker's monologue, periodically say, "No kidding."
- Cup your chin in your hand and squint at various times.
- When the person speaking pauses, say, "This is really good stuff."
- Say "hmmm" periodically but not frequently enough to sound like a psychotherapist.
- Should you daydream while the person is speaking, ask, "Could you go over your main points again? I want to make sure that I have understood exactly what you are saying."

Do not restrict your listening to people who report directly to you. Listen also to lower-ranking workers including office assistants, store associates, checkout counter personnel, and custodial workers. Not only will these people frequently have direct information about problems, they will often spread the word of your fine leadership qualities if you listen to them. (Of course, company executives will also have to listen to lower-ranking workers for their praise to do you some good.)

## BE SENSITIVE TO HUMAN RELATIONSHIPS ━━━━━━

Many a manager has made a mistake in handling people while trying to be too productivity-minded or rational. If you take literally all scientific notions about management, the result could be so mechanistic that you could lose the support of the people you are trying to manage. Stan, a newly appointed manager at a branch store of a chain of home-improvement service centers, fell into this trap. Shortly after arriving on the scene, he decided to reorganize the branch. In doing so, he broke up the old cliques of people who had worked together as teammates on various projects. Here is what happened, as described by one of the team leaders:

> Stan thought he was a productivity expert. He concluded that we were goof offs because the members of each team had become buddies as well as work associates. Stan hoped that by forming new teams, productivity would increase. The opposite proved to be true. We missed the loose and easy work practices that we had in the past. When I was out on assignment with my team, it was more like fixing up your own house than being paid an hourly wage to fix up somebody's else's place. Now the old feeling of camaraderie was gone.
>
> I tried to explain to Stan that his reorganization was a mistake, but he wouldn't listen. Instead, he kept mumbling something about the importance of increasing productivity and the fact that he wasn't in the happiness business. With four new teams created, many problems arose. Cooperation declined. People became huffy about which responsibility was theirs versus which responsibility was somebody else's. All of a sudden people became very rigid about taking a full lunch break and leaving a job early enough to wash up.
>
> Stan pleaded with us to improve productivity, and threatened us with firings if the situation didn't improve. Profits were sinking and he was looking bad in top management's eyes. The more he urged us to get our work accomplished faster, the more we dragged our heels. Nobody was willing to rescue Stan because he had ignored our requests to maintain systems that had worked well for several years.
>
> Recognizing that breaking up the old teams and forming new ones was unworkable, Stan reorganized us back into our original teams. Something had been lost in the process. Even though the time we spent completing a job showed a spurt of improvement, we never reached the level of productivity we had before Stan arrived. He finally resigned. I think management helped him reach that decision.

Being sensitive to human relationships has increased in importance recently as many companies are using production work teams. Team members tackle an entire task—such as building an automobile or processing a mortgage—in contrast to the assembly line approach to doing the same thing. For production work teams to fulfill their promise, the team workers have to get along well with each other. The politically astute manager therefore grants the workers some authority in selecting their own team.

## BE COURTEOUS

Many people are rude to people of lower rank than themselves. Consequently, if you show common courtesy to lower-ranking people, you may be at a substantial advantage in gaining their respect and support. Seven key facets of courtesy should be kept in mind in order to be perceived as a courteous person.

### Answer Memos and Letters

Many managers answer memos and letters according to the rank of the sender. Correspondence from the higher-ranking people is answered within one week; correspondence from lower-ranking people is often ignored and discarded. Answer the memos of lower-ranking people promptly and you will have an advantage in cultivating their support. It generally requires only a little more time to give a quick answer to a memo than to earmark it for later action. An efficient technique is to handwrite a brief response on the bottom of a typewritten or word-processed memo. A photocopy is then made for your files and the original is returned to the sender.

A curious phenomenon in large organizations is that the powerful people do answer correspondence. People at lower levels in the organization are often much less courteous. This is one reason outsiders to the organization often send their complaints straight to the top.

### Write Notes of Appreciation

An almost sure-fire technique of developing a loyal following is to courteously write notes of appreciation to lower-ranking people who have served you well. Be careful, however, to use the memo-writing technique judiciously. Some managers err on the side of stuffing dozens of people's in-baskets with virtually identical notes saying "Thanks for a job well done," or "Great show on that assignment." As in other types of compliments, notes of appreciation should be sincere and individualized to fit the specific good deed.

President George Bush is a prime example of a person who makes deft use of notes of appreciation. On the way back from a successful European trip in May 1989, he took the time to personally write 40 thank-you notes to staff members. Later on several of the aides compared the notes, and not one was the same.[1] A less adept office politician than Mr. Bush might have indiscriminately sent the same note to each of his staff.

## Return Telephone Calls

"I wonder what that pest from Philadelphia wants?" said middle manager Chet. "He's already called three times." If Chet would take three minutes to answer the Philadelphian's call, he might discover that it's a person from another branch of the company who wants to transfer to Chet's branch. The job-seeker also happens to be a talented individual who has a potential contribution to make to Chet's team.

Failing to return telephone calls of sales representatives is a common practice in most organizations. Even if you are not interested in the message, saying, "I'm not interested" will at least end the matter and not brand you as a discourteous person. The message sender may prove to be someone who can someday help you.

## Minimize Keeping People Waiting Outside Your Office

If you have earned the right to an office, it does not automatically grant you the privilege of keeping people waiting to see you. The man who waits until 2:15 in the afternoon for his 1:15 appointment may be inwardly seething with anger and humiliation, despite the fact that he is catching up on paperwork while he waits for you. Unless you are a top executive, most lower-ranking people will perceive you as discourteous for keeping them waiting. Waiting for a top executive is often rationalized because the executive's time is thought to be in high demand.

## Acknowledge the Presence of People Outside Your Office

"Heather can take a flying leap over a cliff" said Jill. "Ever since she received her promotion, she ignores me unless she wants me to do some work for her. My boyfriend and I were sitting together in a restaurant across from our office building. In walks Heather, carrying an attache case and looking so important. I asked my boyfriend if he would like to meet my former boss. I beckoned to her, but she walked right past me as if I were a street beggar."

Heather's act of discourtesy—treating Jill as if she were a nonperson—is not uncommon among pretentious individuals. Such a strategy will usually backfire: As you advance in your career, you need every vote you can get. The more people you have alienated, the fewer people there are around to make positive statements about you to others. Many an individual has been denied a choice promotion because of having developed the reputation of being disliked by people of lower rank.

### Offer an Explanation for Your Actions

"Get my office painted before anybody else's," said Fred to the maintenance supervisor. "Don't make any excuses, just get it done. I want my place looking right." The maintenance chief obliged, but he assigned his sloppiest and slowest painter to Fred's work order. In addition, Fred's office was painted blue instead of the beige he requested. When Fred complained, the maintenance worker said it was an honest mistake that could not be rectified for another three years which was the normal interval between office paintings.

Fred might have received better service from the maintenance department if he had offered a logical explanation for the urgency of his request. Fred neglected to tell the maintenance department that he had been recently assigned responsibilities that required more customer contact. A freshly painted office would therefore create a positive impression for the company. A small act of courtesy on Fred's part might have resulted in his getting the kind of service he needed. Few people willingly comply with orders if not handed a logical explanation of why the order is given. The person who develops a reputation of giving illegitimate orders (those without proper authority or justification) may wind up with more enemies than allies.

### Avoid Being Abrasive

An abrasive personality goes one step beyond being discourteous—he or she literally "rubs people the wrong way." The primary characteristics of the abrasive personality are self-centeredness, isolation from others, perfectionism, contempt for others, and a tendency to attack people. In a study of top executives, psychologists compared "derailed" executives with those who had progressed to senior management positions. The leading category of fatal flaws was insensitivity to others, characterized by an abrasive, intimidating, bullying style.[2]

If you have a true abrasive personality, you may not be able to change your stripes. However, you can learn to keep your abrasiveness under control. Be especially careful to bite your tongue when experiencing heavy job pressures. Otherwise you might repeat the error of a plant manager, who faced with a recall of thousands of parts, blurted out to a supervisor: "You've asked me the same thing three times today. You're like a mosquito bite on my backside. I know you're there, you're annoying, but you're not important enough to do anything about."

## PUBLICIZE YOUR CONNECTIONS

People with the right connections are impressive to others, providing they publicize their connections in a tactful, nonoffensive way. All things being equal, other workers prefer to befriend you if you have influential friends. (This observation applies to people above you, at your level, or below you.) People both admire others who have influential friends and also entertain the vague hope that one of your contacts will help them if you two are allies.

The recommended procedure for office name-dropping is to mention the influential person's name in a work context. Doing so gives the person below you the impression that the influential person relies on your advice. A person below you will be less impressed with a social mention of your connection as it may not transfer to the work environment. Many a high-placed executive has an influential niece or nephew working for the company. The niece or nephew who tries to capitalize on that type of connection might come across as a weak individual.

Assuming it is not an outright lie, you might try making a few vague statements about your work-related connections, provided each statement is accompanied by the true nature of the connection. Allow the listener to interpret the statement anyway he or she desires. You may receive more respect around your office. A few examples:

- J. P. and I were discussing the problem of industrial contaminants the other day. (You coughed continuously during a recent meeting. After the meeting, J. P. asked you if your cough stemmed from a work-related illness.)
- Murph (the president's nickname) is talking a lot about zero defects these days. I guess he found my input useful. (Just to create the impression that you are alert, without being asked, you sent him an article on zero defects that you found in a business meeting.)
- Should Blackstone visit our department this fall as planned, I'd like to introduce you to him. (True. It is only organizational protocol for a department head to introduce subordinates to a high-ranking official when that person pays a visit to the department.)

## BE ESPECIALLY NICE TO
## ADMINISTRATIVE ASSISTANTS ━━━━━━━━━━━━━━━━━

Despite all that has been said about the importance of cultivating administrative assistants in order to win favor on the job, many insensitive people continue to alienate them. Assistants whom you have treated unkindly and unfairly seek, and usually find, revenge. The revenge often takes the form of bad mouthing. Penny tells us how she and another assistant in her department avenged Linda's wrongdoing:

> Linda was a counselor who thought she was the queen of the college counseling center. She had her eyes set on becoming the assistant director of the center. Bit by bit she made herself more useful to Dr. Kilbourne, the director of the counseling center. Linda was always the first to bring forth new ideas and potential programs from the center. Whatever new fad appeared on the scene, she was there with a proposed package.
>
> Linda's downfall was that she was a Janus. The face that looked toward the boss was smiling and pleasant. The face that looked toward the secretaries was snarling and mean. She would order us around as though she was our boss—which she wasn't. Once she overhead us talking about a weird student and proceeded to chastise us for being unprofessional.
>
> One fact we knew about Linda that Dr. Kilbourne did not know was that she was not too well liked by the students. They frequently complained that Linda forced herself and her programs on them. She went through the dorm begging for people to take her workshop in stress management. The students really took offense when she tried to develop a list of gays on campus who could be approached for a minicourse on gay rights.
>
> Melissa, one of the other assistants in the counseling center, and I began to drop hints to Dr. Kilbourne that Linda was kind of pushy and offensive both to us and the students. We don't know if she believed it, but soon Linda's influence began to shrink. She no longer ran workshops, but was confined to doing mostly routine things such as assisting students who wanted to change majors. If she had treated us decently, Linda might now be the assistant director of the counseling center.

## HAND OUT REFRESHMENTS ━━━━━━━━━━━━━━━━━━

A widely held belief is that if a person is being paid more than a starvation wage, you cannot motivate him or her with food. Experience suggests that this is a faulty generalization, particularly because people equate food with appreciation, friendship and recognition. An inexpensive way of cultivating many workers is to find a suitable occasion to provide them with free pastry, oat bran muffins, and beverages during normal working hours. Brent, a management consultant, explains how he used a few bags of doughnuts to cultivate a group of supervisors:

> My assignment was to discover the true nature of the problems facing the manufacturing division of a company located in a small town. Once the problems were uncovered, we would be in a position to make some constructive recommendations for improving conditions. My program called for a series of weekly meetings with different groups of supervisors until I had met with every supervisor in the plant twice.
>
> The first two meetings were dreadfully dull. No matter how much I explained my purpose in being there, the supervisors just made comments about mundane matters such as particular machines that were in need of replacement. One night on my way home, I noticed a bakery shop down the corner from the plant. On my next trip to the plant, I stopped at the bakery to purchase a dozen assorted homemade doughnuts.
>
> When I entered the conference room and told the supervisors I had brought some doughnuts, their faces lit up like children watching seals at the zoo. After they ate their doughnuts, they opened up to me and began a steady stream of conversation about the problems *really* facing the plant.
>
> The information spread quickly throughout the plant that the sessions with the consultant included fresh doughnuts. I knew I had broken down the communication barrier with the supervisors when one of the old-timers said to me that the supervisors were treated like mushrooms. Perplexed, I asked for an explanation. He said, "management keeps us in the dark and feeds us a steady diet of horse manure."
>
> Since that experience with the supervisors, I now incorporate free doughnuts into similar consulting assignments. It seems to facilitate communication and create some instant friends.

## MAINTAIN OLD TIES

A mistake made by some newly appointed managers is to ignore former co-workers because the manager feels that he or she is no longer "one of them." To ignore former co-workers is to lose an important base of support, as discovered by Willy. Willy was ecstatic about his promotion to head of the shipping department. He had worked in the department for seven long years with the hopes of someday becoming the boss.

Willy's co-workers gave a party in his honor to wish him well as the new department head. The group was happy to know that one of their own rather than an outsider had received the promotion. As Willy savored his new status, the workers in the department began to notice substantial changes in the way he acted. Ed, one of the department members, describes what happened:

Poor Willy let his little bit of power go to his head. He began by wearing fancier shirts than we did. He also wore a jacket to work and kept it on. Soon he decided to have lunch alone or with his boss. He even pulled out of his standing Thursday evening bowling date with us. It irritated us, but we figured it was just a stage he was going through. Basically we still liked Willy.

Then he began to turn us off completely. Willy brought a spindle to the office, like the type they use in quick order restaurants. He would place orders on the spindle for us to pick up instead of speaking directly to us.

Willy had forgotten who his friends were. We taught him a lesson at the company picnic. Not one person from shipping showed up except Willy. The way I heard it, Willy was very embarrassed. It made it look as though his department wasn't company-minded. We all figured so long as Willy had forgotten us, we would forget him.

# CHAPTER 8

## BASIC
## POWER-GRABBING
## TACTICS

Power is like money. Not everybody is obsessed with power or money, but few people would refuse more of either if it were offered to them. Another similarity is that power, like money, is an almost universal currency. Possessing power helps get you what you want. Power can also be useful in helping you avoid unfavorable situations. Without attaining power, you run the risk of early dismissal in a business downturn or corporate takeover, or when political infighting is intense.

Power is also vital because it is not uncommon for a person in a high position to make an early exit from the organization because he or she was unable to acquire a solid power base. You also need a modicum of power at lower levels in the organization in order to qualify for more responsibility or your share of the budget.

Tactics and strategies for attaining and retaining power can be divided roughly into basic and advanced tactics. The basic tactics are more frequently used at lower organizational levels, while the advanced tactics are used more frequently at higher levels. Judicious use of the basic tactics and strategies described in this chapter should help you move far enough up in the organization so you can apply some advanced techniques described in the next chapter.

If you think planning, plotting, and scheming to acquire power is distasteful, it will nevertheless help you to acquaint yourself with power-grabbing techniques other people might be using to take away what little power you have.

## DEVELOP EXPERTISE

The launching pad for acquiring power is to develop expertise is some specialty such as selling, computing, accounting, purchasing, or fund raising. Almost every powerful and successful person began by being particularly good at some tangible skill. Nobody will give you a chance to display your executive skills until you have displayed a reasonable degree of technical competence. At times the expertise that attracts attention to yourself is unrelated to the field of your ultimate power. Outstanding athletes and movie actors, for example, have become powerful politicians.

Even after being promoted into administrative work, it is important to develop a specialty other than being a good administrator or inspired leader. The most powerful executives today often possess such expertise as being able to turn around an ailing company, understanding consumer preferences, negotiating with government officials.

## FORM ALLIANCES WITH
## POWERFUL PEOPLE

You will recall that an important part of planning your political campaign is to identify the powerful people. Power stems from forming alliances with one or more of the powerful people you have identified. Forming alliances with the right people, in fact, is one of the most important power-grabbing strategies. It is the essence of influence peddling in government and of making giant sales in business.

Henry Kissinger is the quintessence of somebody whose alliances with powerful people bring him extraordinary power in business. As president of Henry Kissinger and Associates, Dr. Kissinger is able to rely on his many high-level contacts to open doors for clients. The door-opening often involves allowing a company to bid on a government contract, or facilitating being allowed to trade in the foreign country in question. His firm also offers advice, but the door-opening capabilities allow for much higher fees than does the advice giving.

During his years as Secretary of State, Kissinger formed alliances with many top government officials including those of China, Italy, West Germany, and France. The client list of Kissinger and Associates has included Union Carbide, Fiat, Volvo, Midland Bank, Coca Cola, H. J. Heinz, ITT, and Hunt Oil—all firms with multinational operations.[1]

## THINK, ACT, AND LOOK POWERFUL ━━━━━━━━━━━━

If you have reached the top of your field and you control vast resources, it may no longer be necessary to think, act, and look powerful. People already know who you are and how much you can influence their lives. On the way up, there is something to be said for acting the role of a powerful person. If you act the part, people will treat you as a powerful person or will grant you power.

Thinking powerful centers around looking at the big picture instead of worrying about practical details. For example, a dealmaker who buys a company for $80 million, and then intends to sell it for $100 million one year later, thinks in terms of grossing a quick $20 million. He or she does not fret, "What a mess. I would have to go through all the paperwork involved in buying and selling a company twice within six months. Think of all the time I would spend in conference with lawyers and accountants." In short, the powerful-thinking person lets others worry about details.

Almost any behavior that makes you appear to control resources is a power act. Such acts include throwing a grand party, picking up the restaurant tab when dining with a person of higher rank than yourself, signing letters with a $150 fountain pen, and giving your broker power of attorney to make investments for you (even if the amount invested is $300), and purchasing an automobile for cash.

Looking powerful is tricky. If you take literally the advice of wardrobe consultants, you will look like a sales associate in Bloomingdales or Brooks Brothers, or a young professional in almost any metropolitan law or investment banking firm. On the other hand, if you ignore conventional wisdom about looking powerful you risk looking unimportant—and therefore powerless—in the eyes of others. Specific ways of increasing your power look include:

- Wear glasses. Eighty percent of a group of corporate recruiters believed that eyeglasses help the wearer focus on making a power statement during a business presentation.[2]
- Decorate your office with stainless steel, leather, and polished glass. Leave all family photos, mementos, and souvenirs home.
- For accessories, use a gold pen; solid color, leather briefcase; gold watch of simple elegance.
- Hair should be short for males with no sideburns or beard; and short and away from the face for females.
- On occasion when standing, place hands on hip, and place your feet apart about 18 inches.

- For emphasis when speaking, point the index finger parallel to the ground, and thumb at a right angle similar to aiming a gun.

A useful general principle is not to ignore the Dress for Success look, but to supplement it with something that helps differentiate you from others. Creativity is often necessary to find a point of differentiation that makes you distinctive, and therefore somewhat powerful. Terry, a federal economist, faced a problem shared by thousands of individuals who aspire to occupy a big job in a vast bureaucracy—how to distinguish himself from other people with similar ambitions. As an economist, his work did not lend itself to theatrics and Terry had no unusual physical features that would make him particularly easy to remember. However, he did develop a social skill that helped him gain recognition. Terry explains:

> For several months, I wrestled with the problem of how to become distinctive. Browsing through a D. C. bookstore, I happened upon a book about remembering people's names and faces. It dawned on me that such a skill would be very helpful working for a mammoth, impersonal organization. I already had some talent in this area. I had always been better than average in recalling a person's name after only one meeting.
>
> Remembering the names of many people I came in contact with in my job became an intriguing game. Gradually, a number of people commented on my facility for remembering names and faces. My skill helped me phase into assignments that interfaced with people outside my department. My outside contacts led to a position with a much higher GS rating than that carried by the position of an entry-level economist. My career with the government had been launched because I finally found a way to stand out from the crowd.

## PLAY CAMEL'S HEAD IN THE TENT

Just as the camel works his way into the tent inch by inch, beginning with his nose, you might grab power in a step-by-step manner until you acquire the amount of power and responsibility you desire. "Camel's head" has become widely practiced in organizations where large numbers of people are trying to enlarge their empires or become the surviving manager in a downsized organization. The machinations of Charlie provide some illustrative details of how "camel's head" is played.

Charlie was hired as the sales manager of a camera and video products company. Nat, the company president, was keenly interested in the customer aspect of the business and had sales, customer service, advertising, and marketing research departments all report to him. Charlie regarded the arrangement as unusual, but welcomed the opportunity to work as sales manager for this prosperous company. Inherent in this arrangement seemed to be an opportunity for Charlie to increase his power.

Charlie's first power-grabbing maneuver took place when the manager of customer service suddenly resigned. He suggested to Nat that he would be willing to serve as acting manager of customer service until a suitable replacement could be found. Although Charlie had to work extra-long hours, his temporary takeover of customer service proved to be a winning strategy. After a new manager of customer service was appointed, Nat approved Charlie's request that customer service now permanently report to the sales department.

Charlie next took after the marketing research department. His strategy was to have his sales department begin to conduct their own market research. Charlie then explained to Nat that because market research was already being conducted by the sales department, why not have the marketing research department report to sales? It made sense to Nat, particularly as Charlie continued to turn in a fine performance for the company.

At last report, Charlie had submitted a proposal to Nat suggesting that a marketing vice-president be appointed. Reporting to the marketing VP would be sales, customer service, market research, and advertising. A new sales manager would need to be appointed because Charlie had recommended himself as the vice-president of marketing. Should Charlie pull off this coup, he will no longer be using basic power-grabbing tactics, but will have become an advanced player.

## ACQUIRE LINE RESPONSIBILITY

In almost every organization, those people whose work is tied in directly with the primary purpose of the organization (line personnel) have more power than service groups and advisors (staff personnel). Many staff people, nevertheless, do become powerful. A vice-president of human resources of the chief legal counsel usually has considerable power, but yet not as much power as their counterparts in line units (such as operations or marketing).

If you spend your entire career in staff jobs, you may never have as much power or make as much money as people in line positions. An executive assistant who works for the director of manufacturing (a line unit) is usually paid more than the executive assistant who reports to the head of maintenance (a staff unit).

The nature of the work you are performing is not the crucial factor in determining whether you are line or staff. What is significant is how vital that function is to your employer. A photographer is a staff person when she works in the photo department of Black and Decker. When she works for a photo studio, she is a line person.

Working as a market researcher in a consumer products company, Mannie received some disheartening news. "Sorry Mannie," said his boss, "you won't be invited to the sales conference in Boca Raton. Because business conditions aren't that great, we can only afford to send people to the conference this year who are directly involved in customer contact. Maybe next year we'll be able to send along some staff people."

Mannie had no choice but to accept the company decision and silently suffer this blow to his dignity. He vowed to himself that he would not face such an insult again. Mannie's solution was to find himself a line position—one where his particular discipline would be considered crucial to the success or failure of the organization. As Mannie recollects:

> It didn't take long for a man of my background to find a position with a market research firm that provides services to a number of companies. Now when I work on a client's account, I may be a staff function to them, but I'm a line function in my own firm. A market research firm cannot exist without market researchers. My job may not be as secure as an industrial job, but I feel more appreciated. I'm also treated with more respect and I feel more powerful. I have an equal chance of rising to the top of my firm.

## MAKE A QUICK SHOWING

Staff groups are forever scheming about ways to increase their power. A standard technique is for the staff group to prove its mettle by taking care of a minor problem, thus gaining the confidence of the line unit. Having demonstrated merit on the minor problem, the staff group is in a strategic position to take on more major, and consequently more power-yielding, problems. "Make a quick showing" can thus be used as a steppingstone to being granted more power and influence by the organization.

As manager of management science in his company, Brad found himself with a department consisting of himself, one full-time professional, and the part-time help of an assistant shared with another department. Brad's thirst for power was far from quenched. He describes his path to glory:

> I was sadly disillusioned by the little respect paid to management scientists in our company. I thought my small department would be deluged with requests to solve important corporate problems. No such luck. We were creating work for ourselves. One day, I finally received a request to work on a true operating problem. An executive in the marketing department wanted to compare our growth to the industry as a whole.

The other professional in the department and myself took on the problem enthusiastically. We had an accurate answer back to the executive in three days. She was quite happy with our analysis. Capitalizing on the good relationship we had begun, I asked if we might help the marketing department with its sales forecasting. The executive agreed, and before long, we had two marketing researchers assigned to my staff.

Several months later, manufacturing asked us to work on a small problem concerning machine obsolescence. We solved that problem. Shortly thereafter we were conducting analyses to tell manufacturing how many spare parts should be stored in inventory. We took over one of their inventory control specialists. Aside from seeing my staff jump from one to five in one year, plus our own full-time assistant, we were performing more interesting work.

## DEVELOP A NETWORK OF USEFUL CONTACTS

Networking is widely recommended for finding a job. Making systematic use of contacts can also pay big dividends in obtaining more power for yourself. The people gathered into your network can be a useful source of information about potential customers, reliable suppliers, and can help you solve difficult problems. Being able to obtain customers, find the right suppliers, and solve important problems gives you some power. Here are some additional ways you can benefit from your personal network, all of which could give you a power edge:

### Exchange of Information

What is top management thinking? What personnel changes are forthcoming, and what implications does this have for your group? Are there any takeover rumors circulating? Answers to these questions have given you some "gossip power."

### Quick Answers

How reliable is a given vendor? Whom should I call at headquarters when I can't get satisfaction at the division level? Where can I locate reliable temporary workers for production work in a hurry? Obtaining quick answers helps you solve problems rapidly—thus you look good in the eyes of your boss.

### Support for Your Ideas

You have an idea you would like to try out but you're skeptical that your boss will react warmly. Support from others might be just what you need to sway your boss.

**Emergency Assistance**

Two of your key people are out sick, and a crash assignment hits your desk. You need to borrow help from another department. Or a major customer is irate about a matter you can't resolve. Or, your department runs out of supplies during a rush project, and you lack the time to wait for the requisition process. Well-placed people in your network can help you resolve such problems. Unless these problems are resolved, you could experience an erosion of your power.[3]

Almost any person of power, influence, competence, luck, charm, or wealth is worth incorporating into your network. Lisa, a person with a strong power drive, explains how she "networks" (another verb that has become a noun in modern life): "Networking is my *shtick*. My handbags, wallet, attache case, glove compartment, and athletic bag always has a fresh supply of my business cards. Whether at a trade show, restaurant, or singles bar, or traveling, I'm always alert to contacting with somebody who could help me get my job done better. My networking is two-sided. I exchange cards and stand ready to help out anybody else in my network.

"One of the crown jewels in my network surfaced on a business trip. I was flying back to Chicago from Cincinnati. Seated next to me was an earnest looking middle-aged man who was poring over some impressive looking balance sheets. When he put his work down to order a drink, I eased into conversation with him. It turns out that Jim was a business broker who specialized in buying and selling medium-size companies. His dealings put him in close contact with a lot of CEOs. As a consequence he had a lot of useful information about the financial condition of many companies.

"As a benefits consultant, it's helpful for me to know something about a company before I make a pitch. I therefore kept in occasional touch with Jim after the plane trip. Jim is a man of integrity, so he wouldn't reveal any financial details of a company to me. However, he would furnish me some general ideas about which companies might be wanting to increase their employee benefits, and those who were looking to economize. I can make a pitch to a company in either condition.

"As part of the exchange with Jim, I would answer general questions he might have about any of my clients. Like Jim, I wouldn't release confidential information, but I would comment if I thought a particular company was ripe to be bought or was looking to buy a company itself."

To build a wider network, consider the business-card exchange technique of Lisa, along with these suggestions:[4]

- Get connected through friends and acquaintances you already have. Being a friend-of-a-friend is a quick way of getting mutual trust and cooperation.

- Stop to chat briefly with anybody who you think would be a worthwhile inclusion into your network.
- Take the initiative by discussing common problems and asking friendly questions. Being the first to offer assistance is a good tactic.
- Share credit with people outside your workgroup for accomplishments that involved the outsiders in any way. When other people offer congratulations, mention anyone else who deserves to share the credit.
- Stay honest and trustworthy. Effective networking is based on trust. If you have a reputation for discretion, your network will continue to expand. One small indiscretion, on the other hand, can wipe out an entire network of relationships.

## CONTROL FUTURE ASSIGNMENTS

Rightly or wrongly, many people believe that human resource specialists have a great deal of influence over who gets which future assignments.[5] Because of this belief, some people go along with the requests of personnel staffers to stay on their good side. A human resource specialist—or anyone else whose job deals with future assignments—can gain a moderate degree of power because of this perceived control over the future. However, a person who influences future assignments must move cautiously in exercising this power. It can backfire.

Mike was a human resources planner, a job that included filling requirements for future job openings. During one two-year period he was heavily involved in staffing a new company plant located in the South. Mike spent much of his time processing recommendations from managers for transferring people to this new plant. Another part of Mike's job was his responsibility as manager of his own personnel department. Five people reported to Mike. One day he approached Cal, a manufacturing manager, with this proposition:

"I'm in the process of developing my own staff. One of my people, Jeff, needs some manufacturing experience. Will you please accept him as a first-line supervisor in your department? I'd like him to get one year of experience. That will give him the hands-on manufacturing experience he needs to move up in my department. Could he start next month?

"Hold on, Mike. Right now, I don't have the room for you to move an untried supervisor into my department. It would mean bumping somebody else to give your man what amounts to a training program. By the way, since when do you have the authority to arbitrarily assign people to my department?"

"Cal, let's lay the cards on the table," said Mike. "What we're talking about here is a little reciprocity. I get good assignments for your people, especially with that new plant location. All I'm asking for is a little cooperation in return."

Cal replied, "Mike you're not doing me any favors. It's your job to help staff the organization. Because the payroll department gets the paychecks for our group, it doesn't mean that I owe them a favor."

Cal did not let the incident drop. He brought it to the attention of the vice-president of personnel who agreed that Mike was abusing his power. Mike received a verbal reprimand. His error was in being so blatant about his demands. If people wanted to grant him favors because of his influence over future assignments, Mike should have let such favors emerge naturally.

## COLLECT AND USE IOUS

Another way of looking at Mike's error was that he was trying to cash an IOU while the other person felt he owed Mike nothing. Properly used, IOUs can be used to bargain for favors, favorable assignments, and even raises and promotions. After you have done somebody of higher rank an important favor, that person then owes you a favor—the equivalent of gaining some power for yourself. The IOU technique is the same political method as exchanging favors, with the exchange being made with a more powerful person. Covering for your boss is one way of collecting chits that can be cashed in the future.

Joan was an assistant to Roy, an executive with a penchant for being out of the office when an important person needed his assistance. Without being specifically asked by her boss, Joan had developed a variety of effective excuses to cover for him. Among her favorites were:

- Roy is on his way to an interdepartmental meeting. Perhaps I can get your message to him.
- I know Roy had said something about meeting with the internal auditors. I'm sure he'll get back to you later this afternoon.
- Roy just phoned me. He said the meeting he is attending is running late.

Roy usually did get back—in a reasonable time—to the people who sought his assistance. He welcomed the smooth manner in which Joan kept suspicions to a minimum as to his true whereabouts. He hoped that he could probably reciprocate. His opportunity came when Joan made the following request:

"Roy, I'm facing a ticklish problem. My daughter has started nursery school, and I don't have a ride for her three mornings a week. This means I will have to do the driving, and I will have to begin work about one-half hour late on Mondays, Wednesdays, and Fridays. Of course, I'll eat my lunch at my desk to make up for the lost time. I know this is asking a lot."

"Joan, let's keep this request within the department. The company hasn't yet initiated a flexitime program. I think I can answer my own phone for such short periods without making this a formal request. I'll make mental note of the change, and nobody else needs to be informed. You've given me extra-good service so you deserve a concession now and then."

## LET SOMEONE ELSE DO YOUR BIDDING

Another way to gain a moderate amount of power is to win favor for your point of view or program. It is doubly impressive when a supposedly neutral third party makes the pitch for your program. This prevents you from being accused of acting out of self-interest. The more credible the outsider, the more impressive it is when the outsider agrees with your point of view.

Product designer Lloyd recommended that his company's new automatic coffee maker be constructed with a stainless steel housing. The manufacturing department noted that a plastic housing would be much more economical and look better after wear. But Lloyd, believing that the distinctiveness gained by a stainless steel coffee maker would lead to a higher sales volume than that possible with a plastic one, recommended that a design consultant be brought in to settle the issue.

Lloyd also suggested that the executive involved in negotiating the dispute call in any design consultant he wished. (Lloyd realized that relatively few industrial design consultants existed and that most of them disliked products made of plastic.) Jacques Borzoff, a design consultant, was called into the company. After studying the relative merits of stainless steel versus plastic housing, he concluded:

"I will have to side with the concept of a totally stainless steel coffee maker. It is so sleek and glistens when properly cleaned. It will add to the distinctiveness of any kitchen."

Lloyd was pleased with the recommendation. The product was successfully launched, and Lloyd was a more influential person in the company because he was associated with a successful new product.

## USE TENDER POWER

A small movement is taking place for managers to influence others by being tender and kind, instead of harsh and unyielding, and highly competitive. The new influence process involves sharing power and glory, and is labeled "tender power" by Sherry Suib Cohen.[6] Tender power is the type of power frequently used by women in their private lives. Standard feminine tools such as mollifying, empathizing, and accommodating can work very well on the job. The experience many women have had in smoothing over family conflicts can also be used to manage and influence others.

Males, too, can use tender power on the job. The basic idea is that you tune into the feelings of people you are trying to influence. And when people are influenced by you, it gives you more power. The power sharing aspects of tender power also can give you more power. Empowering people often gives you more power because as a consequence of receiving more power, the group members produce better results.

Carol, a commercial loan analyst at a bank, explains how she focused in on the feelings of people—and therefore used tender power—to get her mission accomplished: "Our bank decided to appoint a taskforce to decide how to get a larger share of low-risk loans to business. We had noticed a clear trend for a greater percentage of outright defaults, and slower payments in recent years. After meeting for five weeks, several hours each time, our group was in a deadlock. Any proposal brought to the group resulted in lengthy bickering about its merits.

"I suggested to the group that we purchase a new software package that is supposed to accurately evaluate the credit worthiness of commercial loans. The program was based on more factors than a loan officer will usually take into consideration. Hank, one of the task force members, began to shoot down my proposal saying that it would be too much of a gamble. He said the taskforce would look foolish if the program proved to be less accurate than the current method of evaluating credit risks.

"Rather than retaliate, I said to Hank, 'Let's hear more about why you don't like the idea of the software. What are some of your real concerns?' Hank seemed so relieved. He began to pour out his concerns that soon software would be replacing loan analysts. He was also worried about looking foolish if the software was more accurate than he at predicting credit worthiness.

"I was then able to reassure Hank and the rest of the group that decision-making software of this kind would only be a supplement to our professional judgment. Shortly thereafter, the group voted favorably on my proposal. We bought the package, and it did improve our predictions of credit worthiness to some extent."

## PLAY THE MONEY GAME

Profit and nonprofit organizations alike are strongly money-conscious. Almost all decisions are related to their financial consequences. Even acts of social good such as funding a public museum may be gauged in terms of their tax deductibility and the good will they provide.

You can gain more power for yourself by tying your proposal to financial gain than by ignoring its financial consequences. Earning money and saving money are equally blessed virtues. Many more people are in a position to save money for the firm than to earn it. Unless you are directly involved with customer or client contact, it is difficult to categorize your contribution as a money-making one.

A standard approach to acquiring some power for yourself by playing the money game is illustrated by executives within the Internal Revenue Service. Increasing the number of auditors and collection agents increases the sphere of influence, and therefore the power, of IRS executives. To justify the additional staff members, IRS officials calculate how much additional tax revenue will most probably be brought in by each new auditor or collection agent. Such financial justification for hiring is doubly important: Internal IRS people have to be convinced, and then funds have to be appropriated from Congress.

Karen, a director of employee training, used a money-game approach to justify a stress-management seminar for all support personnel. Her justification for the program made some reference to the humanitarian aspects of helping employees cope better with job stress. Karen's emphasis, however, was on how much money the stress workshops would save the company. She noted that the job of secretary is classified by the government as one of the most stressful occupations. Consequently, the program would save about $400,000 annually including decrease in insurance premiums, increased productivity due to less absenteeism and better concentration, and decreased company payments to health-care providers. Karen's workshop was approved, and her sphere of influence greatly increased.

## CONTROL ACCESS TO KEY PEOPLE

A standard approach to garnering power is to occupy a position whereby people have to go through you to conduct business with a key person. People tend to be nice to you, including granting you favors, when you control their access to powerful figures. To see the CEO, the appointment almost inevitably has to be cleared through an administrative assistant. Unless that administrative assistant thinks you have an important reason for seeing the chief, or likes you personally, he or she may reject your request without even checking with the boss. Administrative assistants, furthermore, exercise particularly tight control over their boss's luncheon calendars.

Cybil is an executive assistant to Phil Gray, the chief financial officer of a major corporation. All major and some minor expenditures have to be personally approved by Phil. His phone rings constantly from 8:30 A.M. until 6 P.M. Cybil allows very few people to get through to Phil immediately. She frequently says, "Mr. Gray will not be returning any phone calls until later this week. Even the president is waiting to see him. Perhaps you can call again next week."

When Phil is legitimately busy in top-level matters, he often asks Cybil which appointments ahead are the most expendable. Cybil exerts her power by canceling the appointments of those people she thinks have the least justifiable reason for conferring with her boss. Asked what hidden benefits she derives from her position, Cybil explained:

> I guess you could say I'm in a powerful spot. I see myself performing a very valuable service for Phil and the corporation. Top executive talent is one of the company's most precious resources. My job is to see that people don't squander one particular resource, Phil Gray. Knowing the service I perform, people treat me with much respect. I am no longer one of the "girls," nor am I treated like a word processor.
>
> People smile at me, open doors for me, and send me little gifts. I have an important job in the corporation and I enjoy every minute of it. Twenty years ago I began as a file clerk in this company. I felt like a nobody. Today, I am somebody.

## USE THE HOME COURT ADVANTAGE

A power tactic for the person who wants to gain advantage at every turn is to try to conduct business negotiations in your own office, seated at your own desk. If you don't have an office, then negotiate in a rented office, motel room, or restaurant of your choice. When a person enters your office, you are the home team and the other person is the visitor. A successful financial services sales representative explains how the home court advantage works for him:

> It's not an easy trick to pull off, but I always give my prospect a choice of discussing an insurance program or related investment in my office or the prospect's office. Most people are accustomed to insurance people visiting them. When a prospect does consent to visit my office, it automatically becomes a situation whereby the person is coming to me for advice. Also he or she cannot retreat from our conversation by answering a phone call.

It's much like visiting a bank to ask for a loan. The loan officer seems to have the backing of the entire bank and you sit there virtually begging them to take your business. My biggest sales have come from situations whereby we close the contract on my premises.

## ACQUIRE SENIORITY

The most low-key method of gaining power is to acquire seniority. Executives who remain with the same organization tend to receive higher salaries and out-rank job-hoppers. The additional income and rank are a source of additional power. Also, longevity on the job still commands respect and privilege. Labor unions have long emphasized the rights of seniority, and most pay systems give some weight to seniority.

Although seniority alone will not prevent you from being ousted from your company or guarantee you more power, it helps. The compulsive job-hopper always works against the implicit threat of "last in, first out" in both managerial and individual contributor jobs. After a corporate takeover, the newly hired manager is more likely to be cut loose than a manager with longevity. Rick, one of the key players in an investment firm that buys other companies, explains his company's position on protecting the jobs of senior workers:

"After we buy a company, it's inevitable that we trim down the management workforce in order to reduce overhead. The managers we feel the least guilt about terminating are those who have recently joined the company, or who have a prior history of moving from company to company. We assume that job-hoppers will most likely be leaving us in the near future. Of course, any manager who is an absolute superstar will not be asked to leave, no matter how long he or she has been with the acquired firm.

"If we decide to fold the job of a senior manager, we encourage the operating executives in the acquired company to look for another job for that person. Sometimes the executive can be demoted to a position where he or she is really needed. We gave one middle manager the chance to become a warehouse manager, and he jumped at the opportunity. In another situation, we gave a 50-year old division controller the chance to demoted to a credit manager. She was happy to take the job, thus avoiding a long and uncertain job search.

## SQUEEZE POWER OUT OF
## A COMMITTEE ASSIGNMENT

Committee assignments are much less vapid than generally realized. In reality, they often represent a good opportunity to increase your power and influence. As described earlier in regard to the tactic, shine at meetings, committees can be a good place to get noticed. After becoming noticed you might be promoted thus providing you an instant surge of power. In governmental and academic institutions, a substantial amount of the important work gets done by committees. Being an outstanding contributor, or the head of a committee such as the one responsible for finding a new chief executive officer, is a power enhancer.

One of the easiest ways to squeeze power out of a committee assignment is to volunteer to become its leader. The opportunity arises because many committees are given the authority to appoint their own chairperson. Paul, a hospital administrator, explains how he has quietly slipped into becoming the chair of important committees on several occasions:

"After the first 15 minutes or so of banter, the committee members realize it is important to appoint a leader. Inevitably, people start to stare around the table at each other. Some people then look down because they don't want to be elected. The participants who want to be appointed chair seem to feel self-conscious about nominating themselves.

"What I do is mention that I have developed a handy little group decision-making technique that saves loads of time in putting together any report we might have to file. The committee head first gathers group opinion, and then whips together a word-processed report reflecting the consensus thinking. The draft of the report, in double space, would then go out to the committee members for their editorial comments and input. All they have to do is make their notations by pencil or pen. The committee head would then retrieve the computer file, and modify the report including everybody's suggestions.

"Group members usually see right away that they won't have to spend their time submitting individual reports. Yet their opinion will be incorporated into the report. With a sense of relief, somebody will usually nominate me, since I have volunteered to accept the report-writing burden. Having been head of several important committees, has given me much more clout in the hospital."

## TITLE YOUR WAY TO POWER

Another way of acquiring a modicum of power to carry a powerful job title. In general, uncomplicated job titles are among the most powerful. People respect your power when your title reads, "president," "chairman of the board," "chief engineer," "head coach," or "ambassador." Titles such as these are granted to a clearly defined organizational role.

Your discretion for giving yourself a more powerful title, and, therefore being thought of as having power is limited. At times you can request a more powerful title. For example, if you are the sole company representative in New Mexico, you can request the title, "Regional Manager, New Mexico." In some instances you can grant yourself an unofficial title to gain power. Under the best of circumstances, your unofficial title will become official.

Laboratory technician Dale was assigned the laborious task of writing a pest control manual for a food plant. Following the dictates of Dale's manual could prevent embarrassing problems such as a customer finding rat hairs in a can of stewed tomatoes. A wide range of other annoying sanitary problems could also be prevented. Despite the importance of this mission, the only official recognition Dale received was to affix his signature and job title to the manual.

To increase the chances that people would take his manual seriously, Dale upgraded his job title from laboratory technician to "plant sanitarian." Within two weeks people began to phone Dale with questions about pest control and other health problems. Dale's supervisor noticed some of the memos addressed to the plant sanitarian.

The supervisor conferred with his superior, and both agreed that Dale deserved the form job title *and job* of plant sanitarian. He would now spend about 80 percent of his time as a laboratory technician and 20 percent of his time dealing with pest control problems. Other people's pesky problems had now become a source of power for Dale, the newly crowned plant sanitarian.[7]

## MARRY INTO POWER

For the sake of completion, we are compelled to mention the ageless tactic of marrying an offspring of a powerful person in order to catapult into a key spot in the organization. However, marrying a major executive's daughter or son will probably not help you unless three conditions are met.

*First,* you must have a good relationship with the person you marry. If your wife or husband complains continually to the Big Boss that you are mistreating him or her, your position may be in jeopardy in that company. If you split with your spouse, you may also split with your job.

*Two,* you must win the respect of other people in the organization based on your good performance. If you are perceived as completely undeserving of your position, you will soon lose the support and cooperation of too many people. At times you will not even be taken seriously.

*Third,* you must be able to work effectively with your prospective in-law. Gil, a manufacturing representative in a small, prosperous firm, began to date the president's daughter. After a year of going together, they announced their marriage plans. The president said to Gil:

I welcome you into our family, but not into our business. As long as I am president, you will always be a sales representative. I may give you a territory that is easy on your home life, but that will be your last concession. I think you will make a fine husband to Diana. She loves you very much.

When I retire, this company will be sold to an outsider. During the three years you have worked for our firm, you have given me no indication that you have what it takes to be the president of our company. It has taken me 25 years to build up this business and I will not see it hurt by handing it over to the wrong person.

But son, don't take my comments the wrong way. I want you to have a happy marriage and a successful business career.

Gil had a sinking feeling in his stomach as he pondered whether to back out of his marriage plans, find a new job, or do both. Because he truly wanted to marry the owner's daughter, he went ahead with the marriage but quit the firm. Gil was then forced to take a lower-paying sales position. For Gil, marrying the boss's daughter backfired in the short run. In the long range, however, he may be better off because he can forge ahead in another direction. But this time he will be more politically astute.

# CHAPTER 9

# ADVANCED
# POWER-GRABBING
# TACTICS

People who have already tasted power are rarely satiated; instead, their appetite for power intensifies. Thus, the offensive thrust for power continues. To mount this offensive, it is often necessary to rely on advanced power-grabbing tactics. Simultaneously, people who have worked their ways into powerful positions must now practice several defensive strategies to remain in power.

Techniques of gaining favor and grabbing power used at lower levels are not necessarily discarded when a person achieves high rank. Many forms of office politics, such as cultivating influential people, are applicable at all job levels. In addition to the basic power-grabbing tactics described earlier, it is also important to rely on some advanced maneuvers.

## THINK BIG AND WIN BIG

"I like to think big. I always have," says Donald Trump. "To me it's very simple: If you're going to be thinking anyway, you might as well think big." Trump's legendary big thinking has helped him amass skyscrapers, hotels and casinos, an airline, a professional football team, several helicopters, and a 282-foot yacht. In addition he has thought big enough to write a book about his philosophy, and enter into show business.[1] All powerful people do not think in the grandiose manner of Donald Trump, but they do think about making big deals, and controlling the fates of large numbers of people.

Closely aligned to thinking big is winning big to pull yourself away from the pack. A case in point is Cliff, a corporate vice-president of manufacturing who was younger than most of his colleagues and subordinates. Despite the short length of time he had held his position, Cliff was well accepted. When he visited a plant, the key manufacturing people generally gave him their full cooperation. As a consequence, Cliff felt confident and powerful in his new position.

Ron, the corporate vice-president of engineering was about the same age as his colleagues and older than most of his subordinates. During the short period of time in which he held his position, he had received no indication that people were going to accept him. When he visited company plants and laboratories, the cooperation he received was really a form of minimal compliance. His administrative and engineering suggestions were countered with explanations as to why they would not work locally. Ron felt uneasy and uncertain of how much power he really held as vice-president.

Personality and ability could conceivably account for the difference in acceptance received by Cliff and Ron. A more important difference is that when Cliff was appointed to his position, he won big. When Ron was appointed, he won small. Cliff was considered the outstanding plant manager in the company. He had established himself as a person who operated at a level a full notch above his competitors. Ron was an unpopular choice for the top manufacturing job. He was a plant manager at a plant plagued by labor disputes and associated with an unglamorous, marginally profitable product. People begrudgingly accepted the authority of a vice-president they considered not better, if not worse, than themselves.

## GAIN CONTROL OF
## ORGANIZATIONAL RESOURCES ━━━━━━━━━━━━━━━━━━

Power is sometimes defined as the ability to control resources. It therefore follows that controlling resources makes a person more powerful. The resources to be controlled include money in the form of budgets, physical space, employees, and equipment. "Camel's head in the tent," as described previously, is one way of acquiring resources. In some instances, power grabbing can actually begin before you take a job—assuming you move deftly and carefully. Cynthia illustrates how to execute such an advanced power play:

> Cynthia was offered a promotion to general manager in her company. Prior to accepting the position, she spent a day with the outgoing general manager,

Mel, who was retiring. As he walked Cynthia through the department, she noticed that Mel had a small office with a single window. He then introduced Cynthia to Dave, his staff assistant (assistant to the general manager). As she looked into Dave's eyes she could see a penetrating chill.

During a wrap-up session, Cynthia asked Mel to assess each of his five subordinates. She quickly learned why Dave had been so cold. "He has applied for my job, too" said the general manager. "Dave doesn't know it yet, but I'm not going to recommend him. Not even if you decide to turn down the job, which I hope you don't. I think you're perfect for it."

The next morning, Cynthia met the company president for breakfast. She informed him, "I would need a bigger office so I could hold meetings there. I like to meet often with my staff, so I'd need extra seating, too. And if you don't think I'm asking too much, a personal computer. If that suits you, I'll take the job at the salary Mel specified."

Cynthia had considered asking for 5 percent more than the salary Mel had specified, and she knew she could have received it. But Cynthia decided the night before the meeting with the president, that a highly visible office and the addition of a computer would leverage additional power into the position. More pay would follow naturally as she used the additional power to increase top management's dependence on her.

As the president pondered over her counteroffer, Cynthia explained how the existing office could be expanded—by breaking down the wall between the office and Dave's adjacent office. She noted in an innocent-sounding voice, that Dave could be moved to another nearby office that was now vacant. "Deal," the president said, extending his hand to Cynthia. "When can you start?"[2]

# DEVELOP POWERFUL ALLIANCES

Rarely can someone attain or hold on to power without forming alliances with one or more other powerful people. The more powerful your ally, the better. If you are aligned with a powerful person, you become an extension of that person's power. The techniques described earlier for impressing the higher-ups are valuable because they help connect you to a person more powerful than yourself. When the time comes for exerting influence, the powerful ally can be invaluable.

Jeff, the chief financial officer (CFO) of an automotive company, expanded his power considerably several years ago. At the time his title was company controller. The automotive company he worked for faced a decrease in sales so substantial, that its existence was in peril. Jeff's company needed some large orders in a hurry. Although not in marketing, Jeff's alliances brought in some promises of orders in a hurry. Three of Jeff's close friends were former classmates at Harvard Business School, and were now company presidents. Jeff pleaded with them to give favorable consideration to purchasing fleets of cars from his firm when they needed new company cars. After Jeff established a favorable climate, these potential accounts were turned over to the vice-president of marketing.

Jeff's company shortly received promises of orders for 3000 cars, which were enough to enable his company to weather their financial crisis. Soon thereafter, Jeff was promoted to corporate vice-president and elected to the board of directors. His powerful alliances give him an extra surge of power.

Playing the "social power game" is an important aspect of forming powerful alliances. Government officials in Washington, D. C., are particularly adept at forming alliances with the right people, particularly at the onset of a new administration. The social power game is crucial to how the city operates, from court appointments to foreign aid. Henry Kissinger acquired huge amounts of power during the Nixon years, and has retained much of that power, by playing the game well. President Jimmy Carter allegedly could have been more effective if he had been more adept at forming alliances. President Ronald Reagan possessed consummate skill in forming powerful alliances. On his first full evening as President, Reagan entertained 50 of Washington's most influential leaders at the exclusive F Street Club. George Bush has devoted much of his career to forming alliances with powerful people.

A reporter for the *New York Times*, Lynn Rosellini, contrasted the success of Henry Kissinger and Zbigniew Brezezinski (the former national security advisor) in forming alliances. She observed that nobody played the power game better than Kissinger. Powerful himself, he was also brilliant, witty, and accessible. From the earliest days of the Nixon administration he made social contact with important people. All the while, Kissinger was working—picking up a tidbit of information here, dropping an item there, and building his network someplace else.

Kissinger's powerful social contacts paid off handsomely. President Nixon had planned to remove Kissinger from his post as national security advisor. Yet when Watergate erupted, Kissinger was named secretary of state instead. Presidential aides reasoned that Nixon apparently hoped to ease his other problems by choosing such a respectable candidate—a man who was so much part of the Washington establishment. The impact of Kissinger's connections were also apparent when his nomination as secretary of state faced little opposition from liberals in Congress or from the press.

Brzezinski was much less successful in developing powerful alliances. When he arrived in Washington as President Carter's national security adviser, Brzezinski attempted to duplicate Kissinger's prowess on the social-political circuit. He began successfully by staying at the home of Averell Harriman for almost six months. Later on he viewed

Washington society as a stage from which to entertain admirers. He never attempted to cultivate his influential dinner companions as they courted him. Instead of being witty and charming, he appeared wooden and heavy-handed.

His worst political mistake was to ignore the counsel of his former host, Averell Harriman. He also openly challenged Secretary of State Cyrus R. Vance, who had many friends in the Washington establishment. Before long, Brzezinski's latest indiscretions became fodder for Washington gossip. Unfavorable gossip in turn led to unfavorable press clippings, and Brzezinski's power eroded.[3]

## FORM COALITIONS AND OBTAIN COOPTATIONS

Alliances are high-level contacts in which two parties become friendly enough to help each other out should the need arise. The advanced political player also needs to form coalitions, or more specific arrangements of parties working together to combine their power. Cooptations, in which a potential adversary is brought into the fold, is a variation of coalition formation.

Coalitions in business are a numbers game—the more people you can get on your side the better. Bart, the dean of continuing education at a private university, watched woefully as the enrollment at his college declined. Part of the problem was that state schools were offering comparable programs at one-fifth the price; another was that local industry was cutting back on tuition reimbursement for employees. After studying what other colleges of continuing education were doing to combat declining enrollments, Bart formulated a new plan. His college would establish education programs tailor-made for the demands of senior citizens.

When Bart first brought up the idea to the president, she sighed, "Are you sure catering to senior citizens isn't just another fad? I'd like to see you do some more careful thinking on this issue." Sidetracked, but not deterred, Bart thought to himself that facts alone would not convince the president. Instead he sought to gain the cooperation of other deans within his university. One by one, he held discussions with the other deans to obtain their support for the idea of offering programs to fit the educational demands of senior citizens.

Bart developed a strategic plan for attracting senior citizens that included input from all the other colleges. The plan for his college was to offer mostly part-time programs, whereas the other colleges drew plans for attracting seniors to full-time study for both bachelor's and master's degrees. The president was so impressed with Bart's strategic plan that she approved seed money for his college to set up a trial senior citizen educational program. The program proved to be successful enough to reduce the enrollment decline by one-third. Consequently, Bart is a more powerful dean than previously.

Obtaining a cooptation requires even more finesse than forming a coalition. A true cooptation means that somebody who was not on your side does an about face and becomes your ally. A frequent form of cooptation in business is for a company facing financial trouble to invite one of its bankers to sit on its board. As a board member, the banker then tries to get the bank to act mercifully. Another type of cooptation in recent years is for a nuclear power plant to attempt to get a media representative on its board. Cooptation is not a form of payola, but simply an ethical method of getting a potential adversary to better understand your point of view. Understanding may then lead to backing off from attempts to erode your power.

> Tom, the director of human resources planning, wanted to keep running an extensive career development program during a period when all nonessential expenses were being challenged. Although convinced of the value of the career development program, Tom knew that it was not popular with all managers and executives. Several regarded the program as a way of stirring up discontent among people who could probably never reach their career goals. Several other executives characterized the program as fluff.
>
> To garner a broader base of support, and to convert a few of his potential enemies, Tom established an advisory board to guide the career development program. He extended invitations to managers and staff specialists from many different units within the firm. In addition, he invited the program's most vitriolic critics to become members of the advisory board. (The letters of invitation were tastefully engraved on egg-shell white stationary.) Nobody declined Tom's invitation, and his program withstood the next swath of the budget knife.

## CONDUCT A MASS, CONCENTRATED OFFENSIVE

Power holders must occasionally carry out activities that both they and the people affected find distasteful. To minimize lingering animosity toward the power holder, it is often best to get the distasteful task accomplished in as short a period of time as possible.[4] Under such circumstances, people may forget the reprehensible act after the initial sting has worn off. Layoffs represent the best case in point. Executives who are forced to lay off a substantial number of the work force often try to do it all at once, rather than dismiss people in small groups over a period of time.

Preston, an executive who conducted such an offensive, recounts what happened to him when he took over as president of a large commercial printing plant and was forced to take some drastic personnel actions:

> One month after I arrived as president, the owners of the parent corporation told me I would have to trim down the size of the executive group. According to their analysis, seven people in top jobs within the company were not needed. This was half the management team above the first-line supervisory level. However, I thought the analysis was essentially correct. The company was top heavy.
>
> After negotiating with my bosses for a couple of weeks, it was agreed that five managers and two supervisors would be laid off. We anticipated two problems. First, a layoff of these oldtimers might create morale problems within the company. Second, the company was located in a small town, so we figured there might be negative community reaction.
>
> Concerned though I was, one Friday afternoon I announced the termination of all seven people at once. Each person was briefed individually the morning the announcement was made. By Monday, the entire company was buzzing about the incident. My wife told me she heard some pretty negative things about me in the supermarket. People in the office stared at me as if I had done something terribly wrong.
>
> The company began to operate more efficiently than at any time in the past. Both sales and profits picked up and people received bigger salary increases than they had ever received before. After one year, people were complimenting me on having improved the company. If I was ever a villain in their eyes, it was apparently all forgotten.

## AVOID DECISIVE ENGAGEMENT

At times a mass, concentrated offensive will backfire. The people surrounding the power holder may not be ready for sudden and major changes. Instead, an evolutionary rather than a revolutionary approach will work best. In these circumstances, the person seeking to expand or hold on to power must avoid ruffling feathers. The potential pitfalls to avoid—such as irritating a slow-moving president—can be learned through networking. A trusted source can tip you off as to the soundness of your proposed methods to create the needed changes.

Avoiding decisive engagement can sometimes be used successfully by a group who seeks power. In one business firm when a man was promoted over qualified women, the women decided to use political skills to deal with the problem. The women organized an after-hours discussion group, with invited speakers to talk about women's careers. Most of the discussion dealt with relatively safe issues such as career planning, and balancing the demands of work and family life.

The underlying political strategy of these meetings was to get people to believe that the career development of women in the company was held back by a congenial, but chauvinistic, personnel manager. The women were convinced that a formal confrontation would have produced much conflict, but little change. Instead of a head-on strategy, the women set out to change the manager's behaviors and attitudes systematically. At first they teased him; in time he recognized that he had been targeted and labeled. Consequently, he really had no graceful alternative but to recommend a woman for the next significant promotion.[5]

## USE CONSTRUCTIVE CHAOS

A report prepared by the National Institute for Business Management, recommends the use of "constructive chaos" to increase your power.[6] Two key rules govern constructive chaos. First, it must not hurt the organization although you might create temporary disruption. Second, it must be planned to make you emerge as a hero or heroine to the benefit of yourself and the organization.

Constructive chaos may appear to be an extreme technique, but it may be necessary if you find it difficult to create your niche in an organization where the existing managers and their power bases are deeply entrenched and difficult to overthrow. You need to overturn the existing system, method, or procedure, and convince top management to replace it with a better way. The "better way," of course, is a system you and your staff have designed. As the traditional way of doing things is replaced, the old power bases will dissipate.

An effective way of implementing constructive chaos, is through *technofright*. One way of frightening people with technology is to introduce a major new computer system to your organization. (To pull off this power play you would have to first become quite knowledgeable about computers.) Many executives are still threatened by computers because they have still not learned much about them. These executives either delay the introduction of computers or refuse to apply them in a meaningful way to their operations. The most resistance is likely to come from senior managers who themselves would have to operate computers. "With all my responsibilities, I've got little time to learn how to use a computer," is a typical response from a senior executive who is not part of the computer generation.

Another way to implement constructive chaos is to suggest a major way to cut costs. Such ideas are often too profitable for top management to reject. The trick is to detect opportunities that will not be a loss to your budget, but which dilute the power of others. Look first for potential cost reductions that would have an organizationwide impact. For example, make a suggestion that neighboring units within your company share equipment and services. Point out that this move would allow your company to reduce the total amount of computers, fax machines, and so on used by various departments. (Neglect to mention, however, that it would also serve to increase the amount of equipment available to your unit, while diluting the assets and autonomy, of your neighboring department.)

Constructive chaos may have some appeal, yet the political player who wants to use only ethical tactics, will avoid the technique. The method is akin to pretending that problems exist, so you can be the heroic person to solve them. For instance, a manager might return from a field trip and report that major problems have erupted with distributors. He then is given authority to spend several months in the field repairing the damage. He returns a hero, stating that relationships with the distributor are better than ever.

## GROOM PRINCES AND PRINCESSES

An indirect, long-range, but often successful high-level power play is for an executive to become known as a person who grooms successful managers for the organization. Managers who are adept at developing younger managers are in short supply. If you have both the patience and talent for such work, you might be at a power advantage. Princes and princesses may remember your contribution to their development when you need their backing.

At age 33, Debbie had become the Equal Employment Opportunity manager at company headquarters. Her job focused on encouraging managers throughout the corporation to promote women, minorities, and the physically challenged into responsible, high paying jobs. At times it was necessary for Debbie and her small staff to apply pressure to recalcitrant managers.

Debbie felt that being young, black, and female made it difficult for her to establish a good working relationship with some of the older plant managers. She thought she needed a trouble shooter who could work closely with the more traditional plant managers and personnel managers in dealing with sensitive problems. The troubleshooter would spend as much time as necessary at plant locations where plant managers and human resource specialists were having difficulty implementing EEO programs.

Jack, the man who gave Debbie her start in the organization, came to mind as an ideal candidate for the troubleshooter assignment. He was compassionate, intelligent, and well accepted by older management personnel. Debbie asked Jack if he would be interested in trying such an assignment. He replied:

"Debbie, how thoughtful of you. My term as labor relations manager for the division is coming to an end. Top management thinks this is a job for an attorney, which I am not. So you could say I've just begun to explore possibilities for myself in the corporation. I'd be very interested in looking into that troubleshooter assignment with you. I enjoyed having you work for me before. I think our relationship would be just as good if we switched sides of the table."

## MAINTAIN A MYSTIQUE ABOUT YOUR JOB

The most powerful executives have an element of mystery about them. Somewhat by intuition and somewhat by design, powerful people are not entirely candid and easy to understand. Although they are not necessarily devious, they sparingly let others know of their plans. If not done to the point of appearing paranoid, maintaining a mystique about your job can add to your aura of power. A typical way in which people in powerful positions cultivate this mystique is by alluding to impressive negotiations in the offing which cannot be fully disclosed at present.

Vivian Ballantine appeared on the university campus with the job title, Director of Development. She reported directly to the president. The news release announcing her arrival talked in glowing terms about many other affiliations. Her credits included membership on the boards of two businesses and three community organizations. The announcement of her appointment included a statement by the college president indicating what an important impact Vivian was expected to have on the college community.

At a luncheon meeting given in her honor, Vivian made a statement to the public about how much she hoped to facilitate communications between the college and the community. She waxed ecstatic about the chance this job would give her to become better acquainted with members of the college and business community. An assistant professor of economics who was attending the luncheon, stood up and fired this salvo:

"Okay, Vivian, we have heard those fine platitudes expressed and we all wish you luck in carrying out your mission. But will you please tell us what your mission is? Are you a good-will ambassador at an embarrassingly high salary? Are you a fund raiser? Let us know what service you actually intend to perform for the college."

"Professor, thank you for your concern about my contribution to the college. I wish I could pin it down as neatly as you would like. I hope to make my biggest impact in terms of directing funds from the business sector to the educational sector."

"Thank you for your answer, Ms. Ballantine," responded the young professor. "Now, could you tell us exactly how you intend to raise funds for the college?"

"It is premature to divulge my plans now. However, rest assured that I have a few major projects in the mill. You will hear all the details, once the project has entered the implementation stage."

The economics professor left the luncheon in anger but Vivian stayed on. In fact, she stayed with the college for three years and did raise a surprisingly large sum of money. Nevertheless, her exact function and the manner in which she carried it out seemed unclear. The next power spot Vivian occupied was a key mental health post with the state.

## WORK ON KEY PROBLEMS

In most business firms, the people who occupy the most powerful positions are often those who have been identified with the solution to pressing organizational problems. Similarly, those people who were associated with breakthrough developments in the company tend to become the most powerful executives. The breakthrough development does not necessarily have the glamor of a personal computer or a sporty car.

Young attorney Steve worked for an industrial company whose product line included commercial pumps. The company developed a pump to be used in the manufacture of trucks and trains that held promise of being highly successful. Steve's contribution to the pump project was to establish an elaborate set of patents to prevent other companies from making an almost identical pump.

After extensive negotiations with the patent office in Washington, D. C., a 15-year protection agreement was formulated for the company's line of pumps. High demand for the product combined with the patent protection engineered by Steve led the company to unprecedented profits. As the company was carried along by the pump, so too was the young attorney's career. He became a corporate vice-president and a member of the board. Steve ultimately left business for local politics, as a happy, wealthy, and powerful person. His contribution on one key project had turned around his career and lifestyle.

## BEND RULES AT THE RIGHT TIME

The advanced power player—and the effective leader—knows when to risk bending the rules, and when not to. Subordinates will regard you as more powerful when you bend rules to meet an important customer requirement or deal with an internal emergency.[7] Gina Husby, a senior vice-president of Bank of America, tells the story of a department head who jumped on an airplane to solve a problem with a printer. "She didn't ask permission. She just knew she had to get the job done, so she made an executive decision. The trip created additional costs not allocated in her budget. But we had customers and deadlines, so we had to find a way to make up for it later. You can always do that if you are creative.

"We're in a customer-service environment, and the customer comes first. You certainly never try to break rules. But bending them is a way of getting things done."

Husby offers a guideline for knowing when to take a shortcut or make an exception: "If you are 80 percent sure, you'd better go for the decision, especially if you're in operations. If you wait until you are 100 percent sure, you may miss the window of opportunity."

Getting around budget limitations is an important skill of the powerful manager. An observer of the budget process says that when it comes to budget for personnel and other resources, nothing is really fixed. "When I was in my first supervisory role, I recall watching the more experienced manager I worked with chip away at built-in budget limitations to his head count and budget, treating them as temporary roadblocks. Year by year he justified adding a fraction of a body here, a fraction there. Temporary vacation help and a part-timer during our busiest months became part of the "written in stone" budget. So did a full-time staffer who was available to be lent to another department when it was shorthanded in the summer.

"He understood the rules, and when it came to legal and fiscal restraints, he was cautious. But he didn't treat all rules as if they were concrete pillars limiting his movement. "But what if it were thought of this way?" he would say to the company head's veto.

"He was also able to shrug off the dreaded crackdown of the accounting department. Once he took the staff out for a morale-building lunch to celebrate an award he had won; the bill came to $600. When he got flack from the accounting department, he said, 'We just got a little exuberant. We celebrated next year's award, two for one.' He didn't make excuses, whine, cry, or blame his staff for being extravagant. He took his medicine—and laughed about it later."[8]

Working around the budget will often make you appear powerful. Keep in mind, however, the outer limits of such bravado: if the CEO is vehement about staying within the budget, overspending in any form can cost you some power.

## BRING IN AN OUTSIDE EXPERT ━━━━━━━━━━━━━

In a power struggle, one or more executives attempt to get their point of view or program accepted, and the adversarial points of view or programs rejected. If the opposing points of view appear plausible, a consultant might be called in to help settle the issue. The consultant's role then is to study the issue or problem facing the organization and make an independent recommendation. Usually the recommendations provided by the consultant are solutions that have been circulating through the organization for some time, primarily because most consultants confer with company workers to obtain their opinions and recommendations. The consultant's suggestions are therefore not shocking, and they are welcomed for their objectivity.[9]

The adept power player attempts to bring in a consultant who has the wisdom to agree with his or her recommendations. It is therefore critical for the person who seeks additional power to help select the consultant. If a third party selects the consultant, it is more difficult to choose a consultant sympathetic with one's point of view. Because a consultant must be professionally objective, it is necessary to find one with a track record of making the type of recommendations one wants to hear.

The CEO of a manufacturer of telephone equipment was concerned about quality problems as perceived by many of its customers. Because the CEO had a marketing background, he decided to ask those managers who were more knowledgeable about manufacturing to make recommendations for improving product quality. Several different sets of recommendations emerged. Dan, the head of the quality control department recommended an elaborate program of quality improvement that involved many high-tech improvements such as the use of robotic inspections, and advanced statistical techniques. Ricardo, the head of manufacturing recommended a program of quality improvement that emphasized changing attitudes and values of employees toward greater quality awareness.

Sensing that the president would probably be receptive to hiring a quality consultant to help the company decide on a suitable program of quality improvement, Ricardo researched and developed a list of six quality consultants, five of whom generally espoused quality awareness programs. He submitted this list to the president and the quality control director, suggesting that the president choose a consultant.

Don, Ricardo, and the president then interviewed four consultants most experienced in the electronics field. The consultant chosen was not the one with the high-tech approach to quality improvement. After a one-month study, the program he recommended fit more the quality awareness approach sought by Ricardo.

A companywide quality awareness program was successfully implemented, and Richard eventually became the company's quality guru, with Dan's group playing a lesser role.

## PLAY THE POWER GAME

This entire chapter, and almost the entire book, is about enlarging one's share of power. There is also a specific power game in which the person makes decisions in favor of the option that gives him or her more power.[10] (Power in this sense means that the individual has control over people and situations and that other people comply with the power seeker's wishes.) If you want to obtain something from a person who plays the power game, your best bet is to cater to that person's quest for power. You get what you want—and acquire more power in the process—by giving the other person a chance to gain more control. Playing the power game is an advanced tactic because one must usually be highly placed before power options are available.

Division manager Sloan was happy to learn that the demand for his company's line of decorative telephones was enjoying a seemingly endless boom. His biggest problem was to find more manufacturing space because corporate headquarters had ruled out any new construction for the next two years. One alternative facing him was to use the manufacturing space of another division in the company that was willing to grant a request. Sloan describes his solution to the problem:

> The only suitable space belonged to one of our oldest divisions, located approximately 40 miles away. Bill, the division head, was hardly a cooperative person. He gloried the days of his past when he was the biggest, most profitable division. I knew it would hurt him to see my division become even bigger and more powerful by taking over some of his space. Yet Bill had more space than he needed for his division's manufacturing requirements.
>
> Knowing that Bill likes to control things, I cooked up a deal I thought might attract him. I explained to Bill that our division could use about 10,000 square feet of his manufacturing floor. What I would do in exchange would be to have mostly his employees work on our product. We would be using his factory, but his workforce could be expanded. In this way, we would both enhance the stature of our divisions.
>
> When Bill realized that the deal would expand his sphere of influence, he jumped at the opportunity. He talked to other people about the deal as if he were making a big concession in order to save my division from embarrassment. The truth, of course, is that we were helping him take care of his biggest problem—unused plant capacity. Bill is happiest when he thinks he's in control of the situation.

Sloan's tactic worked because he played the power game from two directions. He gave Bill an opportunity to increase his power, while he simultaneously increased his power by producing more telephones. Sloan thus achieved a win–win solution to a problem, thus being both political and ethical.

## BE FEARED RATHER THAN LOVED

In 1515 (or thereabout), Niccolo Machiavelli suggested that a prince is better off being feared than loved. He reasoned that it is nice to be both feared and loved; but it is easier to maintain control when you are feared. Here are seven useful techniques if you want to be feared:[11]

1. Give subordinates frequent reminders of how dispensable they are.
2. Announce that expense reports will be carefully audited at irregular intervals.
3. Discuss early retirement with people over age 55 when they openly disagree with company policy or philosophy.
4. Threaten to have every department justify its function at the start of each fiscal year (zero-based budgeting).
5. Mention that you are using an executive color chart. Each team member will be given one of three ratings: green for promotable, amber for "wait and see," and red for not promotable.
6. Keep a book about "slash and burn" or turnaround management prominently displayed on your desk.
7. Make frequent mention of cash flow and bottom-line management during your staff meetings.

## GIVE PROOF OF PROWESS

The top-level power seeker of today might also heed Machiavelli's advice that you provide people an outstanding example of your greatness.[12] If you are not great, it is difficult to provide such an example. Here are five possible ways of exhibiting greatness:

1. Have a newly announced company policy rescinded for your area of responsibility because you believe it disregards local circumstances.
2. Obtain the highest raises possible in the company for your team members.

3. Suggest to people that they set their own working hours because they are so mature and intelligent.

4. Become a member of the board of directors of a large business firm or bank.

5. Build a monument to yourself such as having a brass statue of you in the lobby, or name a manufacturing or service process after yourself, such as the "Glickstein Delivery System."

## CONTROL THE AGENDA

A subtle way of preserving power is to prevent matters that would erode your power from even being discussed.[13] For example, most organizations face the issue of centralization versus decentralization from time to time. Decentralization takes decision-making authority and resources away from the centralized group. If the executive in charge of policy-making meetings blocks the centralization versus decentralization issue from appearing on the agenda, centralized power can be retained. Controlling the agenda is usually a stalling tactic, because a pressing issue will eventually have to be dealt with. In the following example, however, the stalling appeared to be indefinite.

In a large financial organization with relatively few stockholders, the president and the assistant determine the agenda for executive committee meetings. These meetings were comprised of the chief operating officer and staff personnel. This control over the agenda ensured that reorganization and strategy and planning would be discussed only when both the president and assistant were ready with prepared reports.

Controlling the agenda meant that the president exerted considerable power because the content and timing of items for discussion were under his control. Topics were brought to the surface only when he was prepared with a position and supporting documentation. At the same time, it was difficult for other executives to submit agenda items. The culture of the organization dictated that it was in poor taste for another executive to insist on attention to a special issue not introduced by the president.

## SELECT A COMPLAINT
## BOARD OF DIRECTORS

If you are fortunate enough to be a chief executive, you may be able to capitalize on the ploy of selecting a board of directors who comply with your most important requests. Without a cooperative board, it is difficult for a company president to expand his or her power.[14] CEOs attempting to use the board for aggrandizing their power opt for as many inside board members as possible. If you report to the president, it is awkward to cross swords with that person in a board meeting.

The president of an insurance and financial services company helped pack the board of directors with people who were aligned with his thinking. His tactic was to casually recommend new members of the board as old ones retired or resigned. The people recommended, of course, were individuals whom the president knew were compatible with his thinking. Selecting a complaint board enabled him to retain his CEO position for many years, and resist takeovers from other financial services firms.

## AVOID BEING DEPOSED

An unspoken, and at times unsavory, part of any boss's job is self-protection against those subordinates plotting to take over his or her job. Being deposed results in an automatic loss of power, and the climb back to power may be rough. If you're a boss who doesn't own a company, it might be worthwhile to ponder the suggestions below for holding on to your job. Even if you own the place, a relative or two you have brought into the business might have designs on your job.

### Don't Spend All Your Time Managing

A popular myth about effective managers is that they spend the total workday managing people. According to this idealistic belief, an effective manager is a full-time administrator—one whose primary function is to make sure that subordinates are doing their job properly. In reality, executives lead hectic, busy workdays. Although executives spend about 50 percent of their time in conference with either subordinates or other executives, they still carry an enormous burden of individual work. This type of work includes deal making, handling customer service problems, reviewing reports, and preparing budgets.

### Keep Your Department Lean

A lean department is a less likely candidate for a reduction in force than a department where too many people are handling too little work. In the past, a simple solution to an overstaffed department was to dismiss a few support personnel. The modern trend is to play organizational musical chairs. Top management decides to move everybody in the department up one notch in responsibility. Unfortunately the department manager is the one exception. The manager may be moved out of the department and into the street.

## Transfer Your Competition

The job-security conscious executive must guard against having too many ambitious, competent subordinates. Such individuals frequently reason that their best chances for upward growth are to undermine and eventually replace their boss, rather than moving to another firm. To cope with this problem, you can actively campaign for the transfer of highly ambitious and competent people from your department. In this way, the organization does not lose their talent, and your job security improves. However, use the tactic sparingly to avoid having a weak department that detracts from your stature.

## Cultivate Your Superiors

Cultivating superiors is a singularly effective way of protecting yourself against those people trying to depose you. A manager who is well-known and well-liked by superiors has the best chance for survival.

## Be a Developer of Talent

A politically wise manager makes frequent mention to superiors about his or her development plan for each subordinate. In other words, if you are a manager trying to hang on to your job, make others aware of how you try to develop the capabilities of your subordinates. To the extent that you are helping others develop, you are the wise superior, grooming group members for bigger things. Ideally, the "bigger things" would be transfer to another department or taking over your job once you are offered a promotion.

## Do What Your Boss Thinks a Manager Should Do

You are vulnerable to threats from below when you are not fulfilling your boss's expectations of what a manager should be doing. Quite often it is difficult to objectively measure what a manager is accomplishing. If your boss wants to replace you despite departmental achievements, he might argue that the team would get results without your help. As a safeguard do those tasks your boss prefers managers to do—for example, if your boss thinks strategic planning is important, devote a lot of time to talking about the future of your unit.

# CHAPTER 10

# BOOSTING
# YOUR CAREER

Job performance remains the most important factor for moving ahead or staying on the payroll. The combination of hard work and few breaks along the way will usually enable a competent person to earn salary increases and promotions. Despite the validity of this observation, many hard-working, talented people still go nowhere in their careers. Without the extra ingredient of using sensible political strategies, an ambitious person could remain trapped in an unfavorable job situation.

Practically all the strategies and tactics described so far can be used to advance one's career. However, the tactics presented now are aimed directly at giving your career a boost. Many of these career advancement strategies and tactics are not highly political. Instead, they relate to proved techniques for career management. Do not dismiss the relevance of these time-honored tactics—use them wisely. Be the exceptional person who not only knows what should be done for career advancement, but actually *does it.*

## STICK WITH WHAT YOU DO BEST

Let's begin with basics. The surest path to career success is to identify your best talents and build a career around them. Becoming wealthy and achieving recognition are by-products of making effective use of your talents. As many people at the top of their fields have said, "I'm having so much fun, it's hard to believe I'm getting paid." (Use that line with your boss to show how much more you are concerned with job satisfaction than money.) The late Sydney Harris claimed that he had only one piece of advice for young people who came to him for career counseling.

159

It consisted of ten one-syllable words: "Find out what you do best and stick with it."[1]

## BE A CONSISTENT PERFORMER

Consistency in performance helps your boss and the organization and therefore is likely to boost one's career. The manager of a television station recalls, "Several years ago, I had to choose between promoting an employee who was competent and one who was spectacular. I promoted the competent woman because she was consistent. Her rival was only spectacular when the mood hit her. Because I couldn't schedule crises, I needed someone who could handle problems any time, not just when they coincided with her blazes of glory."[2]

Consistency is a career booster in another important way. It contributes to your reputation as a person who can be counted on in an emergency. And during an emergency a tough assignment is more likely to go to a good performer than someone who is political in a transparent, self-serving way.

## EXHIBIT ETERNAL VIRTUES

Certain basic, nonpolitical, behaviors are important for career advancement in almost any organization. It is important to obtain a first-rate education, set realistic goals, have good attendance, be punctual, appear committed to the organization, and prepare a sparkling resume when job hunting. Any book about career management is replete with Innocent Lamb tactics that make sense even for a Machiavelli. It is politically unwise to deviate too far from the image of the ideal employee. Gatekeepers give an immediate edge to the clean-cut, cooperative, appreciative, well-mannered, healthy looking, well-dressed, smiling, obedient, alert looking employee. Several suggestions for creating the image of the ideal employee are in order.

### Exercise Self-Control over Emotion

Robert Jackall observes that in a bureaucracy, managers who get ahead exercise tight self-control and have the ability to mask all emotion behind bland, smiling, and agreeable public faces. They believe that it is perilous to one's career to lose control of oneself, in any way, in the presence of other workers.[3] Nevertheless, in carefully selected situations, it is helpful to display a burst of emotion—either positive or negative—for the specific purpose of motivating others. Note carefully that the purposeful display of emotion is a form of emotional control—not lack of control.

### Select the Right Style

To be considered promotable, it is also important to be fast on your feet; well-organized, give slick presentations complete with computer graphics and slides; and give the appearance of knowledge even in its absence. Part of selecting the right style also includes possessing a subtle, almost indefinable sophistication, characterized especially by an urbane, witty, graceful, engaging, and friendly demeanor.[4] Sales associates in posh retail stores and models exhibit such behavior.

### Display a Total Commitment to Your Job

All it takes to reach the top in corporate America is a career of hard work, a willingness to sacrifice family life for job, and years of planning, according to executive search consultant, Lester Korn.[5] If you have excellent work habits, you can probably shave at least ten hours from the standard executive workweek of 60 hours. Many of those hours of hard work are never seen by people who judge your performance. To appear totally committed to the organization, do things occasionally that imply a disregard for personal life in favor of the organization. Tony, an executive in a chain of instant auto service stores, gives us the benefit of his experiences:

> Being a strong family man, I got into some difficulty with my previous employer. When somebody would suggest an after-hours meeting, or an extra trip into the field, I balked at the idea. My boss told me on my performance review that such actions suggested I was not totally committed to the company. Figuring that my reputation was less than golden at that company, I shifted fields and joined a rapidly growing company in the rapid-auto service field.
>
> Although I still thought that my time with my family should not be sacrificed, I created the impression that I was eager as anybody to attend meetings. Several times I suggested that we have a breakfast meeting to discuss customer service problems and the competition. My pitch was that breakfast meetings interfere very little with normal working hours. Fortunately, we only had two breakfast meetings during the year. But suggesting the idea made me appear very enthused about the company.

## PROJECT A SUCCESSFUL IMAGE

An aspect of displaying eternal virtues that deserves separate attention is the art of looking successful. Your clothing, your desk and/or office, your speech, and your attitudes toward money should project the image of a successful but not necessarily flamboyant person—at least in most organizations.

Appearing too sexy and glamorous can often block a woman from being promoted into a high-level management position. Some male executives are concerned that if they promote a glamorous woman into a top-level position, they will be accused of being influenced by her appearance. Also, some male executives have difficulty concentrating on their work when they work closely with an outrageously glamorous woman. Good looks for women, however, are an asset for being hired into and retaining secretarial and sales positions. As a sales manager analyzed the situation, "It's hard for a male customer to say no to a beautiful woman."

However unfair, an exceptional personal appearance is an asset for a male being promoted into a high-level managerial position. A disproportionate number of good looking men occupy executive positions. And being considered a hunk or "cute" helps men get sales positions as well as office jobs. A store manager told us, "I love to hire cute guys who wear tight pants. It turns on the other women in the store, as well as many of our customers."

Your standard of dress, and other accoutrements of success, should be appropriate to your particular career stage. You may do harm to your career if it appears that you are trying to upstage your boss by dressing or living better.

The recent emphasis on appearing successful is to look healthy, which is more complicated and time-consuming than simply wearing fashionable clothing. Regular physical exercise and a healthy diet contribute to a healthy look but it may take years for improved exercise and diet to make a difference in one's appearance. As a quick-fix, many career people are turning to cosmetic plastic surgery. Today, almost one-third of those seeking facial plastic surgery are men.[6] Many of the men and women opting for cosmetic surgery admit their motive is to look younger and more energetic to their employers. (Personal rather than career reasons are of course still a primary motivator behind cosmetic surgery for many people.)

Another important consideration in looking successful is to not appear cheap. Thus the aspirant to an executive position should not be seen writing with ball pens inscribed with advertising, carrying a brown bag with lunch into the company cafeteria, using an attache case mended with duct tape, or wearing worn-out shoes. Moaning about high utility bills, increases in parking fees, and higher postal rates will also detract from your success image. It is best to suffer all these problems in silence or with people outside the company.

## MAKE OPTIMUM USE OF CONTACTS ═══════════════════

Networking has become such a standard technique that a haphazard approach to making contacts will no longer achieve results. To obtain the best career-boosting payoff from networking, put these points into action:[7]

- *Be prepared.* Keep your business cards and company material on hand. Prospects for your network can spring up at many places including parties, airports, and resorts.
- *Meet as many people as you can.* Networking is a numbers game. You need to meet dozens, perhaps hundreds, of people in order to cash in on a few contacts who might help you propel your career forward.
- *Tell people what you do.* One of the first things to tell a prospect for your network is your occupation and employer. You then exchange business cards. Generally avoid attempting to conduct business during the first meeting. Instead, telephone the person at a later date to set up a meeting for exchanging favors, solving problems, and so forth.
- *Jot down facts about each person in your network.* Keep a careful file on basic facts about people in your network such as how they might be able to help you and vice versa.
- *Follow up.* Make a second contact with the new person in your network, and record in your file the outcome of the follow-up meeting or telephone call. If the person helped you, give the person positive feedback.
- *Sort out your contacts.* Sort your contacts into categories such as "useful," "useless," and "inactive." Also update your file information for changes in job title, address, and type of help available.
- *Engage in new activities that will enhance your network.* Your network is liable to become stagnant if you do not place yourself in new environments. Joining a golf club and becoming a decent golfer remains the number one networking activity. However, you may not have the skill, time, money, nor inclination to play golf. Another potentially fruitful source of contacts is to form or join a breakfast club. These clubs usually feature some sort of program with outside speakers or other members providing information on a wide range of topics. Club members sell and buy from each other, and help solve problems.
- *Avoid overburdening your contacts.* An unfortunate aspect of networking is that a few influential people are being approached by

dozens of ambition junkies. An antidote is to tread lightly when attempting to incorporate an influential person in your network. Begin your initial contact with a thought such as, "I suspect you must be besieged with people asking for advice and help. Let me know if one more person wanting to make you part of his network would be too much." In this way you are less likely to be perceived as a pest.

- *Be candid about what you want.* Be specific about what type of help you want from a contact. In this way the contact is free to accept or refuse your request. If you specify what you want, the other person would then feel freer to ask for reciprocity later.

## JOIN OR START A BREAKFAST CLUB

A promising new method of finding important people in your network is to become a member of a breakfast club. The purpose of these clubs is unabashedly to make valuable contacts. Club members attend periodic breakfast meetings that usually feature some type of program, with outside speakers or other members providing information on a wide range of business and general topics. Breakfast clubs give members an opportunity to talk about and seek advice outside an office environment.

The key purpose of most clubs is political because they emphasize reciprocity. The idea is to conduct as much business as possible with club members. A studio owner commented that her banker, insurance agent, and lawyer all belong to her breakfast club. The owner of a Cadillac dealership said the the Reciprocity Club to which he belongs has meant, "Literally hundreds of thousands of dollars of sales, and we've made hundreds of thousands of dollars of purchases from other members of the club. If everything else is equal, the call goes to members of the club."[8]

A breakfast club can also boost your career should a member offer you a better job or recommend you for one. The sponsor you pick up might even be an executive from your company who has joined the same club.

If there is not a breakfast club in your community, consider starting one. Hard work may be needed to establish a big enough membership to make the club effective. In recruiting members, be sure to send out posh-looking invitations to people you think could conceivably give your career a boost.

## BE VISIBLE

A major strategy for career boosting is to bring favorable attention to yourself. Any method that highlights your abilities and talents to key people can help you gain a promotion. Among the standard techniques are volunteering for projects, task forces, and committee assignments, getting your name in print for favorable reasons, winning a company athletic tournament, or getting your name on memos read by influential people. The committee route to visibility is sound because it demonstrates your actual capabilities:

Competent and industrious Alex worked as a computer analyst for a large company. Although performing adequately in his job, he was intent on attaining managerial responsibility in the company's data-processing center. Alex was concerned that analysts did not get sufficient exposure to higher management, and that his sterling performance was going unnoticed by people who could influence his career.

Eventually Alex's attitude began to affect his work. His productivity declined, and he began to voice some frustration. His growing dissatisfaction led Alex to seek a managerial position by registering with an employment agency. At approximately the same time Alex began looking for a new job, he was reassigned to a different computer project. As part of his new assignment, he was appointed as a member of a committee whose responsibilities covered several company divisions. It quickly became apparent to Alex that the work of his committee would be observed by several members of higher management. He therefore took steps to put himself in a position to be part of the decision-making body within the committee.

Alex volunteered to be the secretary for the group. His responsibilities centered around taking notes and distributing them after meetings. Because the committee was large and a wide variety of opinions were expressed at each meeting, Alex had the opportunity to synthesize the various ideas into a policy which gave the committee direction. In the same way, he was able to set dates by which important decisions could be reached.

After the work of the committee progressed, members began to think of Alex as one of the committee leaders. He supplied each member with a list of problems to be resolved at each meeting. When serious questions arose in a division about a particular aspect of the committee's work, Alex would call a meeting with members of that division's management. In these brief meetings, he would resolve some problems prior to committee evaluation. The committee's work was completed on schedule, and Alex wrote the final report which had to be approved by top management. When the committee received praise from management for its accomplishments, Alex was noted as being one of the key members.

As a result of this committee exposure, Alex was given additional responsibility within his own department, and an opportunity to move away from the more technical aspects of data processing. He stopped seeking new employment and began to enjoy his job. Several months later, Alex was appointed as the supervisor of a small systems analysis group within his department. He now intends to stay in his present position.[9]

Committee membership and the visibility it produced gave Alex the exposure he needed to facilitate his attaining that all-important first supervisory position.

## FIND A SPONSOR

The major positive consequence of visibility is that it may help you find a sponsor to not only nominate you for a higher job but also to look out for your welfare once you are there. (Mentors are not quite the same as sponsors, and are described later.) The techniques outlined in Chapter 5 for impressing higher-ups can also be used to find a sponsor. A sponsor is usually placed in the organization at least one step higher than your boss. However, an influential boss can also be a sponsor.

Despite the potential contribution of a sponsor to your career acceleration, finding a sponsor can backfire. A case in point is Foster, who was a planning specialist in an international corporation based in New York.[10] By age 27 he had worked himself into a key assignment as a special assistant to the vice-president of corporate planning at world headquarters, who sponsored him for a six-months assignment in the international division as an operations auditor. Foster's job was to investigate and oversee problems and plans with selected operating personnel from various overseas subsidiaries. Upon completion of this assignment, Foster returned to headquarters. One week before his return, his sponsor was dismissed from the company.

Foster was never even asked to report on the results of his investigation. The new executive in charge of corporate planning did not require the services of a special assistant. Foster's credentials were therefore sent to the human resources department. After a month of waiting for reassignment, he was offered an opportunity to work as a financial analyst at a company plant in Pittsburgh. Foster resigned, quite disgruntled about having lost the forward momentum in his career.

If Foster made a mistake, it was in having only one sponsor. It can be a perilous policy to be perceived as too closely aligned with one company executive who if forced out will most likely result in your exit too. Ideally, you should cultivate sponsors from at least two different factions in an organization.

Another problem with the find-a-sponsor technique is that it is often difficult to be noticed by an influential person from a low vantage point in the organization. If you are preparing invoices, it can be difficult to be discovered by the vice-president of finance. However, it might be possible to be noticed by somebody who does have a sponsor. The trick is to find somebody who appears to be headed for big things, and to be noticed or develop a relationship with that person. As he or she climbs the organizational ladder, you will follow. Hal provides an apt example:

> I work for the city. In my department, the head of the internal audit section of the finance division was the protege of the Director of Finance. An individual in the internal audit section, because of family ties, became the protege of the internal auditor. When the position of assistant to the Director of Finance opened up, the internal auditor's protege was chosen over five senior members of the department.
>
> People sometimes think office politics doesn't apply to civil service jobs because civil service is based on merit. So a lot of people were surprised when this young man from another department was selected for the assistant position.

## FIND A MENTOR

Finding a sponsor helps you get nominated for promotion, whereas finding a mentor helps you develop skills and knowledge necessary for promotion. Being visible, combined with the display of a genuine love of learning, helps you locate a mentor. Mentors are bosses who take subordinates under their wings and guide, teach, and coach them. An emotional tie exists between the less experienced person and the mentor. Your relationship with a sponsor involves much less teaching, coaching, and formation of emotional ties. It is possible to have more than one mentor at a given point in your career. The dual-mentor approach helps you minimize the chances of your falling out of grace if your mentor topples.

Although mentors usually outrank their prodigies, peers can sometimes take over some of the functions performed by mentors. Co-workers can coach and counsel, provide useful information, and support you in handling personal problems and attaining professional growth.

If you cannot find a mentor yourself, or are not discovered by one, there is an alternative. Many large companies today have implemented formal mentoring programs whereby a senior executive is formally appointed as mentor to a few junior managers. There is usually some choice in this unusual form of corporate matchmaking. Mentors and mentorees are matched somewhat on the chemistry between them, as determined by exploratory interviews. Never, of course, state that you dislike one of your prospective mentors. Refer instead to the "really solid chemistry" between you and another prospect.

Some career women have expressed concern that it is difficult to find a mentor for two reasons. First, many male senior executives are hesitant to take on a female mentoree because they fear being suspected of romantic involvement. Second, there are still relatively few female senior executives, making it difficult to find a woman mentor. Barbara, a 28-year-old product manager, puts this dilemma in proper perspective:

> Hogwash. Don't be concerned that people will think the mentor and men-toree are having an affair. People have to accept the fact that the world has changed. Men and women today are able to form work relationships that are not sexualized. My advice for the opposite-sexed mentor and mentoree is to appear together publicly in a manner that shows yours is a work relationship. No flirting, no touching. Just appear professional.
>
> Besides, when an older male has a younger male as a mentoree, do people think they are romantically linked? With so many gay men in the work-force today, it's more than a remote possibility.

## TOOT YOUR OWN HORN (SOFTLY)

"Buck, you're too nice a guy," said his wife. "You're a harder worker and much better qualified than some of the other people in the office who have been promoted more rapidly than you. When are you going to get out there and sell yourself a little better?"

The advice offered to Buck is regularly repeated by managers' spouses who believe actions speak louder than words. Ideally, good performance should be recognized. The most competent people in any organization should be offered the most responsible jobs. Because most organizations are not meritocracies, it is important for career-minded people to find subtle ways of tooting their own horns. If your toot is too loud, you will give an earache to influential people, thus losing your audience.

A low-key, yet highly effective, method of tooting your own horn is to document your accomplishments. If you want to convince people above you that you deserve a promotion or large salary increase, docu-ment your accomplishments to strengthen your case. Documentation is also helpful to defend yourself against misdirected blame from another individual—such as accusing you of being responsible for a project miss-ing its deadline. Documentation can take the following forms:[11]

### Keep Separate Copies of Everything You Initiate

Establish a "personal accomplishment" file of every letter, memo, or report that specifies your contribution. Objective data, such as cost sav-ings achieved by your idea, is much better than an opinion about your contribution. If your file is computerized, also obtain two hard copies (one for the office and one stored at home). It is not unknown for compa-nies to purge computerized files.

### Establish a Diary of Special Projects

The diary, or work journal, might take the form of a daily or weekly listing of the nonroutine work you do. Provide extra details for all the *big problems* you tackle. Use corporate buzz words such as "initiated system for optimum utilization of human resources" (you found some productive tasks to fill the idle time of warehouse workers).

### Maintain a Current List of Your Regular Responsibilities

Although this file may contain many routine items, it can show how your job has grown over time. You might therefore be able to convince others of your increased responsibility and experience which enhances your promotability.

### List Your Skills Semiannually

Skills, such as computer skills, negotiating skills, and interviewing skills, are not accomplishments. Nevertheless, they make accomplishments possible. If you work for a company where Japanese-style management is practiced, skills may count as much as accomplishments. According to the Japanese philosophy of human resource management, a person's skills are valued as much as his or her tangible results.

### Create a "Recognition Folder"

Although other people's subjective opinion of your work is less convincing than a list of tangible accomplishments, such opinions are worth a separate file. The recognition folder might contain copies of your performance appraisals, thank you letters, notations of awards, notes of appreciation from customers or clients, and awards from professional or trade associations.

## TAKE SENSIBLE RISKS

People who make it big in their career usually take several sensible risks on their journey to success. Among these risks would be to work for a fledgling company that offers big promises but a modest starting salary accompanied by stock options. Another sensible risk would be to take an overseas assignment with no promise of a good job when you return. Industrial relations manager Michael Oliver offers this advice:[12]

If you want to achieve something really creative, thus enhancing your profession, then try a little risk taking. This doesn't mean you should pick up a lance and seek out a windmill. Balance your risk taking with good sense so you will be able to reach a new comfort level somewhere between the role of a bureaucratic follower and leaper of tall buildings. The goal should be to develop credibility without perpetrating a maverick reputation.

Sensible risk taking sometimes means avoiding jobs where the probability of failure—or looking bad—is high. Considerable judgment is required because certain risky jobs (those where the probability of looking good is small) usually carry high potential rewards. Safer jobs usually have smaller potential rewards. The offshore oil driller may someday strike it rich, while the first-line supervisor in an oil refinery will be relatively safe and secure. The supervisor has avoided high risk but has also avoided the possibility of high reward. Product manager Harry learned about the downside risk of taking on a job with a low probability of success. About three years ago Harry became supervisor of a group with responsibility for developing new product ideas.

Harry noted that a raw idea is not enough. The product has to ultimately wind up as a successful product in the field. In his opinion, getting a new product idea accepted by people outside one's department can be more difficult than getting it accepted by customers. Although Harry had reservations about taking on the new product assignment, he was still eager to give it a try. It seemed like the best possible opportunity for him in the company at the time.

The agony for Harry proved to be that his group was not performing as expected. His score was zilch after three years. No new product idea surfaced that appeared to be worth the investment required to launch it. Harry was then faced with the gruesome reality of being reassigned because he failed. A new manager was appointed the group, and Harry was offered and accepted a sales position in his company. Instead of the product development position boosting his career, he now faced a lengthy career plateau. Harry had failed when asked to tackle a glamorous assignment.

## CHOOSE THE RIGHT PATH TO THE TOP

Organizational superstars—those who make it to top-level executive positions—rise to the top from a number of paths. About 95 percent of CEOs were formerly marketing, financial, manufacturing, engineering, or legal managers. A small percentage of top executives came from diverse fields such as personnel, purchasing, and information systems. In the future, however, we can anticipate more CEOs being promoted from CIO (chief information officer) positions.

The key point is that for different fields—and for different firms within that field—the most likely path to the top is not the same. If a person is good executive timbre, the person is best advised to work for an organization that seems favorably disposed toward his or her discipline.

Clinical psychologist Bernie had impeccable credentials for his position as chief psychologist in a large hospital. In addition, his administrative skills were solid; he was well liked by others around him; and patients thought he was doing a good job. One day, Bernie announced his resignation, stating that he was accepting a position as the chief psychologist in a community mental health facility at a 15 percent cut in pay. Asked if the irrational behavior exhibited by some of his patients had become contagious, Bernie replied:

> Not at all. Mine is a well-thought-through, rational decision. My basic reason for leaving my fine position at the hospital is that I want a chance to rise to the top. In this hospital—or any other hospital—no psychologist will ever get the top job. Top executive positions in hospitals are occupied exclusively by physicians. No psychologist, even if he or she won a Nobel prize, would become the hospital chief.
>
> In a community mental health center, the cards are not stacked against psychologists. Many such centers are headed by psychologists. I'm not going to work any place for the rest of my life where I'm guaranteed second-class status.

Bernie's plan worked despite the fact that it took him one more step to reach his goal. After two years of administrative experience in one community mental health setting, Bernie moved to another health center as director. By the age of 41, he had achieved his goal of reaching what he considered a top position in his field. Bernie used the tactic of being in the right discipline to get to the top. Several other approaches can also help a person move along the right path to the top.

## Develop Breadth Through Mobility

Your value to an organization increases to the extent that you acquire broad experience—such as holding jobs in finance and marketing. Ideally, breadth is achieved by performing different kinds of work for the same organization. Project and committee assignments rank favorably as broadening experience. To achieve the necessary breadth, you sometimes have to take the matter into your own hands. Timidity can be a serious career detriment. You can achieve breadth by volunteering for assignments or letting your boss know your eagerness to receive cross-training by working in another department.

## Profit from a Lateral Move

A lateral move is often a career booster because it helps you develop breadth. Selecting the right type of lateral move is important.[13] One option is to gain experience in a field closely aligned to your present one. A product manager might earn valuable experience by shifting from marketing to sales, thus preparing him or her for senior management.

Also consider moving farther away from your discipline if you think you have a good chance at performing well. Transferring laterally from managing a research and development group to managing a marketing group would be helpful to both the individual and the organization. Too radical a departure from your field of expertise, like switching from communications to procurement, could backfire. The farther you move from your area of expertise, the more time it could take to become a standout performer.

Another important consideration is to gain experience in a different type of situation, in order to broaden your experience. A manager of financial analysis recognized she needed experience in managing people who were not college graduates. She requested a one-year transfer to supervising an accounts payable group and benefitted greatly from the experience.

## Volunteer for an Undesirable Tour of Duty

If you are a particularly patient person, it might be worthwhile to volunteer for an undesirable position in order to later obtain a desirable one. A long-range perspective is required to successfully implement this tactic. You have to be placed in the relatively unusual situation where there is an undesirable assignment to volunteer for that is not also a dead end.

Zoology professor Crandall worked in a small zoology department where the chairpersonship of the department was lowly regarded. Professors were generally rotated through the job. The position paid a modest premium over a person's regular salary, and offered only a one-third reduction in teaching load. Yet the time demands of the job were quite heavy in comparison to other faculty positions. Crandall told the administration that he would like the opportunity to serve as department head. He noted that his long-term desires were in the direction of becoming a college administrator, not a professor and researcher. Crandall recounts his experiences:

It was three years of hard work, modest pay, and very little gratitude. I set up course offerings and schedules, listened to hundreds of complaints from students and faculty alike, and acted as an intermediary between the faculty and the administration. I even taught freshman zoology. My hours were long, and at times I wondered if I had made a mistake. Finally, my judgment was vindicated. Three years after volunteering to become the head of the zoology department, I was chosen as dean of the College of Biological Sciences. I was where I wanted to be after three years of sacrifice.

## Refuse a Promotion for the Good of the Company

A twist to choosing the right path to the top is to avoid assignments that could detract from your forward thrust. One such delicate maneuver is to refuse a promotion, because in your opinion, the overall good of the organization could best be served by your staying where you are.[14] The payoff is that your superiors will be struck by your loyalty and unselfishness. Because you think the promotion will not help your career, your sacrifice is smaller than it appears. Along these lines, Jack, a supervisor of a parking violations department, explains why he refused a promotion:

> Last year, I was offered a promotion to unit chief of the parks and recreation department, a one-step promotion. My first thought was that the position would help me in my career to advance further in the municipal government. Talking it over with a few knowledgeable people, I found out that in our city, it is difficult to get promoted from parks and recreation to a top-level administrative position. Somehow the parks and recreation department has less prestige than most of the other units.
>
> I told my boss that I would like to decline the offer because of the many problems facing the parking violations bureau at the time. A citizens' group was placing pressure on us to soften our approach to enforcement, and the Mayor was carefully reviewing our procedures. Some of our people were worried about dealing with all our problems. I explained to my boss that a change in leadership was not a good idea at the time.
>
> My judgment proved to be sound because two years later I did get promoted to a top-level position in city government. An assignment in the parks and recreation department might possibly have hurt my chances.

## ANALYZE THE COMPETITION ═══════════════════════════════

An important strategy for career boosting is to compete in an environment in which you have an edge over the competition. Age can sometimes work to your advantage. If you are middle-aged, you might have a competitive edge over a group of very young people in a department. Your lengthy experience might be associated with wisdom and emotional maturity. However, being a young person in a department where most are considered too old to be promotable can also work to your advantage. You might be selected for an important promotion. Many a young executive has sought a new job in an organization where most of the top executives are close to retirement. Among the most important relevant factors for analyzing the competition are the capabilities and aspirations of the other people trying to get ahead in the organization.

The company consultant asked Phil his primary reason for wanting to join the company. Phil confidently said, "Bartow Industries is ideal for an ambitious and well-trained manager. Like cream, I will rise to the top. The financial analysts tell me Bartow is a company with great potential but immature management. If Bartow doesn't get some capable management soon, they may not be able to capitalize on the opportunities facing them. I've been looking for a chance to prove myself in a company that needs me."

Phil's brashness irritated the consultant, but he saw some truth in his pronouncements. Bartow Industries did need to recruit a goodly number of ambitious and confident young managers. Five years later, the brash young job candidate was a manufacturing vice-president at Bartow. His analysis of the competition in relation to his capabilities proved to be devastatingly accurate.

## SWIM AGAINST THE TIDE

A careful analysis of the competition can lead to a risky, but effective, career boosting technique called "swim against the tide." The basic idea is that you take an unconventional path to career success based on your analysis of the conventional path pursued by others of similar backgrounds. Twenty-four year old Sharon is one such swimmer. Her college placement director said to her, "A person with a master's degree in business administration is in demand in many large corporations. Major banks like Chase and Citibank hire hundreds of MBAs. It would make sense to apply to institutions such as those if you want to maximize your chances of finding a job."

"Mr. Prichard," replied Sharon, "I don't want to work for an organization in which I'll be doing the same thing as everyone else. I'm afraid I'll get lost in the crowd if I join a bank that already has 800 MBAs on board. I want to try something a little different. Do you have any requests from a lumber mill, foundry, or meat-packing plant for an MBA?"

Adventuresome Sharon was intuitively choosing an unconventional path to career success. Women with MBAs are in short supply in the industries she mentioned. Another example of swim against the tide is for an outgoing, personable individual to enter accounting, engineering, or computer science, *not* sales. Assuming the person can make the grade in a technical field, his or her chances of rising up in management are quite good. Personable and outgoing accountants, engineers, and computer scientists have a good shot at managerial positions.

Conversely, if you are highly analytical and reflective, as well as personable, sales might be your path to success because sales departments are usually in search of such people to promote into managerial assignments.

A potential disadvantage of swimming against the tide is that you might drown, as Bud discovered. He was a successful middle manager in a large business corporation and a onetime college baseball player. Much of his emotional energy was devoted to baseball. An opportunity came along for Bud to become the general manager of a minor league baseball team at a modest salary. Despite the pay cut, Bud welcomed the chance to apply his professional management skills to something he loved. Few people with Bud's big company background could be found managing a minor league baseball team. After one year, he found himself at the start of a tedious job search because his contract was not renewed. As Bud saw the situation:

> I made a bad mistake. The owners of the minor league team told me they wanted some professional management, but they were only paying lip service to the idea. They second-guessed every move I made. If I made a decision that went counter to their beliefs or the coach's, it was they who got their way. Before I arrived on the scene, every business decision was made on the basis of intuition. Apparently, the owners and the coaches wanted to continue along those lines. After I left, they brought the former general manager out of retirement.

Bud's situation indicates what can go wrong with "swim against the tide." You may place yourself in an environment where the uniqueness of your background is not welcomed and you are not accepted. Before jumping into a situation, try to discover if the cards are stacked against you.

## KNOW WHEN TO APPEAR INDISPENSABLE AND WHEN TO BE DISPENSABLE

One of the complexities of winning at office politics is that sometimes one tactic is effective, while another time just the opposite will achieve results. Such is the case with appearing indispensable versus being dispensable. Let's look at both choices, remembering that you have to size up your environment to decide which action to take.

## Appear Indispensable

Few people are really indispensable, but you can appear to be. If the big decision makers believe that you cannot be replaced, your career will receive a boost. The most effective means of appearing indispensable is to acquire knowledge, including personal contacts and secret techniques that top management believes no one else possesses to your extent.

It pays to combine the appearance of indispensability with the perception that you are in demand by other employers. As Steven Robbins observes, "Combining perceived mobility with perceived indispensability lessens the likelihood that your rise in your present organization will be stalled by the excuse, 'We can't promote you right now because your current unit can't afford to lose your expertise.'"[15]

## Appear Dispensable

The downside risk of appearing indispensable, or very difficult to replace, is that it can hamper your chances for promotion. Most managers are reluctant to part with a star individual performer. Solid talent is difficult to replace in any field. Many a branch manager has been secretly bypassed for promotion because he or she is doing such an outstanding job for the company. Top management is often unwilling to break up a winning combination. By being effective, yet dispensable you increase your chances of being eligible for promotion.

Audrey was the manager of the municipal bond department of a substantial sized bank. During one of her discussions with her superior about advancement opportunities, Audrey heard a familiar refrain, "But Audrey, 'munis' is a specialized business. You know more about that operation than anyone else. We need you where you are. You're too valuable to transfer right now." Having heard these same attitudes expressed a year earlier, Audrey had prepared her rebuttal. She explained to her boss:

> I agree that the field of municipal bonds is a specialized business, and I agree that I have accumulated considerable knowledge abut it. Recognizing these facts, I have shared all my knowledge with two subordinates, George and Kathy. George is ready right now to take over my job. Kathy should be ready in about six months. I have given each one of them a turn at running the department while I was out of the office on vacation or a business trip. I could be transferred or resign tomorrow, and the department would run very smoothly.

Top management at Audrey's bank became aware of its oversight. Three months later Audrey became manager of correspondent banking at her bank (relationships with affiliated banks). George was moved up into her slot, and Kathy took over George's job. Her new position gave Kathy additional breadth and a high salary.

## HELP GET YOUR BOSS PROMOTED

An indirect, difficult-to-apply career-boosting tactic is to help your boss get promoted in your own organization. Getting your boss promoted, however, will only benefit you directly if *you* are the logical successor. A variation of the same tactic is to help your boss be recruited away to an outside company. The latter tactic is Machiavellian since it serves to weaken your organization by removing a presumably competent manager. The highly ethical strategy of "help your boss succeed" is the most effective way of getting your boss promoted. Under the right circumstances, a more focused approach can be used to vacate your boss's job.

Mike attended a management development conference at a hotel. Seated at a poolside luncheon, he chatted with his table mates, one of whom was the vice-president of human resources. The conversation turned to the plant in Colorado that would be opening in a year. Mike said to the vice-president, "I know these things are confidential, but I'll bet I know who will be chosen to manage the Colorado plant. Bill Grimsly (Mike's boss) would seem to be the logical choice. He's the best plant manager I've worked for. I would say Bill could successfully run any operation in this company."

The vice-president of human resources dutifully scurried back to the home office with this valuable input from Mike. Bill was, in fact, one of the contenders for the plum position in Colorado. Mike's unsolicited endorsement helped influence the decision in Bill's favor. The company began screening internal and external candidates as a replacement for Bill. Mike was one of the contenders, but an outsider was chosen. Mike was disheartened, but only temporarily. One month later, the outsider decided not to join the company, and Mike was selected as Bill's replacement.

## CAPITALIZE ON LUCK

Good fortune weighs heavily in most successful careers. Without one or two good breaks along the way (such as your company suddenly expanding and therefore needing people to promote into important jobs), it is difficult to go far in your career. One factor in being lucky is to accept the idea that luck is what happens when preparation meets opportunity. Another is recognize that "If you're in enough places, you're bound to be in the right place at the right time."[16]

The effective career strategist manages luck to some extent by recognizing opportunities and taking advantage of them. The unlucky person is often the individual who, out of timidity, lets a good opportunity slip by. Taking advantage of good opportunities today includes the many executives who leave large corporations to purchase a franchise at a reasonable price. Some of these people are forced to enter a new business because they are laid off from their corporate job and cannot find another job. Instead of bemoaning their fate, they parlay their severance pay into a thriving new business. Some of the "luckiest" of these former executives took a chance on a lesser-known—and therefore more reasonably priced—franchise.

## AVOID TAINTED MEMBERS

Every organization has people who are in disfavor for political or work-related reasons—for example, bad attitude, association with failed projects, appear to be disloyal, or obsolete. Keep your distance from them.[17] Your effectiveness and judgment might be called into question if you associate with such tainted co-workers.

Janet, a former drug abuse counselor, left counseling after ten years because she felt burned out. She searched for a new career, and found a job as a marketing planner in a pharmaceutical company. Janet's natural orientation toward helping people led her to drift toward spending a lot of time with a marketing manager who was being neglected by influential people in the company. The two of them lunched together frequently, often talking in great detail about his career problems. At Janet's year-end review she was told that her performance was judged to be marginal, partly because she was allocating too much of her time to managers who couldn't profit from her assistance. It took Janet two years to overcome that perception of her work.

## KNOW WHEN TO QUIT

Dogged persistence is a virtue in many aspects of career management: Never give up until you find the right job; keep calling on prospective customers until one says yes; keep coming back until you finally get your budget approved. Nevertheless, there is a time to leave an organization, or transfer to another division or agency within the larger organization.

From a political standpoint, the time to quit is when it is certain that your power and influence has been substantially reduced or is beginning to erode. When you are on the "outs," get out. Find a suitable

new position before you are demoted, fired, or laid off. Telltale signs
that you are losing power include:

- You hardly ever receive a luncheon invitation from an important
  organization member.
- You are no longer appointed to high-level committees.
- You are bypassed for promotion more than once.
- Your highly competent assistant is transferred to work for a highly
  regarded manager.
- You are moved to a smaller office.
- You are not invited to a major reorganization meeting.
- Your budget and staff are reduced.
- Influential people hardly respond to your memos.
- Only routine messages appear in your electronic mail.
- You ask a subordinate to help you on a project, and that person says
  that your boss has pulled him or her away from your department
  temporarily.
- One week you find that you have no important work to do. Instead,
  you while away your time doing busy work.

## HITCH YOUR WAGON TO YOURSELF

The ultimate career-boosting strategy is to have faith in what you are
doing and persist in doing it well. If you hitch your wagon to yourself,
you will not be bothered by your detractors. Eventually your contribution will be recognized because what you are doing is worthwhile and of
value to the world.

Hitching your wagon to yourself is your career foundation. Other
tactics and strategies of boosting your career are designed to supplement
this basic strategy. If you lack technical, administrative, problem-solving,
or human relations skills you are lacking the basis of a successful career.
As noted by one observer of power and politics in organizations:[18]

> "While dramatically illustrated by Galileo and Pasteur who persisted in
> their experiments despite the criticism of their associates, the technique
> [hitch your wagon to yourself] has been used by countless other people
> who have faith in what they are doing and put their efforts into doing it
> well."

# CHAPTER 11

# MAKING POLITICAL USE OF INFORMATION

Information is a major source of power. The would-be power seeker recognizes that information is vital in every organization. Considering that the 1990s is truly the age of information, the deft management of information makes more political sense than ever before. Important information at your disposal enhances your status. If the only information you control is that readily gathered by others, you will be deprived of one more potential source of power.

A person with trade secrets is more valuable to the organization than the staff assistant who reviews periodicals in search of public information. Merely recognizing the fact that information can be used for personal advantage and power grabbing is the first step in playing the information game. The strategies and tactics described in this chapter, if properly applied, will help you capitalize on this subtle aspect of office politics.

## OBTAIN INSIDE INFORMATION

Making political use of information often begins with obtaining information that is not readily available to others. You will impress, and therefore be able to influence others, if you are privy to consequential information they lack. Obtaining such information may require careful planning.

### Cultivate Information Sources

To gain political advantage from information, you need to develop sources who can provide useful raw material. Direct payments to sources for information would quickly stamp you as highly unethical. A more subtle approach is to befriend people who have a pipeline to valid and useful information. The best source is likely to be an executive, but other sources are also important. Among those individuals outside of the executive suite likely to overhear tidbits are nurses in the medical office, systems analysts (they visit other departments regularly), executive assistants, executive dining room servers, and communication specialists.

## Use the Right Probes

After you have cultivated information sources, you can then employ probing techniques to obtain some needed facts.[1] One such probe is to act as if you already know the facts. State what little you know about a situation, and pretend to know more. You might say, for example, "Too bad about the layoff, isn't it?" It is also helpful to guess out loud. Matter-of-factly mention something that could be true, such as, "It looks like a search committee has already been formed to find a new president." Your source is then likely to contribute whatever information he or she has on the topic.

Name dropping is another subtle approach to eliciting information. If you've overheard a juicy morsel from an executive, mention it in conversation with a knowledgeable co-worker, and act as if you personally overheard the comment. You might way, "Jane was telling me about a drastic cut in our advertising budget for this year."

Assuming you have a trusting relationship with a key person, you might ask directly for information that can be used to enhance your power: "My senses tell me there is going to be another reduction in force. Can you tell me if this will affect my job, or the jobs of my group members?"

## Interpret Body Language

In your quest to obtain useful information, don't rely exclusively on the spoken word. Carefully observe also how people say things and various aspects of their body language. Almost any aspect of nonverbal behavior could be significant: gestures, twitching of the eyebrows, breathing rate, and blushing. A person's squirming could mean that the information they are giving you is very important, and potentially very upsetting to the people involved.

Speaking in a low tone usually indicates that the information you are hearing is truly confidential, and that your source could get in trouble if identified. When your source appears too calm, it could mean that you are getting stale or invalid information.

Interpreting nonverbal messages is most accurate when you are very familiar with another individual. One organizational politician told us, "I know when Natalie is giving me untrue or worthless information. She can't look at me directly."

## CONTROL VITAL INFORMATION

After obtaining vital information—either tidbits or expertise that can help the organization—power is acquired by keeping it under tight control. Blackmail is an unethical example of how power accrues to the person who has very sensitive information under his or her control. Of a more ethical nature, many people work themselves into secure and powerful positions because they are the only ones who understand what is going on. Many a sales representative has coasted along in a territory, even though overpaid, because the representative possessed so much unrecorded information about customer relationships. As companies demand more and more documentation about accounts, fewer sales reps than in the past keep so much useful information recorded.

Up until several years ago when computer experts proliferated, computer specialists often held onto information that made them seemingly irreplaceable. A company that did not submit to the demands of a key computer expert risked having that person leave. Along with that person would leave esoteric knowledge about the computers on which the company had become dependent. As the field of information systems has become amply supplied with competent people, computer knowledge has become less esoteric. Except in the fields of robotics and artificial intelligence, few computer people in business control information that cannot be obtained elsewhere.

Specialists today who control vital information include those who can pinpoint new products and services that will be in demand, and those who can provide accurate estimates of the values of companies and other properties to acquire. Ray, a financial analyst who works for a business broker, earns far more money than other employees in the 25-person firm. At his own admission, he is an irritant to other employees. When asked by another professional in the firm why Ray is retained, the president answered:

> I know that Ray has a few rough edges, but he is still a valuable contributor. We're in the business of matching buyers and sellers of businesses. Quite frankly, Ray does this better than any financial analyst I know. Like you and several other professionals in the firm, Ray has a bunch of analytical tools. Just like the rest of you he can juggle financial ratios and spew out

from his personal computer all kinds of fascinating data. But Ray is unique because he can arrive at a more accurate estimate of the fair price of a business property for sale better than anybody I know.

We almost never get a complaint from a client that he or she paid far too much for a business. Ray has the intuitive skill to cut through all the fancy data and smokescreen provided by someone who's attempting to sell a business. The ordinary number cruncher cannot touch Ray's uncanny knack for helping our clients find a good buy. He has information in his head that you can't purchase elsewhere. If Ray left us, he could easily set up shop for himself and become a tough competitor. That's why Ray remains with us as long as he wants.

## BE A CONFIDANT

Being privy to sensitive information yields power because many others in the organization want to know your inside knowledge. Another power advantage is that the person who is in on the biggest company secrets also develops additional job security. A major reason J. Edgar Hoover stayed in office so long as the FBI director is that he had collected so much negative information about so many people. The powers above him feared that Hoover might release some of the unsavory details about political figures should he be deposed.

Bruce, the former head of the research division of his employer, was thinking of using personnel manager Craig as a sounding board for confidential company matters. Before trusting him, however, Bruce tested his trustworthiness. He explains how:

> I liked Craig from the start. I was looking for somebody out of the main-stream of events to listen to me about delicate personnel problems. Craig was the logical candidate. But my 30 years of experience told me not to conclude that a person will respect confidences until you have had some solid evidence. I told Craig that I was giving some careful thought to terminating his boss, but not to tell anyone. If Craig told his boss, I knew I would hear about it. His boss was not a timid soul.

> After three weeks, I heard nothing about the alleged firing, so I proceeded with my plans for Craig. In the meantime, I revealed my little deception to Craig, and we both had a good laugh. Next, I went over my master plan for reorganizing the company. I explained to Craig that I wanted to remove one layer of management which would involve terminating about ten middle managers. Craig and I shared impressions about the strengths and weaknesses of the entire staff.

> Finally, we got down to the personnel department. If somebody was to go, the logical choice would be Craig because of his level of management. The idea shook me up. It reminded me of a gangster movie in which a criminal kingpin gives a contract to a hit man to kill another hit man the kingpin has hired to kill somebody else. It seemed like bad business to declare as surplus the man who had helped me pare down the organization. So we let

somebody else in Craig's department go, and reorganized Craig's position. He wound up with a bigger job.

The lesson I learned from all this was that when you share top secrets with somebody, that person has something on you. It becomes awkward to later make an objective business decision about the person.

## INITIATE WORTHWHILE INFORMATION

Power stems from being in control of or privy to important information. It also derives from initiating information that others can use. For example, as the National Institute for Business Management reports, by creating useful information, you can turn your company's slow pace into an advantage for yourself.[2] If your organization is slow-paced, you can gain power through establishing a better system for monitoring department or companywide costs, productivity, or quality. Higher-ups crave this type of information because they need it to make accurate decisions. You can vastly enhance your power by creating new data or finding faster ways for executives to get existing information.

One way to create new information is to enlist the cooperation of a knowledgeable administrative assistant to run a spreadsheet analysis on what would happen if the company took certain actions. Top management is likely to be impressed by stunning forecasts, even if they are only partially accurate. Here are examples of the type of information derived from a spreadsheet analysis that could impress people enough to enlarge your power:

- If we bought $100,000 worth of advertising on BET (Black Entertainment News) we would generate approximately $2 million in sales in the black population.
- If the medical staff encouraged five percent of our patients to stay in the hospital an additional day, our annual revenues would increase by $500,000.
- If every employee in the company took three days of unpaid vacation next year, our payroll costs would decrease by $8 million.
- If we increased the length of our turkey franks to "bun length" we could increase revenues 20 percent on the product, resulting in additional yearly sales of $19 million.

## ACT ON ADVANCE INFORMATION

A deft power-grabbing strategy is to capitalize on information that is not widely circulated. If you can react to an event before others are aware that the event has taken place, you will be at a power advantage.[3] Suppose you hear through an informant that your company will be actively recruiting a Hispanic woman to fill an important post. Fortunately for you, a friend of yours—a Hispanic woman with managerial talent and experience—is currently looking for a better job. If you introduce her to the company president, you will appear prophetic in your judgment.

Acting properly on advance information is an advanced political tactic. You need both a pipeline to the top and the resources to capitalize on such information. Harriet, a branch bank manager, was able to act on advance information provided by one of the board members. In her bank, a board member is required to conduct an audit or trustee examination of officials at the branch locations where technical information, general procedures, and future projections are discussed in detail. The trustee who visited Harriet's bank mentioned in passing an item of importance: The board had indicated to the home office marketing department how important it would be to obtain the payroll account of a large local retailer.

Without any flurry or mention, Harriet made appointments with several department stores in the community. She was able to sell the human resources executive of the largest store on the idea of having a payroll deposit account with the bank. Harriet then called the marketing department at the home office to describe her accomplishment. Within three days, the bank president sent Harriet a personal note, congratulating her breakthrough accomplishment. Harriet's timely response to advance information had instantly made her a more powerful branch manager.

## BE AN INFORMATION HUB

An ideal way to gain control over information is to set yourself up so that information passes over your desk on the way to other people in the office. Rarely will your position allow for this much control over information. However, you can move toward being an information hub by collecting as much information as your position will allow. The effectiveness of this strategy varies. How much do the people in your work environment value information? Tidbits, rumors, gossip, and other items of information are particularly valued in governmental settings. People rise and fall from power in Washington, D.C., in direct proportion to the amount of seemingly useful information at their disposal. A former political appointee, Howie, explains how he played in the information game in Washington:

> To earn my share of power, I found it necessary to cultivate fresh sources of information. Combing the newspapers and government reports was one way of bringing important information to my boss. But that wasn't good

enough. I was expected to produce information that wasn't available to the public. After a while, I functioned like a gossip columnist. One source was an administrative assistant; another was a barber; another was a hairdresser; another was an office assistant in a public relations firm that provided speech-writing services for key people. I paid cash for most of my bits of information. Sometimes gifts like perfume, fountain pens, and hand tools were more appropriate forms of payment.

I was not purchasing secret information nor engaging in character defamation. I was just plucking information before it became public knowledge or was leaked to the press. For instance, I found out four days early that one trade union was going to write a formal letter of protest about a new government law relating to employee safety. My boss gobbled up the information.

After a while it hit me that my job as a special assistant was really that of an information broker. I would dig around for information, often buying it. In turn, I would figuratively sell it to my boss. The better my information, the more power I acquired. The less significant my information, the less my power.

Another version of being an information hub is to serve as a conduit for information from lower-ranking people to a top executive. Marty, a management consultant, acted in such a role. One method Marty uses to impress a member of a client firm is to reach inside his breast pocket, grab for his appointment book, and say, "Incidentally, is there anything you would like me to pass along to the president? It looks as though he and I have a luncheon appointment next week. Let me make a note of any thoughts you might have."

Marty, of course, wants people to know that he and the president exchange information, giving him power at the top of the company. His technique generally works well, but it backfired at least once. On that particular occasion, the person Marty was trying to impress said, "Are you a consultant or a messenger service? If I have something to tell the president, I will write or phone him personally. No use something getting lost in the translation or your taking credit for my information."

## STOCKPILE A FEW IDEAS _____

No matter what the extent of your craving for power, you will probably find it morally acceptable to save some of your best ideas for a rainy day. One reason underlying this tactic is that if you are engaged in creative work, there is no guarantee that you will always have a fresh idea in your desk, or in back of your mind, waiting to be implemented. If you have the good fortune to think of a number of useful ideas over a brief time interval, it is a wise strategy to save a few for when your idea bank is at a low ebb.

Many college professors are required to have at least one good research project per year. If a new project is not reflected in their year-end report, their performance evaluation and salary increase may suffer. Professors therefore often distribute their good ideas evenly over the years to avoid the risk of having one year in which no new research project is initiated. One professor put it this way, "Sure, it's a temporary high to report on two or three new projects in one year. You receive some praise and a decent raise. But should you turn up nothing the next year, you get zapped even though it's supposed to be the yearly average [of research projects initiated] that counts."

Another good reason for stockpiling ideas is that sometimes the timing may not be right to receive maximum credit for a good idea. George worked for Joe, a man who systematically took credit for the ideas of group members, conveniently forgetting that he was not the source of the ideas. George once suggested to Joe that the company should channel through ducts the heat generated by some of the largest machines on the factory floor. This otherwise wasted heat could then be used to heat a colder, more difficult-to-heat section of the factory. The suggestion worked, but Joe took about 80 percent of the credit. His boss did state, however, that George provided valuable input into the problem. Recognizing that it is difficult to complain to upper management that your boss is stealing your ideas, George tried this approach:

> I asked Joe if I might have an opportunity to rotate jobs. I explained that I enjoyed working for him, but that I felt a six-month assignment in another department should make me a more valuable contributor to the company. I said that I then would be happy to return to the department if there were still an opening for me. Joe did get me assigned to a manufacturing control department which happened to be a good place to practice creativity. Basically the department was concerned with setting standards and making sure we weren't wasting time, money, or material.

> While still working for Joe, I figured that the company was using too much control in some areas. For instance, we were weighing every box of nuts and bolts or nails that came in from a supplier. That took considerable time, especially when we would repack and ship back the occasional underweight box. I recommended that we abolish weighing items like nuts, bolts, and screws because it was an uneconomical procedure.

> I also recommended that we stop dispensing nuts and bolts to our employees as if the nuts and bolts were precious stones. Instead of having a full-time worker handing these out in metered quantities, I thought it would be more economical if everybody took all the nuts and bolts he or she needed.

> Two weeks after I was assigned to my new job, I followed through and made these two recommendations. Both ideas were tried and found to be money-savers for the company. I was given a special citation by the head of

manufacturing. If I had launched these ideas while working for Joe, he would have gobbled up the credit.

## DROP A FEW BUZZ WORDS

A person intent on being successful needs effective communication skills. Overloading your speech with jargon will usually alienate you from generalists. Nevertheless, dropping a few of the latest buzz words will often help you sound more professional.

The buzz words you choose should be those used by powerful people in the organization. Avoid the jargon of the technical specialist, the clerk, or the operative (a buzz word for production worker). If an influential person uses a particular phrase in a speech, be one of the first to incorporate that phrase into your own language. Below are five pairs of statements, expressed in neutral and powerful (incorporating buzz words) organizational language:

*NEUTRAL:*   Our department takes care of customer service problems.

*POWERFUL:*   We interface with the public served by the organization.

*NEUTRAL:*   Our company makes many products; we have some plants scattered around the world.

*POWERFUL:*   We are a diversified, multiproduct, multinational corporation.

*NEUTRAL:*   We expect people to do their jobs around here.

*POWERFUL:*   We hold every employee of this corporation accountable for his or her results.

*NEUTRAL:*   Our supervisors often ask employees for their opinion about how to solve a problem.

*POWERFUL:*   Our management philosophy emphasizes power sharing at all organizational levels. Employee input is a vital part of every manager's decision-making process.

## ASK IMPRESSIVE QUESTIONS

Yet another way of making political use of information is to ask questions that imply you are linked to important forces within the organization, or that you are aware of hidden realities. No matter what inference people may draw because of the questions you raise, the questioning tactic is not devious. Asking intelligent questions usually serves the good of the organization. Part of the rational decision-making process is to question every assumption you make. Asking the right questions is also part of the operating procedure of an effective manager or staff person.

Impressive questions can be broken down into two categories. One category is questions based on detailed technical or administrative information, such as, "How does your proposal fit into our new retrofit program for the MK–14 project?" A second category is general purpose questions that fit many situations in many organizations. Unless you have some specific inside information, you are better advised to use general purpose questions. Here are ten sample questions designed to orient you toward the habit of asking impressive questions:

1. How will (name the highest-ranking executive in organization) react to your proposal?
2. How might your proposal sit with the various interest groups we serve?
3. How cost-effective is your idea?
4. What are the alternatives facing us?
5. What input from below and above did you receive before reaching your conclusion?
6. What might be some of the negative consequences if your plan were totally accepted?
7. Are you being unduly optimistic?
8. Are you being unduly pessimistic?
9. What is the environmental impact of your proposal, however remote it might be?
10. Is your perspective broad enough to meet the overall good of the organization?

## BECOME A BEARER OF GOOD NEWS

A subtle political use of information is to become associated with opportunities and solutions rather than problems. Every organization faces many problems, and many people are willing to focus on these problems in their contacts with peers and higher-ups. You might be able to gain advantage if you develop the reputation of being associated with good news. Artfully done, being a good-news bearer can increase your power base.

Within three years after he joined a small company that manufactured parts for other companies, Maury was appointed assistant general manager. His new appointment made Maury the leading contender for the company presidency. Good-natured Maury agreed to give a talk to a group of college students enrolled in a marketing course. One of the students asked how a person as young as he, who had been with the company for such a relatively short length of time, was promoted to the assistant general manager position. Maury answered:

> I owe my promotion to my philosophy of life. I try to emphasize the positive. I think that is what should be expected of a professional marketer. Too many people at Lawhorn Products dwelled on problems. I emphasized what *could* be done, rather than what could *not* be done. The president, who promoted me, found that to be a welcome relief. He faces enough problems without my adding to his burden. I can recall two vivid examples of my philosophy in action.

> One time, the company was hit with a bombshell. We were in the process of manufacturing thousands of parts for a company that suddenly declared bankruptcy. They cancelled the order too late—85 percent of the parts were ready to be shipped. It would make no sense to force the company to honor its contract because they were bankrupt. I heard that Mr. Harding, the president, was furious. He was plagued by others in the company bemoaning our fate. Instead of joining the crowd of people telling the president how bad things were, I telephoned all the companies who had a product line similar to ours. I explained our situation and asked each company if they could find any use whatsoever for our cancelled inventory.

> Finally, I hit a company in Cleveland who could modify our product for their own use. All they offered to pay was 20 percent of the unit price we were to get from the bankrupt company. I asked for a conference with Mr. Harding, saying that I think I found a customer for the seemingly useless inventory. My pitch was that my prospective customer was willing to pay nearly four times the scrap value of the inventory. To add to the value of the deal, we might still be able to capture some money after the assets of the original customer were sold and bankruptcy proceedings concluded. The president was very pleased, and approved the deal. He thanked me for getting rid of the biggest headache in years faced by the company.

> Another time the company encountered the problem of a downturn in sales. It appeared we would have to lay off about 50 of our experienced production workers, and also to make some cuts among sales and administrative workers. The president did not want to take such a drastic step because he believed strongly that all the company really had to offer was the abilities of its people. Instead of being another gloom peddler, I developed an action plan. I told Mr. Harding that I had a plan capable of saving our workforce. He listened intently.

> I proposed that we run an advertisement in several newspapers in boom areas of the country, such as Atlanta, indicating that we were willing to subcontract work at close to cost. Harding approved the plan and we did get enough subcontracting business to keep our workforce intact. As our own business picked up again, we raised our price for subcontract work. We still do occasional work for an aerospace firm located in the Georgia area.

When Mr. Harding promoted me, he stated clearly that every company needs somebody who can search for opportunities at times when others are mired in problems.

## USE "INITIAL POWER"

A curious twist to politicizing information in bureaucracies, both public and private, is for an executive to initial photocopies of memos and route them back to the sender.[4] For instance, you rearrange things so you receive a photocopy of all correspondence that concerns the purchase of capital equipment. When you receive your copy, you initial and return it to the sender along with the comment, "I concur. Good decision." It could be then inferred that you have some decision-making power about the purchase of capital equipment.

If you can convince enough people to send you copies of memos, your initial-signing tactic could make you appear powerful. At its worst, initialing memos and returning them to their sender could create the impression that you are a pest who is looking for activities to perform. Another hazard of the initial power tactic is its instability. A current cost-cutting fad in business and nonprofit organizations is to place tight controls over the use of photocopying machines. Thus your vehicle for displaying power could be subject to the cost-cutting whims of the controller.

## TAKE COUNSEL WITH CAUTION

Gaining political advantage through information includes both offense and defense. A way for a manager to prevent the erosion of power is to be very selective about accepting information in the form of advice from group members.[5] Asking advice sometimes results in decisions actually being made by subordinates. The strategy, "take counsel with caution," is at variance with the current trend toward participative decision making. Nevertheless, it is helpful to recognize that, the more advice you accept, the more power you surrender. Because of this fact, many astute (and power craving) managers are resisting a full swing to participative leadership.

Dorothy, the head of a community action group, received a suggestion from two of her staff members that their group should organize a "sleep-in" at local merchants. The point of the demonstration was to protest the fact that very few youths from poorer sections of the city were finding employment. Dorothy's group noted that in some neighborhoods, teenage unemployment ran as high as 40 percent. (In these neighborhoods there were no major employers of teenagers such as fast-food restaurants or large retailers.) Sleeping in the doorways of the local merchants and other small businesses supposedly would dramatize the problem.

The sleep-in idea was implemented and proved to be a fiasco. Several merchants pointed out that the retailers and other small businesses represented the best hopes for teenage employment. Such behavior was therefore self-defeating. A widely quoted editorial stated that sleeping in the doorways was associated in the minds of prospective employers with sleeping on the job. The agency learned that some of its funding was not to be renewed as a direct result of its recent unfavorable publicity. Upbraided by her boss, Dorothy said in defense, "But don't you see, it wasn't my idea. I was just approving some plans suggested by my staff."

Dorothy's boss countered, "I'm going to recommend to the board that your appointment not be renewed for next year. It doesn't matter if the people who work for you are crazy. When you're the boss, you are held accountable for what they do."

## DO NOT TRUST OTHERS
## TO KEEP A SECRET

Making political use of information also includes preventing the loss of power through slips of the tongue. To repeat, there are very few secrets in organizations. If you would feel uncomfortable, embarrassed, or anxious if thoughts of yours were repeated, do not express them to an insider. Almost inevitably, your trusted confidant will disseminate the controversial information to at least one other person. In turn, that person is likely to pass along your secret to at least one other person. Before long, the controversial message and its original sender will be widely known throughout the firm.

Ted, a supervisor in the motor vehicle department, said to a coworker that the director of the local branch of the agency appears to be suffering from Alzheimer's disease. After a staff meeting one day, the director said to Ted, "You may think I'm suffering from Alzheimer's disease. But one fact I'll never forget is that you were the person who said it." Ted apologized profusely, and claimed that he was jesting because everybody knew what a sharp mind the director had. Ted's defense didn't work; his scheduled promotion was delayed indefinitely. The explanation offered was that Ted had not quite developed the maturity of judgment required of a supervisor in the motor vehicle department.

Ted probably never knew how his comment about Alzheimer's disease leaked back to the director. To help prevent yourself from falling prey to the problems of secret information being passed along, recognize that there are at least three reasons secrets are so rarely kept. First, many people attempt to gain power by spreading gossip. A good tidbit today (such as "Ted said that the director appears to be suffering from Alzheimer's disease") can give the person dropping the tidbit a modicum of fleeting power.

People also pass along secrets by honest mistake. They may forget who told them the secret or that it was highly confidential information. For example, you might casually mention that an acquaintance was leaving her husband for one of her team members because you simply forgot it was not public knowledge.

Finally, letting out secrets is a favorite weapon of the back stabber —particularly if the secret will put you in an unfavorable light. Nora, a financial analyst, was stressed out from a week of exorbitant demands. With a sigh of exasperation she told a co-worker, "The way the financial picture is headed, I may not have to worry about being overworked in this company anymore. If my projections are correct, we'll have zero sales within four years." The co-worker later told the president, "Are you aware of the grim financial picture Nora Beckworth has painted of our company. I hope she hasn't been interviewed by the *Wall Street Journal.*" The president demanded an explanation from Nora. Her explanation was that the projection was simply a humorous comment made during a moment of extreme fatigue.

The president seemed placated. Nora learned from the incident how loose talk to the wrong person can conceivably damage one's career. Information had more power than she realized.

# CHAPTER 12

## DEVIOUS POLITICAL TACTICS

What constitutes an ethical or unethical political tactic is a question of values. To an Innocent Lamb, almost all forms of office politics are dishonest, dirty, or devious. To a Machiavellian, any maneuver that helps you gain advantage without getting you into legal trouble is fair game. One useful way of judging the ethics of a given tactic, is to ask, "Would I want myself or a loved one to be handled this way?" Also, one might ask, "Does this tactic show a respect for justice and human rights?"[1] Negative answers to these questions suggest that the tactic is unethical and perhaps devious.

Here we describe techniques for which negative answers to the above questions would be given by approximately 99 percent of the workforce. The person who practices such devious political tactics does so at considerable career risk. Practicing unsavory office politics may lead to your being unwanted, unloved, and fired. In extreme cases, you might even be sued for libel or punched in the face.

### STAB RIVALS IN THE BACK

The ubiquitous back stab requires that you pretend to be nice, but all the while plan someone's demise. A safeguard against being stabbed in the back is to ask yourself why a particular person is trying to befriend you. If the reason seems legitimate, forget your suspicions. The most common form of back stabbing is for a person to initiate a conversation with you about the weaknesses of your common boss. The back stabber encourages your negative commentary and makes a careful mental note of what you say. Later, he or she casually passes these comments along to the boss, making you appear disloyal and foolish.

Sometimes the back stabber is more subtle. After enticing you to make negative comments about the boss, he or she says to the boss, "I hope you can work out your problems with Ben. I know he's a difficult person to supervise."

## EMBRACE OR DEMOLISH

The ancient strategy of "embrace or demolish," suggests that you remove from the premises rivals who suffered past hurts through your efforts. Those wounded rivals might retaliate at a vulnerable moment. The origin of this strategy is found in Machiavelli's advice regarding the conquest of smaller nations:[2]

"Upon this, one has to remark that men ought either to be well-treated or crushed, because they can avenge themselves of lighter injuries, of more serious ones they cannot; therefore the injury that is done to a man ought to be of such a kind that one does not stand in fear of revenge."

Owen, a vice-president of finance, bitterly opposed the takeover of his firm by another company. Despite his protests, the acquisition took place. The president of the acquiring company learned of Owen's displeasure about the acquisition. One month after the deal was consummated, Owen was fired. His boss told him: "They are forcing me to put one of their people in the top financial spot in our company. It's a question of somebody experienced in their way of implementing financial controls."

## TAKE UNDUE CREDIT

Perhaps the most widely practiced unethical political tactic is to take credit for work performed by others. A manager who uses this tactic often takes full credit for the successes of team members, but disclaims any responsibility for their failures. One way of taking undue credit is to adopt a consultative decision-making style. In the process of making a decision, ask team members and perhaps co-workers for their input. Skim their best ideas, and then take full credit for the best ideas. After all, you did collect and synthesize their ideas.

Another way of taking undue credit for ideas is to tell people you would like to "pick their brains" to get some ideas for a tough problem you are facing. You thank the contributors, and then take full credit for the best ideas.

The person who takes undue credit for the ideas of others quickly develops an unsavory reputation that invites retaliation. Vince was one such scoundrel. To get even with him, two co-workers plotted to present Vince an idea that had been tried in the past with disastrous results. He would receive the same specious suggestion from either person. The bad idea involved the company owning and maintaining its own fleet of trucks instead of allowing an outside company to own and operate the company trucks.

When Vince brought his purloined idea to the company president, she replied: "That bummer of an idea has been floating around for 15 years. We tried operating our own truck fleet once before and we lost a fortune. Do your homework more carefully the next time."

## DISCREDIT YOUR RIVAL

Many devious political tactics are aimed at discrediting a rival or any other person you would like to see made uncomfortable, put out of the running for a promotion, or stripped of power. Specific techniques for discrediting one's rival can take several forms, including both overt and covert thrusts.

### Direct Accusation

Only a naive boss would accept a damaging statement about a team member without corroboration of the adverse information. For the record, here are a few discrediting statements made by people desperate to gain advantage:

*Plumber talking to his boss about another plumber*: "I wonder if on my next assignment, I could work with somebody other than Jack. I've tried working with him, but he just doesn't seem to be any good with his hands."

*Team member talking to boss after she returns from a trade show*: "I couldn't find Ginny at any of the meetings. Was she called back early? I hope she didn't take ill."

*Manager talking to his boss about an ambitious team member*: "When Marty's around, he's a terrific worker. But he's hard to find. I guess he's usually in some other office, politicking to find a good job for himself."

### Raise Questions About Your Competition

A mild form of discrediting your opposition is to simply raise questions about his or her capabilities. Raising questions is an effective technique because it allows the other person to reach his or her own conclusions. If you declare outright that your rival is incompetent, the boss may resent the implication that he or she made a serious judgment error by hiring the person. Among the penetrating questions that might be asked about a rival are these:

1. Has he or she trained a replacement to take over the job should he or she receive a promotion? (It is usually difficult to demonstrate that one has a ready replacement.)
2. Is he or she overloaded? (In other words, could your rival possibly take on any more responsibility without risk to efficiency, physical health, or mental health?)
3. Is he or she more of a specialist than a generalist? (A good criticism to make about any technically competent person. Most people become good generalists only after years of being a specialist.)
4. Is he or she losing enthusiasm for the job lately? (If you look hard enough, you can find some signs of burnout in most workers.)

**Character Assassination**

To be an effective character assassin, you move one step beyond raising questions about your competition. Instead, you make derogatory hints about your rival. Should you have no ethical qualms about this technique, get right to the heart of your rival's competence. In talking about the team with group members, you might say, "We all still like Jim a lot. But it's difficult not to criticize his judgment in handling customer service problems. He seems to have some hidden agenda that we can't figure out."

**Keep a Blunder File**

A methodical way of discrediting others is to keep a blunder file on everyone in your office. Almost everybody commits a blunder once in a while. In one company, a group of managers had a background investigation run on a recently hired manager. Although nothing derogatory turned up, the older managers were looking for a way to depose the new manager should he prove to be a menace to their cause. Here are a few specific items found in a blunder file:

- On January 8, Betty Lou turned in her department budget three days late. It contained several inaccuracies and vague projections.
- On May 20, Jerry returned from lunch at 3 P.M. He appeared glassy eyed and had difficulty walking. An administrative assistant from another department was with him.

- On August 8, at Sea Island, Georgia, Glenn made a presentation to the salesforce on forecasts for the upcoming year. He was so nervous that he had to leave the stage temporarily.

## DIVIDE AND RULE

The age-old strategy of encouraging team members to scrap among themselves so they will not form alliances against the boss is still with us. In this way the boss might be able to push through programs that require full cooperation from subordinates, or gain full support from team members. The person who uses divide and rule skillfully gains the balance of power. The strategy requires finding a valid way to create dissension among subordinates without being transparent. A major problem with divide and rule is that it can backfire.

> During a meeting called to discuss the production schedule on a new product, Vic, the general manager, said to Don, the head of manufacturing: "They tell me engineering isn't holding up its end of getting things ready for production." Two weeks later Vic dropped another conflict arousing comment, this time to the head of engineering: "It's too bad you're having so many problems with manufacturing trying to figure out how to build the product you've designed."
>
> Vic's techniques did create rivalry and hard feelings between engineering and manufacturing. Ultimately, his top staff saw through his divide and rule tactics and his effectiveness as a leader diminished. Realizing that he was no longer effective as a general manager, the CEO asked Vic to submit his resignation.

## SPY ON YOUR RIVALS

It is sometimes necessary to find out what your rival is thinking, or whether that person has done anything to make him or her vulnerable in relation to dealing with you. Spy techniques used to conduct political battles include surveillance devices, hiring a detective to dig up adverse information about your rival, and stealing copies of written or computer files. Discovering, for example, that a rival was arrested for soliciting a same-sexed prostitute could give you an advantage in negotiating.

Al Neuharth, the former chairman of Gannett Company, at one time serendipitously spied on a rival. In 1978, Neuharth faced a prodigious personal threat when Combined Communications Corp., a television company, merged with Gannett. Karl Eller, the CEO of Combined

Communications, was intent on replacing Neuharth as the top executive of the merged company.

Before the merger was completed, Eller was a guest at Neuharth's palatial estate in Cocoa Beach, Florida. Eller telephoned his wife from the guest room but neglected to push the privacy button on the room-to-room intercom. His end of the conversation was broadcast to Neuharth's study. Neuharth listened carefully as Eller proclaimed to his wife that he would run the entire show within six months. Knowing that Eller was out to depose him, Neuharth used all the tricks in his bag of hard-hitting political tactics to ultimately defeat and banish Eller.[3]

## USE BLACKMAIL

Extortion has been a long-standing criminal activity. It has also been used by devious office politicians to gain power and favor, or boost their careers. A curious aspect of company blackmail is that one deviant threatens to make public the deviant behavior of another, unless the former makes certain concessions to the latter. Grist for the blackmailer includes evidence that your rival has done such misdeeds as sexually harassed another employee, received kickbacks from a supplier, dumped toxic wastes, used company property for personal use, uses cocaine, or cheats regularly on an expense account.

Blackmailers lead a hazardous existence. A major problem is that blackmailing is usually considered a worse offense than the basis for blackmailing somebody. Don, an accountant, noticed a few major irregularities in the expense account submitted by an executive in his firm. One abnormality he noticed was that the executive's daily expenses were higher than those of others taking similar trips. A more pronounced problem Dan discovered were two hotel receipts with smudged-in areas over the dates. In addition, the hotels seemed unusually far from any company location.

Dan phoned these hotels to verify the receipts submitted by the executive. Dan's hunch was correct. The executive was submitting phony hotel receipts that he had collected while on private travel. He had apparently stayed with friends in place of using a hotel. Dan even suspected that the executive might be submitting expenses for phantom trips.

Dan confronted the executive with his findings. He demanded a promotion into his department and threatened to disclose the expense-account irregularities if his demands were not met. Dan did receive a promotion to a supervisory position. Four months later, he and the executive were both fired. The executive was caught receiving a bribe from a company supplier. On the way out, he revealed Dan's act of extortion.

## ABOLISH THE JOB OF INGRATES ━━━━━━━━━

A current method of squashing people you dislike is not to fire them, but to eliminate their jobs. In this way, they can be sacrificed even if they are outstanding performers, and they cannot sue the company for wrongful discharge. Vera explains how her job was abolished because of a personality clash between herself and her boss:

> My boss had three computer programmers and one systems analyst report-
> ing to her. She and I clashed from the first moment I joined the group. It
> seemed to be a case of negative chemistry between us. The analyst quit, so
> one of the programmers was promoted to that job. My boss then phased
> out one of the programmer positions, saying it was no longer needed. I was
> let go. The department still accomplished all its work because the person
> who was promoted to systems analyst really spent most of his time pro-
> gramming. There really wasn't enough work for a full-time systems ana-
> lyst. If the system analyst's job had been eliminated, my boss would not
> have been able to dump me. The department would still have needed all
> the programmers, and my performance evaluations indicated that I was
> meeting the expectations of my position.

## MAKE LIFE MISERABLE
## FOR YOUR RIVALS ━━━━━━━━━

Many devious political acts are designed to make life so miserable for a rival or enemy, that the person leaves the organization voluntarily. Making life miserable for someone else becomes necessary when the person you want to banish is performing satisfactorily, or his or her job cannot be eliminated. Five of these misery-creating tactics are worth knowing should you want to make someone else miserable, or someone is trying to make you miserable.

### Use a Frontal Assault

A vice-president in a multinational company disliked one of his most talented team members. To make life miserable for him, the executive conducted a relentless assault. The subordinate describes his version of what happened:[4]

> The conflict affected my work and personal life. He controlled my living
> conditions and my expenditures. Company executives abroad get an over-
> seas package which includes housing and living expenses, furniture al-
> lowance, sometimes a car and other benefits. If you really want to hurt

someone, you can make his or her home life miserable by delaying the person's car or not approving housing expenditures and so on, which is exactly what this man did to me and my family.

For 14 months, he moved my wife, our son, our dog and cat from city to city, hotel to hotel. He never allowed us to stay in one place long enough to settle down and rent a house. And since I was traveling 28 days out of 30, my wife was always alone.

The badgered manager succeeded in telling his version of the story to top management, but soon thereafter did leave the company. He had created too much ill will in the process of defending his reputation.

Making life miserable for an unwanted person by forcing heavy travel is also practiced in federal civil service. In one application of this technique, the disliked person is sent on a prolonged fact-finding mission to hundreds of small towns. Anybody who values family life, or who lacks the stamina to cope with such a hectic pace, eventually resigns.

## The Transfer

Another approach to making life miserable for an unwanted person in your command is to transfer that person to an undesirable location. A location can be undesirable for a number of reasons, including distance from relatives and friends, weather, expensive living conditions, or a high crime rate.

An unwanted political rival who owned a gracious home near Louisville, Kentucky, was told he would be transferred to a corporate staff job in New York City. He and his wife soon discovered that a suitable replacement for their $150,000 Louisville home would cost $450,000 in nearby suburbs of New York. When he explained the circumstances to the executive who ordered his transfer, the regional manager was told, "Sorry, your job is now in New York." Rather than disrupt his way of life, the manager cashed in some of his savings and opened a men's clothing store in a suburb of Louisville.

## Assign a Person a Meaningless Job

A high-level power play at the expense of stockholders or taxpayers is to transfer an antagonist, or entire department, into an activity that seems meaningful but is essentially meaningless. Ultimately, some of the victims of this technique will be sufficiently frustrated to resign at their own accord.[5] Brian, a former business executive, describes how he and his small department were transferred into a meaningless new activity:

My job had been the manager of strategic planning. I had a small staff, and we were engaged in helping to plan the future of the corporation. When people listened to us, we had a real contribution to make. A new president who thought very little of our activity was appointed. He transferred our department to another building and gave us the new title of Quality Assurance. We were to audit the quality standards in every department. It quickly became apparent to us that everybody felt they were already doing a good job of meeting quality standards.

We felt awkward and uncomfortable. My three team members all requested a transfer to more solid jobs. I finally resigned because I couldn't take the insult to my job of not having a real job. Things did work out for the better. I obtained a job with a management consulting firm that was helping clients with their strategic planning.

## Make a Department Superfluous

Although this technique was formalized for governmental use,[6] it has also been tried in industry. The underlying assumption is that an entire agency can be isolated and bypassed by making it superfluous. A parallel agency is established that will take over the work being performed by the now-obsolete agency. Soon an organizational taskforce looking to excise waste will discover that the group has no legitimate purpose, and it will be jettisoned. Or, as the department members discover they have no legitimate work to perform, many of them will seek productive employment. The obsolete department therefore withers away quickly. This technique can only be used in a large complex organization.

## Snub a Rival

A diabolical way of making a productive person appear unwanted is to minimize his or her accomplishments. If the "rival" productive person is a subordinate, the manager is ethically obliged to make a performance appraisal. However, that manager can snub the person's performance publicly without appearing too unethical.

Gabe, the manager of a packing design group, felt threatened by the exceptional creativity of Jessica, a designer within the group. When Gabe reviewed recent accomplishments during staff meetings, he made almost no mention of Jessica's outstanding package designs. On one occasion, a package designed by Jessica received recognition from an association of packaging engineers. Gabe never acknowledged her success, privately or in a department meeting. Jessica felt so snubbed and unappreciated by the incident that she began a job search, and subsequently left the company. Gabe's misery technique worked, but the company lost the contribution of a talented packaging engineer.

## CREDIT AND REMOVE THE OPPOSITION ────────────

Earlier, we described the career-boosting strategy of helping your boss get promoted by singing his or her praises to others. When you carry this strategy one step further—finding a way to get the boss hired by another organization—you are using a devious tactic. Assuming your rival is effective, you are weakening your own organization by facilitating that person's leaving the firm. Maggie explains how a rival used this tactic to get her out of the way:

> Sharon and I worked for the same company as first-level supervisors. We were both eager to be promoted but our company had very limited advancement opportunities at the time. Sharon invited me to a cocktail party at her house. During the evening, she introduced me to Barry, a human resources manager from a local company. Barry mentioned to me that Sharon had told him very impressive things about me. He handed me his business card and asked me to call him to discuss an exciting job opportunity.
>
> Barry was truthful. His company had an exciting opportunity—an open requisition for a female manager in a high-level position. It seems that Barry's company was underrepresented by females in management and they wanted to correct the situation. I wound up taking the job. It dawned on me that Sharon had set me up so she would have a better chance at being promoted.
>
> I guess Sharon didn't want to risk leaving the company herself or she might have applied for the outside position. I think she pulled a dirty trick, but I proved to be the winner since the meeting with Barry did give my career a shot in the arm.

## EXCLUDE THE COMPETITION
## FROM MEETINGS ────────────

A sometimes practiced, underhanded maneuver is to keep the competition away from important meetings without actually using physical restraint. Assume you know that your rival is scheduled to be on vacation or away on a business trip on a particular date. You schedule a meeting on that date, knowing it would be important for your rival to attend. Danny explains how excluding the competition can advance your own cause:

> Our place is such a political jungle, people are afraid to go away on vacation. You don't know what you're going to miss while away. The purpose of keeping the competition away from important meetings is so you will look good in the eyes of important people who attend the meeting. Your rival, of course, will not be noticed because the person is not present. A former

boss of mine set up a budget meeting during the time I was sent out of town to audit a branch operation.

At that meeting I was told that he presented the figures from the department and did not mention that I was the person who really assembled them. He received the compliment for having done a good job while I did all the work. It was a missed opportunity for me.

## THE SMOKESCREEN

Another approach to excluding somebody from something important is the smokescreen. It works this way: "Say, Craig, have you and your wife ever tried Dante's, that little Italian restaurant near Lake Avenue?" asked Stan. "It seems like they have ten different Italian dishes. Linguini is their best pasta dish. You need reservations, but it's worth it. Did you know the boss wants us to stop giving discounts to small-volume buyers? When you were at Dante's you should order their spumoni. I hear it's the best in the city."

Stan is not deficient in communication skills. He knows that an important message from the boss should not be sandwiched between linguini and spumoni. Stan is using the smokescreen on his rival.[7] Later, when Craig continues his policy of offering discounts to small buyers, he will be criticized by his boss for not following orders. Craig will contend that he never heard about the policy. Stan will insist that he carefully mentioned the new policy to Craig. "Don't you recall: We were also having a discussion about Dante's restaurant."

## BE THE DEPARTMENT WATCHDOG

A department watchdog keeps the boss informed about big problems within the department (such as who is out to backstab the boss, or which individuals have conflicts). The purpose of the watchdog technique is to make you appear loyal to the boss by reporting on the wrongdoings of others. If you are a watchdog, make sure your information is correct or you will soon be written off, appropriately enough, as a SOB. A manager within an insurance company explains why he was forced to recommend that a watchdog in his department be transferred to another kennel:

> At first I trusted Ted. He was a valuable ally. He would tell me if two of my department heads were too much in conflict with each other. I would poke into the matter and try to get things straightened out. Once he told me that one of my managers was saying nasty things about me to the personnel department. I confronted him without identifying the source. The accusations to the personnel department stopped.

Ted told me that Ann, my claims manager, was mailing out her resume to a large number of insurance companies. I asked her if she were discontented with the company, as reflected in her job hunting. Ann told me she hadn't looked for a job in years. Furthermore, she told me to contact any insurance company I wish to see if she had written them. She also invited me to search her desk.

My conclusion was that Ted was using desperate tactics either to get rid of Ann or to impress me that he was highly loyal to me. Whatever the reason, I asked him to resign.

## LET THE COMPETITION HANG

The old adage, "give them enough rope and they will hang themselves," is put to good use in organizational warfare. Specifically, it takes the form of failing to point out a person's errors to facilitate his or her making a big mistake. Rick, a human resources specialist, was hoping that his boss Fred would fade away. His dirty trick was to let Fred make a fool of himself in front of top management. Rick explains how:

> Fred went through a rehearsal with me of his upcoming presentation to management about the problem of managerial obsolescence. Our company was suffering from too many managers who lacked the technical and human relations skills to perform their job properly. In his trial run, Fred kept saying "adolescence." My first reaction was to laugh at the malapropism, but instead I decided to say nothing. After all, was it my job to correct my boss?

> I attended Fred's presentation. He made a royal fool of himself in front of management. When Fred mentioned the term managerial adolescence the second time, the people in attendance roared with laughter. The president said it was better than a problem of managerial senility.

## THREATEN TO GIVE
## NEGATIVE REFERENCES

One way to force a political enemy to resign is to promise a favorable reference if the person complies. Conversely, if he or she does not resign, a strong negative employment reference is promised. According to the *Federal Political Personnel Manual* used during the Nixon administration, there are three key steps in using a frontal assault on an employee victim:[8]

*First,* you promise that the person will leave with honor and with highly favorable recommendations. A farewell luncheon is advisable, perhaps coupled with a department award.

*Second,* you indicate that should the person not accept your offer, and is "forced to resign or retire through regular process or on his own volition," then the person's references given by the department will be much different than if he or she cooperated.

*Third,* there should be no witnesses in the room when you make your offer. A caution is offered to the government official: "This technique should only be used for the timid at heart with a giant ego. This is an extremely dangerous technique and the very fact of your conversation can be used against the department in any subsequent adverse action proceedings."

## COVER UP THE TRUTH

Lying might be the most frequently practiced devious tactic people use to look good. "Bury the truth" is the gambit of the dishonest office and public politician. "Your check is in the mail," "your order has already been shipped," and "_____ left the firm for personal reasons," are such common lies that few people become upset when the truth is uncovered.

A variation of covering up the truth is to fake information to indicate that a project has been successful. Faking success in this manner is particularly important when you are measured on the basis of achieving tangible objectives. At the time of performance review one might make such statements as:

- "Depending on the yardstick used, we have definitely achieved all our milestones."
- "The best I can interpret it, morale has definitely increased over the last quarter."
- "Although we have not quite reached the breakeven point, the rate at which we are losing money has declined substantially."
- "From a long-range perspective, we are well on the road to achieving all our objectives."

## GIVE SELF-SERVING ADVICE

A chilling power play is to give people advice that is geared more toward solving your problem than theirs. If the other party follows your advice, you obtain more power whether or not that power redistribution helps the organization. A case in point is Darwin, who was the manager of a quality control department. He wanted a bigger empire, but felt that advancement opportunities were limited. His master plan was to make a proposal to the company president outlining the importance of a corporate quality assurance department. The purpose of the new department was to guarantee the quality of the machines produced by the company. The quality assurance department would have more power than the quality control department.

Darwin advanced the argument that because quality control reported to manufacturing, it could not be truly objective in its pronouncements about product quality. The CEO bought the idea. As he had hoped, Darwin was appointed the quality assurance director of the corporation. He reported directly to the president, and began with a staff of six people.

The people closest to Darwin got a chuckle out of his new assignment. This was the same Darwin who one year ago said a quality assurance department was redundant providing the quality control group was doing its job properly.

## GIVE SHAM SUPPORT

A manager is often caught in a squeeze between a superior and team members. The boss wants support of a specific program but the team members are opposed to the program. A devious solution to this conflict is for the manager to pretend to support the program. Yet in dealing with team members, the manager behaves in an opposite manner. Such a situation of sham support took place at a bank:

> The corporate office announced a new check-cashing policy. When cashing a customer check, tellers were to obtain a computer reading on their present balance. Tellers were not to cash checks in excess of anyone's present balance. Tellers disliked this policy because they were the ones who bore the brunt of the angry, established customer who considered the procedure an insult. New customers generally accepted checking their balance as a reasonable business practice. Long-term customers who are also large depositors objected very strongly to the policy. The procedure got particularly sticky when a good customer did not have a balance large enough to cover the check to be cashed.

> Terry, the branch manager, openly agreed with the corporate officials that such a policy was long overdue, and that he and the staff would have to learn to live with the policy. When one of the tellers would complain to Terry that the new policy was creating problems, he would wink and say, "Do what you think is best." After a short period of time, very few balance checks were made in the branch.

## UNDERESTIMATE THE COST OF YOUR PROJECT

Many automobile dealers and appliance dealers have been accused of bait-and-switch tactics. A variation of this technique is also used for gaining power on the job. It takes the form of underestimating the true cost of a project you wish to undertake.[9] The organizational bait-and-switch schemer hopes that once the company likes the project, it will agree to go along with the added costs.

Underestimating costs should be done infrequently and selectively; otherwise one loses credibility. An amusing incident is reported by an engineer who worked for a low-ball cost estimator: The first time he submitted a cost estimate to his vice-president, he was asked, "Is this a true estimate or is it a W. H. (his supervisor's initials) estimate?"

## ALLOW A PROJECT TO DIE ON THE VINE ———————————

In some circumstances an executive finds it wise to agree with a plan or program only because disagreeing would precipitate too much of a harangue. So the executive engages in the devious maneuver of saying that the program will receive the go ahead, then plays a stalling game. The executive is always in the process of getting the program implemented.

Gerry, a company president, received a petition from an employee representative that demanded a modern cafeteria in place of the current substandard employee lunchroom. He realized the request was legitimate but thought his company was not in a position at the time to assume such a large capital expenditure.

Concurrent with the employee demand for a better cafeteria was a demand from the board of directors to improve profits. Gerry agreed that a cafeteria should be built. He assigned a committee to study the problem and suggest several different types of cafeterias. Whenever approached about the status of the project, Gerry would point out that roadblocks were being encountered and that many complications had arisen. Two years later, ground was actually broken for the cafeteria at a time when the company's financial situation could absorb the costs of such an improvement. Gerry's stalling tactics had created considerable ill will, but he was able to keep peace with the board of directors and prevent employee discontent from getting out of control.

## TRIGGER A RIVAL'S FLARE-UP ———————————————

As mentioned previously, temper tantrums are viewed negatively in most work places. You can score against your rival if you don't mind the sight of emotional bloodshed. The trick is to provoke your antagonist into a public outburst of anger or rage so others can appreciate his or her immaturity. Before executing this devious stunt, you have to be aware of your rival's most sensitive areas. An incident of this nature took place in a departmental engineering meeting, the purpose of which was to reorganize the department.

Ken, one of the contenders for more responsibility in the department's reorganization, knew that Fritz was also under consideration. Fritz, a self-made engineer with very little formal technical training, had taken some mechanical engineering courses in Germany but did not have an engineering degree. Ken knew that Fritz became indignant any time the subject of importance of formal education for an engineer was discussed. As the group conversation turned to the nature of the changes that would be made, Ken said to Fritz, "Could you tell us something about your background? Some people here may not be familiar with your past experience."

Visibly irritated, Fritz went into a rage. He sputtered and said, "What business is it of anyone's what my background is? When I want people to know about my background, I'll be the first to tell them. Anybody who thinks he is a better engineer than I, please step forward. I learned engineering the hard way. I'm qualified and that is all there is to it."

Fritz looked so weak to the group on the basis of his tirade, that he could not be seriously considered for an administrative assignment in the department's reorganization.

## TRY THE BOGUS INTERDEPARTMENTAL MAIL TRICK

A tactic for the bit player attempting to create a big impression is to appear important because of the people who send him or her mail.[10] One way of implementing this devious trick is to place the name of VIPs on an interdepartmental envelope that is used repeatedly until all the name spaces are filled. Your name is written in the space just above the name of the person who is receiving your message. Directly above your name is the name of a highly influential person. Above that person's name are those of other company bigwigs. (All names have a thin cross-out line through them.) Hopefully, the recipient of your envelope will be impressed by the list of people from whom you receive memos.

One person who tried the bogus interdepartmental envelope routine said it has one pitfall: "Writing down the names of important people is easy. The catch is to find influential people in the company to receive your correspondence. It's no use trying to impress people of less importance than yourself. Yet who can send memos to powerful people if you have no genuine message for them."

A variation of this technique can be used with electronic mail. At the bottom of selected electronic messages, create a distribution list containing the names of key people. The people who receive your electronic mail might be impressed that you are sending copies of this message to such important people. Electronic mail is preferable to paper mail for this caper because there is less hard evidence floating around that you are creating an inflated distribution list. If you should get nailed, simply blame the problem on an "input mistake."

## HOLD A GUN TO MANAGEMENT'S HEAD

A heavy-handed approach to boosting your income or advancing your career is to force management into submitting to your demands by threatening to quit at a crucial stage in the project. Lloyd, a computer science manager who worked for an aerospace firm, was assigned a project with a tight deadline. The customer was the U. S. Air Force. A penalty clause was attached to the contract whereby the company would be fined $2000 for each day the completed project was overdue.

As the project approached its most critical stage, Lloyd asked his boss for a promotion and a $4000 salary increase. He threatened to quit if his demands were not met. The company reluctantly met his demands but asked for his resignation 24 hours after the project was complete.

## FAKE A ROMANTIC INVOLVEMENT

In the past it was widely recognized that some women in every industry would trade sex for political advantage. This technique was possible as long as lecherous males occupied positions of power. In recent years, many fewer women are willing to trade sex in order to advance. One reason is that the human rights revolution has made such behavior seem unnecessary. Many men in power are also hesitant to request sex in exchange for favors. A major reason is that the person in power can readily be charged with sexual harassment, even if the woman proposes the idea of conducting an affair in order to advance her career. Few executives want to face charges of sexual harassment.

A much more effective devious tactic is to fake a romantic involvement with a person in power in order to obtain preferential treatment. If two people are conducting a regular relationship outside of work, and one grants preferential treatment to the other, charges of sexual harassment make little sense. One person helps a friend get promoted—a frequent and generally accepted political arrangement. The promotion facilitated is usually one to another department.

A devious, time-consuming yet workable tactic is to conduct a regular romantic relationship with somebody who can help you achieve an important work goal. We emphasize the term time-consuming because one might invest up to several years and achieve no results. The faking technique is therefore recommended for up to several months. If no additional power is granted on the job as a result of the relationship, the romance-faker can find a plausible reason to end the relationship. Frequently used sign offs to relationships include:

- I guess I needed more space than I thought. It's best that we break up for now.
- Somehow our relationship just isn't working; the magic has disappeared and it bothers me.
- I thought I was ready for this level of intimacy, but I guess I just can't handle it. It's my fault, not yours.
- You're really a great person, but our values mesh so poorly that the only sensible alternative is to end our relationship.
- I'm getting so involved in my career, that I've decided I don't have the energy for both a career and a relationship.

## PLAY DISHONEST GAMES

Faking a romantic interest to gain power might be considered just one game. A game, in this sense, means that one has an ulterior motive for seemingly honest and forthright interaction with another person. Until people get on to your particular game, you are able to exert control over them. Four games frequently played in the office are described below. Many other games are variations of these four.

### The Setup

One way to get rid of the opposition is to set them in a situation where they are likely to look bad or fail completely. The person who fails loses some power and becomes a less threatening rival. Ricardo, a sales representative for computer-based training programs, was establishing a solid record of accomplishment. His commissions were the highest among five other sales reps in the firm. Based on his knowledge of management, his education, and ambition, he was also a strong contender to be promoted to the director of marketing—his boss's job. Fearful that Ricardo might replace him, Len decided to set Ricardo up to look bad.

Len assigned two major, but troubled, accounts to Ricardo. In one account, a newly appointed training director was bitterly opposed to computer-based training. She believed that learning skills by computer was too impersonal. The other account was with a financially troubled company that was intent on slashing costs wherever feasible. As expected, Ricardo performed poorly on both accounts. He was unable to retain the previous level of sales with both of them.

Len noted on Ricardo's performance evaluation, "He does an outstanding sales job on easy-to-sell accounts, but can perform poorly when faced with a tough account. Ricardo appears to need more experience before he can be considered a serious contender for promotion to sales management."

## The Double Cross

The idea underlying the game of double cross is to feed incorrect, or partially correct, information to a rival. By so doing the rival makes mistakes. Tim, a market researcher, wanted his rival to look bad. Consequently, he volunteered to take a number of questionnaires dealing with preferences for different types of bread along with him on a vacation. He contended that the bread preferences of campers would contribute to the scope of the sample. The campers chosen to complete the questionnaire were people who were not concerned about bread and teenagers who wanted to have some fun. Enough of these almost invalid questionnaires were collected to contaminate the results of the rival market researcher's study. The study proved to be valueless, much to the satisfaction of the friendly vacationer.

## Blemish

This is an extremely simple game to play and is widely used by managers to keep team members in line. All the boss has to do is to find some small flaw in every assignment carried out by team members. The game-playing boss stays one up with comments such as "Nancy, you did a great job on that report except for your conclusion. It just didn't seem to fit the body of the report."

## Yes, But

The game of "yes, but" is ideal for a meeting in which the leader wants to prove that the other members are far from being perfect problem solvers. In this way, the leader avoids sharing too much power with the group, and also zaps team members. In its purest form, the game player begins by telling others about a vexing problem. Those who fall for the bait begin to offer advice: "Why don't you . . . ."

To each proposed solution, the experienced game player responds with a plausible reason as to why the proposed solution will not work. The reservation is usually prefaced with "Yes, but . . . ." If the leader can reject every proposed solution, his or her superiority is proven by putting the other players down. Another implication is that if the game player does solve the problem, he or she is a superperson because no one else present could arrive at a worthwhile solution.

## WHEN IN DOUBT, SMILE

A disarming cover-up technique is to smile when confronted with a serious problem, never really committing yourself. Smiling in this context is devious because the person who wants an answer is really being deceived. Here, smiling is used as a holding action until a counterattack can be launched against the person with the audacity to bring a delicate issue to the surface.

Dolores, a certified public accountant, recalls with a mixture of anger and indignation an application of "When in doubt, smile": "We told the president that our audit revealed so many irregularities in the company's books that a favorable report could not be sent to the stockholders. His response was a big smile and a polite thank you. The next day my firm received a registered letter from the president saying that his company decided to switch accounting firms. Consequently, our services would no longer be needed."

# CHAPTER 13

## POLITICAL
## BLUNDERS

An important part of winning at office politics is knowing which actions to avoid. The victorious office politician practices offense, defense, and also senses what actions will lead to disfavor. Most positive tactics and strategies mentioned so far have hinted at what kind of behavior is taboo. If you conduct yourself in a manner opposite to most of the major strategies of office politics you are committing a political blunder. For example, if you upstage your boss instead of supporting him or her in a meeting, your behavior is taboo. Here we concentrate on fourteen blunders that if carried out could create your disadvantage and loss of power. Avoiding blunders in an era of downsizing is very important because managerial and professional workers are often squeezed out for minor reasons.

### SURPRISING THE BOSS

"No surprises, please" is the tacit wish of most bosses, whether the surprise is pleasant or unpleasant. Organizational psychologist H. B. Karp observes that the last thing your boss needs is to be uninformed about topics of major concern to your unit. This is particularly true when the surprise involves bad news. Empathize with your boss's perspective. Suppose at a staff meeting, your boss is confronted by his or her boss who says, "I understand you just lost a million dollar account. What happened?" Your boss is stunned because this is the first time he or she has heard about the lost account.

Not only does your boss have to absorb the shock, an immediate defense is needed to explain what happened. It is going to be difficult for your boss to escape this incident without appearing to be a weak leader.

Good surprises are better than bad surprises, but should also be avoided. Take the same scenario, but this time your boss's boss says, "Congratulations. I just heard you pulled in a one million dollar account." In this case, unless your boss is a good actor, it is going to be difficult to avoid appearing out of touch with what is happening within the unit.[1]

## BYPASSING YOUR BOSS

Protocol is highly valued in multilayered organizations. Going over your boss's head to resolve a problem is a hazardous political ploy. You might carry it off, but if you fail your career can be damaged and your recourse limited. In a court case an oil company's dismissal of a manager was upheld because the manager had repeatedly ignored the chain of command by going over his superior's head directly to the president.[2] Avoid making an end run around your boss unless you are sure this behavior is acceptable.

An important exception is when you are faced with an emergency situation such as working for a highly incompetent or illegally behaving boss. Under those circumstances, a gentle confrontation with your boss's boss might be appropriate. A general principle is that going over your boss's head is taboo, but may be necessary when you get no satisfaction from speaking directly to your boss about an important problem. Asking your boss for permission to speak to a higher-up is another workable alternative. A sneak play will often backfire.

Henry, a telemarketing specialist, wanted to work as an outside sales representative. He took his request to his boss who replied, "That doesn't sound too unreasonable, but I think you should spend another six months on the sales desk before we give serious consideration to your request. This way you can learn a lot more about our product line and handling customers."

Henry did not like what he heard. He was concerned that his boss was stalling. Henry waited for Larry, the branch sales manager, to drop by his department before further pursuing his transfer request. Henry casually asked Larry if he might speak to him for a few moments. Larry obliged, and Henry informed him, "My boss won't let me out of the department, and I want to become an outside sales rep. How do I get past the guy?"

Predictably, Larry simply reported the conversation back to Henry's boss. His boss in turn, called Henry into his office and delivered a straightforward message: "Larry tells me that you think I've locked you up in this department. It so happens that every sales representative in this company has served at least one year on the sales order desk before being assigned an outside territory. In your case, we think you need a little extra seasoning. Larry and I agree that you need a lot more improvement before you are ready for outside selling. Bring up the matter again next year if you are still interested."

Henry's sneaky end run thus backfired. His career was stalled further and his next performance appraisal was more negative than he anticipated.

## BEING DISLOYAL

Being disloyal to one's boss or company is a basic blunder. Disloyalty takes many forms. Attacking your boss publicly, going out of your way to admit that your unit's position on an issue is wrong, or emphasizing the virtues of a competitor's products are common forms of disloyalty. You may not get fired, but one sign of overt disloyalty to your boss and you may fall into permanent disfavor. Seemingly trivial situations are often tip-offs about the depths of your loyalty.

Kristen had a promising career in the human resources department of a giant food company. Working as a wage and salary analyst, Kristen was also assigned a few miscellaneous duties. Among them was the coordination of the annual company-sponsored picnic. Up to 500 people were known to attend the picnic, particularly if the weather was favorable.

Recognizing that a good company person never turns down an assignment considered important to top management, Kris never publicly expressed her true feelings about the annual picnic. Privately, she was less guarded. One day while having lunch in a restaurant with a friend from another company, Kristen was asked how things were going at the office. She replied:

> Yeech, I'm assigned to that dreadful company picnic again. I wish the company would send every employee who wanted a picnic the $16 per head it costs us. That way they could have a cockamamie hamburger and frankfurter roast in their own backyard or balcony. I have never seen so many people make such fools of themselves at once. You get these pasty-looking, out-of-shape people clumsily playing softball and volleyball. Hundreds of children run about shrieking and, at the same time, stuffing themselves with ice cream, soda, and hot dogs.
>
> I don't think the whole affair contributes anything to employee morale. Only creeps attend a company picnic. And here I get the assignment of organizing it every year.

Three days later, Bill, Kristen's boss, sent her a message over the intercom to report to his office immediately. Bill wasted no time with a warmup. Faces reddened, Bill said, "Kris, I'm both disappointed and irritated. A friend of mine overheard your conversation in the restaurant about our annual family picnic for employees. You undoubtedly misunderstood the importance of what the human resources department is trying to do for the company. Perhaps a person of your values should not be a member of the human resources department. Never in my 26 years of corporate experience have I heard such a blatant display of disloyalty to the company. It's too late to pull you off the assignment now, but rest assured you will never be asked to coordinate the company picnic again."

Bill was true to his word. Kristen was never again asked to coordinate the company picnic. Nor was she given any other important assignment in addition to her regular duties. After two years, it became apparent to Kristen that she was going to be a career wage and salary analyst in her company and nothing more. People were promoted around her when she was not even aware that an opening existed. Kristen now faced the decision of looking for employment elsewhere despite her general liking for the company.

## COMPLAINING ABOUT A FORMER BOSS

A blunder of moderate intensity is to make frequent complaints about a former boss. Strident complaining about a former superior might be interpreted as an act of disloyalty. It also suggests that when you move on to another department, you will make similar complaints about your new boss. Complaining about your former boss is also a poor idea when you are trying to be hired into a company. Ron, a financial manager, tells of an interesting experience along these lines:

> I spent six months looking for a new job. I needed a job because I worked for an impossible manager. He did about everything a manager could do wrong. He was tyrannical, dishonest, and played favorites. I couldn't take the pressure any longer.
>
> When I went for a job interview, inevitably they asked me why I was looking for a job. I explained the situation about my incredibly bad boss. They seemed to show some sympathy, but I received no job offers. It dawned on me that I should stop complaining about my situation. I changed my strategy. I told prospective employers that everything was wonderful at my company. I said I was learning a lot from my boss but that I wanted more responsibility. I received two good job offers within 30 days after I changed my tune. The lesson I learned is that people are reluctant to bring a complainer into their organization.

## BEING A PEST ————————————————————————————

In an era when being assertive about your demands is considered a virtue, many people are overzealous in making childlike demands on management. Workers who insist on always being granted every possible benefit or advantage legally coming their way often are viewed as pests. For instance, if you are on the exempt payroll (which means exempt from overtime pay), it would still be possible to receive some premium pay if you work overtime on a systematic basis. However, if you made a plea for overtime pay after working two Saturday mornings, the damage you would do to your reputation would outdo your few small dollars of gain.

Two industrial psychologists conducted extensive research suggesting that refusing to take no for an answer (being a giant pest) can be costly both personally and professionally. People who were persistently assertive were labeled as "shotguns." It was found that such people received lower salaries and poorer performance evaluations than people who were more diplomatic and ingratiating. Shotguns also experienced high levels of job tension and personal stress.[3] We asked a marketing executive for her interpretation of these findings. She replied, "I don't think the findings are surprising. It's nice to get revenge on people who are a pain."

Another form of job pestiness is chronic complaining about work-related matters such as the amount of snow accumulation in the company parking lot, quality of food served in the company cafeteria, benefits package, or the caliber of top management.

Mickey, a cost accountant, was happy to be working for a small company. He believed his talent and hard work would be noticed by top management, giving him a good chance to work his way up the corporate ladder. Mickey's first important misstep occurred when his manager was two months late in formally reviewing Mickey's work performance. He told his boss that by delaying his performance review, his salary increase would automatically be delayed. He was therefore being underpaid for the period of time in which his review was overdue.

Mickey once put in a request for a mileage allowance to cover his expenses for the few days per month that he worked at another company plant located in town. Mickey reasoned that any work assignment not at his regular office must be categorized as authorized travel and compensated for by the company. Mickey's boss recalls the incident that finally branded him as too small-minded to be considered management timber:

One day in July I received a call from Mickey while he was on vacation. He told me that he had taken ill and it seemed that his illness would last two days. He wanted to know if it would be all right to extend his vacation time to make up for the two days of illness in which he could not take advantage of his vacation. Mickey said that his previous company had such a policy. I explained to Mickey that our small company was not General Motors or IBM.

He became adamant about extending his vacation but did consent to return to work on time. Still, he did not let the matter drop. He wrote a memo to the human resources department protesting my decision.

Mickey had a keen legal mind in terms of attempting to squeeze from management everything coming to him. In contrast, his political sensitivity is that of a dullard. The few small advantages he might gain for himself with his demands will not compensate for the blocked opportunities (such as promotions) attributed to his being a pest.

## DISPLAYING A LOOSE TONGUE

At several points we have mentioned that there are no secrets in organizations. Nevertheless, if you want to preserve your reputation as a trusted individual do not let it be known that *you* are a betrayer of confidences. One negative consequence of having a loose tongue is that you may lose the trust of people who count in your career. This is true despite the fact that most other people cannot be trusted to keep secrets.

The political blunder of loose lips does not imply that there are no situations in which candor is beneficial. If you tell a co-worker that her performance is substandard, negative repercussions are unlikely if she tells others of your evaluation. However, if you tell that same person that your boss is incompetent, your message may be relayed back to your boss, causing you trouble.

Priscilla, a talented computer programmer, worked for a software consulting firm that provided services to companies without large programming staffs. After the birth of her second child, Priscilla decided that she needed to spend more time being physically present in her house, and therefore wanted to become a telecommuter. She made this pitch to her boss:

"Over the last two years I have been doing an increasing amount of programming at home, particularly during rush periods. At this point I can keep an eye on my children without my work suffering. What I would like to do is spend Wednesday, Thursday, and Friday afternoons working out of my house. Because my work can be measured quite accurately, you would be able to tell if my working at home was lowering my productivity.

Ted, Priscilla's boss, agreed to the plan, but cautioned her that the arrangement was an informal one and should not be interpreted to mean that this constituted a permanent arrangement. Priscilla expressed her gratitude for the flexibility Ted showed her. Ted describes what happened next:

> About two months later, two more programmers on my staff came to me with similar requests for working out of their homes. One was a woman with a small child, the other was a man who had a particularly long commute to work. I turned both down, but they countered with the argument that Priscilla was being granted the privilege of doing some of her programming at home. They both took this as evidence that our firm had initiated a program of telecommuting.
>
> I asked them what made them think that we had embarked upon a telecommuting program. Each one replied that Priscilla had bragged to them about her new hours. I was so angry with Priscilla that I wanted to fire her. Instead, I passed an edict that all employees were required to work in the office during normal working hours. I explained that it would be a long time before we could seriously consider a telecommuting program.

Priscilla's loose talk ruined a good thing for herself and placed her boss in a compromising position. He did not wish to be seen as a manager who treated his subordinates unequally. Nothing was gained by Priscilla's sharing her good news with her colleagues.

## BEING A NAYSAYER

Some people in an organization are expected to review the plans of others and make critical judgments, often asking them to temper their judgments and curtail spending. A typical scenario is for a marketing person to propose a bold new program of customer service, or beat the drums for a possible new venture. A financial specialist then reviews these ideas and decides they would be a poor investment of company money. Even if it is within your role to pass critical judgment on the proposed plans and dreams of others, don't become the abominable naysayer. If you become branded as one, it could hurt your future. A politically wise person therefore knows when to stop saying no to others' dreams.

Al Neuharth, the founder of *USA Today*, gives us insight into the potential self-destructiveness of being a naysayer.[4] Neuharth was struggling to overcome obstacles in advertising and circulation, and was also fighting internal battles with naysayers. "There was a category of people who were enemies from within," he said. "They took a hell of a lot of my time keeping my backside covered; time that I could have used more productively. There were people in finance who would ask, 'Why do you need 135,000 vending machines? Couldn't it be 99,000?' That was disruptive. The enemy from within didn't keep the job from getting done, but it made it a lot more difficult.'

Much of Neuharth's anger was focused on Doug McCorkindale and his staff in the corporate financial department of Gannett. They had been opposed to the launching of USA Today from the beginning. Even after the newspaper was in print for two years, the financial people were still using stalling tactics. Although McCorkindale and his staff did not do anything to deliberately sabotage USA Today, they took a detached stance that hindered its progress. They treated the paper as Gannett Unit 121—not that different from Unit 120 or Unit 122.

When the corporate financial people did get involved in the newspaper's problems, the approach they took often complicated things rather than resolve the problem. Where USA Today was involved, they would "tie sandbags to their accounting procedures."

The split between believers and nonbelievers had a substantial impact on the careers of two top Gannett executives, Doug McCorkindale and John Curley. McCorkindale had been a wunderkind at Gannett. At age 37 he had become one of the youngest chief financial officers of a Fortune 500 company. In the late 1970s, many insiders believed that McCorkindale was a strong contender to succeed Neuharth as the CEO.

McCorkindale, however, did not seem to grasp the significance of the new venture's news potential. He paid little attention to the extraordinary reaction USA Today had received from readers. Instead he focused on its heavy financial losses. The combination of McCorkindale's opposition and John Curley's enthusiastic support, gave Neuharth the confidence to favor Curley. Several years later when Neuharth retired from Gannett, he appointed Curley to replace him and McCorkindale remained as chief financial officer.

Another form of being a naysayer is to openly criticize your firm or some of its most important people. Such candor may damage your reputation and make you a less desirable team member because most people dislike working with a pessimist. "How do you enjoy working for our firm so far?" said the founder of the CPA firm to Norm, a young accountant who had recently joined the firm. "To tell you the truth," said Norm, "I like everything around here except for some of the management attitudes."

"Could you elaborate on that," requested the founder. "I'm glad to have the opportunity to give you some idea of how I see the firm," said Norm. "I get the feeling that we are suffering from organizational arteriosclerosis. Some policies around here are right out of the Dark Ages. It looks as though an accountant would have to work four years before being given any independent assignments.

"Another problem is wages. We're about five years behind the times with respect to the wages paid junior accountants. With some new blood in top management, I think this firm would be just fine."

Norm's acid comments went beyond the requirements of good sense. He was being too pointed in criticizing policies that obviously the founder of the firm had been instrumental in developing. Norm's insensitive display created conditions whereby he was unlikely to become a person with enough power in the firm to change the conditions he thought needed changing.

## DECLINING AN OFFER FROM
## TOP MANAGEMENT

Consider yourself fortunate when top management makes a request of you individually or as a manager of a group. The surest way to get recognition is to perform well under the scrutiny of a higher-up. Yet there are times when you or your department is already so overburdened with work that more responsibility would test your breaking point. According to a well-accepted principle of time management, under these circumstances one should learn to say no. You thus have to balance saying no against committing the blunder of refusing a request from top management. A simple resolution to the problem can sometimes be found to avoid saying no to top management when saying yes might result in an insufferable burden.

Matt, the executive vice-president of a manufacturing company, was spearheading a move to relocate company facilities. One day he approached Jason, the manager of facilities planning and one of the busiest people in the company. Frank had a request:

> Jason, I know your group is already overloaded, but we need to do a quick feasibility study of taking over an old pasta factory in the center of town. I know that place doesn't look like much, but if we did move some manufacturing down there, we would be able to hire a number of people from the inner city who badly need jobs in their own neighborhood. If we don't make a decision within 60 days, I think the building will be demolished and converted into a parking lot. What can you do about the situation?

Jason's first impulse was to scream that if he asked his people to take on one more project they would quit in protest and he would suffer a nervous breakdown. In lieu of such histrionics, quick-thinking Jason thought of a more politically astute response. "Of course, our group would be more than willing to take on the assignment. It's just a question of a crushing workload at this time. Do you think we could get authorization to subcontract some of our more routine work to an outside consulting engineering firm? In this way we would be able to tackle the pasta factory project.

"You're the professional in this area," responded Matt. "You have my backing to do whatever you want to get this study done. Anybody who gives you a hard time will have to answer directly to me."

By saying yes to the pasta factory feasibility study, Jason had created a strong bond between himself and an influential member of management. Had Jason rejected the recommended feasibility study, he would have violated the taboo of saying no to top management.

## CHALLENGING FOND BELIEFS

Most organizations, profit or nonprofit, have certain fond beliefs that are implicit rather than stated. These beliefs constitute an important part of the organizational culture. Within several months of employment, you should be able to ferret out the nature of these beliefs, possibly from a friendly old-timer. People who are blindly loyal to the organization will rarely admit that these beliefs exist. Nevertheless, their comments often suggest these beliefs are cherished. If you make public statements challenging the folklore of the organization, you may be branded as disloyal or unappreciative. Seven common fond beliefs contribute to the folklore of many organizations, large and small.

1. *We are the best in our field.* Many a hapless organization finds some rationalizations to delude itself into believing that it is the best in its field. A marketing manager might show belief in this statement by a comment such as, "True, our model KFG is priced higher than that of the competition, but the quality-conscious buyer will always choose it. It is the best in the field in the minds of the sophisticated buyer." A president of a mediocre college will often state, "Our graduates are welcomed by employers across the country. We have developed an enviable reputation for the practical mindedness and solid values of our graduates."

2. *People at the top of our organization are wiser and stronger than people at the bottom.* A fascinating children's toy is a closed cylinder containing four sets of marbles, each with a different color. When the toy is inverted the marbles pass through a series of multiholed shelves. The holes for each layer are of slightly different size. Within three minutes the blue marbles lie on the first shelf, the red on the second,

and the white on top. Each shelf then consists of marbles homogeneous in color and size.

Most organizations lead you to believe that their hierarchy is arranged in such a manner: The wisest and most talented people are at the very top, followed by a group of the second-most talented and wise people at the next level, and so on, down to the bottom. You are expected to speak of high ranking people with awe, acknowledging that only those people of superior talent, ambition, and moral character rise to the higher levels. In short, hold dear to the belief that your organization is a pure meritocracy. Only an Innocent Lamb would be iconoclastic about the myth of the meritocracy.

3. *Administrative skill is more valuable than technical skill.* A man who became president of one of the ten largest industrial companies in the work once commented to me, "I wish I knew what to do with all the programmers we have in our company. They are like carpenters. When you need some carpentry done, they are very useful. But if you don't need any carpentry, what do you do with them?"

Business and governmental organizations fondly hold the belief that administrative skill is more valuable than technical skill. In such organizations, one way to slight a rival is to say that the person "is a good technician." Within universities and scientific laboratories, this belief is much more tenuous. Eminent researchers in these two types of organizations might become better known and earn a higher incomes than administrators.

4. *The founder of our firm is (or was) a genius.* Speak with a tone of reverence when you refer to the founder for your firm. Revere that oil painting in the lobby or the president's office depicting the founder is a noble pose. The *true* founder of the firm is often the founder's father who left him or her with $500,000 in cash with which to start a business. The struggling young entrepreneur—with barely enough money for groceries—thus bought a fledgling company and turned it into a great one.

Despite the truth, it can serve you no good to challenge any old-timer's belief that the founder was (or is) a genius. Never make the young professional's impulsive mistake of saying, "If we got the old man to retire, this place would make some real progress." Reserve such impulsiveness for an exit interview after you have secured employment elsewhere.

5. *Most people who leave our organization are people whom we prefer would leave.* The implication of this statement is that the most competent people stay and the least competent people leave. Once an organization passes its rapid growth phase and enters a plateau,

the opposite is more nearly correct. Highly competent and ambitious people tend to leave an organization when they believe that opportunities for advancement are limited.

Even if you are objective enough to praise the virtue of the person who voluntarily leaves the organization, never imply that those who remain are of lesser caliber. One manager in a mammoth corporation was reprimanded by his boss for stating at a management development conference that "Most of the people with guts and talent left us long ago."

6. *Other organizations in our line of work who do things differently are faddists. The fads they have embraced will soon disappear.* Carried to extreme, this belief destroys an organization. If you are concerned about the progress of your firm, you may have to delicately inform the traditionalists around you of new developments by your competitors that need watching. Never rub against the grain of this belief by making the inference that your firm is weak because it ignored the competition.

A marketing manager in a bank noticed that a competitive bank was establishing a program of credit cards for teenagers. When the marketing manager brought this new development to the attention of management, he abrasively said his own bank was falling behind the times. Management countered with the idea that credit cards for teenagers was a fad that would soon fade. Two years later, the bank finally had to join the "fad." Had the marketing manager been more diplomatic about criticizing his own bank when trying to sell a competitor's approach to his bank, he might have emerged a hero. Instead, the bank was slow to participate in this extended approach to customer service.

7. *We are a lean and mean organization in which all the waste and excess has been trimmed away.* In an era of organizational downsizing, most firms like to think of themselves as trim and efficient. Company executives believe that every member of the organization has an important role to play and is productively occupied. In reality, too many high-level managers still spend much time in trivial pursuits. If this were not the case, why wouldn't the organization suffer when several managers voluntarily leave the company and are not replaced?

When the topic of downsizing surfaces, it is a blunder for an insider to suggest openly that the company suffers from management bloat. Instead comment, "We are already running lean and mean, much like a finely tuned machine. However, should we have to trim back even further to enhance earnings, I think we can pull together and survive. Our managers are accustomed to stretching the outer limits of their capabilities."

## DEVIATING TOO FAR FROM CUSTOM

Rigid conformity is no longer a virtue in most successful organizations. The intellectual maverick often forges ahead because of his or her innovativeness and enthusiasm. Despite the merits of this generalization, it is still a political blunder to deviate too far from accepted customs dealing with dress, speech, or courtesy. "Custom" also includes such things as carrying your lunch to work versus eating out. Either practice may reflect current custom. The organizational culture is composed primarily of customs, along with shared beliefs.

Some organizations are more picky regarding customs. In one bank, a junior officer was sent home to change clothing because he appeared at work in a jeans suit. The price one pays for violating custom is to be branded "difficult to get along with," "immature," or "stubborn"—all potentially damaging labels to your career.

Vic, a tax attorney who worked for a prestigious Boston law firm, chose to wear short-sleeve shirts to work during June, July, and August. His supervisor advised him repeatedly that short-sleeve shirts did not constitute proper attire for lawyers in their firm. Vic brushed aside these comments as an infringement on his personal freedom. The supervisor retaliated by placing a note in Vic's file that he was not a good candidate for partnership in the firm because he did not fully respect its values. Several years later, Vic was still not invited into partnership and left the firm to enter into solo practice.

## DUMPING A PERSON WITH CONNECTIONS

"John, I'm sorry," said his boss, Tom. "I've given you four warnings so far. I've told you that if your attendance and punctuality did not improve, I would have to recommend that you be dismissed. What good is an engineering technician who isn't around when we need him? I will recommend to the personnel department that they give you 30 day's severance pay. If you prefer, I will accept your resignation. Let me hear from you by noon tomorrow."

At 10:00 the next morning, John said politely to Tom that he liked his job too much to resign. Tom, in turn, sent a letter to the personnel department recommending that John be fired. One week later, the personnel department had still not acted on Tom's request. During the week John was absent once and late three times. Furious, Tom went to personnel demanding an explanation. The personnel director told him, "You've created quite a problem for us. We've had to turn down your request, but the news leaked to the chairman and he's on our back to get on your back."

"Why?" asked Tom. "Doesn't an engineering manager have the power to recommend that we get rid of a loafer? We're not running a welfare department."

"We may not be running a welfare department," answered the personnel manager, "but neither do we try and fire the nephew of the chairman of the board without first getting his permission."

## BURNING YOUR BRIDGES ════════════════════════════

A blunder in all but the most cut-throat organizations is to create ill will with people who have helped you or employed you in the past. The best known form of bridge burning occurs when a person leaves an employer, either voluntarily or involuntarily. A person who leaves involuntarily is prone to express considerable anger toward those responsible for the dismissal. Linda, a vice-president of marketing at a consumer products company had a basic disagreement with the president about her job. Linda thought she should concentrate on the future of the company's marketing efforts. The president, in contrast, wanted Linda to spend more time dealing with present problems.

The dispute between Linda and the president ended when he asked her to resign. Upset by the incident, Linda wrote a letter to the board of directors accusing the president of being a "short-range thinker, preoccupied with matters that should be taken care of by lower-ranking workers." The president retaliated by inserting a memo in Linda's personnel file stating that she was asked to resign partly because she was a dreamer, who also showed poor judgment in handling differences of opinion. The employment references he gave Linda were so lukewarm that it prevented her from obtaining one position she really wanted. Eight months later Linda finally found a position as a director of marketing at a small competitor. She regrets to this day having left her marketing vice-presidency in a huff.

Another form of bridge burning is to forget the people who helped you move up the ladder.[5] People who behave in this way fail to give credit where it is due. Even worse, some people ruthlessly try to crush those who supported them along the way. Crushing might be having rivals transferred to lesser jobs, abolishing their jobs, or making their life so miserable they resign. With this kind of bridge burning when a crisis comes, there are no allies—hence you become an easy target for a layoff.

Burning bridges with people who helped you advance has another potential negative consequence. The person you offended may later become your boss, thus creating an ideal opportunity for revenge. Bruce, a division president, requested that his financial vice-president, Kurt, be transferred to another division because in his opinion, Kurt lacked flexibility. Kurt objected strongly to the insult and the transfer, but Bruce had his way. Kurt rightfully claimed that he had played a key role in helping Bruce make the division profitable. The company president thought highly of Kurt, and he found a new position for him as the vice-president of finance at another division.

Kurt performed well in his new position, and was promoted to division president when the president resigned 13 months after Kurt joined the division. Four months later, the company decided to merge Kurt's division with Bruce's division. Kurt was appointed as the president of the new merged division. When asked his opinion of what to do with Bruce, Kurt responded, "I think we can find a spot for him as the warehouse manager. The present one is retiring next month."

## EXPENSE ACCOUNT CHISELING

Manipulating expense accounts to personal advantage has become so common a practice that the topic is no longer secretive. Expense account chiseling has become a stronger taboo recently years as companies try to trim costs to stay competitive. One widespread maneuver is: A person charges the organization the price of a full dinner, perhaps $17, eats at a diner for $5, thus making a $12 "profit." (Many diners contribute to this practice by giving out blank receipts that allow the chiseler to create a convenient dinner price. Many business travelers regularly eat at low-priced diners to subsidize their use of escort services.

Sensible office politics suggests that you do not jeopardize your career for the sake of pocketing a few unearned expense-account dollars. Governmental agencies and some large business firms have reduced such temptations by granting employees a standard per diem for travel. A middle manager with big hopes, Luke severely damaged his reputation in his company. His boss tells us what happened:

> Luke attended a five-day trade show in Chicago on company business. He seemed to have profited from the experience because he brought back a few tentative orders and much useful information about new developments in our line of business. One of my chores is to approve the expense-account reports of my group members. Usually the process is quite routine. Unless something is way out of line, I approve it without question.

In this particular case, something struck me as curious. I noted that Luke made an entry for five days of cab fare back and forth from the hotel to the convention center. I used to work in downtown Chicago and I know that the hotel was only one block from the convention headquarters. I confronted Luke with this discrepancy. He said to remove his request for reimbursement, that it must have been a mistake.

Ever since that incident I have never fully trusted Luke. It made me wonder if this discrepancy was only the tip of the iceberg. What was to stop him from being dishonest on a larger scale? Luke resigned from the company about one year after the incident. He must have realized that I no longer had full confidence in his judgment.

## YELLING AT THE BOSS

In most organizations, however justified, one should not yell at the boss. For example, your boss might have dumped all over a report you thought was a masterpiece. If you do commit the blunder of yelling at your boss, reflect on what triggered your anger. Was your ego bruised? Are you enraged about having to work for such an ungrateful boss? Whatever the reason, apologize, then act as if it never happened. You can apologize in person, in writing, or use a combination of both if you really blew your lid. Don't try to justify your behavior even if you think the boss deserved the shout.

Co-workers who witnessed your tantrum may not be willing to let the incident die. If you can't escape probing about the incident, simply inform curious co-workers that you were wrong to yell at the boss, and that you wish the incident never happened.

The next time you are being pushed to the breaking point by your boss, try an on-the-spot relaxation technique to relieve the tension. Exhale, count to ten, bath your face in water, or take a walk around the block. Then write a note to your boss, seal it in an envelope, and don't mail it. Most likely, you will be happy the next day that the envelope stayed in your desk.[6]

## AN INDISCREETLY CONDUCTED
## OFFICE ROMANCE

Despite all the concern about sexual harassment and sexually transmitted diseases, office romances are on the rise. According to researcher Cate Bower, the office is becoming the primary place for people to form relationships.[7] Several reasons underlie this upsurge in finding love on the job. More men and women work as equals today than in the past, thus allowing more friendships to form. Another factor is that so many career-minded people are so preoccupied with their careers that they have limited time for pursuing romance off the job. Searching for dates or mates on the job can be a real time saver. Many people prefer to prospect on the job because they know more about their potential dates than if they met through personal ads, introduction services, bars, and resorts. Furthermore, blind dates arranged through friends have fallen into disfavor.

Despite the popularity of office romances, many employers discourage them. Executives of 100 large corporations were surveyed by an executive recruiting firm. Asked about their company's general attitude toward office romances, approximately two-thirds ignored them, one-fiftieth encouraged them, while one-third discouraged them.[8] Top management and co-workers may have negative attitudes toward office romances for a mixture of valid and invalid reasons.

Above all the office romance may interfere with productivity. The two lovers may waste a lot of time conversing, flirting, and engaging in romantic activities including love making. Productivity also suffers when co-workers gossip about a couple conducting an office romance.

An analysis of several hundred office romances revealed that the partners involved do less effective work, fail to meet deadlines and other commitments, and make foolish errors.[9] Another problem is that co-workers become anxious when a superior and subordinate become involved. Others feel angry, jealous, and worried that the boss's lover will receive unequal treatment.

Some companies have formal policies against office liaisons because of the possible conflict of interest. For example, a person in the payroll department involved with someone from another department might divulge sensitive salary information to his or her lover. Or a top executive might leak information about a major shakeup to his or her office paramour. In many situations, a company will fire or reassign one of the co-workers involved in the romance.

The corporate treasurer in one company told his girlfriend, an office supervisor, about a pending takeover of the company. Acting on this information, the supervisor invested all of her savings, and a home equity loan into the company stock. The stock increased 25 percent in value in three months, and the supervisor made a quick profit. A jealous co-worker reported the incident to the company president. Nothing was proved, but both the treasurer and his girlfriend were placed under a distrustful, watchful eye.

What should one then do if a great romance, or even an ego-building brief fling, happens along on the job? Keep these suggestions in mind for conducting an indiscreet office romance:[10]

- Act very professional with each other. Avoid walking around holding hands or kissing, patting each other's rumps (especially if your lover is of the same sex), sending sweet notes through electronic mails, or making frequent telephone calls to each other.

- Maintain a high level of productivity so others cannot accuse your romance of lowering your productivity.

- Don't arrive or leave with your lover, and don't discuss your glorious weekend trysts with co-workers.

- Don't sit next to each other in a staff meeting and play footsies or rub each other's necks.

- Be especially discreet if you are on a business trip together. Each take your own room, perhaps even on a different floor or in a different hotel, if there are other company members present.

- Have lunch together only occasionally; lunch with other co-workers more frequently than with each other.

- Consider keeping your relationship secret unless it's a committed relationship. It's usually not worth being the subject of office gossip for a short-term relationship.

- Remember that a great relationship is worth more than one mediocre job. If the two of you are from the same department, one of you should request a transfer to another distant department or division.

- Remember that a mediocre relationship is worth less than one great job. Don't proceed beyond the first date if you are convinced that the relationship will never last more than three weeks. Why commit an organizational taboo for a brief surge of excitement, followed by a sense of embarrassment and defeat?

# CHAPTER 14

## OUTWITTING
## DIFFICULT
## PEOPLE

The executive director of a community agency was attending a management development program about goal setting and planning. Toward the end of the session, her irritation had risen to the point whereby she blurted, "Okay, you've been telling us all day about how to establish goals and plans. If you're talking about doing that with rational people, that's so easy, we don't need your help. Do us a favor by telling us how to deal with the crazies. Those are the people who make doing my job strenuous."

The executive director just quoted points to one of the most important truths about the workplace. It's relatively easy to work with normal, healthy, well-motivated people. The difficult ones—including your boss—create most problems.

Difficult people include anybody in the workplace who create problems for others because of their personality, attitudes, and values. Frequent types of difficult people—about 5 percent of the workforce—include liars, cheats, totalitarians, backstabbers, sexual harassers, and manipulators. Dullards are not included because there is very little they can do about their condition. Neither are substance abusers nor compulsive gamblers classified as difficult people. Aside from poor performance, they do not go out of their way to make life miserable for others.

Dealing with difficult people is part of winning at office politics because the tactics required exceed typical human relations or management techniques. First we'll classify ineffective bosses, study how to handle them, and then move on to co-workers and lower-ranking people.

## DIFFERENT TYPES OF
## INEFFECTIVE BOSSES

Many meritable approaches have been used to classify difficult bosses. The most systematic approach was used by two Center for Creative Leadership researchers, who based their ten types of intolerable bosses on interviews with 73 experienced managers. These types of intolerable bosses, listed in order of how frequently they are found, are given next:[1] (to this list we have added the Jekyll and Hyde boss):

### Snakes in the Grass

"Snakes" lack basic integrity. They lie, fail to keep their word, use authority to extort confidential information, create compromising situations for their team members, or otherwise cannot be trusted. One such snake kept a dossier of mistakes by each subordinate and would often use the information to the person's disadvantage.

### Attilas

Intolerable bosses in this group are not slowed down by being wrong, and are offended if others make decisions or look good in any way. Unlike a modern boss, they attempt to take power and freedom away from group members.

### Heel Grinders

This type of boss forgets that group members are human beings desiring at least a modicum of respect. A heel grinder mistreats others by belittling, demeaning, and humiliating them. Such managers are unforgiving of mistakes and intolerant of people who do not share the same view of the world as they do.

### Egotists

Bosses who already know everything, won't listen, and parade their pomposity are egotists. One egotistical boss would play the ruthless game of bringing up a seemingly insurmountable problem and then disparage every solution proposed by team members. When they ran out of suggested solutions, he would present them with the solution he had in mind all along.

## Dodgers

Bosses of this type are intolerable because they shirk responsibility, and are either unable or unwilling to make decisions. One Dodger was found who openly announced that he would never make a decision unless absolutely forced to.

## Business Incompetents

Incompetent bosses do not understand their job and are afraid to admit it. Their incompetence leads them into defensiveness because they worry about being discovered. When asked an opinion on a technical matter, they often say, "What do you think?" or "Use your best judgment. It would be a disservice to you if I solved your problems."

## Detail Drones

Those who manage strictly by the book, savor petty details, and enjoy making big issues out of little ones are detail drones. It is difficult to please these Drones because they can always find one more detail that requires improvement. Their favorite game is Blemish.

## Unrespecteds

This type of intolerable boss manages to lose the respect of virtually all those around him or her. Often the disrespect comes from being both incompetent, obnoxious, and insincere.

## Slobs

Bosses in this category have personal habits, appearance, or prejudices that are intolerable to others. One reputed Slob is forever munching food, even while talking to a group member in the halls. Another Slob takes frequent naps on a cot in her office.

## Personality Clasher

Bosses of this type have personality clashes with many different team members and co-workers. Somehow they have negative chemistry with most subordinates, and the subordinates never seem to know why.

It is natural to wonder how intolerable bosses hold on to their jobs in an era when organizations are supposed to demand so much productivity from everybody. However intolerable and incompetent many of these bosses are, they have enough political skill to be on the good side of one or more powerful people. Consequently, they can remain on the job much longer than common sense would predict.

### Dr. Jekyll and Mr. (or Ms.) Hyde

Jekyll and Hyde managers have a split personality. When dealing with superiors, customers, or clients, they are pleasant, engaging people—much like Dr. Jekyll. Yet when carrying out the role of a boss they become tyrannical—much like Hyde. Employees who deviate from Mr. or Ms. Hyde's expectation are publicly reprimanded. The basic strategy of these individuals is never to allow superiors or peers to see their Mr. or Ms. Hyde side. Consequently, superiors tend not to believe a subordinate who complains that this manager is being tyrannical.[2]

## COPING WITH AN INCOMPETENT BOSS ⸻⸻⸻⸻⸻⸻

Strictly speaking, an incompetent boss is not a difficult person because the person may not have any personality or attitude problem. Nevertheless, such a boss can make life difficult for you if you cannot find a way around the incompetence. To prevent being dragged down by an incompetent boss implement the tactics described next.

### Show Compassion

Political advantage can be gained when working for a poorly performing boss if one acts meritoriously. Instead of finding subtle ways of exposing the poorly performing boss, it is preferable to offer professional and emotional support. Although the boss may not admit to others that you bailed him or her out, your contribution probably will be recognized. Your help when needed may prompt your boss to give you an outstanding performance evaluation.

### Fortify Your Boss's Weakness

You may secretly delight in seeing your ineffective boss fail, but the failure could hurt your career. If your department fails, it could harm your reputation to be associated with a losing effort. If there is something that your boss is doing wrong that could ultimately shroud you in failure, intervene before the situation gets out of control.

Andrea, a product development specialist, and her boss Roy knew that their product, a heavy-duty curling iron, was fighting for its life. The company decided to jettison all new products that did not show promise of becoming profitable in the near future. Roy was scheduled to make a presentation to management in ten days to defend the continued funding for their curling iron. Andrea knew that Roy's weakest skill was making oral presentations under pressure. She reasoned that with Roy making the presentation, the curling iron was headed toward a quick grave.

Confident of her own ability to make an oral presentation to top management, Andrea approached her boss: "Roy, I'm willing to put my head on the block over the deluxe curling iron. I'd welcome the opportunity to make the presentation to top management about our need for more advertising money. With you at the meeting to fortify me with any additional facts I might need, I know we can swing management around to our way of thinking."

Roy replied, "Good idea Andrea. I have a few commitments coming up in the next ten days that would make it difficult for me to make the presentation. I'm sure you'll do a first-rate job. I doubt I could do a better job myself."

## Take over Part of Your Boss's Job

A pernicious form of incompetent boss is one who jealously guards exciting portions of the job and delegates only its routine aspects. As one frustrated middle manager expressed it, "Nobody has a worse boss as far as making life interesting for subordinates. He wouldn't delegate a decent assignment if he were in a body cast."

To the organizational climber, the nondelegator is a curse. Until you get meaningful assignments, you can't improve your competence. Worse, until you perform well on important assignments, you are unable to establish a solid reputation. There is a way to combat the problem of a boss who won't let go. Begin by looking for a task currently performed by your boss that you are confident you can handle well. One reason many nondelegators hold on to important work in their department is that they have an underlying fear that anybody else who attempts to perform such work will fail. If the team member fails to perform satisfactorily, the boss will suffer because he or she is still accountable for the results of the unit.

After you have identified tasks your boss is performing that you know you can perform well, select an appropriate time to ask for the takeover. An ideal time is when your boss is overwhelmed with work and beginning to falter because of a burdensome workload. Move tentatively by asking a question such as, "My schedule is clear enough whereby I can handle an extra assignment. Would it be helpful if I took over those past due accounts you've been working on?"

### Sell Yourself to Other Managers

A basic tactic for getting away from any type of undesirable boss is to promote yourself and your credentials to other managers in the organization. Make others aware of your accomplishments by volunteering for committee work or getting your name in the company newsletter. In essence, you would be applying the technique of "find a sponsor." Another method is to make personal contacts by joining company teams or clubs.

While you are developing your contacts, speak to your boss about a transfer. Point out that although you are satisfied with your job, you value broad experience at this point in your career. A related approach is to speak to the human resources department about your dilemma. Suggest that you could make a bigger contribution if you worked for a superior who gave you more responsibility. However, never say anything derogatory about your boss. Also, check your intuition to see if the human resources specialist can be trusted not to get you in trouble with your boss.

## COPING WITH AN INTOLERABLE BOSS

An intolerable boss is one who is difficult to work with because of personality, attitude, and values. Such a boss is likely to be touchier than one who is incompetent for reasons such as lacking the appropriate skills. If you try a combination of the coping tactics described below, you are much more likely to come out ahead than if you ignored the problem of an intolerable boss.

### Schedule a Communication Session

A good starting point in coping with an intolerable boss is to schedule a meeting to discuss job responsibilities. Explain that certain areas of responsibility require clarification. Prepare for the meeting by listing questions or subjects for clarification. For example, suppose you are a sales manager and your boss has been berating you for not spending enough time with major accounts. You might point out that you have also been instructed by him or her to spend more time recruiting and training sales representatives. Ask tactfully which activity should receive more attention—calling on major customers or working with the sales reps. A session of this type, according to Henry Rogers, should lessen the tensions between you tremendously.[3]

## Relate Your Criticism to Job Performance

You may arrive at a point where it is necessary to criticize an intolerable boss. Extra tact is needed for those who are extrasensitive to criticism. Explain how your boss's behavior, however well intended, is hampering your job performance. A case in point took place in a retail store chain. The loss-prevention managers in each store were supervised by a zone manager, who in many ways behaved in a counterproductive manner. One of his worst practices was to swear at loss-prevention managers (LPMs) when losses were above average at their store.

One of the LPMs decided that she could no longer tolerate her boss's tirades. Confronting him after one of the verbal reprimands, she said calmly, "Karl, when you swear and scream at me, it interferes with my ability to perform my job well. My records show that I make my biggest mistakes in counting inventory soon after you have screamed at me. Especially when it's not even my fault." Karl did temper his criticism in the future.

## Talk to Your Boss as a Group

Many people would feel uneasy and self-conscious conducting a one-on-one meeting with an intolerable boss. If other team members share your opinion that the boss is intolerable, try to organize a group discussion with your boss. Although there may be more security in confronting the boss as a group, it is still important to be tactful and relate your concerns to job performance.

Business psychologists Mardy Grothe and Peter Wylie point to several advantages of meeting as a group. The group meeting can have a more powerful impact than an individual meeting. Some employees would rather let a problem fester than face an individual meeting. There is also safety in numbers; it is more difficult for a boss to be vindictive toward the entire department! Be cautious, however, that it is not apparent that you are the leader who brought along others just to support your position.[4]

## Send Indirect Feedback

Indirect feedback is a method for sending a message to your boss so the boss will not be able to identify the source, and therefore retaliate. This highly effective method works simply.[5] A company president had become obsessed with trimming costs, to the point of making life miserable for many employees. He would march through the office and factory challenging both large and small expenses.

One day while inspecting the company garage he took an air-pressure gauge from his pocket and proceeded to measure the air pressure on the tires of several vehicles. After his inspection was completed he berated the transportation supervisor publicly for allowing tires to be underinflated: "Don't you realize that underinflated tires can lower gas mileage up to 5 percent. We're wasting precious pennies on every trip." Another time he ordered Judy, an office manager, to take discarded paper from a wastebasket and convert it into scrap paper for office memos.

Judy later composed a letter to the president on a neighbor's electronic typewriter, to avoid tracing the letter back to herself. The letter read,

> Dear Mr. Calhoun:
>
> I realize that our great company needs to avoid spending unnecessary money. But I think you are going overboard. You have become a tyrannical cost cutter. Besides, if you want to cut costs so much, why don't you and the other executives cancel your company-paid club memberships. How about taking a 5 percent cut in pay, and stop paying for so many company meals with your expense account?"
>
> > Sincerely,
> >
> > Concerned employee

The letter appeared to have an impact. The president became less picayune about cost cutting, and announced that the top management planned to keep all business travel to a minimum.

## Send Public Indirect Feedback

A more outrageous method of getting an outrageous boss to change his or her intolerable behavior is to make a public statement of what you think the boss is doing wrong. As with the "private" example above, bosses are unable to get even with any one in particular because the source of the feedback is anonymous. Here are a couple of examples of the group feedback technique, offered by Grothe and Wiley:[6]

> The "problem boss of the month" award. Using this technique, employees surreptitiously post the monthly award on a company bulletin board or send it through electronic mail to all people on the system. The offending boss is named as well as what he or she did to earn the award.

Employees develop stickers with appropriate messages they want to get through to their boss. Examples include, "Watch out, I bite when I'm not having a perfect day." or "Yes, I'm the boss but I'm so disorganized I don't know what I'm doing." These stickers are affixed to the boss's door, car window, and office furniture.

## Going over Your Boss's Head

When the situation is serious and other tactics have failed, you may have to confer with your boss's boss about the former's intolerable behavior. Be aware that most of the time, upper management will side with your boss, and your conversation will be reported back to your boss. Consequently, your boss will hold a grudge against you. In extreme cases of managerial ineffectiveness or intolerable behavior, upper management usually has some inclination that a problem exists. They may welcome corroborative evidence.

Marlene worked for Ned, a hostile and unappreciative manager. When group members did something right, he almost never offered praise or accomplishment. When an employee accomplished something outstanding such as winning a large suggestion award, Ned's most lavish compliment was "Your contribution has been noted." When a group member did something that did not fit Ned's standards, he would berate them and insult their intelligence. Furthermore, he would write a memo to the file stating that the employee was a "poor corporate citizen."

Marlene took the initiative to discuss the problem with Ned several times. His only response was to insult her for not being tough enough to handle the demands of her job. Marlene's final step was to ask for a private discussion with Ned's boss. The vice-president listened sympathetically, and said he would investigate the problem further. Several weeks later, Ned was given a one-month leave of absence from the company and assigned to work with a counselor to help understand and control his behavior.

## Don't Leave in a Huff

One of the political blunders described earlier was burning your bridges. The temptation to burn bridges is greatest when one quits an organization to escape an intolerable boss. If you complain too vociferously about your boss to executives or to a member of the personnel department, officials in other companies might be given the word that you are a loud mouth who is not to be trusted. Being placed on an industry "bad list" can place a low ceiling on your career.

## HOW TO TELL THE BOSS WHEN
## HE OR SHE IS WRONG

Generally it's not politically astute to say "No" to your boss. Yet it may be necessary for your long-range good to express disagreement when a boss makes a request that either won't work or is unethical. You could be branded as having done something wrong even though it was your boss who ordered your actions. The wisdom of a group of experienced managers who pooled for suggestions on how to disagree with the boss without creating too much conflict. These suggestions are even more important with a difficult boss, because that person is more likely to be thin skinned. Consider these approaches to telling the boss he or she is wrong:[7]

1. *Express doubt in the form of a question.* Instead of flatly disagreeing with your boss, ask a question that will allow him or her to make the final decision. An example: Your boss wants you to get all the orders shipped before the end of the month, which is two days away. You know the task is almost impossible. Pose the question "Do you think it would be better to postpone shipping a few of the orders until next month? We've had a fantastic quarter, and we could use a few shipments to start the next quarter off right."

2. *Suggest the assignment be referred to a more appropriate person.* Instead of saying that a request doesn't fit into your job description, offer this kind of analysis: "O.K. I'll take on the assignment, but Gloria does this kind of thing regularly in her job. She has already established the contacts and could probably get quicker results for you. Do you mind if I ask her to place these calls?" In this way you are not refusing an assignment, but referring it to a more appropriate person.

3. *Ask your boss to explain the idea's merits.* Instead of saying that the boss's idea won't work and you have a better idea, say something like, "Help me to understand why we are going to do it this way." In this way you are not implying that you will not do it your boss's way. After your boss has explained the reasons, suggest that you are willing to comply but that you know a way that might be faster, cheaper, or more efficient. A manager recalled that once he presented an idea to a boss who didn't think it would work. A few days later the manager came back with the same idea restated, acting like it was original. Although the manager rejected the idea at first, it had registered in her brain.

4. *State your ethical code.* If you adhere to an ethical code of behavior you may find yourself in conflict with many difficult bosses. Despite all the lip service paid to the importance of business ethics, many executives push ethics right to the borderline of illegal behavior. From the viewpoint of some executives, high ethics are too expensive.

   A manager found that in one job, lying to vendors was the norm. Before he was ever asked to commit an ethical violation, he took the initiative to confront the issue with his boss: "I notice it is common practice here to tell vendors that payments are coming when they are not. I have a personal code that prevents me from doing that. I want you to know so you won't unknowingly put me into a position where I can't do what you want." Notice that the manager neither demanded that the boss change his ethic or apologized for his own code. Nevertheless, proceed cautiously because some difficult bosses might become defensive when approached in such a way about ethics.

## COPING WITH TOO MANY BOSSES

Having more than one boss often results in being caught between conflicting assignments. Such a predicament has become typical because so many people are assigned to projects and taskforces in addition to their regular job. Also, you might have an administrative boss along with a functional boss (one in your area of specialty). Here is how it works: A purchasing manager reports to a plant manager, who in turn reports to a vice-president. But she also reports to the group director of purchasing, who reports to the same vice-president. The group director of purchasing and the plant manager then become co-workers on the same staff. When the group director tells the purchasing manager to seek the lowest bid whenever possible, but the plant manager begs for high quality parts, whose instructions should she follow?

   A manager who gives you directions that conflict with those given you by another boss is not a "difficult person" in the ordinary sense. Nevertheless, the net effect is the same because you may wind up bitterly frustrated. If you find yourself being pulled in two directions at once, give serious thought to the following tactics:[8]

1. *Explain that you have been given conflicting assignments.* Your boss might ask you to tackle an assignment that conflicts with an assignment given by another boss. For example, you can't visit two

different company locations at the same time. When caught in such a potential squeeze, you might request, "I'd be happy to take on this assignment, but first you and Dave (the other boss) will have to come to an agreement as to whose project gets priority. I'm concerned that I don't have the authority to drop Dave's project."

2. *Focus on the problem, not the people.* It could be politically unwise to focus blame on either manager for your predicament. Instead, explain that you cannot execute your assignment well because your priorities are not clear. Alan C. Filley recommends that you outline the problem on a flip chart or chalkboard. In this way the two superiors are looking at the problem rather than combatting each other.

3. *Focus on the costs of not confronting the problem.* If you emphasize your own conflicts, you may be perceived as a complainer or someone who cannot handle multiple demands. To appear strong, and help get the problem resolved, try a statement such as, "If I receive opposing signals, there may be costly delays on this project." Then pull together some figures that support your position. Don't lie, but use a little creative cost analysis if necessary.

4. *Ask open-ended questions.* Avoid being dogmatic about the right or wrong way to resolve the problem of conflicting directions. Such an approach results in one boss being perceived as a winner, and the other a loser. A recommended approach is to ask a question such as "How can we solve this?" or "What can we do?" Observe that the use of "we" helps create a feeling of teamwork, and it is very desirable to be perceived as a team player.

5. *Don't run away from the problem.* It usually makes more career sense to attempt to resolve the issue of multiple bosses than to change jobs. Resolving the problem will help build your reputation as a person who can overcome adversity.

6. *Be tolerant—the confusion may not last.* Consultant Jewell G. Westerman observes that intentional ambiguity sometimes exists when management is trying to resolve issues. Top management may be trying to decide on new reporting relationships. Another possibility is that one of your bosses won't be around much longer. Therefore, cool it and see what happens.

## GETTING THE CREDIT YOU DESERVE

Imagine you have been assigned the job of making the arrangements for a company meeting. Everything runs so smoothly that at the banquet your boss is praised for his or her fine job of arranging the meeting. You smoulder while the boss accepts all the praise without mentioning that you did all the work. Not receiving appropriate credit for a job well done or for a useful idea is an omnipresent problem.

Before taking action remember that in one sense your boss deserves some of the credit. Managers are responsible for the accomplishments and failures of their subordinates. Your boss had the good sense to delegate the task to the right person, or to select you as a team member. To get the credit you deserve for your ideas and accomplishments, try these tactics:[9]

1. *Supply the pieces, but let others fit them together.* Suppose, for example, you were talking to your boss's boss at the company meeting mentioned above. You might state, "I'm happy that people enjoyed this meeting. I enjoyed being given so much responsibility for helping our department arrange this meeting." Your boss's boss may get the point without your disputing what your boss said.

2. *Try a discreet confrontation.* The boss who is taking credit for your accomplishments may not realize that you are being slighted. A quiet conversation about the issue could prevent recurrences. You might gently ask, for example, "At what point do I get recognition for doing an assigned task well?" I noticed that my name was not mentioned when our department received credit for setting up a new billing system. (It was you who did 95 percent of the work on the system.)

3. *Take preventive measures.* A sensible way to receive credit for your accomplishments is to let others know of your efforts *while* you are doing the work. This is more effective than looking for recognition after your boss has already taken credit for your accomplishments. Casually let others know what you are doing, including your boss's boss and other key people. In this way you will not sound immodest or aggressive—you are only talking about your work.

4. *Present a valid reason for seeking recognition.* By explaining why you want recognition, you will not seem unduly ambitious or pushy to your boss. You might say, "I am trying to succeed in this company. It would help me to document my performance. Would it therefore be possible for my name to also appear on the report of the new billing system?"

## DEALING WITH VERBAL BULLIES

Another type of difficult person is the verbal bully, as described by Suzette Haden Elgin.[10] Verbal bullying is akin to physical bullying, and can be carried out by your boss or a co-worker. Instead of physical force, the bully uses language to inflict damage. Verbal bullies resort to nasty insults for several reasons. Bullying may be an ingrained part of some people's personality; it is their traditional way of dealing with people. Bullies sometimes persist in their behavior because it satisfies their sadistic impulses. Another reason is that the bully may be treating you the same way he or she is being treated by somebody else. The victim gets even by striking out at a safer target. Unfortunately the safer target might be you.

Here are several bullying statements:

- "If *really* wanted to become a manager, you would put more effort into your job."
- "Don't you even care that our costs are skyrocketing while our sales are flat?"
- "How can you call yourself a manager when you can't even get your own act together?"
- "Everybody *knows* that hardly anybody wants to work for you for a long time."

To handle the verbal bully, advises Elgin, take action and short-circuit the attacker. Begin by analyzing the verbal assault. The first part of each sentence usually contains a negative presupposition. ("If you *really* want to become a manager" implies that you are not serious about becoming a manager.) The second part of each sentence is a direct accusation which acts as bait. If you respond to the bait, you are accepting the negative supposition, and you are embroiled in conflict—just what the bully wanted.

Every verbal attack has two parts: (1) what the bully expects you to go for and what gets you in trouble (the bait) and (2) the true attack (the presupposition). Respond to the real attack rather than the bait, as shown by this example:

The bully says, "If you *really* wanted to become a manager, you would put more effort into your job." If you respond by saying, "What do you mean? I put a lot of effort into my job," you've fallen for the bait. Instead, respond to the negative presupposition: If you *really* wanted to become a manager." Come back with a question, "When did you start thinking that I am not interested in becoming a manager." By avoiding the bait and responding neutrally to the real attack, your attacker is disarmed and defused. He or she expected another type of response.

The general approach is to avoid the bait and respond to the presupposition with a neutral statement. Your retort will throw the verbal bully offbalance and save you from an emotionally exhausting argument.

## DEALING WITH MANIPULATORS ═══════════════════

Manipulators are in every office, and every Machiavellian engages in some manipulation. A manipulator attempts to influence people and circumstances and gain benefits through dishonest and often unfair means.[11] For example, an employee might imply that if given a promotion his father's company might become a good customer of your employer. Or, an employee might fake tears and talk about heavy child-rearing responsibilities when asked to work every other Saturday.

Manipulative employees often attempt to dupe managers into disclosing information, making a decision favorable to them, or bending the rules against their best judgment. An example: Kevin had recently joined the local purchasing manager's association. He wanted to impress other members by bringing an executive from his company as a guest. He approached the vice-president of marketing and casually mentioned that the next meeting of the purchasing managers could prove quite worthwhile.

Kevin hinted that several members might be present who were interested in finding a new vendor (for one of the company's products). The vice-president asked to attend the meeting with Kevin, and Kevin impressed many of his associates with the fact that he brought the vice-president of marketing along.

At the end of the evening, the vice-president inquired as to when he was going to meet the interested purchasing managers. Kevin replied, "Somehow those two purchasing people must have changed their minds about coming at the last moment. However, I wouldn't be surprised if they called you later this week."

According to George Bell, if manipulation goes unchecked, it sets off a series of negative events: The manipulators discover threat scheming is effective, so they continue to manipulate. Team members who witness the manipulation lose respect for the deceived manager. Seeing that dishonesty is rewarded, the more honest employees become discouraged. A few of the most moralistic might quit. Some onlookers get the message that manipulation works, so they give it a try. To combat this problem, Bell has identified common manipulative tactics, and appropriate countermaneuvers:[12]

### Bandwagon Technique

The employee informs you that "all other company managers" are doing something such as granting personal time off to visit a lawyer. If you do not go along with this request, you are therefore wrong. The way to handle the bandwagon thrust is to close the case, and not being manipulated into defending your position. An effective response here would be,

"What you say may be true for other managers, but here we don't allow personal time off for appointments with lawyers."

### "Always" Technique

The manipulator might say to you, "I always get assigned to the least important projects." Here the manipulator attempts to gain control of the discussion by indirectly prompting you to respond to a general accusation. The antidote is to demand specifics. Begin by asking "What do you mean by always?" and continue digging until you reach the person's true concern. By forcing the person to be quite specific, you remove all the ammunition. You might probe, for example, "How many times have you been assigned an unimportant project?" The employee might only be able to point to one or two poor assignments.

### Threats

The most brazen of manipulators will sometimes use threats in order to intimidate and gain control. A manipulator might see you as passive and therefore threaten to go over your head, quit, or disclose embarrassing information about you. To deal with manipulative threats, stand firm and repeat your position as many times as necessary. "No matter how you threaten to retaliate, I will not change my evaluation of your performance." When the manipulator realizes that you will not succumb to threats, he or she will usually back off.

### Psychological Sabotage

Highly manipulative team members may attempt to control your actions by purposely making you look bad or delaying on the completion of work projects. These methods of psychological sabotage include intentionally overlooking, losing, or forgetting things intended to impede your productivity. Another form of this type of subversion is to ignore an important problem, such as not bringing a consistent customer complaint to your attention. The swiftest antidote to psychological sabotage is to invoke discipline, such as a written reprimand or suspension.

### Biased Reporting

In order to achieve his or her way, the employee presents information that supports an issue while omitting opposing data. For example, the employee brags about shipments in order to achieve a bigger budget, but does not refer to the high rate of customer returns. To handle this type of manipulation, reserve judgment until you have investigated an unfamiliar situation further.

In all of the above manipulations, the villain has been a team member. You can also be subject to manipulation from superiors and co-workers. Generally, the same countermaneuvers can be used against people at and above your level. For example, if your boss threatens to discipline you for requesting vacation during a busy season, you might say repeatedly, "I have made no unusual demands on the company before, and it is my right to take some vacation during the fourth quarter."

## DEALING WITH THE DISSENTER

Constructive criticism is welcome in any healthy organization. Nevertheless, there are "pills" out there who raise dissent just to breed conflict and make life miserable for the manager. A vociferous dissenter can embarrass you and erode your power. A critical employee who has the good of the organization in mind can be handled without much difficulty. Explain to the person that sometimes he or she appears too harsh and disgruntled and that it would be better to express criticism privately rather than at a staff meeting.

In contrast, a worker who repeatedly creates animosity by deceiving, lying, and accusing probably wants to achieve personal gain rather than be helpful. The most effective way to deal with this type of person, observes Ralph H. Kilmann, is to warn the employee unequivocally that such behavior will not be tolerated.[13] Back up a spoken message with a stiff letter.

A gentler approach can be used with less difficult dissenters. Help them realize that it is preferable to express strong disagreement within the confines of their organizational unit. Point out that the unit could be weakened if outsiders perceived substantial intragroup disagreement. Also discuss the value of constructive rather than destructive criticism.

## NEUTRALIZING SNIPERS

An organizational sniper makes nasty attacks on another person. If the sniper is aiming at you, handle that person as you would most other types of difficult people. Confront him or her about the attacks being made behind your back, and don't take the insult personally. If you are a manager, you may receive a request from a team member who is intimidated by the sniper. A supervisor of yours might say, "Jessica is bad-mouthing me to other employees, and I don't know what to do. I've told her about the problem, but she denies everything."

If you recognize that your supervisor is stressed out and decide to intervene in the situation, here are several approaches to take.[14] The first thing to do is verify the incident. Confront the source in a manner such as, "Word has gotten back to me that you've been making derogatory remarks about your supervisor behind his back. Is that true?"

Next, explain the consequences of the sniping. Jessica may admit the charge, but dispute the details. ("I never said he was an incompetent supervisor, just inexperienced.") Inform Jessica that malicious gossip can damage others and interfere with productivity. The next step is to request an apology. Point out that the supervisor would be justified in filing a formal complaint, but that a written apology might take care of the matter.

Finally, continue to monitor the situation. One apology may not end the sniping. Investigate to see if the employee's disruptive behavior persists. If the sniping continues, advise the errant employee that disciplinary action is next.

By giving the sniper an opportunity to make amends, you have shown your fairness, thus lowering the chance that he or she will talk behind your back. You've also demonstrated your concern about the well-being of the department. The offender now knows that he or she is in trouble if the sniping continues.

## HANDLING THE PERSONALITY QUIRKS OF OTHERS

Both on and off the job, many people have personality quirks that are difficult to deal with. The manager is usually in the best position to help these people control their quirks so that job performance does not suffer. As a co-worker, however, you can also prevent the quirks of others from getting the best of you.

Your best defense, either as a manager or a co-worker, is to show sympathy for employees with these quirks without submitting to all of their demands. Be understanding even if you do not find all of their behavior acceptable. Here are four frequently observed personality quirks, along with a counterthrust for each one:[15]

1. *The person who has a strong need to be correct.* Employees with this quirk set up situations so that people who disagree with them are made to look naive or foolish. For example, "All well-educated and intelligent people believe as I do that this is the way we should go on this project. If anybody disagrees, please speak up now." (You can sympathize in this manner: "I recognize, Jennifer, that you

research everything before reaching an opinion, and that you are usually right. Nevertheless, I want to point out another perspective on this problem."

2. *The person who has a strong need for attention, whether the attention be positive or negative.* Attention seekers may shout louder than others, play the role of the office clown, or tell co-workers all their woes. (You can sympathize in this manner: "We all know, Gus, that you like to be in the limelight. You do deserve our attention, but now it's Amy's turn to speak.)

3. *The person who resents control, direction, or advice from others.* Employees with this quirk are so oversensitive to being controlled that they misinterpret hints as suggestions, and orders as direct challenges to their intelligence and self-worth. (You might express sympathy—yet still get through to a co-worker with this quirk by a statement such as: "Carlos, I know you like to be your own person. I admire you for it, but I have a teeny suggestion that could strengthen the graphics that you just put together.")

4. *The person who views everything management does as negative and also questions every action in an attempt to uncover the true reason behind it.* Employees with this quirk create doubts in other workers similar to the ones they exhibit, thus contributing to morale problems.[16] (You can sympathize with cynics and perhaps help them achieve insight into their behavior with a comment such as: "I appreciate your analytical attitude Faye. But did you ever think that management does sometimes do something kind or generous? Is management really always the villain?"

## NEGOTIATING WITH DIFFICULT PEOPLE ━━━━━━━

Many times in a successful business career you will have to negotiate with a difficult opposing party. The negotiations could take place in contexts such as buying and selling, attempting to get the size budget you need, obtaining the right salary increase, or preventing your department from being decimated during a downsizing. If the difficult negotiator has more formal authority than you, getting your fair share of resources will be extra difficult. As in any negotiations, you will have to use such techniques as play hard to get, compromise, and show that you are bargaining in good faith by beginning with a plausible initial demand or offer. However, negotiating with a difficult person also requires a few special tactics:[17]

1. *Get the other side's attention.* Until you get the difficult person's attention you are wasting time. Shock the other side out of his or her self-centered mental set and let them know you intend to be taken seriously. The way to get the other's attention is to set a boundary as to how much you will tolerate. Create a negative consequence that far outweighs whatever benefit the other side is deriving from his or her current actions.

   Your boundary will vary with the situation. Yet the basic idea is to figure out what is important enough to get the opponent's attention. Ann was negotiating a budget to establish a company child-care facility. The budget offered by the vice-president for human resources was totally inadequate according to Ann's perception. She countered, "If you don't come up with a sensible outlay for the center, I'll personally let employees know that the company is paying only lip-service to the needs of working parents. Word will leak out to the press, and you'll be sorry."

   One week later, the vice-president begrudgingly renegotiated. This time he began with a sensible offer that was within 80 percent of the funds Ann thought would be needed. The on-premises day-care center was built, and the vice-president now brags about the company's concern for the problems of working parents. (Difficult people like to receive all the credit they can get.)

2. *Insist on playing by the rules.* Difficult people will attempt to force you to accept unreasonable agreements in a negotiating session. Instead of succumbing to the pressure, insist on fair rules for both the negotiating process and the final settlement. Assume you are negotiating a price for freelance work that your firm would be performing for another company. The negotiator is intent on making you grovel. You might say, "I would rather not conduct business with you than accept a payment for our services that results in a loss for our company. Conduct some research of your own. I doubt any other company could do the work for the price you offer."

3. *Put the ball in their court.* When the opposing party takes extreme stands and makes unreasonable demands, ask that person to explain the logic behind his or her position. You might say, "In order to understand your demand, I need to understand how you arrived at those points. Why do you need $25,000 for redecorating your office? Most people can get the job done for $8000." When the person answers you, demands that cannot be justified lose their credibility.

## GIVE RECOGNITION AND AFFECTION
## TO NEEDY PEOPLE ━━━━━━━━━━━━━━━━━━━━━━━━━━

Difficult people, like misbehaving children, are sometimes crying out for attention. By giving them recognition and affection, their counterproductive behavior will *sometimes* cease. If their negative behavior is a product of a deeper-rooted problem, recognition and affection alone will not work. Other actions need to be taken. The most direct strategy is to give the misbehaving individual attention and affection. If the difficult behavior stops, you have found the proper antidote. The successful resolution of such a problem took place in a photo studio:

> Rich, one of the commercial photographers, had an annoying habit of interrupting the conversation of other people during staff meetings or with customers. In one instance during negotiations with an important customer, Rich blurted, "I'm the local expert on nature photographs. If you want anything done along those lines, your best bet would be for me to shoot the job."

> Rich's boss Mandy then tried spending a few minutes each week telling Rich how great a photographer he was and how much the studio needed him (not a lie because Rich was talented and valuable). In addition, Mandy arranged for Rich to have some of his work put on display at a local photo show.

> Rich changed his behavior toward that of a more subdued and contented worker. In the words of one of his colleagues, "I can't understand what happened to Rich. He's become much easier to live with."

# CHAPTER 15

## BOUNCING BACK
## FROM CAREER
## ADVERSITY

Playing it cool and rolling with the punches when adversity strikes is part of playing sensible office politics. Rebounding from setback is also an essential aspect of career management because almost every successful person encounters some job adversity. The manager who rants, raves, pounds the chest, or throws a temper tantrum when things don't go as planned is paving the way for harder times ahead.

Nobody always wins on the job. At one time or another, you will be passed over for promotion, demoted, fired, chastised, sent to corporate Siberia, or abandoned by a favorite subordinate. If you are self-employed, add bankruptcy to the list of potential adversities. If you are currently facing a career setback, the strategies described in this chapter could help you make a comeback. Also, it might be worthwhile to think in advance how you will handle the next downside episode in your career. Only a lucky few can sidestep adversity in the turbulent 1990s.

### RECOGNIZE WHEN YOU ARE
### BEING DUMPED

A beginning point in overcoming career adversity is to recognize when adversity strikes. Sometimes the adversity is subtle, such as when you are being eased out of power. Large organizations in particular are adept at removing from the mainstream people whose contributions are no longer valued but who are considered immune from being dismissed.

Valuable contributors, too, are sometimes shunted to the side rather than fired. The valuable contributor may get dumped because he or she was the victim of an internal power struggle. Whether a particular assignment is a dumping ground depends on the organization and the specific circumstances.

An ambitious manager was assigned to an important project simply because his manager no longer wanted a troublemaker in the department. The project itself was important, but one manager used it as a dumping ground. In organizations with large corporate staffs, it is not uncommon to place an out-of-power manager into an internal consulting role. (These shenanigans may take place when the firm is attempting to trim costs.) The displaced manager may carry an impressive job title, but requests for consultation with the former manager are infrequent. In other instances, an internal consultant may be making an important contribution. In short, you have to recognize whether your new assignment means you are being groomed for even bigger responsibilities or simply being cast aside.

Communications (public relations) manager Welby was the son of the largest stockholder in the company. His boss, the president, was displeased with Welby's performance but unwilling to undertake the delicate task of asking a person of his connections to resign. According to Welby's boss, he is deficient in this manner:

> Welby is a difficult person to have on your staff. The only communications people who stay working for him are docile, noncreative types. Anybody with a little spirit or talent quits after about a year. They claim he tries to make all the decisions and rejects any idea that departs from the ordinary. Another problem is that we receive a lot of muted complaints from the public relations firm that supplements the efforts of our internal staff. The owner once told me that Welby rejects all their good ideas. They figure that they cannot serve our corporation well if they are not treated as professionals.

Welby's boss found a temporary solution to his problem. Welby was appointed to a taskforce that would study the future of the corporation. It would attempt to answer such questions as, "What products and services should we be offering in the next two decades?" "What demands will be made on us by the public?" "What new laws will be influencing us the most?" Because of the importance of his project, Welby was released from his responsibilities as director of corporate communications.

When asked if Welby could make a contribution to such an important assignment, his boss responded: "No problem. I just want him to coordinate activities and collate the opinions and information that the committee digs up. He'll be more of a recording secretary and historian than somebody who provides input to the project. His tendency to veto ideas won't hurt on this effort."

Welby's attitude toward his new role was positive at first: "I welcome the opportunity to serve the corporation in this important capacity. I envision the job as integrating the information from a wide variety of sources. We will leave no stone unturned in uncovering information that will help us adapt to the demands of the future." Later, when Welby recognized his opinions were neither welcomed nor valued, he realized he was being cast aside. His response was to sell off some family stock and open his own one-person communications consulting firm.

## DEAL WITH THE EMOTIONAL TURMOIL
## ASSOCIATED WITH ADVERSITY

Adversity has enormous emotional consequences. The emotional impact of severe job adversity can rival the loss of a personal relationship or attending the funeral of a close friend. The stress from adversity leads to a cycle of adversity followed by stress, followed by more adversity. A vending machine sales representative who lost his major account, explains the cycle in these terms:

> During a period in which times were mediocre in our industry, I lost my largest account. It had been generating about 30 percent of my commissions. Losing the account really hurt. The company had been on my back and accused me of being negligent. I even heard hints that I might lose my job. Another problem was that I couldn't withstand the loss of 30 percent of my commissions and still cover all my living expenses.
>
> I panicked a little which only made things worse. I started pushing my smaller accounts to install more vending machines than they needed. Soon a few complaints were trickling back to the office. I was getting in deeper trouble. Two of the receptionists at my accounts even told me that I was looking bad. I felt I was going downhill faster than I could handle.

The tactics described next can help you cope better with the emotional aspects of adversity.

### Accept the Reality of Your Problem

Dealing constructively with the emotional aspects of crisis does not mean denying the reality of your adversity. A resilient manager or professional is likely to self-admit: "My problems are real; my crisis is a biggie; I'm hurting inside, and I deserve to hurt; life is temporarily a mess; after I lick my wounds, I'm going to do something about the mess." Unless your boss is unusually supportive and can respect confidences, do not communicate these feelings to him or her. Keep them to yourself or share them with a confidant.

### Do Not Take the Setback Personally

When adversity strikes, many people take the setback personally. They feel they are being punished for wrongdoing or incompetence. In the midst of adversity it is sometimes difficult to recognize that you have been set back because of outside forces such as political favoritism. Remember that setbacks are inevitable as long as you are taking some risks in your career. Not personalizing setbacks helps reduce some of its emotional sting.

John William Poduska, Sr., chairman of the board of Apollo Computer, was fired three times before he founded his own company. Although he was personally hurt by being fired, it was a constructive force toward his founding Apollo. Poduska was not overly concerned about the financial consequences of entrepreneurship: "The dollar risk of failure is almost nothing," he says. In a new business backed by venture capital, the investors assume the financial loss. Poduska believes that you can anticipate some failure. "It's like skiing," he says. "If you ski all day and don't fall once, then you're not skiing hard enough."[1]

### Treat Failure as a Temporary Setback

Many successful people do not even use the labels "failure" or "defeat" to describe their adversities. Instead, they treat failure as a temporary setback on the journey toward what they really want to accomplish. Treating failure as a temporary setback is more than a semantic game. By looking at adversity in a more favorable light, its emotional intensity is decreased. Just as failure or rejection is treated only as a temporary setback, stumbling blocks are treated as steppingstones.[2]

Aside from the inner peace achieved by regarding failure as a temporary setback, it also enhances one's image. Instead of saying to your boss, "I failed. My biggest account went with the competition," say, "I've got a tough challenge ahead of me. I have to replace my biggest account. They went with the competition."

### Don't Panic

A sense of panic overcomes many people when they experience emotional trauma. Panicking is understandable because it is a normal human response to trauma; however, because panic is normal it does not make it useful. Larry, a sales promotion manager in consumer products, provides an example of the counterproductivity of panic.

> The company Larry worked for was bought by an industrial company whose managers were not highly knowledgeable about consumer products. After six months of leaving Larry's company intact, the acquiring company decided to reduce costs and increase profits by consolidating some departments. The vice-president of administration of the parent company decided that the consumer products company did not need both an advertising and a sales promotion department. Shortly thereafter an edict was issued that advertising and sales promotion departments would be consolidated.
>
> Larry was filled with a sense of panic. Although his job was not terminated, he would be demoted to a sales promotion coordinator. In his new job he would perform less administrative work but would still spearhead sales promotions such as consumer rebate programs. To ward off what he perceived as a career disaster, Larry sprung into action. He wrote the company president a letter explaining why the company needed a separate sales promotion department; he sent messages throughout the company's electronic mail system criticizing the merits of the consolidation. Larry also attempted to discredit the advertising manager to top management, hoping that he would be appointed as the manager of the new combined department.
>
> Larry's panic action almost led to his dismissal. He calmed down in time to save his job but not his reputation. A note was placed in his personnel files that he should no longer be considered promotable to management.

How could Larry have handled this situation better, considering that strong emotions were shaping his actions? Most importantly, he should have said to himself, "I'm experiencing heavy stress now, so I had better watch out. People can do crazy things when they are stressed out." He also might have listened to his wife who asked him repeatedly, "Are you sure you are all right?" If Larry had overcome his sense of panic, he could have begun the long hard route back of performing well in his new position in order to qualify for a future promotion. Or he could have performed well while patiently searching for a new position in another company.

## Get Help from Your Support Network

Asked how he put the pieces back together after his company went bankrupt, and his wife skipped out on him—both in the same month— Art replied, "It was rough, but I talked over my problems with my best friend and my children. Even though it seemed that the rest of the world had deserted me, they hadn't. Talking to my friend and my kids gave me the strength to figure out what to do next."

Art's matter-of-fact statement sums up years of research and observations about overcoming setback: relying on others for emotional support is necessary to survive the trauma. After interviewing hundreds of people about how they bounced back from both career and personal setbacks, we reached an important conclusion: Getting emotional support from family members and friends helps people overcome the emotional turmoil associated with adversity. No other technique was even a close second to talking out your problems with a trusted listener.

## WELCOME THAT ROCK BOTTOM FEELING

Wanda, the owner and president of a company, turned to her assistant, and noted with a tone of optimism. "Cheer up Mary. It looks like we have finally hit the bottom of the barrel. From now on things are going to get better. We have laid off half of our workforce, our business has shrunk 45 percent this year, and our new computerized inventory system has caused endless problems.

"The future looks better. Business conditions are improving, and the people still in the company are mostly our better employees. It's a good feeling to know that things won't get any worse."

Wanda is doing more than wishful thinking. She is developing an attitude that is almost indispensable in bouncing back from adversity. When you are truly convinced that your problems have bottomed out, you are preparing yourself emotionally for a recovery. That "nothing-else-can-go-wrong feeling" helps you mobilize your energy for your counterattack. Similarly, hurricane victims experience a sense of relief when the winds have died down to normal, and they can begin shoveling away the debris.

## TAKE CRITICISM GRACEFULLY

Handling criticism makes you appear unflappable—a highly desirable characteristic of a winner. A Machiavellian, it must be cautioned, may take criticism gracefully but is probably plotting revenge while appearing to be graceful.

Agreeing totally or partially with the criticism made of you is generally the most effective way of appearing graceful when under assault. Part of a criticizer's fun is to watch you squirm and become angry when under attack. Take away that fun and the criticizer feels ineffective. Another advantage of agreeing with criticism is that it may appear you have nothing about which to feel guilty or defensive. Some specific examples:

CRITIC:    You didn't even listen to what our client was saying. If you don't listen to the clients, how can we ever retain their business?

YOU:       You're right. I could do a better job of listening to clients. I'll keep that in mind next time I speak to a client.

CRITIC:    I notice your expense account shows a charge to the company for a double occupancy rate at the Sheraton. Do you expect the company to pay for your sleeping with another person while on a business trip?

YOU:       I did charge the company the double occupancy rate. It's very restful when you're away on a trip to bring along company. Would you like me to write you a check for the difference in price between a single and a double room?

CRITIC:    A bank representative called today saying you are three months behind in your car payments. How do you explain that?

YOU:       They are probably right. I think I owe them for May, June, and July. I'm thinking of making a jumbo four-month payment in August.

## PLAN YOUR COMEBACK

After the emotional turmoil associated with a crisis is adequately controlled, it is time to focus on the rational, analytical side of your comeback. A constructive, detached perspective is that career adversity is but another major business problem to be solved. If you apply the same planned approach to overcoming your setback as you would to a vexing job problem, a workable solution will emerge. Planning helps you figure out what went wrong and sketch out an improved path for the future.

### Analyze the Reasons Behind Your Setback

A carefully planned comeback begins with an analysis of why the reversal took place. Discovering the setback causes is also the logical way to learn from your past mistakes. Getting an accurate answer may not be easy, but it could help avoiding a similar setback later. Despite all that has been preached in recent years about the importance of honesty and openness in management, you may still have to probe to get an authentic answer as to why you were thrust backward. Gary, passed over for promotion, did just that.

"How can I tell my wife?" he thought to himself. "It's the third time I've been passed over for a regional managership. Each time the company told me that I would be warmly considered for the next promotion."

Gary's reflection was followed by sullenness and then finally by action. He demanded a conference with his boss, Ed, to discuss why he was passed over again. With some hesitation, Ed did agree to review the reasons why Gary was not selected for the position of regional manager.

> "Your work performance has been fine," began Ed. "It's just a few little things that made us decide to give somebody else a chance this time around. It's not too much to worry about."
>
> "Ed, that is precisely why I came to see you. It *is* something to worry about. Is there something holding me back in the company? I must know. Maybe it's something I can correct. What are these little things you refer to?"
>
> "Gary, this may hurt, but you asked for it. My boss and I think you are rude to top management. It's this rudeness that is keeping you back."
>
> "I don't recall being rude to anybody. Could you give me a couple of examples?"
>
> "The best example I can think of is when Marv Finney, the executive vice-president, joined us for lunch. When we were returning from lunch, you barged through the revolving door ahead of him. During his presentation you clipped your nails. Just like you do in other meetings, you interrupted him before he had a chance to finish what he was saying. Do you get the point? We think you need more polish."

Gary thought the company was being needlessly picayune. Yet he developed a clear understanding of what aspects of his behavior were holding him back. Gary could quit in a huff or conform to what the company thought constituted good manners in dealing with higher management. By taking the latter course of action, Gary's hopes of becoming a regional manager were reignited. At no sacrifice to his sense of morality, Gary did become more deferent toward higher-ranking executives. Fourteen months later, a new region was formed and Gary was selected to become a regional manager.

### Analyze Who You Are and What You Want

The early stages of a comeback represent an excellent opportunity for taking a candid look at who you really are and what you want out of your career. Many people who have been fired or laid off take the opportunity to switch careers. Lola, an administrative assistant to a top executive, faced an emotional crisis when her boss was forced into early retirement. She identified more with him than with the company, and was so angry with the organization that she quit. While walking the streets two days after she quit, Lola realized that she really didn't want to be somebody's assistant again. It was time for her to occupy center stage. Her solution was to sell interior designs for offices.[3]

## Engage in Creative Problem Solving

An inescapable part of planning a comeback is to solve your problem. Typically an off-the-shelf-solution is not available. Instead, you need to search for creative alternatives. In review, a widely used problem-solving method follows these steps:

1. *Diagnose and clarify the problem.* What is the real problem created by your adversity? Are you suffering losses in income, self-esteem, job satisfaction, personal relationships, and well-being (or any combination of the preceding)?

2. *Search for creative alternatives.* What options are open? To be resilient you may have to find a creative solution to your problem. Lola, for example, decided to sell creative designs for offices.

3. *Make a choice.* If your career crisis is to be resolved, you must make a tough decision at some point.

4. *Develop an action plan and implement.* What steps must be taken to get out of this mess? For Lola, it meant talking to dozens of people in the office interiors field to find suitable employment.

5. *Evaluate outcomes.* Did your recovery plan work or will you have to try another alternative? Within six months you will usually know if you made a workable choice.

## Reestablish the Rhythm in Your Life

People become more dependent than they realize on the natural rhythm of their lives—the daily routines they establish for themselves.[4] Commuting, answering mail, logging in on the computer, attending staff meetings, drinking coffee, telephoning friends, are but among the many activities managers and professionals need to feel healthy and alert.

People have different activities in their routine, but most accomplished people have a consistent pattern to their daily activities. Break these routines for a considerable period of time, and the individual is liable to suffer depression. The lesson to be learned from the importance of life rhythms is to do what is necessary to maintain your daily pattern of living when faced with adversity. For example, job counselors urge the unemployed to arise at a regular time every day and get to work conducting their job campaign. Telephone calls (toll free) to business associates should also be conducted as regularly as possible. Groom yourself everyday so you don't look as if you are falling apart.

## SWING INTO CONSTRUCTION ACTION

As implied in the problem-solving method just described, the all-purpose principle of managing adversity is to take direct and constructive action toward resolving your problem. Taking direct action is particularly applicable to obtaining immediate results to help you weather a crisis. A company that does mass mailings for magazines and advertisers committed a major blooper in handling one of its largest accounts: It sent out hundreds of pieces of mail with a mismatch between the addresses on the envelopes and letters. For instance, an envelope addressed Ms. Dolores Wing might contain a letter addressed to Ms. Evelyn Wingate. The error was caused by an unintentional human mistake of mixing up the order of a large batch of envelopes. Nevertheless, the client was irate.

The president of the letter-mailing company was concerned about both losing his major account and tarnishing the reputation of the quality of his services. The president took immediate action to rectify the situation. At no expense to the client, he ran a corrected mailing of the envelopes and letters. The following insert was enclosed in each envelope:

> Recently you received a letter which is the same as the letter enclosed. You may have noticed that your name and the address on the letter and envelope did not match. This was due to an inadvertent mistake by one of the employees when matching and inserting the letter.
>
> We regret any inconvenience this may have caused and we apologize for the mistake.
>
> Sincerely,
>
> Apex Letter Company

The client was happy with the patchwork done by the letter company, and not one addressee lodged a complaint about the mix-up. Admitting one's mistakes, and then rectifying it, is an effective way of getting quick results to combat adversity.

## BE WILLING TO ACCEPT SOME JOB SLIPPAGE

Many managers and professionals who face the adversity of job loss have difficulty finding a comparable position. Although there is a shortage of people to fill low-paying service jobs, and some well-paying technical jobs, managers and professionals are in ample supply. Many unemployed managers and professionals who want to return to work quickly must therefore accept some job slippage—another name for being underemployed.

What happened to Jim, a 54-year old former plant manager, illustrates the problem. As a result of his dedication to his job, Jim rose from a production worker to a manager responsible for the operation of all the plant's assembly lines. He was proud of the status he achieved as a manager. Jim was laid off after 38 years with the same company because of a corporate merger. Jim steadily searched for a job for five months, assisted by GROW, a support group for middle-age job seekers. "After the fifth month I felt like I was washed out," he said. "You wake up in the morning and you wonder why you bother to get up. You just don't feel like you're a whole person. Maybe it was just the way I was brought up, but sometimes I don't feel I deserve to eat at the table."

During the five-month search, Jim said he applied for 350 jobs from production management—his area of expertise—to private detective work. At one point he made 75 phone calls in two days of searching for a job. Jim finally found a position as a sales associate in a home-improvement supply store at one-third his former pay. However, his problems were not over. Jim laments, "The job was a killer. We were expected to help set up the entire store in addition to taking care of customers. After working here a few months, a buddy of mine who worked for a small manufacturing company helped me get hired as a production coordinator."

Four years later Jim was still with the same company and had been promoted to purchasing agent. His salary is now 60 percent of what it was before he was laid off. Jim sizes up his job in these terms: "It isn't perfect, but at least I'm working. A lot of people my age who were laid off, never found anything."[5]

Jim's story doesn't have a magnificently happy ending, but at least by accepting job slippage he preserved his self-respect and met his financial obligations.

## RECOVER THROUGH POSITIVE THINKING

Great comebacks are fueled with large amounts of optimism and positive thinking; and lesser comebacks are fueled with less amounts of optimism and positive thinking. In contrast, failed comebacks are often fueled by pessimism and negative thinking. The contribution of optimism and positive thinking to overcoming adversity is reflected in many cliches and aphorisms. Among the most uplifting are:

- Don't give up.
- Keep trying.
- You can succeed if you try.
- This too will pass.
- Happiness is just around the corner.
- Wishing will make it so.
- If you think you can, you can.
- Goals make wishes come true.
- Keep up your spirits.
- Believe in yourself when the going gets rough.

Simply repeating these cliches may not be sufficient to engineer a comeback. It is also important to be convinced by some facts about optimism and positive thinking, and to understand how others have used these forces to bounce back from adversity.

## The Healing Power of Optimism

The power of positive thinking might be even more effective than Norman Vincent Peale believed. Peale and many others have touted the contribution of optimism to leading a successful life. Psychological research has shown that optimism has a specific beneficial effect on a person's health and ability to overcome the stress associated with adversity.[6]

"If I were lost at sea in a lifeboat, I'd much rather be stuck with an optimist than a pessimist," claims Michael Scheier. "I would expect an optimist to be able to row, and for a long period of time, because that person believes it will pay off. A pessimist would lay back in the sun, taking it easy because he or she would say, 'What's the use?'"

Closely related, Charles Carver observes that "People's optimistic or pessimistic orientations are not just faces we display to the world. They have lots of implications for what people do, how they feel, and potentially they may have important health implications."

Psychologist Martin Seligman says that the link between optimism and performance is basically persistence. "Optimists keep at it; pessimists give up and fail, even if they have equal talent. And because optimists are always hopeful about the outcome, they tend to take more risks and try new things."[7]

## Make an Optimistic Interpretation of Events

A specific way to use optimism and positive thinking to energize a comeback is to make an optimistic interpretation of events that others might interpret pessimistically. At a late stage in his career, John Z. DeLorean provided a classic example of optimistically interpreting events. As most business people recall, DeLorean left a promising career at General Motors Corporation in 1973. He devoted much of his work time during the next 15 years building the DeLorean Motor Co., and then handling its bankruptcy.

During the time DeLorean was spearheading his automobile company, he had been on trial for cocaine dealing, racketeering, and fraud. The company went bankrupt, his wife left him, and he fell behind in his mortgage payments. Despite these problems, in 1987 DeLorean received back $22 million in assets and the right to continue to manufacture under the name DeLorean Motor Co. By that time he had plans underway to build a high-performance, limited edition auto designed and built in West Germany. Called the "Isdera," the car was to have a Mercedes-Benz engine and a Porsche suspension. Before proceeding further with the car, DeLorean needed to raise large sums of money from investors— a feat he was confident he could accomplish.

When asked how he felt about all the difficulties he had faced in the years since he had left General Motors, DeLorean who was age 62 at the time, said: "That was just a stage I went through. The main accomplishments in my life are still ahead of me."[8]

Undoubtedly, DeLorean's optimistic interpretation of past events helped give him the courage to attempt a comeback. His optimistic spirit is also part of his charisma that enables DeLorean to attract investors despite his shaky financial record.

Making optimistic interpretations of events that could readily be deemed pessimistic involves developing the right mental set. Studying the optimistic interpretations of events listed below will help you develop the right mental set for interpreting events optimistically:

| *ADVERSE CIRCUMSTANCE* | *POSSIBLE OPTIMISTIC INTERPRETATION* |
| --- | --- |
| You get fired. | Here is an opportunity to find a job I really want or start a new career. |
| You lose out in a political power play for the third time in your career. | The other players in this game are much better office politicians. Since I'm not very political, I should concentrate more on technical than managerial work. |
| The last 38 leads you pursued refused to buy. | Not to worry. In this business, you have to call on lots of prospects to make one sale. I'm one step closer to a yes. |

| *ADVERSE CIRCUMSTANCE* | *POSSIBLE OPTIMISTIC INTERPRETATION* |
|---|---|
| You take over as general manager of a division that is losing large amounts of money. | After studying the situation for a month you inform your staff, "Don't be discouraged. My analysis is that we are a smooth-functioning organization internally. We therefore have the capacity to be very successful. The only thing lacking right now is orders. Once we get some orders, we will be able to handle them quite well." |

## Visualize a Happy Outcome

One of the most important new techniques in mental training is visualization—imagining the outcome you want to achieve in order to facilitate making it happen. Visualization is widely used to improve sports performance. In playing tennis, for example, you select a spot on the opponent's court and then visualize the ball you hit landing precisely on that spot. In playing basketball, you similarly visualize the ball going through the hoop or a pass getting to the right teammate. The process is also referred to as *feedforward* because the person creates powerful images of a desired future reality—before actually trying to achieve that reality.[9]

Visualization can also be used as a method of overcoming career adversity, and moving yourself toward peak performance. The process is uncomplicated. Imagine yourself having a successful outcome to your current adverse circumstances. Carefully imagine the minute details of your comeback victory, such as a judge reading a verdict that you the defendant are not at fault. Furthermore, the plaintiff must pay you the damages.

Imagine yourself sitting in a vice-presidential office, while in the interim you are scrambling around searching for a new position in the company because the project you headed has completed its mission. Think of yourself delivering a flawless presentation to the budget committee, justifying the budget you need to continue operating.

Although visualization is uncomplicated, do not confuse it with idle daydreaming. Visualization projects you into such a specific set of actions that it serves as a pinpointed goal toward which to direct your mental and physical energy. The process also works because it elevates your self-confidence by giving you a taste of the victory you seek.

## COOPERATE WITH THE VICTOR ━━━━━━━━━━━━

A political street fighter will not quickly throw in the towel, but once he or she is temporarily set back, the victor will get the person's full cooperation. To do otherwise is foolish. Holding a grudge against a boss or co-workers who has won over you in a political fray can only worsen your situation. One of the most damaging labels to be tagged with is *uncooperative*. An equally bad reputation to acquire is one of being *difficult to supervise*.

Faith and Gail both wanted to become department manager Hal's personal assistant. Gail was selected for the position, a decision that upset Faith. She told a friend from another department in the company, "Gail got the job because she's forever playing up to Hal's ego. She laughs at his worst jokes, serves him coffee, and compliments him on his creative ability. She is not nearly as efficient as I, but because of politics, she was given the job."

After Faith was promoted, a minor reorganization took place within the department. All word-processing technicians and support personnel reported to Faith. Gail seethed in anger. She expressed her indignity by dragging her heels when Faith gave her assignments. In contrast, if she thought an assignment came directly from the department manager or a supervisor in the department, Gail was her usual efficient self. Faith reported Gail's poor cooperation to Hal.

Hal counseled Gail about the importance of cooperation, but she responded with stone-faced silence. After two more months of negative attitudes on Gail's part (but not substandard work), a four-way conference was held among Gail, the personnel manager, Faith, and Hal. Gail protested that she wanted to become a personal assistant and that her attitude would improve if given such an assignment. The personnel manager retorted that only a highly cooperative secretary could be recommended for promotion to a personal assistant (private secretary).

Gail suddenly recognized the folly of her ways. She had become embroiled in a departmental feud so big that the personnel department had to intervene. She had done permanent damage to her reputation in her department and her company. By giving Faith her full support, Gail perhaps would have been next in line for a personal assistant position.

## TAKE STEPS TO CLIMB BACK INTO POWER ━━━━━━━━━━━━

To many people, the loss of power is a major adversity. One reason behind the hurt is that losing power is a blow to one's self-esteem. To lose power, in the eyes of many, is to be less worthy than previously. Another reason power loss creates adversity is that it results in shame and humiliation for those who crave power—and most managers crave power. The tactics and strategies described next can help a person regain lost power through such means as demotion, being ignored by upper management, or being handed a drastically reduced budget.

## Earn Back Your Reputation

One way to understand how to climb back into power is to look into a worst-case scenario—earning back one's reputation after being stripped of power because of illegal or quasi-legal activities. President Richard M. Nixon is an excellent public example. After resigning from office to ward off the threat of impeachment proceedings, Nixon slowly regained his reputation as a world leader. Another person we can learn from is Bob, the owner of a company that sells cleaning supplies and calcium chloride used for ice and snow control.

To maintain sales, Bob made cash payments to company and local government officials. Although he preferred not to make these bribes, he wrote them off as business expenses. An audit by the Internal Revenue Service led to his eventual conviction for tax evasion. He was sentenced to five years in prison for white-collar criminals, and was released after 18 months. While serving time, Bob left the running of the business to two of his managers. He explains how he rebuilt his reputation:

> The first thing I did when I returned to work was to call a company meeting. I explained to my employees that I had made a mistake and paid for it. I told them that by being sent to prison I wasn't going to have a scarlet letter tattooed on my chest. During my prison term, our sales had slipped badly. Our company had lost much of its market share, and I was feeling powerless. Showing the team that I was eager to rebuild the business was the first step in earning back my respect.

> Rebuilding the business was no picnic. About one-third of my former customers never talked to me again. I showed my other customers that I had products they needed to conduct their business, and that I was willing to deal generously with them. But I told them I had to stay within the bounds of business ethics.

> It was as if I was restarting the business. In those early days when I was trying to establish the reputation of my company, I gave cuts in prices. I threw in extra favors such as free delivery. I had to prove to our customers that I wanted to rebuild our reputation by winning their business in an entirely aboveboard manner.

> My attitude rubbed off on everybody in the company. We began to get our original customers back and developed new ones also. Within two years after I returned from prison, our sales had reached an all-time high.[10]

### Perform Well in Your Demoted Position

A sensible comeback strategy is to regain your former position by turning in excellent job performance as a demoted employee. Although this strategy may appear obvious, the bitterness often experienced after a demotion can interfere with performance. Demoted people often drag their heels, sometimes without realizing it (you will recall that Gail made this error). Not so with Conrad, a man who faced a big surprise on returning from a business trip to Mexico. Another man was seated in his office, performing his job. Conrad had no warning before his trip that he would be replaced.

Conrad had been corporate standards manager for several years and had received above-average performance evaluations. Prior to this position he held the post of manager of information systems. His work was well received by management. When Conrad checked out what had happened, he discovered that his boss had been replaced with a new vice-president and the latter had brought in his own people. All the changes had taken place during Conrad's two-week business trip.

Conrad was told that he had six months to find another job within the company. Having been on the corporate staff for ten years, Conrad decided to switch fields within the organization. He sought a position in the company's education department. Conrad finally was able to secure a position as an information-systems trainer. Although he was not forced to take a pay cut, Conrad's new position was a three-step demotion and his pay would be frozen for three years.

Conrad dug into his new job with the enthusiasm of a person who has been given a new lease on life. Within 18 months, due to his hard work and diligence, Conrad was promoted to the manager of the education department and his job was upgraded one level. He confesses, "I'm happier as a manager of a small, effective department than I ever was as a member of the corporate staff. There is less pressure on me, and I think I'm actually making a bigger contribution. If I had left the company in a huff, I might not be in such good shape today."[11]

### Move Out of the Graveyard as Soon as Possible

Conrad's strategy of staying put in his new assignment and performing well obviously worked. In other situations, the best strategy is to find a quick way out of a *graveyard* assignment. There is a nuance of difference between an undesirable assignment and a graveyard. Many positions may be undesirable but a graveyard position is clearly a dead end. A large business corporation established a salvaging department staffed mainly by employees with disciplinary problems, or those whose illnesses made them unsuited for stressful jobs (such as those with cardiac disease). From the outset, the department became known throughout the corporation as The Graveyard. Managers in the department were generally considered unpromotable.

Fifty-five year old Judd was appointed against his wishes to a supervisory position in The Graveyard. A friend in the human resources department gave Judd her honest opinion about the situation: "Judd, you've been put out to pasture. The only way you will ever get out of this department is through retirement. But if you like that kind of work, your future with the company is assured. Besides, the workers there are stable and appreciative. You might feel like you're doing good for them."

A vigorous man, Judd did not wish to see himself placed in a terminal position; however, he did enjoy the challenge of a salvage operation. He decided that he would stay in his graveyard position until he acquired enough knowledge about salvage operations to enter business for himself. Two years later, Judd, his brother-in-law, and a close friend established a metal recycling business. Judd had bounced back from the graveyard.

### Develop New Expertise

A time-consuming, but fundamentally solid, approach to regaining power is to develop new expertise valued by your employer. Because you possess this esoteric knowledge, you are in a position to regain some or all of your eroded power. For example, a manager in an investment firm, might be demoted to a financial analyst in a political battle. She accepts her loss temporarily, but in the meantime acquires arcane knowledge about several industries. Her recommendations about buying and selling securities in her industries are so profitable that she is invited to become a partner in her firm.

### Wait for Your Enemy to Leave or Self-Destruct

A strategy for climbing back into power when one person is responsible for deposing you is to take no offensive action at all. Simply perform well in your demoted position and wait for somebody else to depose your deposer. Or, your antagonist might self-destruct. If sending you to corporate Siberia was unjust, arbitrary, and politically motivated, your deposer may commit many other similar acts. Eventually the person who demoted you will begin to falter and others will help him or her plummet from power. His or her abrasive, intimidating, or manipulative tactics will backfire when tried against the wrong person. Under these circumstances you may be able to regain power providing you have told your side of the story to the right people.

Let key people know that you did not welcome nor deserve your demotion. Tell them you were involuntarily stripped of the power you cherished. Explain that you want more responsibility so you can continue to make all the important contributions you were making before you were moved out of the mainstream. If your record shows you are indeed Mr. or Ms. Clean, the replacement for your antagonist may give you a second chance.

## BECOME AN ENTREPRENEUR

For a growing number of people (like "graveyard Judd"), the best antidote to career adversity is self-employment. In fact, entrepreneurship is said to thrive on adversity. Many new businesses are started by executives, managers, and professionals dropped by larger corporations. People who have the right personal characteristics, managerial skills, and funding have a decent chance of rebounding from adversity by entering self-employment. Those who don't may find themselves drowning in new adversity.

Because the type of businesses founded by entrepreneurs differ so widely, an accurate stereotype of the ideal entrepreneur does not exist. However, there is enough consistency among their core attributes to help you appreciate whether you are entrepreneurial material.[12]

- Heavy motivation to get work accomplished, combined with a direct approach to giving instructions to employees.
- Intense sense of urgency that motivates many people and discourages some. Many entrepreneurs have such an intense sense of urgency themselves that they expect others to feel the same way about work.
- Impatience and brusqueness toward employees because entrepreneurs are always in a hurry. Many entrepreneurs operate more on hunches than careful planning; they therefore become discouraged with employees who insist on studying problems for a prolonged period.
- Charismatic personality that inspires others to want to do business with the entrepreneur despite his or her impatience.
- Strong dislike for bureaucratic rules and regulations, which makes the entrepreneur impatient during meetings.
- Much stronger interest in dealing with customers than employees.
- Strong achievement drive which translates into being a self-starter driven by the need to succeed and accomplish something. Entrepreneurs are constantly keeping score.

- Willingness to assume personal responsibility for the success or failure of a given activity or event.
- Ability to spot problems and opportunities that others overlook.
- Belief that one's accomplishments and failures are under one's personal control and influence, and that luck is not such an important factor in contributing to success or failure.
- Ability and willingness to live with some uncertainty in life. This uncertainty can relate to job security, business deals, and personal life.
- Willingness to take calculated and sensible risks. A calculated risk means that the chances of winning are neither small enough to represent a big gamble nor so large as to be almost certain.
- Willingness to accept setback, and then to recover and keep going. The entrepreneur embodies the spirit of the resilient person.

The more of these traits, characteristics, and behaviors you possess, the greater the chance that entrepreneurship will rebound you from adversity.

## LOOK FOR SIGNALS OF GOOD NEWS

A curious, almost mystical, way of bouncing back from adversity is to receive subtle signals from the outside world. The right signals will provide you with a burst of optimism that can help ward off the depressive elements of a crisis. Only a mind finely tuned to the outside world can notice these signals. Once they appear, you can face others with renewed confidence and realize that good news is imminent. Just as a bird chirping signals the end of a heavy rainstorm, the world of work offers its own indicators of good times ahead. Not everybody gets the same signals, but here are a few that could mean the turning point for you:

- You have been trying to get an appointment with a key executive for two weeks. One morning his assistant phones you and says, "Mr. Evans will be able to see you at 11:15 this morning."
- A manager whom you insulted in a meeting last week smiles at you with forgiveness and invites you to join her for lunch.
- A prospective customer for a large account returns your phone call and asks to learn more about your product.

- Your request for additional staff support is approved.
- Your name is included on the distribution list of an important company document.
- Your rival for promotion resigns.
- Your boss informs you that you have been placed on a list of key people who will not be included in the next company layoff.

# CHAPTER 16

# SURVIVING A CORPORATE TAKEOVER

In today's corporate world a separate set of tactics are needed to survive takeovers, mergers, acquisitions, leveraged buyouts, and restructurings or downsizings. Your job and the services provided by your department can be on the line any time your company is taken over by or merged with another, or is even being threatened with a takeover. One reason is that the new owners attempt to squeeze more profits out of the new corporate entity by laying off people, and cutting back on programs and services. A related reason is that takeovers, including leveraged buyouts are very expensive. The acquiring company may go heavily into debt to make the purchase. In order to pay back debt, the company is forced to drastically reduce costs.

The perils of organizational reshufflings to the individual have become common knowledge, and have instilled fear in many employees. In a study conducted by Robert Half International, Inc., 100 highly placed managers were asked to specify their greatest fears from a list of typical executive nightmares. The number one worry is that they will lose their jobs through mergers and acquisitions. Fifty-four percent of the respondents mentioned a fear of takeovers. This fear vastly exceeds concerns about being fired, losing a promotion, becoming ill, or not making sufficient income to cover expenses.[1]

Many forms of politicking described in previous chapters can help you cope with a change in ownership of your firm. For example, all the information about developing a good relationship with your boss, and impressing higher-ups is relevant. In addition, you may also need to strengthen your armamentarium with the strategies and tactics described in this chapter.

## DEVELOP A CRISIS MENTALITY

Crisis management expert Gerald Meyers observes that crises in business are so frequent they are almost inevitable. (Meyers should know, he was the former CEO of American Motors.) Because of their inevitability, politically wise managers need to learn crisis management techniques. One of Meyer's suggested strategies deals with managing an individual's own crisis. He recommends that managers develop a crisis mentality because job security is a fictitious state in our present business environment.

"Once you accept that crisis is not beyond the realm of possibility, you can deal with it positively," says Meyer. "We're taught to think success, which is good as far as it goes. But it's not complete. You must also develop an attitude that takes into account the unexpected disaster. It's not just the chief executive officer who must cope with it, but all the company executives."[2]

A good way to prepare for an expected disaster is to accumulate a large cash reserve to tide you over between jobs should your position be eliminated. Another is to continue to make contacts in your industry that you can rely on should you need to make a sudden job switch. Perhaps even more important is to position yourself so strongly in your organization that you will be asked to help the firm cope with a disaster rather than being asked to leave.

## SELL YOUR QUALIFICATIONS TO THE PREDATOR FIRM

Henry Kravis, one of the most successful and toughest deal makers, contends that leveraged buyouts (LBOs) do not spell doom for everybody. He contends, "We're not going to take the heart out of a corporation. People who produce things will stay. We look at the people who report to people who report to people. We'll often cut fat at the corporate level."[3] The hidden message behind Kravis's comments is that you have to prove you are worth keeping after the corporate buyout.

Even when your position seems worth retaining, you are still in peril of being replaced by a manager from the acquiring firm. In an LBO engineered by the present management team, this is less likely because outsiders do not enter the picture. However, in other LBOs an outside buyer gains control of the firm and may immediately begin to swing a cost-cutting ax.

Barbara faced a potential erosion of power when the fashion store she worked for was bought by a nationwide firm and converted into a subsidiary. The new owner's initial move was to replace existing management with its own people. As a result, Barbara was on the verge of losing her assistant manager's job. She explains what happened and how she survived:

> One week after I graduated with a degree in fashion merchandising, I obtained a job as a sales associate in a local retail store. Within a year I was promoted to assistant manager, and business was quite good. Three months after I was promoted, we were informed that a new company was buying the store. We were told not to worry about our jobs being disturbed.

> What we didn't know was that our job security was not guaranteed by the terms of the sales agreement between the companies. Upon acquiring our store, the new owners decided to move its own people into key positions. You can imagine the chaos that hit when we were told our jobs had been virtually eliminated with the stroke of a pen!

> The day the new company representative came to give us exit interviews we were told that the sales associates would be let go. But Julie (the store manager) and I would be able to work as sales associates. We were informed that if we worked up to their standards, we might be reappointed as assistant managers in the future. Julie considered the offer to be a slap in the face after seven years in the business, and submitted her resignation that day. Who could blame her?

> I told them I'd like the weekend to consider my options; I would give them my decision the following Monday morning. I spent Friday and Saturday fuming about the callous way we were all being treated. By Sunday I got down to the serious business of trying to understand what these changes meant to my career. I had nothing to lose by accepting the company's offer. My one stipulation was that I be hired as a management trainee with the same pay and benefits as before.

> As I explained to the representative that Monday, I had a college degree and nearly two years of merchandising experience. The experience included supervisory duties over sales associates. I felt I was overqualified for an associate's position. I also knew I had good information to offer about local customer attitudes, behavior, likes and dislikes, and preferred lifestyles.

> I can't believe how bold I was. I told that man that I had no qualms about learning another style of management and that working for his company could only add to my career development. I wanted the chance to broaden my experience base, and I could think of no reason why the company and I couldn't enjoy a mutually beneficial association.

> I couldn't believe my nerve, and I guess he couldn't either. I was hired that day as a manager trainee. I have to confess I never thought my pitch would work, but you never know until you try. It's five years later and I am now

the assistant regional manager for this chain. My boss is that same manager who was sent to reorganize the outlet I originally worked in.

My advice to career-oriented people would be to see yourself as a marketable product. Stick your neck out and have enough confidence to take a chance. If you present your qualifications as an asset to an organization, you'll be surprised how much easier it is to get the position you really want. Or at least one which will get you where you want to go.[4]

## REACT POSITIVELY TO YOUR NEW BOSS

After any type of corporate shakeup, you are likely to have a new immediate boss. How you relate to that boss at the outset could determine how pleasant life will be for you in the present and future. For example, suppose you tear into the new boss with complaints about the injustices of the layoffs and your former boss being replaced. You are then likely to be viewed as a troublemaker, and therefore unpromotable. The following suggestions are aimed to help you present a positive image to your new boss.

### Take the Initiative in Getting to Know Your New Boss

A professional style manager will routinely schedule an appointment with key department members shortly after moving into the position. However not all managers think of scheduling these get-acquainted sessions. If this is your situation, take the initiative to have a formal session with the new boss. Explain to the boss's assistant that you would like to be given a 20-minute appointment for a general discussion.

During the session be as nonthreatening as possible. Mention that you would like to get acquainted and describe your function within the unit. Congratulate your new boss on his or her new appointment and pledge your support. Rehearse your words of congratulation and support in advance of the meeting. Otherwise it is easy to appear too political. A sincere-sounding statement along these lines is, "Congratulations on becoming our new department manager. If there's anything that I can do to help you and our department, let me know. I'm here to help, and my job is an important part of my career."

After about ten minutes of conversation, gain control of the situation by asking for another meeting to discuss what you perceive to be the biggest challenges facing the department. Mention that you would also like to discuss your plan for meeting these challenges. All but the most insecure or inept boss will welcome your ideas. Citing problems and recommending solutions, you will recall, is a great way of enhancing your relationship with the boss. A curious boss will often request your preliminary thoughts right on the spot.

Gwen, a customer service representative, explains how she took the initiative to identify major problems within the department. "In my first meeting with Casey (her post-downsizing boss), I gingerly asked if he would be interested in hearing my analysis of our biggest problems. The amount of his enthusiasm shocked me. Casey invited me to have lunch with him the next day to review my analysis.

"During lunch I explained that our company's philosophy emphasized customer service. Yet we had a constant ten-day backlog of unresolved customer complaints in our subsidiary. I suggested that we needed to increase the staffing of our customer service department and develop a set of guidelines and procedures for resolving complaints. As things stood, customers with similar complaints would receive very different treatment depending on the customer service rep they dealt with.

"I also explained that myself and the two other customer service representatives needed more direct access to a supervisor. Our function now reported to Casey, but he also had other functions to manage and was frequently out of the office on other business.

"The upshot was that three weeks later I was appointed as the customer service supervisor. Two new representatives were added to the department. Both reps were transferred from less essential jobs. You could say my advice to Casey was self-serving, but it also helped take care of an important company problem."

## Be Careful About Giving Advice

The above-mentioned tactic suggests that you give advice about solving an organizational problem that *you* have identified. In contrast, move slowly in giving advice when the new boss has an idea for making changes. The new boss may be really asking you to put a seal of approval on a decision he or she has already made. If you make any suggestions you run the risk of interfering with your boss's hidden agenda.

Before responding to the new boss's suggestions, ask questions to learn more about his or her view of the situation. Figure out if the boss has already made a decision or is genuinely looking for fresh input. If your manager presses you to present an opinion, offer suggestions but show that you can adapt to decisions that have already been made.[5] Assume that your boss asks for your opinion about the usefulness of centralized purchasing. In response, you ecstatically describe the benefits of centralized purchasing, such as better pricing because of volume purchases. With a shrug of her shoulders, your boss then explains that the policy of mostly decentralized purchasing will remain.

Slowly extracting your foot from your mouth, you respond, "I see your point of view. Some companies find decentralized purchasing quite effective, while centralized purchasing works for others. There are distinct tradeoffs for both philosophies. I guess the important thing is how well we monitor our decentralized purchasing."

## SELL YOUR STORY TO THE
## OUTSIDE CONSULTANT

The statement "Your check is in the mail" is now rivaled in sincerity by "Don't worry, very few changes will be made after the acquisition. We intend to leave everything intact. No personnel changes are anticipated." Shortly after a takeover, a common practice is for the acquiring company to hire a consultant to assess the contribution of various departments and to make suggestions of excising noncontributing or redundant operations.

Staffing decisions are likely to be made quickly, based on sketchy information. You have to think and act rapidly if you want to be one of the survivors. Many people err by taking the passive approach of waiting to see what happens. They assume a low profile at a time when they should be attempting to excel. Consultant Price Prichett offers four survival pointers for dealing constructively with the consultants invited in to study your operations.[6]

1. *Decide if you fit in with the new corporate culture.* Before even worrying about what to tell the consultant, decide if you are compatible with the culture of the acquiring firm. If you are truly incompatible with the new regime, staying could frustrate you and damage your personal and professional life. However, exiting too quickly can be a mistake because you might lose out on a generous severance package given during postmerger shakeouts.

2. *Retain your composure.* When discussing your organizational unit with consultants, avoid being defensive, argumentative, or panicky —at least visibly. Instead, offer a balanced evaluation of your department, covering both its strengths, areas for improvement, and potential. Explain how your unit can be made more productive to meet the demands of the new owner. Point out that the team members are willing to support the necessary changes.

3. *Explain how your unit is contributing to the organizational strategy.* Most consultants get turned on by "strategic thinking." In practice this means explaining how your unit fits in with the master plan of your company. If you are managing a customer service department explain how the company philosophy emphasizes the importance of satisfying customers. Also show how your group makes an everyday contribution to the quality of customer service.

Emphasizing quality is important because by now virtually every company includes quality as part of its strategy.

Present as many facts and figures as you can about your unit's productivity. As the customer service manager, you might display a graph of the increasing number of customer complaints handled by your department over a period of time. Prepare a scrapbook of thank-you letters from customers you have helped. Above all, gather some figures about the annualized financial contribution of your unit to corporate profits. The consultant is likely to incorporate your data into the report submitted to management.

4. *Avoid a cover-up.* If you know deep down that your position or unit is redundant—and therefore likely to be eliminated—frankness may help. Suggest that the company should consolidate your unit with the duplicate function, or eliminate one of them. Your candor may help your unit survive. Discuss with the consultant what other positions you feel you can handle under a reorganization. Avoid appearing bitter or angry—just keep focused on your organizational contribution, not on your job security.

Neil, a manager of quality assurance in an acquired company, knew that his function duplicated a similar department in the acquiring company. Neil was confident he could find a suitable position elsewhere, but he wanted to avoid sacrificing his ten years of seniority and pension rights. The pitch Neil made to the consultant investigating his department centered on the theme that he wanted to make a different kind of contribution to the organization. He felt he was ready and prepared to work as a "turnaround manager"— one who takes over a troubled unit and returns it to profitability.

Because the acquiring company wanted to squeeze as much profitability as possible out of the combined company, the consultant listened attentively. When the consultant discussed his analysis with top management, he recommended that Neil be given an opportunity to turn around a small troubled division within the organization. Neil took on the assignment gleefully. Within two years the troubled division became profitable, and Neil's stature—and job security—was enhanced. Eventually Neil left the company to join a consulting firm of turnaround managers. The difference was that he left at his own convenience.

## KEEP YOUR BOSS INFORMED
## TO OBTAIN RESOURCES

During lean and mean times not every organizational unit is severely cut back or eliminated. Some managers are able to obtain enough resources to keep their units staffed and supplied. The Innocent Lamb reason for wanting to obtain an adequate budget is to be able to perform satisfactorily your department's mission. The more political reason is to preserve as much of your empire as possible. An executive newsletter offers some useful suggestions for obtaining a healthy budget during lean and mean times.[7]

## Make Top Management's Uncertainty Work for You

Top management knows they can make mistakes. In fact, many organizations have eliminated so many managers and professionals in recent years that innovation and customer service have suffered. Good opportunities go unexplored while the remaining members of management scramble around putting out fires. A chance therefore exists that members of the executive suite are worried that they have thinned out resources too much.

## Fill the Information Gap

Keep your immediate manager informed of your day-to-day operations, yet avoid being a constant bearer of bad news. If you communicate mostly good news, management will be more receptive to coping with occasional bad news. Useful information can be fed to management in several ways. An "FYI" (for your information) memo may seem like a cliche but is still a standard communication vehicle. An FYI is especially good for passing along information that compliments your group or describes unusual activity. An FYI memo is also effective, because you are not asking anybody for a decision; you are just taking the initiative to keep them informed.

Ask your team members to put their cost-savings and dollar-earning suggestions in writing and then pass these along to upper management. Dollar-earning suggestions are noteworthy because about 98 percent of employee suggestions deal with cost savings. Suggestions for earning money (such as holding a garage sale on obsolete equipment and office furnishings) are a welcome relief.

Staff meetings can serve as another way of communicating useful information to top management. If you anticipate an exciting meeting that reflects well on the productivity of your department, invite a powerful executive to attend. Prepare in advance for the dog and pony show, by gathering the most impressive news about the department's activities— such as how your group is solving an important public relations problem, or attracting a major new customer.

Develop an employee newsletter, prepared monthly by your assistant. Useful topics include notable projects being carried out by team members, significant achievements, and future plans. Avoid making the newsletter so elaborate that it appears expensive and time consuming to produce. A heart-wrenching touch is to have the newsletter printed on recycled paper. It adds a hint of cost consciousness to your thinking. Get in touch with Greenpeace for your nearest supplier of ecology responsive office paper.

Make your bulletin board lively with interesting information and newsclips related to your unit or the organization. Update it frequently, and be extra careful not to keep bulletins posted that have yellowed with age. Find a spot for the bulletin board that is likely to be seen by top management.

In addition to all of the above communication thrusts, update your boss weekly on projects completed, those under way, and new ones undertaken. So long as you don't become perceived as a pest, it will appear that you are a vital contributor to the well-being of the firm.

### Air Legitimate Gripes

When the boss attempts to squeeze even greater productivity from the group, subtly remind him or her of the heavy workload team members are already enduring. You might ask, "Should I tell Jessica to push back the date for the completion of the investigation of our new inventory control system?"

### Keep Pressing for More Resources

When you keep top management informed of your constructive activities, it becomes easier to contend that if you had more resources, your contribution could be enlarged: "With just one more field investigator, we could collect another million dollars in taxes owed the government. I know that members of Congress would be interested in a return on investment of that magnitude."

### Translate Requests into Their Financial Consequences

As just implied, translating demands into their dollar consequences is favored by executives. When requesting additional resources, talk in terms of return on investment, increased earnings per share, increased sales forecasts, or ultimate cost savings. Be sure to express your requests in a helpful rather than a complaining mode. For example, don't complain about a filthy warehouse being unsightly. Instead talk about how refurbishing the warehouse might improve employee morale and enhance the image of the firm to visitors.

## AVOID A "THEM VERSUS US" MENTALITY

When one firm engulfs another, antagonisms often develop between managers of the two firms. The antagonisms tend to be more intense when the takeover is hostile and forcible. It is not surprising that conflict should take place between the two firms. Of major significance, the two cultures may clash. For example, key members of one firm might tend to be adventuresome, risk takers, and free-swinging. The other firm members might be much more conservative and risk avoiders. Pay scales and benefits may vary between firms. People who are receiving lower compensation, yet working as hard as workers getting paid more, may become resentful.

Another difference that can lead to conflict is when the systems and procedures between the two firms clash. The predator firm may require two signatures on checks over $5000, while the other firm may impose a $1000 upper limit on checks signed by only one person. Another difference might be one firm emphasizes customer satisfaction while the other emphasizes better engineered products. By so doing the latter hopes to attract more customers.

With so many potential conflicts between the acquiring and the acquired firms, it is understandable that a "them versus us" attitude may pervade the organization.[8] Acquiring such a mentality may be politically unwise. It may peg the individual as narrowminded and unreceptive to change—hardly good credentials for being promoted. Grant, a manager of a large department store, fell into such a trap. For ten years he had helped his company become the leading retailer downtown. One spring, the store Grant managed was bought by a large, out-of-town retail chain.

When Grant's store was acquired, the new owners made the usual pledge of leaving management intact and making few changes. Within three months, however, substantial changes began to take place. As a starting point, the new owners demanded that Grant decrease the number of floor personnel by 25 percent. According to their analysis, customer service could be maintained by operating with a smaller staff of better trained sales associates.

Customer complaints about shoddy service began to arrive in Grant's office. The new owners insisted that as soon as the associates completed their training, they would be able to please customers, and complaints would lessen. Besides, they argued, the increasing profit margins were worth a few isolated complaints. The next big changes imposed on Grant's store stemmed from a change in merchandising philosophy.

The new owners insisted that Grant's store carried too much high-priced, stodgy clothing. Based on the advice of merchandising consultants, the new owners insisted on Grant's store carrying a wide variety of flashy but inexpensive clothing. Large numbers of established customers soon began drifting away from the store. They were replaced in part by youthful bargain hunters who bought mostly sale merchandise.

Grant became increasingly perturbed by the changing nature of his store, and the insensitivity of the new owners to the problem they were creating. Gradually, Grant began to express some hostility toward the new owners to department managers in his store. The women's wear manager asked Grant one day when the new owners would be reviewing the upcoming fall line with them. Grant replied, "Oh, the Champions of Schlock will be getting to that right after they figure out how we can cut some additional costs."

Another day Grant visited the children's wear department. He noticed that many customers were serving themselves, unassisted by any store representative. Grant asked for an explanation from the manager. She explained that the new owners emphasized self-service. Angered Grant said, "I don't care what *they* say. Here is how *we* treat customers." Without realizing it, Grant began to make more frequent references to the new owners as "them" and his store as "us."

Grant's attitudes encouraged "them versus us" attitudes throughout the store. Soon, store employees at all levels began to exchange derogatory jokes about the new owners. Two examples:

"Why haven't the new owners' daughters been married yet?"
"I don't know, why haven't they been married yet?"
"They are all waiting for K-Mart to open a bridal shop."

"Can you give me an example of our new owner's flair for new concepts in merchandising and cost savings?"
"I sure can. Starting this spring, we are offering one-size-fits-all shoes. In this way, we capitalize on economies of scale, and we will never be out of any customer's shoe size."

Word soon got back to the new owner's management team about the recalcitrant attitude so pervasive at Grant's store. Shortly thereafter, he was replaced by a new store manager from the parent company. However, Grant was not fired. Instead, he was offered the opportunity to become the manager of the furniture department, at 75 percent of his current pay. Muttering to himself that "they" are SOBs, Grant decided to accept the position and coast until he would be eligible for retirement in five years.

## DEVELOP A LEAN AND MEAN
## OPERATING STYLE ════════════════════════════════

After a takeover, it is almost inevitable that a big push develops for improving productivity, with an emphasis on trimming costs. If you want to fall into grace with the new management team, a sensible strategy is to demonstrate a lean and mean operating style. In other words, you can get your work accomplished with fewer workers than you or your predecessors required. Even better, perhaps you can get more work done with fewer people. This is a much better strategy than finding ways to beat the system, and run with a "fat and good-natured" operating style.

Adopting a lean and mean operating style is largely a question of raising your level of awareness to accomplish more with fewer resources. Whenever possible, publicize your efforts of operating with a tight budget. However, avoid spending so little money that it is expensive. For example, do not attempt to save money by sending a bid proposal by parcel post or third-class mail. Here is a starter kit of maneuvers and suggestions that could enhance your image as a lean and mean operator:

- Instead of replacing a programmer who quits suggest that the company subcontract the programmer's work on an as needed basis.
- Make shipments of your company's merchandise in boxes you saved that contained shipments from your suppliers. (Use a fresh mailing label, however.)
- Conduct a national sales meeting in a budget motel in a medium-sized town rather than at a posh hotel in a major city.
- Conduct breakfast meetings at a Perkin's or a diner rather than in hotel restaurants.
- Delay performance appraisals by an average of three months, thus postponing salary increases and saving the company lots of money.
- Suggest that your division relocate to lower-priced office space, or that departments be consolidated therefore enabling the company to sublet some space.
- Delay accounts payable as long as possible. At the same time apply pressure to shorten the collection time for accounts receivables.
- Cancel orders for regular shipments of fresh flowers for the reception area. Instead, suggest that employees who have gardens bring in their own flowers to decorate the office.
- Demand that every employee under your jurisdiction take no more time for lunch and rest breaks than required by law. Theoretically,

the additional hours recaptured by this maneuver will lead to increased productivity.

- Work closely with the office manager to control the slippage of office supplies for home use. Put up a poster reminding workers to empty their pockets of company ball pens and pencils before returning home.

- Compose a list of suggestions on how the company can save water, such as eliminating the watering of lawns except for emergencies.

- Despite low profits or a high budget deficit never suggest ways to economize by decreasing top-management pay. If somebody else does make such a suggestion, present an analysis showing that executive pay is a miniscule proportion of the total operating budget.

## CONDUCT AN INTERNAL JOB CAMPAIGN

An organizational shakeup could mean that you will be forced to find a new position. If you are a middle- or high-level manager, this could be difficult in an era when other companies in your industry are also trimming down. Suppose you have advance warning that you may be placed on the hit list, or you intuitively know that your position may be eliminated. It makes more sense to conduct an internal job campaign before looking outside. Instead of pounding the pavement, pound the carpet or vinyl in your own firm. A major plus for your career is that an internal job switch is looked on more favorably than an external one; you appear well-rounded rather than disloyal or unwanted.

Gail, a manager of a group of industrial engineers, faced a reorganization in the corporation. Two industrial engineering units were merged into one in order to eliminate a few support positions and one managerial position. Gail was removed from her supervisory position and reassigned as a senior industrial engineer. The reshuffling upset Gail because she was intent on moving up into manufacturing management. Losing a managerial position therefore represented a serious career setback.

"I didn't let myself slip into a passive mode," said Gail. "I realized the merger was necessary to keep my division cost-effective. I realized that someone had to be demoted. I just wished it wasn't me. The minimum benefit for me from the reshuffle was that I could resharpen my professional skills by working as a full-time engineer.

"Within two months, I launched my plan to get back into management. I sat down with my manager and developed a career path. The path specified the jobs I needed to reach my long-range goal of becoming a manufacturing vice-president. My manager took my path seriously, and gave me permission to interview for a manager's job in other divisions of the corporation.

"After four months I secured a new position as the manager of industrial engineering in the aerospace division of our company. The division had just landed a large government contract and was actually short of talent."[9]

The lessen to be learned from Gail's career-enhancing move is the sophisticated approach she used to finding a new position internally. Instead of simply circulating her resume around the company, she explained her career plans to her immediate superior who then became an ally in her job search.

## ENTER INTO COMPETITION WITH YOUR FORMER EMPLOYER

A high-level way of surviving a corporate takeover or downsizing is to start a new business that competes directly with the firm that squeezed you out. A major advantage of this approach is that you are entering a business in which you have first-hand experience. Equally important, you may have the right personal contacts.

Jay, the vice-president and general manager of a division of an aerospace firm, is an example of a David who took on a Goliath who wronged him. "When I first took charge of the division in 1975," said Jay, "it had been operating at a loss for some time. By 1982 it was profitable, thus helping to balance the books for its parent company which was experiencing severe financial problems.

"The company experienced two major problems the next year. The demand for the products made by the Connecticut division cooled down, and funds were mismanaged. It was therefore necessary to lay off a large percentage of the workforce. The board decided to close the New Jersey facility and consolidate the entire operation in Connecticut.

"To the outsider, closing the New Jersey division didn't make much sense. But you must realize that the corporation was originally based in Connecticut, and the board of directors and top management were located there. The New Jersey division was opened as an offshoot of the Connecticut division to handle a specific product line. When the overall company got into financial trouble, top management knew that a consolidation was necessary. They chose to close my division in order to minimize the personal inconvenience for them.

"A lot of dislocation resulted from that decision. Those with essential technical positions were invited to rejoin the Connecticut division once the product line was reestablished. But people in managerial positions were not offered new jobs because most of them would be redundant with positions in Connecticut.

"As division manager, there wasn't an equivalent opening for me in Connecticut. I might add that personality conflicts between myself and certain people in headquarters had not endeared me to them. I accepted a generous severance offer which bought me some time in finding a suitable job.

"I felt I had several options to pursue. First I submitted an offer to purchase my division from the corporation. I would borrow most of the money, using a leveraged buyout on a small scale. My offer was not only refused, but also generated hostility toward me from top management.

"I still felt I had the knowledge and capability to competently merge a manufacturing business in the aerospace field. Market research indicated there was very little competition in the product niche I had in mind. Another factor in my favor was that I had acquired a specialized technical knowledge of the product, as well as valuable connections in the field. During my years in the industry, I had developed an excellent reputation. The products I managed were of high quality and my personal integrity was good.

"With all these factors in my favor, I decided to launch my own corporation. I arranged an adequate bank line of credit, sold stock, and hired key personnel from the New Jersey division that had closed. I was even able to obtain some of my old equipment through an auction. We began manufacturing on a limited scale, with a modest-sized labor force. To reduce managerial expenses, I functioned as vice-president and general manager. At the same time I was chief product manager, controller, and sales manager.

"Today our company is fairly successful. We've won back most of our former customer base, and have received several large government contracts. During the past year I have computerized most of our budgeting, payroll, and purchasing functions. Our sales have reached the point where we could use a few more good people.

"Looking back, I have almost no regrets. The initial start-up costs were somewhat prohibitive. I still cannot afford to pay myself what I would expect to be earning in an established aerospace company. The job itself can be very demanding because there are no limits to my responsibilities. I work until the job gets done, period. In the long run the risk and the opportunity costs will have been worthwhile. My career had taken a setback, and now I'm at a higher vantage point than ever. I also get a personal kick out of giving my old firm a run for its money."[10]

Jay had thus established a manufacturing company to enter into competition with his former employer—an undertaking that requires extraordinary start-up costs. Financing for such ventures is usually obtained through investors or bank loans for which the new corporation is liable. Opening a retail store to compete with a former employer requires less capital, but personal funds are usually invested in the venture.

Stacey represents an example of somebody who opened a retail outlet to compete successfully with a former employer. She had worked as a pharmacist for an independently owned pharmacy in a small town. The agreement was for Stacey to buy out the owner when he retired in a few years. She would give the owner a downpayment, and mortgage the balance of the purchase price.

One year before the business was to exchange hands, a major pharmacy chain made an offer to purchase the business. The owner was reluctant to sell because it would mean backing off the agreement with Stacey. However, the cash offer was twice the price Stacey had agreed to pay. The owner accepted the offer, and Stacey felt devastated. She saw her dreams of owning a profitable pharmacy disappear.

Stacey was made an offer to continue along as a store pharmacist. Although she preferred not to work for a chain, Stacey accepted the offer. The starting salary was higher than her current pay, and she liked the store's clientele. After working for three months in this position, Stacey realized that working for a corporation did not fit her long-range plans. Her dislike for bureaucracy was intensified by her simmering discontent over having been betrayed by the owner, however justified he was from a financial perspective.

Stacey put her plans for owning a pharmacy back on track. She continued to save money for investment. She investigated other possibilities for purchasing a pharmacy in the surrounding area. Nothing attractive presented itself, so Stacey formulated another strategy. She began to look for store space at a good location that was suitable for conversion to a pharmacy.

It became apparent that the best location would be in the same neighborhood where she was currently working. The only nearby pharmacy (including general merchandise) was the one she worked for. In addition, the population could support another pharmacy, and Stacey had developed a solid base of customers who valued her services.

With the assistance of a real-estate broker, Stacey searched for the right location. Six months later Stacey found empty space in a small plaza that seemed to fit her requirements. The plaza contained a supermarket, launderette, liquor and wine store, and adequate parking—all important back-up features for a pharmacy. Within four months Stacey was in business. She made good use of the experience she had gathered with the chain in handling employees and merchandising. In a four-year period, Stacey has expanded the store twice, and purchased the plaza. She now employs two full-time pharmacists, a store manager, and approximately 30 part-time workers.

Asked if she intends to become a chain, Stacey replied, "No, I've accomplished what I wanted for now. I've got a nice little empire I can wrap my arms around, and I'm competing with a chain in at least one location."[11]

## BECOME A FREE-AGENT MANAGER

"They did it to me, so I'll do it to them," said the jaundiced sales manager as he wooed away three big accounts from his former employer. In today's turbulent corporate environment, it may be necessary to place your own interests above those of the organization. If every employee were entirely self-interested, self-centered, and self-aggrandizing, company effectiveness and competitiveness would decline. As a consequence, every employee and stockholder will suffer. Nevertheless, if you are ready to reject before being rejected, or to jump ship before being shoved overboard, you will be able to soften the blow of a corporate shakeup.

Paul Hirsch labels this the prepared approach, "becoming a free-agent manager."[12] Free-agent managers and professionals have developed skills far different from those taught in traditional MBA and executive development programs. (An important exception is those programs offering a seminar in organizational power and politics.) First, free-agent managers are loyal primarily to themselves because sacrificing personal goals for the organization will no longer be rewarded or appreciated by the organization. After a merger or acquisition, even the most loyal organization person might be put on the hit list.

Second, free-agent managers and professionals protect themselves and learn to survive in their own environment. Previously guaranteed perks such as pension plans and fringe benefits can no longer be perceived as automatic. As a result, managers must develop their own protection plans.

Third, the recommended new breed of managers are still committed to their careers. However, they see the company as a temporary arena in which to apply their skills and knowledge. This attitude is imperative because the organization will not hesitate to fire managers in order to reach its financial objectives—particularly a good return to shareholders.

Fourth, free-agent managers and professionals regard temporary setbacks such as being fired as a challenge—-they realize that downsizing decisions are made by people who do not know them personally and who have very little concern for human welfare. Deal makers are a spectacularly callous breed of executives. Remote-control management is inevitable as mergers and acquisitions place a greater emphasis on efficiency (as measured by headcount) than on effectiveness.

Finally, free-agent managers strive to be in control of their own destiny. Proactive rather than reactive strategies and tactics are required to increase their visibility in their organization and industry.

If you want to pack your own parachute, and thus become a free-agent manager or professional, Hirsch urges you to take the following steps:

1. *Maintain your mobility.* Because jobs are only temporary, assume that you will move on your own terms should the need arise. Try to overcome guilt feelings because you have left the organization short-handed. Most companies can readily adjust to the loss of a few key people. Will the board of directors, shareholders, or top management feel guilty when your division is sold to pay debts, and you are left jobless?

2. *Avoid long-term or group assignments where your accomplishments cannot be clearly defined.* Minimize the number of taskforce assignments you accept. Opt for individual problem solving over group decision making. Avoid attempting to solve the unsolvable.

3. *Become a generalist rather than a specialist.* You will usually need to build your reputation by being an expert about something. After your career is launched, however, branch out into more general assignments. Overspecialization can hinder movement from one corporation to another. Remember that a delicate balance between being a generalist and a specialist must be achieved. Strive to become a generalist who also has a well-defined bag of tricks in his or her repertoire. Headhunters usually pursue an executive with a track record of accomplishing a specific task such as cutting costs, boosting sales, or mobilizing distributors.

4. *Return calls from headhunters thus maintaining your marketability.* Not returning calls is a tip-off that you are not willing to test the waters. If you do not return calls, your name mysteriously gets out of circulation among executive recruiters.

5. *Cultivate networks that enhance your visibility outside your organization.* Participation in professional associations (such as the National Association of Accountants or the Purchasing Managers Association), community activities, and so on, makes you visible as a competent manager or professional.

By following these guidelines for becoming a free-agent manager, you will be better equipped to deal with the ravages of mergers and acquisitions, and other shakeups. The same guidelines can help you cope better with personality conflicts with top executives, and business failures.

# CHAPTER 17

# DEFENDING
# YOURSELF AGAINST
# UNFAIR POLITICS

The astute practitioner of office politics plays defense as well as offense. At many times in your career—perhaps weekly—you may have to counteract the manipulations of people playing politics at your expense. Much effort will be directed at finding antidotes to devious tactics, yet even the reasonably ethical political tactics of others can put you at a disadvantage. For example, too much of your professional time might be gobbled up by honest and ambitious people who want to incorporate you in their networks. In the competitive organizational environment of the 1990s, we can anticipate an increase in the use of devious office politics.

Keep in mind that those who use unsavory political tactics believe in equal opportunity. Men are devious to men and women and vice versa. Nevertheless, some systematic evidence has been gathered that women are meaner to each other than they are to men. According to interviews conducted by Judith Briles, many women used devious political tactics to embarrass the reputations of other women. Men were not so nice either; their unethical behavior often led to the loss of a raise or a promotion for other men.[1]

In this chapter we describe how to counteract political ploys directed against you; the following chapter describes how to stem the tide of too much political behavior in the organization below you.

## CONFRONT PEOPLE WITH THEIR
## POLITICAL GAMES

By now you are aware of most forms of office politics. To defend yourself against such politicking, you might confront people with their own type of game—particularly when they are using devious tactics. It is best to begin with a nonadversarial, or gentle, confrontation. Such an approach takes into account the possibility that the game player wasn't really out to hurt you. The person might change when apprised of the adverse impact of his or her behavior. When a gentle reminder fails to do the trick, proceed with a harsher approach.

Assume that a co-worker tells you about a job opening in another company that fits your background. You might ask, "Why are you telling me about this job: Are you looking for a favor from me? Do you want me out of the way? I'd like to know." If you find confrontation exciting and you do not mind running the risk of alienating an office politician, here are a few sample confrontations:

*Situation 1.* A co-worker invites you to lunch on your birthday. A week later, she brings you two canceled Swedish stamps because she has heard you mention that your daughter collects stamps. The following week she hears that you have been given an exorbitant amount of work to do. She volunteers to pitch in, so you can spend the weekend free of office work. You confront her with the question, "Why are you being so extravagantly nice to me? What favor do you want from me in exchange?"

*Situation 2.* A subordinate of yours says he has a plan to help develop Tim, one of his subordinates. The plan is to have him supervise a department of entry-level workers who were previously receiving public assistance. You know that Tim has an upper-middle class background and has no supervisory experience. You assume he is not prepared for such an assignment. Because of your suspicions, you say to your subordinate, "Is this a sink-or-swim setup designed to have Tim sink? Do you want him out of the way? Do you want him to fail? Are you giving Tim a fair shake?"

*Situation 3.* A support worker from the accounting department sits down next to you in the company cafeteria and says he has something important to talk about. He then says, "I'm looking for a promotion into your department." After you tell him that you have no openings for support workers in your department, he says, "Don't you realize, I'm in charge of auditing the use of office supplies? I know that your consumption of supplies has been a little heavy lately—almost like you've been taking some supplies home. I wouldn't want to report my findings to upper management. Tell me again, are you sure you don't have any openings in your department for a person of my talents?"

You respond, "Let's you and I go to the head of the accounting department right now. I want you to repeat your conversation. Come to think of it, maybe we should bring along a member of the security force. You're accusing me of embezzling some office supplies. In return, you're attempting extortion. This is too important to drop."

## EXPOSE DIRTY TRICKS

The confronter in Situation 3 threatened to expose a political game that fits the dirty-trick category. Some risk was involved in his situation because the extortionist might have had some valid derogatory information about his consumption of office supplies. Exposing a dirty trick is a direct and effective antidote to one of the most unsavory forms of office politics. Usually the dirty trickster will be too embarrassed to repeat the act, as discovered by Grace.

Word-processing technician Grace was happy to find employment in the word-processing pool of a large law office. The job fit in with her plans for becoming a legal secretary. However, her straight-laced devotion to duty and her prissy mannerisms put Grace in disfavor with co-workers. To make life difficult for Grace, on several occasions somebody rearranged the order of work in her in-basket. In this way Grace was processing her assignments out of order. Newer work was being taken care of before older work. The result was a number of complaints about Grace's work by attorneys in the firm.

Grace refused to accept her harassment gracefully. She wrote a report about what she thought was happening and carefully reviewed it with her supervisor. The upshot was that the supervisor called for a department meeting. She angrily told the group that word had gotten back to her about the childish pranks being played with others' in-baskets.

The pranks ceased and Grace developed a better system for placing priorities on her work assignments. She received an excellent rating on her last performance report, and is now on the way toward becoming a legal secretary.

## DON'T PERSONALIZE
## POLITICAL SETBACKS ━━━━━━━━━━━━━━━━━━━━━━━━━━━

A disconcerting problem with political warfare is that one's feelings may hurt after being attacked. Feelings are hurt because people take innuendoes and power plays directed against them personally. If you are passed over for promotion in favor of a top executive's protege, it is easy to think that there is something wrong with you. You might wonder if perhaps somebody has discovered an important weakness of yours that makes you unpromotable.

To cope with this problem, Marilyn Moats Kennedy urges you to create distance between your personal and professional selves.[2] According to her method, leave your personal self, or ego, at home before going to work. Bring your professional self to the job. Because the person who gets caught then in office political battles is not entirely you, the insults and slights are easier to take.

The first step in creating a professional self separate from a personal self is to remember to leave your ego at home. If you are a committed professional this may not be easy to do because your career is such a big part of yourself. Nevertheless, you can model the attitude of Constantine, a manager of international banking.

"I get a lot of heat from other bankers," says Constantine. "They resent the money I make and all the attention I get because our unit of the bank is doing so well. Besides that, we represent the glamour end of the business. I don't take their barbs seriously because I know that they are envious of my success. If they knew the real Constantine, they wouldn't dislike me so much. If I were an ordinary performer, I know I would be subject to much less backbiting.

"If I want to achieve my professional goals, I'll just have to learn to live with ordinary performers who are trying to drag me down."

Second, it is necessary to tell yourself that you are a professional at whatever you do. "Professional" in this sense, simply means that your work is not a hobby—that's for amateurs—but a paid occupation. As a professional you can expect some people to be jealous. It might even help you to see yourself as a soldier of fortune. You wouldn't be invading other countries if you weren't paid.

Third, convince yourself that criticism of your work is not criticism of you as a person. A boss may call your work "sloppy" not because the boss dislikes you, but because he or she is compelled to play Blemish (some fault can be found with everything). Imagine how crushed the mayor of your town would be if he or she took personally every derogatory editorial about the mayor's office.

In short, political attacks, like any other type of setback, should not be taken personally. Should you be compelled to seek revenge for the creep who cast doubt in management's mind about your capabilities, don't take that personally either. The real you is not a revenge seeker. Circumstances forced you to counterattack, much like a criminal is sometimes forced to exterminate the competition.

## CIRCULATE YOUR IDEAS
## TO RECEIVE CREDIT

As mentioned in relation to coping with a difficult boss, credit stealing is a common problem in the workplace. A boss will frequently neglect to inform higher-ups that you are responsible for a breakthrough success. Instead the boss will try to pass it off as his or her own. A one-time public relations executive says he's seen instances in which a team member described some accomplishment in a memo to the boss. The boss, in turn, had it retyped under his or her name and sent it along to the boss. The team member was not even thanked for the contribution.

A West-coast television producer once resigned in protest over a dispute with another producer who was grabbing credit for his ideas. The producer offers this advice: "Defend yourself by becoming systematically less modest. Put your ideas, agreements you've made—everything—in writing, and circulate them to everyone on the staff including the shipping clerk. You never know who will be your ally."[3]

A deft variation of this technique is to protect yourself against the opposite ploy of someone trying to make you the scapegoat for a project's failure. If you've been assigned a job with a high risk of failure, let everybody know in advance in writing. Send photocopies of your risk analysis to every plausible person. Should the project fail, you can point to your advance warning that failure was probable. You have therefore erected a defense against anyone who might zap you because your project failed.

## CLAMP DOWN ON PEOPLE
## OUT TO GET YOUR JOB

A good job is a precious resource, and because precious resources are limited, many people will be in pursuit of your job. Subordinates are the most likely pursuers. It is also possible that a co-worker will have similar designs. On occasion, a higher-ranking person will want your job because your position appears more satisfying. Herb, the vice-president of marketing at a clothing manufacturer became fatigued of constant job stress. His perception of a more relaxed, yet still responsible job, was to be branch manager of the Atlanta regional office.

One alternative facing Herb was to approach the company president directly, and ask to be appointed as branch manager of the Atlanta office as soon as Vera, the incumbent, left. Herb opted against such an approach because he believed Vera to be happily ensconced in her job. The alternative Herb chose was to initiate a subtle campaign of finding good reasons for the company to replace Vera. He put together several contrived reports showing how the growth of the company's business in the Atlanta region was poor in comparison to the general business growth in the area. Herb also looked for ways to discredit the value of reports prepared by Vera.

One day after receiving another berating from him, Vera recollected how Herb had mentioned in the past how wonderful it would be to run the Atlanta region. Particularly in comparison to the pressures he faced as a vice-president. Vera's recollection gave her the inspiration to mount a counterattack. In a lengthy letter to the president she described how Herb may have lost objectivity in his criticism of her region's performance. Vera let the letter sit for two days, edited it, and then mailed it to the president.

Vera received a noncommittal letter back from the president, stating that he received her letter and appreciated the feedback. "Upward communication is always welcome in our organization," said the president. From that point forward, Vera incurred no unwarranted attacks from Herb. A year later Vera received a phone call from the president. He wanted to know if she would be willing to accept Herb in her region as the sales representative for the Miami territory. Herb's cardiologist advised him to get out from under so much job pressure, and the president thought that a sales position in Miami would be less stressful for him.

Vera agreed that her region could possibly use a Miami sales rep, providing he could pull his weight by concentrating his energies on customers rather than on internal battles. However, she could not guarantee that Herb would be out from under all job pressures.

Vera thus fended off the potential loss of her job by delicately presenting feedback on how she was being attacked to the right person. The need to clamp down on somebody else who wants your job arises most frequently in relation to subordinates. Often that person is a trusted subordinate. One tip-off that a team member wants your job is when he or she jumps at the opportunity to act on your behalf, even without receiving your approval.

Bob had just returned from a three-week trip during which he visited the company's manufacturing and warehousing operations in the United States and Canada. The first thing Bob did was to coordinate with his top assistant, Helen, to bring himself up-to-date.

Bob and Helen are not only colleagues, but friends as well. They work together easily and informally. Helen quickly covered the key points on which Bob needed information. Bob then said, "Helen, I guess now one of your top priorities is that problem with marketing. Maybe we'd better . . . ."

Helen interrupted by saying, "Yes, I was coming to that. Charley Ames called me last week and he seemed to want some final resolution. Since he's the top person, I thought a little fast action was in order. So I made some moves." Then, somewhat nervously, Helen proceeded to describe what she had done, concluding with, "Charley says it looks fine to him. And I was sure it's about the same thing you would have done."

With part of his mind, Bob was listening to the words his assistant was saying. But one thought was paramount, and it was an unpleasant and vexing one: "She's after my job!"

The discussion ended with Bob approving the action his assistant had taken. He did not surface the question of whether or not Helen might have waited for his return, or made a stronger effort to get in touch with him. Bob needed time to think.

One approach Bob might take with Helen is to confront her gently about her apparent intention of taking over parts of his job. Bob might say, "It appears that you want to be acting manager in my absence. Perhaps you are looking to replace me when I leave. Whatever your reasons, let's agree on guidelines for handling such situations in the future."

Another way to cope with people out to get your job is to let your boss know of your intentions to stay where you are as long as it pleases the organization. Point out that rumors have been circulating to the effect that you are going to recommend a replacement for yourself. State that although there are one or two people in your department capable of handling your job, you feel that you are making an important contribution where you are now. Should the company decide to promote or transfer you, however, you would warmly consider the idea. Emphasize strongly that you want your career moves dictated by upper management, not by subordinates.

The scenario just described will alert your boss to the political thrusts of any team member who hints at being ready to assume your position. You will also be seen as a manager who is quite observant of what's going on in your department.

Another way of clamping down on would-be deposers is to recommend them for a new permanent assignment. Explain to the ambitious subordinate that it is obvious he or she craves a new challenge. You are therefore recommending a lateral transfer (same level of responsibility) as further grooming for a future promotion. If you are successful in transferring the team member intent on your job, he or she will have to start all over again in plotting to be promoted.

## PUT A LID ON THE BAD MOUTHER

A person who bad mouths you can damage your reputation by inducing others to question your capabilities. Others may not accept in toto all the negative comments, but they may create doubts. If the bad mouthers can manipulate others to say negative things about you, it may be too late to salvage your reputation. It is therefore difficult to ignore the bad mouther. If you have solid evidence that a team member (or a co-worker) is bad mouthing you, it is important to find answers to several questions:[4]

1. *Who is doing the talking?* The bad mouther may be a typical malcontent, forever complaining about something. Or the person might be a marginal employee who seeks attention through controversy rather than through notable performance. In either case, there is a good chance that other team members won't pay much attention to the malcontent's attempts to undermine you. In contrast, if the bad mouther has a generally good reputation, it's time to worry about the negative commentary.

2. *What are your informant's motives?* The person or persons telling you about the bad mouthers could be informing you because they are legitimately concerned about attempts to undermine you. Perhaps they really do not want rumors to disrupt the smooth flow of the department. If this is the case, you may be receiving honest feedback. Another possibility is that they are reporting for some less cooperative reason. Perhaps they want to create trouble for the alleged bad mouther, want you to feel insecure, or, have decided to become the department watchdog—informing you of problems in order to win your approval.

Finding answers to the above questions will require some delicate questioning and intuition. One manager I know relies on her trusted assistant to help find answers to such questions. Over lunch she might say to her assistant, "I'm concerned. Lou is saying that Allen is bad mouthing me. I have a sense that in reality Lou is bad mouthing Allen by pretending that Allen is bad mouthing me. What is your opinion of the situation?"

If it appears that bad mouthing is really taking place, two courses of action might be taken. In the future, make a point of publicizing the reasons behind your behavior. If people understand why you have taken certain actions, there is less likely to be resentment, sub rosa accusations, and negative rumors about you. For example, if you carefully explain why you have been forced to severely restrict travel expenses the grumbling about these actions may decrease. Second guessing decreases when team members understand the reasoning behind decisions.

A more direct action is to conduct a low-key discussion with the probable bad mouther. Avoid betraying informants by mentioning names. Just zero in on the central issue: "Word has gotten back to me that you disagree with several decisions I have made. Would you be willing to tell me directly of your concerns?" Such a line of attack gives the employee a chance to air any legitimate gripes.

In an attempt to stop new incidents of bad mouthing, you might say, "I'm glad we talked over this problem. In the future if you disagree with something I've done, why not discuss it with me? I'm always interested in listening to constructive suggestions."

The reason this approach may resolve the problem is that employees sometimes bad mouth the boss as a way of expressing discontentment. By listening to the employee's gripe, you may have taken care of his or her need to express negative attitudes. Another possibility is that the bad mouther is a difficult person who needs attention. By listening to the person, you may have satisfied that need.

If your tete-à-tete doesn't work you may need to apply sanctions such as the threat of a negative performance evaluation, a written warning, or possible demotion. However, such actions can be politically unwise. You may be seen as a manager who can't keep the troops under control without creating a stir. The stir occurs because formal disciplinary measures usually drag in the next level of management.

## SET LIMITS TO NETWORK JUNKIES

The virtues of networking are so well known that influential and/or knowledgeable people are frequently swamped with others who want to "network" with them. Network junkies hand you their business card, ask for yours, hound you for luncheon or breakfast dates, use you as a reference, call for your advice, make pitches to you as a potential customer, and ask you to help solve their problems. In exchange, they offer to help you should the need arise. But if you are influential and knowledgeable, you will always have a trade imbalance—in their favor.

Why are these network junkies practicing unfair politics? In a subtle way you are being exploited if you are consistently the helper and rarely the helpee. Those people attempting to network with you are sopping your professional time. You could invest that time to improve your job performance or play sensible politics and thus enhance your career. Instead, you are unintentionally engaging in charitable acts.

From one perspective, if you are the target of many networkers, consider yourself lucky. Others perceive you to be a meaningful contact. Nevertheless, you can't spend too much of your time helping others. As one cynical executive said, "How many people in a lifetime am I supposed to help get jobs? Am I an employment agency for the ambitious and the discontent?"

The people hoping to entice you into their network include friends, acquaintances, relatives, former colleagues, and job applicants. You can also expect people you meet at cocktail parties and athletic clubs to want to hit on you. Networkers often beat around the bush, waiting for you to tell them what they want. To decrease the drain on your time, do the following:[5]

## Clarify the Issue

Get the networkers to state exactly what they want from you. Then explain tactfully but explicitly what you will and will not do. For example, "I am not in a position to recommend anybody as a new hire these days. Our company is currently assessing how big we should be, and we have a freeze on hiring." If you are vague about whether or not you can help the networker, you may be kept on the phone a long time.

## Specify Time Limits

You might say over the phone, "My time budget allows five minutes for this type of interview. Go ahead." If you do grant a personal interview, say something to the effect, "I can see you for a maximum of 15 minutes. If you think we can conduct the business you have in mind in that amount of time, I'll fit you into my schedule."

## Set a Time Frame for Your Assistance

Suppose your organization has a one-year hiring freeze. Tell the person you will talk about job openings when the freeze is lifted. Or, make a statement such as "I will be willing to discuss your proposition after June 15th. A major project of mine will be completed by that date."

## Engage in Lateral Networking

Suggest that the person contacting you be in touch with a secondary source of help such as a colleague, the recruiting department, an employment agency, or a colleague at another firm. If you believe that any of these other people might be interested in the person, you will have done your job. However, it is politically unwise to pass a pest on to people in your network. They may not be so receptive the next time you have a legitimate need of your own. In contrast, referring a valuable person to another source can enhance your reputation.

### Don't Feel Guilty

You can't give to every charity, no matter how altruistic you might be. And you can't help every person attempting to incorporate you into their network. Assist only those people you genuinely enjoy helping.

## CONFRONT THE BYPASSER

A manager has to be concerned with bypassers from below and above. The bypasser from below is a subordinate who takes problems, concerns, and ideas directly to your boss without informing you. The bypasser from above is a higher-up who deals directly with one of your subordinates, ignoring you in the process. Both types of political blunders can embarrass you and erode your power.

Keep in mind that an honorable explanation for a bypass in either direction can exist. In the modern, loose and easy organization, people go to whomever they need to get work accomplished. This is a radical departure to the chain of command so rigidly followed in the traditional bureaucracy.

The multipurpose, nonadversarial confrontation is an effective starting point in dealing with the bypasser from below. Discussing the problem with a subordinate may help you know *why* you are being bypassed. Understanding the reason can help you find a permanent solution to the problem. Sometimes a team member goes directly to your boss in an attempt to undermine you and make you look bad. At other times, there may be a less devious reason for the bypass.

Sandy, a high-school French teacher, consistently went directly to the principal with her concerns over matters such as coping with an intimidating student, or the need for modern equipment for teaching a foreign language. Alison, Sandy's administrative superior and the head of the language department, was miffed. She felt that she had little enough power as a high-school department head. Sandy's violation of the chain of command worsened the problem.

"We've got to talk," said Alison to Sandy one afternoon. "You've been doing something lately that makes it difficult for me to do my job as a department head."

"What's that?" said Sandy, innocently. "I may have been a little harsh in my criticism of a few students. But I don't think their parents are after your hide or mine."

"No, the problem isn't with students. It's with me," said Alison. "You keep running to the principal with problems that you and I should be hashing out. When you do this, it makes me look wimpy in the principal's eyes."

"I'm going directly to Bruce for a good reason," responded Sandy. "In the past I went to you with problems such as requesting new equipment for our language laboratory. Your answer was always that you would have to check with Bruce. So instead of going to Bruce indirectly, I chose to use a direct route."

Alison thought to herself that Sandy's explanation did make sense. Nevertheless, she still was being a little underhanded. Alison then said to Sandy, "From now on, come to me directly with problems. I'll give you an immediate answer on everything that can be settled at the department level. Otherwise, I will have to check with Bruce. Often he will have to check with Dr. Chang (the school superintendent). And quite often Chang will have to check with the school board. That's the way the school system works."

Alison's gentle confrontation achieved its intended purpose. Sandy virtually stopped undermining her authority. Alison still thinks Sandy's motives were not as pure as she professes. Nevertheless, the problem is under control.

Coping with a bypassing boss can be more difficult than coping with a team member doing the same thing. In a multilayered organization, the person to whom you report has more rights than you. As with the subordinate bypasser, the boss bypasser may be going around you for different motives. Your boss may go directly to one of your team members because he or she has a legitimate need to get something done in a hurry or requires a quick answer. An executive newsletter points out two more reasons for the bypass: The boss may want to save time or may have doubts about your ability to get the job done properly.[6] Also consider the possibility that your boss may be trying to weaken your authority.

The best approach when being bypassed from above is to talk candidly with the boss about the situation. If the situation is not brought under control, the bypassing will continue. Furthermore, your team members may start bypassing you to deal with your boss. Here are some actions you can take to fend off a bypassing boss:[7]

- *Ask for a formal meeting.* Inform your boss that you have something important to discuss about running your operation. To appear humble, assume that the conference will take place in your boss's office.

- *Describe the problem.* State the general problem of your boss going directly to your team members in order to solve problems, and then give one or two examples. Be factual rather than accusatory. Say, for example, "About ten days ago, you wanted a forecast of how much our department would be over budget for this year. You went directly to Ginny with your request. It's true she had some figures to give you. But she didn't have the complete picture. Ricardo was also working on the budget problem. If you had come to me, I could have put the pieces together." (Notice that you are giving your boss a nonpolitical reason for dealing with you rather than with one of your subordinates.)

- *Discuss the consequences of being bypassed.* Negative consequences of your boss going under you for information and problem solving include: confused employees due to conflicting directions, missed deadlines, incomplete information (as described above), and embarrassment to you and team members.

- *Describe your feelings.* Especially if your boss is psychologically minded, describe how you felt embarrassed, exasperated, frustrated, belittled, or miffed. Don't overdo it, however, at the risk of your boss thinking you lack flexibility.

    After this conversation, your boss will be embarrassed if he or she has merely been insensitive or impatient to get answers. If this is the case, request that work assignments be made through you to clarify work schedule and avoid conflicting priorities.

    Your discussion might also reveal that your boss has lost some confidence in you, or that you appear to be overloaded. Ask what changes your boss would like to see, or what improvements can be made. If your boss realizes he or she has been trying to weaken your authority, perhaps the behavior has become too obvious, and it might stop.

Whatever the reason for the bypass, putting it under control can benefit the boss. You can then do your job more effectively, making your boss look better.

## COUNTERACT NAYSAYERS

Some people in an organization, such as cost accountants and financial analysts, have a legitimate reason for being naysayers. Their formal role is to carefully protect company assets. Other naysayers hurl peccadilloes at the creative suggestions of others for devious reasons. Lacking in imagination themselves, they want others to look foolish or stay mediocre.

Unfortunately, the naysayer is usually correct because very few ideas for products, services, or cost improvements prove to be useful. If you say something won't work, there is a high probability you are right. Yet if you want to gain visibility and get ahead, you have to suggest and help implement some innovations. To get your ideas implemented, be prepared to outmaneuver naysayers. The following guidelines are designed to help you do just that.[8]

1. *Provide ample details to support your suggestion.* Naysayers are lurking in the wings to snap questions at you such as "How much will it cost?" "Has this idea been tried and failed before?" "Does the technology exist to bring your idea to fruition?" "In what way does your idea fit our company strategy?" All of these are valid questions, so have detailed answers before you present your innovative idea to higher-ups.

2. *Think through how your idea fits into the total organizational system.* A contemporary buzz word among managers and professionals is "organizational system." It is therefore politically astute to explain how your suggestions directly or indirectly affect other parts of the organization. Suppose you suggest a rebate program to boost sales. It would be wise to specify who will handle the complaints of people who purchased the product just before the rebate was announced. Also explain how the rebate program can be made palatable to dividend-hungry stockholders.

3. *Get your critics involved in your suggestion.* It's difficult to skirt all the naysayers in your path. You may silence them once, but they will probably strike again with backbiting comments made to a third party. A plausible antidote is to defuse naysayers by incorporating some of their negative thinking into your proposal. In the example about the rebate program, you might ask a critic: "I appreciate concern about some customers being miffed because they made a purchase just before the rebate program. How do you suggest we deal with that problem? I welcome your suggestion, and I will certainly put your name on the proposal."

4. *Anticipate major criticisms.* Skepticism about your grand new scheme is inevitable. Anticipate these reservations so you can be prepared in a meeting to parry the thrusts of the inevitable naysayer. An example: "You say that the rebate program is far too expensive. You point out that the rebate will result in us losing 20 cents on every sale. Your argument does not take into account the fact that only about 40 percent of customers ever send in their rebate coupon. My analysis shows that if only 50 percent of the rebate coupons are cashed, we

will have reached the breakeven point on the promotion. We then will have picked up a large number of repeat customers we would not have captured without the rebate program."

5. *Empathize with a broad range of critics.* In addition to anticipating obvious criticisms of your proposal, think through the type of criticism you can expect from various people in the company. Potential naysayers—in addition to financial specialists—include legal, manufacturing, and quality specialists. How would you react to your proposal if you were in their shoes?

Jess, a hotel manager was making preparations to open a new night club in a company hotel. He suggested that the hotel hire a number of attractive people of both sexes to act as customers the first two weeks. The purpose of these models would be to create a glamorous atmosphere that would spark the enthusiasm of legitimate patrons. Before bringing his proposal to top management, Jess anticipated warnings of possible job discrimination in hiring only attractive people to decorate the club.

His solution was to hire models. In this way, the night club would be relying on the judgment of the modeling agency to select attractive people for the short-term assignment. Jeff would grant full authority to the agency for selecting the models, with the only stipulation being that an equal number of men and women be hired. Because a dancing couple is usually composed of one member of each sex, the request would unlikely be challenged by anybody.

6. *Be prepared to redirect your innovative idea.* Sometimes a naysayer blocking your path to converting an innovative idea into reality has a valid point. You may be upset because the person throwing cold water on your idea relishes putting you down. Sometimes the objection raised just requires that your idea take a detour. A hospital administrator proposed that the hospital put together a crisis team that would be prepared to handle a catastrophe such as several wings of the hospital being closed down because of a hurricane. The Swat Team would be composed of members from both clinical and administrative departments.

The clinical director objected strenuously to his overworked staff investing time in preparing for an emergency that would probably never take place. Rather than give up on the idea, Terry revamped the proposed team roster. It would now consist of members of the administrative staff, and retired medical professionals who had worked extensively at the hospital. The revamped proposal was eventually accepted.

7. *Describe payoffs that outweigh the inconveniences.* An innovation of substance usually requires a lot of people to be inconvenienced. In the SWAT team example, key personnel would have to attend regular meetings, the training director would have to help develop the program, and many people would be upset while the drills took place. You should therefore suggest benefits that will compensate fully for the possible inconveniences in implementing your idea. The administrator who proposed the SWAT team pointed out that the hospital was already facing competitive threats. A long period of interrupted service might create such a financial crisis and loss of public confidence that the hospital might be forced to close.

8. *Be patient, the naysayers may take a long time to convert.* Sometimes even your most severe critic may ultimately embrace your idea. Despite initial dart throwing at your proposed innovation, the naysayers may come to realize that there is merit in your proposal. If you cannot overcome the first set of objections to your suggestion, put the idea away for awhile. Several months, or even a year or two later, your idea might be accepted. Another possibility is that the naysayer who has blocked your idea will have left the scene.

   A story has circulated that when a Sears & Roebuck executive first proposed that the company sell insurance, the naysayers dismissed the idea as preposterous. "Nobody is going to buy life and casualty insurance from the same place they purchase washing machines" said the critic. Several years later, Allstate Insurance became a major business for Sears.

## KEEP YOUR COMMUNICATION
## CHANNELS UNCLOGGED

At times it is necessary to defend oneself against devious political thrusts from below. A politically astute manager therefore keeps informed about problems brewing in his or her organizational unit. A manager who is out of touch with the feelings and opinions of team members is vulnerable to a palace revolt.

Several years ago a corporate executive was deposed by one of his vice-presidents, much to his surprise and dismay. Several of his staff members became disenchanted with his style of management. They felt the executive had become too detached from the people and the real problems of the business. As one insider explained to a company outsider:

"The man had become obsessed with paperwork and controls. He never visited us any longer. He simply called up information on his computer and made pronouncements about what we were doing wrong on the basis of the computerized information. I don't think he had ever seen some of our products. He only made two personal visits to plant locations.

"We finally met secretly with the board of directors and suggested they ax him. Instead, he was given a staff job as vice-president of special projects."

Palace revolts, of course, are more typically found at the highest levels of management. But the same approach can be used at a lower level. To ward off potential revolts (which are a devious tactic), keep attuned to the members of your team.

One self-confident manager I know asks at an occasional staff meeting, "Folks, is there anything I'm doing that interferes with your doing your job as you would like to do it?" By acting on these suggestions (such as "Be more specific about what you want us to accomplish") he is able to prevent a minor annoyance from becoming a revolution. Also, there is an advantage to making top management aware of this approach to upward communication. They are less likely to listen to sniveling complaints about how you manage your unit.

## DOCUMENT YOUR SIDE OF THE STORY

A major accusation made by an unfair office politician is that the person under attack has not performed satisfactorily. Documenting your side of the story may therefore be necessary to prove what you have accomplished. A full dossier of your accomplishments can help settle a dispute as to whether you are performing properly in your job. The time invested in documenting your accomplishments is worthwhile because the same information might come in handy in advancing your career (as described previously). The situation faced by one college dean illustrates the defensive value of documenting one's side of the story.

> Accompanied by his wife and five children, Fred moved across the country to become dean of the college of continuing education ("night school") at a private university. A number of faculty members and administrators in his college were opposed to the idea of an outsider being appointed dean. Slowly, they began a campaign to have him ousted. One approach they used was to let outside people know how discontent they were with their new dean.
>
> A department head under Fred attempted a more devastating maneuver. He reported to the university president that enrollment in the college had declined 14 percent since Fred was appointed dean. The president contacted Fred and told him to be prepared to defend the charges being made against him—declining enrollment and employee dissatisfaction. Fred spent a busy week accumulating facts and figures to answer the charges.

His number one defense of his methods was that his college had experienced a smaller decline in enrollment than other colleges of continuing education: His school showed a decline of 14 percent versus an average of 21 percent for other comparable private universities. In regard to the alleged morale problem, Fred noted that absenteeism and turnover figures were lower than in the previous two years. Case dismissed. However, Fred still had a long way to go to build the support and confidence of his staff.

## BE IMPERVIOUS TO AN EXPOSE

Another person out to get you and your job has the best chance of succeeding when you have something to hide. A simple antidote against this is for you to become Mr. or Ms. Clean. People can extort you only when you have engaged in some deviant or questionable act. Such was the case with contracts administrator Art who imprudently used his position to receive kickbacks from several vendors. In one instance he accepted a large-screen television receiver and home entertainment center from a paving company. The bargain Art struck was to arrange things so they could win a large contract without having to go through competitive bidding.

Paul, the contract supervisor reporting to Art (and at least a contender for Paul's job), asked that he be recommended for a maximum salary increase. Art flatly refused, telling Paul quite honestly that his performance did not justify any more than a cost-of-living increase. In retribution, Paul wrote the chief executive of the agency a memo exposing Art's kickback system. An investigation resulted. Several instances of kickbacks and noncompetitive bidding were discovered. Art was forced to resign.

Paul did not get Art's job, but he did get retribution. If Art had nothing to hide, he would have been impervious to the counterdevious tactics of an irate subordinate.

# CHAPTER 18

## STEMMING
## THE TIDE OF
## OFFICE POLITICS

The appropriate use of office politics contributes to obtaining the resources necessary to achieve such worthwhile goals as developing a new
vaccine or an oat bran muffin. Yet excessive politicking weakens an
organization and injures many innocent victims. When too many people
are playing too much politics not enough legitimate work gets done.
People spend so much time ingratiating themselves to others and protecting their own hides, that energy is diverted from task accomplishment. Political game playing can also detract from creative problem
solving as people focus more on style than substance.[1]

The previous chapter focused on one aspect of controlling excessive politics—counteracting devious tactics directed against you. Here
we describe how to curtail the overuse of politics in the total organization, or in the unit under your control. Controlling the excessive use of
office politics will probably become an even more important aspect of a
manager's job in the organizational climates of the 1990s. Eliminating
politics is an unrealistic goal. You would be attempting to overcome the
forces of human nature, and prevent people from getting the power they
need to do important work.

## ESTABLISH OBJECTIVE MEASURES
## OF PERFORMANCE

Political maneuvering is more pronounced when performance is measured by subjective standards rather than tangible results. This problem

313

was underscored by the comments of Gary L. Ackerman, D-N. Y., chairman of a House subcommittee on civil service. He was concerned about a proposal that all members of the senior executive service undergo a recertification process every three years to keep their higher salaries. The recertification would, of course, involve a supervisory evaluation of a government executive's competence.

Ackerman objected in these words: "It creates a system in which there will be a political litmus test. People will have to snooker up to their supervisors and kiss their rings [the Congressman was being euphemistic] to keep their pay raises. That's not what government service is all about."[2]

A related problem is that more politicking takes place in organizational units with unclear purposes, making it difficult to measure the contribution of people. When workers know what is expected of them, know how their results will be measured, and believe that what they are doing is important, the need for political maneuvering lessens.

The case history of Mildred, the public affairs coordinator, presented in Chapter 1 illustrates how difficult-to-measure work contributes to political behavior. Similarly, some people play politics to impress others because they lack relevant work as a vehicle for gaining recognition.

Media design specialist Alstair spent many a lunch hour trying to cultivate department heads. He flattered them and made frequent reference to the contribution of his department. One day a manager asked Bill, Alstair's boss, "What's Alstair's problem? Why does he spend so much time licking people's boots? Maybe you can help the fellow out. He's a nice guy. Perhaps you should find some honest work for him to do."

The acrid commentary made by this third party gave Bill an idea. He gently confronted Alstair with the comments relayed to him, combining his criticism with a couple of constructive suggestions: "Alstair, they tell me you're spending too much time playing politics. Specifically, you're trying to impress people with your words instead of your deeds. Let me suggest that you change your approach to being a media design specialist."

"What do you have in mind?" asked Alstair. "I thought you agreed that the company needed improved media design."

"That could be," said Bill, "but few people even know what a media design department is supposed to do. Why don't you let it be known that your department is willing to help people with any illustration or art work they might need. Even use the word 'graphics.' Explain that you can also help with computer graphics. I think you would get better requests from other departments if people knew you were willing to take on straightforward work. The way things stand now, people are hesitant to take on your services."

Alstair dutifully let it be known that the media design department was also an art and audiovisual department with a computer graphics capability. Gradually, interesting requests for useful work came to the department. Alstair's contribution was now being acknowledged and he spent very little time at lunch telling people how great they were, or he was. Talking about the captivating graphics he was doing kept Alstair busy.

## TELL THE TRUTH AND SPEAK DIRECTLY

A powerful antidote to excessive office politics would be a climate of openness and trust, characterized by direct, explicit talk. A deep-rooted reason many workers engage in political antics is that they fear the consequences of telling the truth. You might be willing to tell your boss that his proposal is flawed with poor logic if you did not fear that he would retaliate. When an organization welcomes candor, people have less fear of telling the truth. Consequently, they are freer to be less political in their actions.

An emphasis on unvarnished—but not brutal—statements by the boss fosters a climate of openness and trust. Because workers know the boss's true position on an issue, less ambiguity exists, and therefore less need to politick.[3] Suppose you assign a group member a difficult problem to solve. She returns with a pedestrian alternative. An indirect-talk response indicating your dissatisfaction would be, "I see a lot of possibilities there. Perhaps you can develop your thinking even further. Let's talk about it again, real soon." The team member is left hanging. Perhaps if she says something ingratiating to you, you will accept her solution.

Suppose instead, you engage in direct talk, with a statement such as, "I appreciate your effort, but please try again. I need a more creative solution." She knows where she stands, and must return to the drawing board. The ambiguity has been removed from the situation, and political behavior would seem less useful.

The experience of department head Val helps explain how leveling with people can curtail the need for playing politics. When he first took over the department, Val noticed that people went out of their way to please him in addition to performing well. Having attended a management development program aimed at teaching managers how to level with people, Val thought his department was ripe for such an approach. He reports:

> It appeared to me that people were wasting a lot of time politicking. It was apparent in such things as writing memos to me proving what a good job they had done. People were figuring out all sorts of ways to impress me and my boss. After I was on the job about six months, I accumulated

enough information about my people to have a good idea of their strengths and weaknesses. I then held an appraisal session with each department member. I also explained what promotions were possible in the next year or so. Everybody then knew where he or she stood and what the chances for advancement were so long as I was in the saddle.

My talks had a dramatic effect on people. One department member quit because he did not like my evaluation of him. Everyone else seemed to appreciate knowing the truth. Office politics went way down and work performance went way up. Because people knew what I thought of them, going out of their way to please me seemed unnecessary.

## STOP GOSSIP AND RUMORS SHORT

Many political ploys begin with the spreading of gossip and rumors. When gossip is stopped short by ignoring or challenging the gossip, another form of office politics is diminished. Simultaneously a rumor is stopped. Rumors breed politics because people behave politically to ward off the feared consequences of the rumor. For example, in one office the rumor circulated that several workers would be forced to transfer to another city. Several people then busied themselves trying to prove to the boss how much they were needed in their present job.

When the office gossip runs out of listeners he or she might return to productive work. Two examples follow of how to stop gossip short:

| | |
|---|---|
| *GOSSIP:* | Too bad about McGee. I heard his wife has cancer; he's having an affair; and the whole mess is affecting his work. |
| *POTENTIAL LISTENER:* | That is too bad. But everybody has problems. I'm sure he'll work things out. Is there something you wanted to talk to me about? |
| *GOSSIP:* | I've heard from a reliable source that the marketing department is in for another shake-up. Word has it that Todd, the vice-president, will be axed. |
| *POTENTIAL LISTENER:* | Could be. The company always sends out official announcements of organization changes in the management newsletter. |

## BREAK UP COALITIONS AND CLIQUES

The negative side of long-standing coalitions and cliques is that under such circumstances people tend to become involved in political warfare with other departments. A danger sign is when team spirit is *too high* in one department. The team may develop a strong in-group feeling that places more emphasis on serving their own ends than the good of the larger organization. Political warfare among units can become particularly intense when unit heads are competing for a promotion.

As employees receive exposure to different departments, they tend to develop broader perspectives and place less importance on maximizing gain for their own departments. Job rotation is therefore helpful in decreasing detrimental interdepartmental bickering. Rotation is also helpful because it counters a "them versus us" view of other departments.[4]

Four vice-presidents were being groomed for the CEO's job in an energy company, because the current CEO was planning to retire. Each vice-president was intent on protecting his own unit, causing a breakdown in interunit cooperation. The antidote chosen by the current CEO was to play musical chairs at the top. For example, the vice-president of operations was moved to marketing and the engineering vice-president was moved to operations.

All four executives were rotated to another function twice in a five-year period. As a result of this rotation, the four executives developed a more realistic perspective of each others' problems. An important side benefit was that the cross-training helped prepare each vice-president to become the CEO. When one man was chosen for the presidency, he was not beset with the problem of having recently been engaged in interunit rivalries with the other three executives.

## PUT TOGETHER COMPATIBLE TEAMS

A consistent finding is that conflict among people leads to an increase in politicking. (It is also true that a heavy emphasis on politics breeds conflict: People get irritated and may retaliate when they are the victim of frequent political maneuvering.) A sensible way to reduce office politics is therefore to put together teams of people who are less likely to have conflicts with each other. There is less conflict likely when team members:

- Share similar values such as a love of knowledge and a strong work ethic
- Have similar frames of reference because they are of comparable age and education
- Have a similar sense of humor—they laugh at the same kind of comments and jokes
- Have similar goals and dreams

- Share similar outside interests such as a love of the water or professional football
- All like you

It would be a tall order to have a team that was compatible in all the aspects just listed. Such total compatibility might also dampen creativity. People who are too much alike sometimes don't bring enough diversity to problem solving, and tend to let each others' thinking go unchallenged. Nevertheless, compatibility on several factors would reduce team conflict and politicking.

In most organizations the newly appointed manager cannot choose all the team members; they are already present when you take over. However, as team members move on and you hire new ones, it is helpful to look for compatibility. Some executives use the "trip to Europe" test when selecting a potential team member. In sizing up the candidate (either external or internal), ask yourself, "Would I want to sit next to this person for a six or seven hour trip to Europe?" If the answer is yes, that person and you would be compatible. Your intuition counts heavily in making such a choice.

To be brutally honest, ask yourself such questions as, "Would I want to live with this person?" "Would I want to marry this person, assuming we fell in love?" "Would I want this person to marry one of my children?" "Would I want to go into a business partnership with this person?"

As part of the selection process, also have team members interview the prospective new member. In addition to the usual questions about technical competence, ask the team members how much they would enjoy having the candidate as a co-worker.

## RESOLVE CONFLICT BETWEEN FACTIONS ━━━━━━━━━

Just as it is important to minimize conflict within the group in order to ward off excessive politicking, it is also important to reduce conflict after it has erupted. It is not unusual for factions in conflict to waste substantial amounts of time and money fighting political battles.

In one company, a dinner meeting (paid for with company money) was held by a training group. The single agenda was to decide how the people at the meeting could protect their turf against another group within the same company that also wanted to offer computer training to the public. Each group wanted to convince top management it was better qualified to offer such a service. Both groups looked for ways to discredit the other.

If you have formal authority over the conflicting factions, get the groups in conflict to sit down and discuss their differences. A good starting point is what organization development specialists call image exchanging. Each group, with the assist of a leader, writes down

1. How they stand on the issue
2. How they think the other side stands on the issue
3. How they think the other side sees them as standing on the issue

The first exchange of perceptions results in some laughter and anger. For example, one of the groups intent on offering a computer training program wrote of the other group, "Like Sherwin-Williams, they want to cover the world. They already have more work than they can handle, but they want to grab anything new that's hot." After awhile, however, some serious discussion emerges over differences and how to resolve them.

A healthy resolution of the problem under discussion was that the training program would be offered as a joint venture by both groups. Each group would have primary responsibility for different programs, yet still have the option of using the talents of people in the other group.

## CHECK OUT PRAISE AND CRITICISM

An effective way of snuffing out one form of office politics is to determine why one person praises or criticizes another. Ideally, the praise or criticism is factually based.[5] At other times, the comments made by one person about another are aimed toward a devious end. People tend to be naive with regard to receiving compliments about themselves, so you have to work hard at evaluating praise aimed at you. Asking another person why he or she is dispensing praise or criticism is helpful, but a more penetrating approach might be to investigate why a third party is being lauded or chastised.

Late one afternoon, Virgil dropped by his boss's office to chat about some production problems. After making a few routine comments about factory activities, Virgil dropped a few words on behalf of Nick, a first-time supervisor. He said to his boss in an offhand manner, "I'm getting to think this company is sure on the way up. Look at the caliber of some of our new supervisors.

"Take that fellow, Nick, who was made supervisor last year. The guy's an absolute pistol. I wish I had more people like him working for me."

Virgil's boss listened but did not react. Instead, the next day he asked Nick's boss how Nick was doing as a supervisor. He was told,

"Good thing Nick has an old fishing buddy in Virgil. Otherwise he wouldn't have been recommended as a supervisor. I promoted him against my better judgment, but Virgil insisted the guy had lots of hidden talent. In fact, the talent is so hidden I'm thinking of recommending that the company fire him. Maybe Nick can discover the hidden talent at someone else's expense."

Cagey Virgil was trying to protect the hide of his fishing buddy, Nick. If Virgil's boss had not investigated the reason for his song of praise, he might have been deceived into believing that Nick was a capable supervisor. When Nick's boss ultimately recommended that he be fired, Virgil's boss might have mistakenly attributed Nick's problems to a personality clash with his boss.

## PROVIDE EVERYBODY WITH HIGH PAYING AND EXCITING JOBS

A principal of a small company that sells computer-based training packages to private and public organizations told me there is almost no office politics in her company. Asked why this was so, she answered: "People are too busy, and making too much money to bother with kissing up to the boss or taking swipes at each other. Everybody seems to be doing the kind of work he or she wants. We pay very well for a company in this region of the state. There's a good spirit in the office. We all know that we are on the forefront of an important movement in training. We are pioneers and we love the role."

The idyllic state of affairs described by the company principal is not readily achievable. Yet it points to an important way of combating excessive office politics. When people are well paid and enthusiastic about their work, they tend to concentrate more on work and less on posturing. Placed in a job you find stimulating, you too, might have less need to engage in excessive office politics.

## THREATEN TO DISCUSS QUESTIONABLE INFORMATION IN A PUBLIC FORUM

People who practice devious office politics usually want to operate secretly and privately. They are willing to drop hints and innuendoes, and even make direct derogatory comments, about someone else providing they will not be identified as the source. An effective way of putting the lid on character assassination or other forms of questionable information, is to offer to discuss the topic in a public forum.[6]

A team member might say to you, "Everything was going well in terms of having this report prepared and duplicated on time. Ten days ago I gave the word processing and duplicating department my floppy disk with the complete file. Ordinarily they only need five days lead time to get a report of this length word processed and duplicated.

"Actually, their stalling tactics are part of a general pattern I've noticed. I think Marla (the head of word processing and duplicating) really has it in for our department. She's on some kind of power trip."

An effective response on your part might be, "I think I understand the problem you are facing. It sounds like something that needs to be dealt with openly. Let's call a meeting among Marla, several of her people, you, my assistant, and myself. We can then bring this entire problem out in the open."

The person attempting to pass on the questionable information will usually back down, and make a statement closer to the truth. Recognizing that all complaints are subject to open discussion usually discourages people who hope to engage a manager in political games.[7]

## SET FAVORABLE EXAMPLES AT THE TOP

Senior management sets the stage for the type of political game playing that takes place at lower levels in the organization. When top management manipulates people, discredits the opposition, and covers up the truth, similar machinations are found down the line. When senior management plays sensible and ethical politics, a good example is established as to what kind of behavior is acceptable and encouraged.

An influential member of the business community, Helen was appointed publisher of a suburban newspaper. Within four months, according to an insider, the petty politics that had plagued the paper in the past had substantially diminished. The decrease in rampant office politics had improved morale and made it easier for the paper to achieve its deadlines. Helen explains her method of lessening political activity at the paper:

> When I took over as publisher, the political climate was so thick you could cut it with a knife. All the good jobs were held by personal friends of Sean Galsworthy, the former publisher. A reporter had to be extra nice to the editor-in-chief to get important new assignments. You had to buy gifts for the production room people to gain any cooperation. Gifts were no longer a bonus for good performance; they were a requirement for getting the paper printed.
>
> Two weeks after I took over, I told everybody we were starting with a new slate with respect to friendship and personal ties. From now on, all

employees had to prove themselves on their job. After six months, permanent assignments would be made. Many people would hold on to their
jobs, but reassignments would be made according to ability. I said that no
layoffs or firings were planned. Everybody was to write a signed statement
as to what job they were being paid to perform. I asked no one for special
favors and I didn't grant special favors to anyone.

A few people squirmed when I announced my new policy, but for the most
part people sighed in relief. For the first six months, people seemed to
conduct themselves in a businesslike manner. Sure, we would get the occasional plea for a special favor based on personal friendships, but not to a
disruptive extent. I think I succeeded in ridding the paper of office politics.
At least for a while.

The ultimate antidote against excessive politicking ties in closely
with setting an example of being nonpolitical. It takes the form of becoming so secure that you find it unnecessary to play most forms of
office politics. When you are successful, competent, and confident, there
is much less need for you to curry favor with others. It is their turn to
please you.

When you reach the stage in your career where you are satisfied
with your power and recognition, you can play office politics more out of
fun than necessity. When you reach this stage, or if you are already
there, you have truly won at office politics.

# REFERENCES

## CHAPTER 1

1. Stephen P. Robbins, *Organizational Behavior,* 4th ed. (Englewood Cliffs, NJ: Prentice Hall, 1989), pp. 355–357; Andrew J. DuBrin, *Human Relations: A Job Oriented Approach,* 4th ed. (Englewood Cliffs, NJ: Prentice Hall, 1988), pp. 271–273.

2. Robbins, p. 357.

3. Andrew J. DuBrin, "Sex and Gender Differences in Influence Tactics," *Journal of Business and Psychology,* Winter 1989.

## CHAPTER 2

1. Twenty-seven of the items on the original version of the Political Orientation Scale were quoted or paraphrased from two sources: Eugene E. Jennings, "You Can Spot the Office Politicians," *Nation's Business,* December 1959, p. 2; Richard Christie, *Studies in Machiavellianism* (New York: Academic Press, 1970).

## CHAPTER 3

1. Stephen P. Robbins, *Training in Interpersonal Skills* (Englewood Cliffs, NJ: Prentice Hall, 1989), p. 176.

2. Marilyn Moats Kennedy, *Office Politics: Seizing Power, Wielding Clout* (New York: Warner Books, 1980), p. 67.

3. Alan S. Schoonmaker, *Executive Career Strategy* (New York: AMACOM, 1971), pp. 107–109.

4. Kennedy, *Office Politics,* pp. 54–59.

5. Kennedy, *Office Politics,* pp. 132–133.

## CHAPTER 4

1. Christopher Hegarty, *How to Manage Your Boss* (New York: Rawson Wade, 1981).

2. Marilyn Moats Kennedy, "How to Manage Your New Boss," *Business Week Careers,* March/April 1987, p. 94.

3. Shirley Sloan Fader, "What Your Boss Wants You to Know," *Business Week Careers,* October 1985, p. 44.

4. Quoted in Judith Myers, "Corporate Star Quality: How to Shine Better Than Your Competition," *Woman's Day,* March 5, 1987, p. 162.

5. The idea of becoming a crucial subordinate stems from Eugene E. Jennings, *The Mobile Manager* (Ann Arbor, MI: University of Michigan Press, 1967).

6. Quoted in "Handling a Difficult Boss," *Personal Report for the Executive,* October 1, 1985, pp. 1–2.

7. Seth Allcorn, "The Self-Protective Actions of Managers," *Supervisory Management,* January 1989, p. 3.

8. Kennedy, "How to Manage Your New Boss," March/April 1987, p. 94.

9. Gerard A. Santelli researched the incident about winemaking.

10. "Socializing with Your Boss," *Personal Report for the Executive,* June 1, 1987, p. 8.

## CHAPTER 5

1. Stephen P. Robbins, *Training in Interpersonal Skills* (Englewood Cliffs, NJ: Prentice Hall, 1989), p. 172.

2. "The Super Achievers," Special Report from the National Institute of Business Management, Inc., 1988, p. 11; Constance Kurz, "A Business Lunch: Follow the Lead on the One Who Pays," *USA Weekend,* May 8–10, 1987, p. 14; George Mazzei, *The New Office Etiquette* (New York: Simon & Schuster, 1983); Letitia Baldridge, "A Guide to Executive Etiquette," *Business Week Careers,* October 1986, pp. 60–63.

3. E. Melvin Pinsel and Ligta Dienhart, *Power Lunching* (New York: Rawson Wade, 1984).

4. Adapted from Robert F. Reilly, "Teaching Relevant Managerial Skills in the MBA Program," *Collegiate News & Views,* Winter 1981–1982, p. 15.

5. "'Dr. Gloom' May Talk Himself Out of a Job," *Business Week,* December 12, 1983, p. 139; "Professor Feldstein Flunks Politics," *Business Week,* October 17, 1983, p. 219.

## CHAPTER 6

1. Rosabeth Moss Kanter, *Men and Women of the Corporation* (New York: Basic Books, 1977).

2. Andrew J. DuBrin, "Sex Differences in Endorsement of Influence Tactics and Political Behavior Tendencies," *Journal of Business and Psychology*, Winter 1989.

3. Jane Michaels, "You Gotta Get Along to Get Ahead," *Woman's Day*, April 3, 1984, p. 58.

4. Robert S. Wieder, "Psst! Here's the Latest on Office Gossip," *Success!*, January 1984, pp. 22–25.

5. The basic idea here is based on *The Super Achievers*, report published by the National Institute of Business Management, Inc., 1988, pp. 11–12.

6. Michaels, "You Gotta Get Along to Get Ahead," pp. 60–61.

7. The first two points are from "Surviving Company Picnics," *Executive Strategies*, July 18, 1989, p. 7.

8. Niccolo Machiavelli, *The Prince*, The Modern Library (Random House), 1940. The original book was published circa 1510.

## CHAPTER 7

1. David Hoffman, "Bush: Making Himself up as He Goes Along," *Washington Post*, August 13, 1989, p. B4.

2. Morgan W. McCall, Jr. and Michael M. Lombardo, "What Makes a Top Executive?" *Psychology Today*, February 1983, p. 28.

## CHAPTER 8

1. Richard Cohen, "Henry K and the C Words—China, Conflict," *Washington Post*, syndicated column, August 29, 1989.

2. "Got Your Eye on Power? Try Glasses, Survey Says," Associated Press story, April 26, 1986.

3. Toni Apgar (editor), *Mastering Office Politics* (New York: National Institute of Business Management, Inc., 1988), pp. 22–23.

4. *Mastering Office Politics*, p. 23.

5. Henry L. Tosi and Stephen J. Carroll, *Management* (Chicago: St. Clair Press, 1976), p. 214.

6. Sherry Suib Cohen, *Tender Power* (Reading, MA: Addison-Wesley Publishing Company, 1989).

7. Case researched by Wayne Strawn.

## CHAPTER 9

1. Joanne Kenen, "A Gorbachev Host, Trump Is an Icon of Capitalism," Reuters story, December 2, 1988.

2. *The Secret Ways Executives Grab Power*, National Institute of Business Management special report, December 1988, pp. 1–2.

3. Lynn Rosellini, "The Social Power Game," *New York Times* syndicated story, January 2, 1981.

4. William H. Newman, *Administrative Action,* second edition (Englewood Cliffs, NJ: Prentice-Hall, 1963), p. 89.

5. Fred Luthans, Richard M. Hodgetts, and Stuart A. Rosenkrantz, *Real Managers* (Cambridge, MA: Ballinger Publishing Company, 1988), p. 128.

6. *The Secret Ways Executives Grab Power,* p. 16.

7. Jane Ciabattari, "Managerial Courage," *Working Woman,* September 1988, p. 107.

8. Ciabattari, "Managerial Courage," pp. 107–108.

9. Jeffrey Pfeffer, *Power in Organizations* (Marshfield, MA: Pitman Publishing, 1981), p. 143.

10. Jurgen Ruesch, *Knowledge in Action* (New York: Jason Aronson, 1975), p. 158.

11. Niccolo Machiavelli, *The Prince* (New York: The Modern Library, 1940), p. 61.

12. Machiavelli, *The Prince,* p. 82.

13. Pfeffer, *Power in Organizations,* pp. 146–149.

14. Robert N. McMurry, "Power and the Ambitious Executive," *Harvard Business Review,* November–December 1973, p. 142.

## CHAPTER 10

1. Sydney J. Harris, "Career Advice: Stick with What You Do Best," syndicated column, September 16, 1982.

2. Judith Myers, "Corporate Star Quality: How to Shine Brighter Than Your Competition," *Cosmopolitan,* August 1987, p. 162.

3. Robert Jackall, "Moral Mazes: Bureaucracy and Managerial Work," *Harvard Business Review,* September–October 1983, p. 122.

4. Jackall, "Moral Mazes," p. 123.

5. Richard Satran, "Recruiter Charts Path up Corporate Mountain," Reuters story, February 20, 1989.

6. "Cosmetic Surgery Is on the Rise for Male Executives," *Personal Report for the Executive,* May 15, 1986, p. 7.

7. "How to Make Personal Contacts That Accelerate Career Advancement," in *The Super Achievers,* National Institute of Business Management report, August 1988, p. 13; "Networking Tune-Up," *Executive Strategies,* August 1, 1989, p. 7.

8. "Booming Breakfast Clubs Provide Bacon, Eggs, Business Contacts," Gannett News Service story, September 20, 1986.

9. Thomas Busch researched the case about Alex.

10. Jennifer Urbanski researched the case about Foster.

11. "Document Your Accomplishments," *Personal Report for the Executive,* July 1, 1986, p. 6.

12. Michael L. Oliver, "Taking Risks Will Get Your Career Moving," *Personnel Journal,* April 1983, p. 319.

13. "A Lateral Move Can Lead Upward," in Toni Apgar, ed., *Mastering Office Politics* (New York: National Institute of Business Management, 1988), p. 29.

14. Idea contributed by Arnold Smeenk.

15. Steven Robbins, *Training in Interpersonal Skills* (Englewood Cliffs, NJ: Prentice Hall, 1989), p. 173.

16. *The Super Achievers*, p. 16.

17. Robbins, *Training in Interpersonal Skills*, p. 174.

18. William H. Newman, *Administrative Action*, second edition (Englewood Cliffs, NJ: Prentice-Hall, 1963), p. 89.

## CHAPTER 11

1. *The Secret Ways Executives Grab Power*, National Institute of Business Management Report, 1988, p. 3.

2. *The Secret Ways Executives Grab Power*, p. 3.

3. Gerald W. Oakley researched the anecdote about Harriet and developed the basic idea contained in this section.

4. The basic idea contained in "use initial power" is credited to Michael Korda, *Power! How to Get It, How to Use It* (New York: Ballantine Books, 1975), pp. 102–107.

5. John H. Simms, "Thinking Ahead: Power Tactics," *Harvard Business Review*, November–December 1955, p. 28.

## CHAPTER 12

1. Gerald F. Cavanagh, Dennis J. Moberg, and Manuel Velasquez, "The Ethics of Organizational Politics," *Academy of Management Review*, July 1981, p. 372.

2. Niccolo Machiavelli, *The Prince* (New York: The Modern Library, 1940), p. 73.

3. Al Neuharth, *Confessions of an S.O.B.* (Garden City, NY: Doubleday, 1989).

4. *The AMBA Executive*, March 1977, p. 7.

5. This technique is described in *The Federal Political Personnel Manual*. Reported in Doug Shuitt, "Federal Jobs and Politics," *Los Angeles Times* story, December 26, 1976.

6. *Ibid.*

7. The smokescreen technique is credited to Chester Burger, *Survival in the Executive Jungle* (New York: Macmillan, 1964), p. 6.

8. Shuit, "Federal Jobs and Politics."

9. Fred K. Kaltenbach researched the information contained in this section.

10. Mark Kindig contributed the basic idea contained in this section.

## CHAPTER 13

1. H. B. Karp, "Avoiding Political Pitfalls," *Management Solutions*, October 1988, p. 11.

2. "How to Win at Organizational Politics—Without Being Unethical or Sacrificing Your Self-Respect," *Research Institute Personal Report*, 1985, p. 4.

3. Stuart M. Schmidt and David Kipnis, "The Perils of Persistence," *Psychology Today*, November 1987, pp. 32–34.

4. Peter Prichard, "Project Hindered by Non-Supporters in Financial Area," Gannett News Service story, September 19, 1987.

5. "The Importance of Being Earnest About Politics," *Personal Report for the Executive*, June 1, 1987, p. 2.

6. Betsy Bauer, "You Yelled at the Boss? Apologize, Then Forget It," *USA Weekend*, November 22–24, 1985, p. 28.

7. Karen Peterson, "More and More People Find Love at the Office," Gannett News Service story, November 24, 1988.

8. "Love Conquers (Almost) All," *Personal Report for the Executive*, November 15, 1987, p. 5.

9. R. E. Quinn, "Attraction and Harassment: Dynamics of Sexual Politics in the Workplace," *Organizational Dynamics*, Fall 1984.

10. Most of the items in this list are from Gloria Welles, "Love in the Office," *USA Weekend*, April 24–26, 1987, p. 10.


## CHAPTER 14

1. Michael M. Lombardo and Morgan W. McCall, Jr., "Coping with an Intolerable Boss," Center for Creative Leadership, Special Report, January 1984, pp. 1–4.

2. Eric Flamholtz, "The Dr. Jekyll and Mr. Hyde Game Managers Play," *Management Solutions*, November 1987, pp. 4–9.

3. Henry Rogers, *The One-Hat Solution* (New York: St. Martin's Press, 1986).

4. Mardy Grothe and Peter Wylie, *Problem Bosses: Who They Are and How to Deal with Them* (New York: Fawcett Crest, 1987), p. 229.

5. Grothe and Wylie, *Problem Bosses*, p. 251.

6. Grothe and Wylie, *Problem Bosses*, p. 256.

7. Don Michael McDonald, "How to Tell Your Boss He's Wrong," *Management Solutions*, December 1988, pp. 3–9.

8. "Too Many Bosses," *Personal Report for the Executive*, p. 3.

9. *How to Win at Organizational Politics —Without Being Unethical or Sacrificing Your Self-Respect* (New York: The Research Institute of America, January 1985), pp. 7–8.

10. As reported in *Mastering Office Politics: How to Finesse Your Way to Success* (New York: National Institute of Business Management, 1988), p. 46.

11. *Mastering Office Politics*, p. 50.

12. *Mastering Office Politics,* p. 50.

13. *Mastering Office Politics,* p. 72.

14. *Mastering Office Politics,* p. 73.

15. The first three quirks are from Michael E. Cavanagh, "Personalities at Work," *Personnel Journal,* March 1985, pp. 55–64.

16. Shane R. Premaus and R. Wayne Mondy, "Problem Employees: The Cynic," *Management Solutions,* October 1986, pp. 14–16.

17. Len Leritz, "Negotiating with Problem People," *Working Woman,* October 1988, pp. 35–38.

# CHAPTER 15

1. Steve Fishman, "Facing up to Failure," *Success,* November 1984, p. 53.

2. Charles Garfield, "Peak Performers," *Success,* February 1986, p. 54.

3. Leah Rosch, "Turning a Career Crisis into a Chance for Growth," *Working Woman,* September 1988, p. 118.

4. Julius Segal, *Winning Life's Toughest Battles* (New York: Ivy Books/ Ballantine, 1986), pp. 34–39.

5. John Harstock, "Trouble in 'Oasis'," Rochester *Democrat and Chronicle,* September 1, 1985; updated with interview conducted January 15, 1989.

6. These results are described in Tara Bradely-Steck, "Looking at the Bright Side Has Rewards," Associated Press story, June 21, 1987.

7. "Beyond Positive Thinking: New Facts About Ancient Wisdom," *Success,* December 1988, p. 32.

8. Martha T. Moore, "DeLorean Plans New Venture Into Car Making," Gannett News Service story, June 6, 1987.

9. "Beyond Positive Thinking," p. 34.

10. Case researched by Daniel Rosenblatt.

11. Case researched by Nancy Harrell.

12. Andrew J. DuBrin, *Human Relations: A Job Oriented Approach,* 4th ed. (Englewood Cliffs, NJ: Prentice-Hall, 1988), p. 234; Ramon J. Aldag and Timothy M. Stearns, *Management* (Cincinnati: South Western Publishing Co., 1987), p. 801.

# CHAPTER 16

1. "Executives Fear That Mergers Will Take Their Jobs," Associated Press story, September 11, 1989.

2. Quoted in "Crisis Management to the Rescue," *Personal Report for the Executive,* October 15, 1985, p. 7.

3. Rick Gladstone, "Urge to Merge Could Leave a Debt Wasteland," Associated Press story, January 1, 1989.

4. Case researched by Jamie M. Denard.

5. "Unbearable New Boss," *Executive Strategies,* October 3, 1989, p. 2.

6. Several of the suggestions are based on "Postmerger Survival," *Executive Strategies,* August 22, 1989, p. 4.

7. "Keep the Boss Informed in Lean and Mean Times," *Personal Report for the Executive,* March 15, 1989, pp. 2–3.

8. Toni Apgar (editor), *Mastering Office Politics: How to Finesse Your Way to Success* (New York: National Institute of Business Management 1988), p. 66.

9. Case researched by Linda Smith.

10. Case researched by Susan B. Wilson.

11. Case researched by Leon Kentner.

12. Paul Hirsch, *Pack Your Own Parachute* (Reading, MA: Addison-Wesley, 1987). The summary and analysis of Hirsch's work cited here is based on a book review by John W. Slocum, appearing in *Academy of Management EXECUTIVE,* February 1988, pp. 75–76.

## CHAPTER 17

1. Judith Briles, *Woman to Woman: From Sabotage to Support* (New York: New Horizon Press, 1988).

2. Marilyn Moats Kennedy, *Office Politics: Seizing Power, Wielding Clout* (New York: Warner Books, 1980), pp. 78–83.

3. Caroline Donnelly, "Warding Off the Office Politician," *Money,* December 1976, p. 71.

4. *How to Win at Organizational Politics—Without Being Unethical or Sacrificing Your Self-Respect,* Research Institute of America special report, January 1985, pp. 13–14.

5. "Help, I'm Being Networked!" *Personal Report for the Executive,* March 1, 1989, pp. 7–8.

6. "The 'Bypass' Boss," *Personal Report for the Executive,* August 1, 1988, p. 3.

7. "The 'Bypass' Boss," *Personal Report for the Executive,* p. 3.

8. *How to Win at Organizational Politics,* pp. 16–17.

## CHAPTER 18

1. Abraham Zaleznik, "Real Work," *Harvard Business Review,* January–February 1989, p. 63.

2. "Bush Seeks Federal Raises," The Associated Press and Gannett News Service story, July 8, 1989.

3. Zaleznik, "Real Work," pp. 57–76; Marilyn Moats Kennedy, *Office Politics* (New York: Warner Books, 1980), pp. 293–296.

4. Robert P. Vecchio, *Organizational Behavior* (Hinsdale, IL: The Dryden Press, 1988), p. 272.

5. Edward J. Hegarty, *How to Succeed in Company Politics,* second edition (New York: McGraw-Hill, 1976), pp. 189–190.

6. Vecchio, *Organizational Behavior,* p. 272.

# INDEX

Abrasive behavior, 118–19
Acceptance desire, 14–15
Administrative assistants and
  secretaries, 36, 120
Administrative task handling, 111–12
Administrative vs. technical skill, 225
Adversity handling, 255–75
  acceptance of problem, 257–58
  analysis of setback, 261–63
  climbing back to power, 269–73
  comeback planning, 261–64
  constructive action for, 264
  cooperation with victor, 269
  creative problem solving for, 263
  criticism handling, 260–61
  demotion handling, 271
  enemy self-destruction, 272–73
  entrepreneurship as solution, 273–74
  emotional problems involved, 257
  good news signals, 274–75
  job slippage and, 264–65
  optimism for healing, 266
  perception of failure, 258
  personalizing setbacks, 258
  positive thinking and, 265–66
  recognize being dumped, 255–56
  reputation regaining, 270
  rhythm reestablishment, 263–64
  rock bottom feeling, 260
  support network and, 259–60
  visualization for, 268
Advice giving, 207–208
Advice seeking, 92–93

Agenda control, 156
Alcohol consumption, 69
Alliance formation, 124, 143
"Always" technique, 248
Antidotes to office politics, 295–322
  coalition and clique breakup, 316–17
  compatible team formation, 317–18
  conflict resolution for, 318–19
  direct talk, 315–316
  favorable example at top, 321–22
  good jobs for, 320
  gossip and rumor handling, 316
  objective measures for, 313–15
  praise and criticism analysis, 319–20
  questionable information handling,
    320–321
  truth telling, 315
Appearance and success, 125
Attention getting, 252
Attention seeking, 253

Back stabbing, 195–96
Bad news trumpeting, 86
Bad mouthing antidote, 302–303
Bandwagon technique, 247–48
Bias-free language, 80
Biased reporting of facts, 248–49
Big talk, 75–76
Blackmail, 200
Bloopers of boss, 56
Blunder file, 198–99
Board of directors manipulation, 156–57

331

Body language, 182–83
Boss contact, 67–68
Boss promotion, 177
Boss relationship, 42–47, 53–70, 234–45,
    280–85 (see also Higher-ups)
  accomplishment sharing, 63–64
  analyzing boss's objectives, 54–55
  assisting in personal life, 69–70
  blooper covering, 56–57
  chemistry analysis, 54
  compliments and, 63
  confrontation with, 245
  contact with boss, 67–68
  corporate takeover and, 280–82
  criticism handling, 57
  deadline respecting, 57
  deference tactic, 57
  dirty work and, 66
  helping with success, 58
  incompetent boss handling, 236–38
  intolerable boss handling, 288–41
  keeping boss informed, 283–85
  language analysis, 55–56
  listening approach, 55
  loyalty factor, 66–67
  matching boss's style, 59–61
  mood cycles and, 46–47
  objective analysis, 54–55
  personal life assistance, 68–70
  presenting alternatives to boss, 64
  reading vs. listening analysis, 55
  rewards for, 62
  romance avoidance, 70
  role confusion, 70
  self-protection avoidance, 61–62
  sharing accomplishments with, 63–64
  sizing up boss, 42–47
  skill teaching to, 65
  small talk and, 68
  solving boss's problems, 65–66
  subordinate vs. friend role, 70
  style matching with, 59–61
  support of, 56–57
  understanding the boss, 54–56
  upstaging avoidance, 62
Breakfast club, 164
Brezezinski, Zbigniew, 144
Bridge burning, 228–29
Business meals, 41
Buzzword use, 189
Bypassing the boss, 216–17, 241


Career advancement methods, 159–79
  analysis of competition, 173–74
  avoiding tainted members, 178
  breadth importance, 171–72

  breakfast club for, 164
  commitment to job, 161
  diary method for, 168
  eternal virtue display, 160–61
  faith in self, 179
  helping boss get promoted, 177
  image projection, 161–62
  indispensability vs. dispensability,
    175–77
  lateral move for, 172
  luck factor, 177–78
  mentor technique, 167–68
  networking for, 163–64
  path for advancement, 170–73
  perform consistently, 160
  recognition folder for, 169
  refusal of promotion, 173
  right style for, 161
  risk taking for, 169–70
  self-control of emotion, 160–61
  self-promotion for, 168
  sponsor technique, 166–67
  stick with best talent, 159–60
  swim against tide, 174–75
  undesirable assignment and, 172–73
  visibility for, 164–66
Career breadth, 171–72
Causes of office politics, 1–17
  acceptance hunger, 14–15
  belief in external forces, 13–14
  competitive work environment, 3–4
  emotional insecurity, 12–13
  external locus of control, 13
  goof off desire, 17
  imitation of power holders, 6–8
  Machiavellian tendencies, 11–12
  power craving, 9–11
  scarcity of resources, 2–3
  self-interest, 15–17
  subjective performance standards, 4–6
  unclear job definitions, 6
  win-lose philosophy, 8
Character assassination, 198
Chemistry with boss, 54
Children and office politics, 87–88
Coalitions, 145, 316
Cliques, 316
Comeback planning, 261–64
Commitment to job, 161
Committee work, 137–38
Communication channels, 310–11
Company politician, 30–31
Competition analysis, 173–74
Competition hanging, 206
Competitive work environment, 3–4
Compliments, 99–100
Composure retaining, 74, 282

Confidant role, 184–85
Confrontation method, 296–97; 305–307
Connection publicizing, 119
Constructive action, 264
Constructive chaos, 148–49
Consultant handling, 282–83
Control of vital information, 183–84
Coopatations, 145
Corporate culture, 282
Corporate princes and princesses, 234
Corporate takeovers and mergers, 277–94
   competition with former employer, 290–93
   corporate culture fit, 282
   crisis mentality for, 278
   financial consequences of requests, 285
   free-agent manager, 293–94
   information-gap handling, 284–85
   internal job campaign, 289–90
   lean and mean style, 288
   networking for, 294
   organizational strategy, 282
   relationship with new boss, 280–82
   resource obtaining, 283–84
   selling qualifications to new firm, 278–80
   selling self to consultant, 282
   "Them vs. us" mentality, 286
Cost underestimation, 208–209
Courtesy to co-workers, 116–19
Cover-up avoidance, 283
Co-worker relationships, 89–107
   advice asking and, 92–93
   compliments and, 99
   despised and hated behavior, 105–106
   diplomacy and, 97–98
   exchanging favors and, 93–94
   expression of interest in, 94–95
   fire extinguishing and, 98
   gossip and, 96–97
   improving their social life, 104–105
   Innocent lamb technique, 107
   office parties and picnic for, 102–104
   supply handling and, 101
   reservoir of good feelings and, 95–96
   team play and, 90–92
   touching base with, 92
Creative problem solving, 263
Credit sharing, 90–91
Credit stealing, 196–97, 244–45, 299
Crisis management, 278
Criticism handling, 57, 260–61, 309–309

Deadline respecting, 479
Decisive engagement, 147–48

Defensive tactics, 295–312
   bad-mouth handling, 302–303
   circulating ideas for credit, 299
   clamping down on competitors, 299–303
   communication unclogging, 310–11
   confronting bypasser, 305–307
   confronting game players, 296–97
   criticism handling, 309–309
   dirty-trick expose', 297
   documentation importance, 311–12
   expose' imperviousness, 312
   naysayer handling, 307–310
   networking abuse, 303–305
   personalization avoidance, 298
Deference toward boss, 57
DeLorean, John Z., 266–67
Demotion handling, 271
Department watchdog, 205–206
Deposing powerholder, 49–50, 157–58
Development of team members, 158
Devious tactics, 195–214
   back stabbing, 195–96
   blackmail, 200
   blunder file on enemies, 198–99
   character assassination, 198
   competition hanging, 206
   cost underestimation, 208–209
   cover up of truth, 207
   credit stealing, 196–97
   department watchdog technique, 205–206
   die-on-the vine technique, 209
   discrediting rival, 197–99
   divide and rule, 199
   embrace and demolish, 196
   exclusion from meetings, 205–206
   frontal assault, 201–202
   game playing, 212–214
   gun to management's head, 211
   interdepartmental mail trick, 210–11
   job elimination of ingrates, 201
   meaningless job technique, 202
   misery for rivals, 201–203
   negative reference threat, 206–207
   removal by crediting, 204
   romantic involvement faking, 211–12
   smokescreen, 205
   snubbing rival, 203
   spying on rivals, 199–200
   superfluous work creation, 203
   transfer to poor location, 202
   self-serving advice, 207
   sham support, 208
   smiling tactic, 214
   triggering rival's flare-up, 209–10
Diary of special projects, 169

Difficult person handling, 233–53
  attention getting, 252
  attention seeking, 251
  boss bypass, 241
  compassion for boss, 236
  communication session, 238
  confrontation with boss, 245
  criticism of boss, 242–43
  dissenters, 249
  doing boss's work, 237–38
  fortifying boss's weaknesses, 236–37
  incompetent boss handling, 236–38
  indirect feedback technique, 239–40
  ineffective bosses, 236–38
  informing boss of wrongness,
     242–43
  intolerable boss, 238–41
  Jekyll and Hyde boss, 236
  manipulators, 247–49
  multiple boss problems, 243–44
  negotiating tactics, 251–52
  personality quirks, 250–51
  recognition and affection giving, 253
  receiving deserved credit, 244–45
  psychological sabotage, 248
  selling self to other managers, 238
  sniper neutralization, 249–50
  verbal bullies, 245–46
Die-on-the-vine technique, 209
Diplomacy, 97–98
Direct talk, 315–16
Dirty-trick expose', 297
Dirty work, 87
Disclosure of questionable information,
   320–21
Discrediting rival, 197–99
Disloyalty to organization, 217
Dispensable worker, 176
Dissenters, 249
Divide and rule, 199
Documentation for defense, 311–12
Downward relationships, 109–22
  abrasiveness toward, 118–19
  administrative assistants and, 120
  connection publicizing, 119
  courtesy and, 116–19
  customer-treatment toward, 109
  fighting for worker demands, 111
  listening approach, 114
  old ties and, 121–22
  participative management and, 114
  prompt action for, 111–12
  recognition giving, 112–14
  sensitivity to relationships, 115–16
  refreshment serving, 120–21
Dumping of employees, 227–28,
   255–57

Embrace or demolish, 196
Emotional insecurity and politics, 12–13
Emotional self-control, 74–75
Emotional turmoil handling, 257
Enemy elimination, 196, 204, 206
Entrepreneurial characteristics, 273-74
Eternal virtues, 160–61
Ethical code, 243
Etiquette and manners, 78–80
Exchange of favors, 93–94
Expense account chiseling, 229–30
Expertise in job, 124
Expose' avoidance, 312
External locus of control, 13–14

Failure perception, 258
Faith in self, 179
Favorable executive model, 321–22
Feedback to difficult people, 239–41
*Federal Political Personnel Manual*, 206
Feldstein, Martin S., 86
Fire fighting, 98
Fond beliefs, 224–227
Free-agent manager, 293–94
Frontal assault, 201–202

Games, 212–14
Goals and objectives of boss, 42
Goals of office politics, 34
Good news bearing, 190–92
Good news signals, 274–75
Goofing off, 29
Gossip and rumors, 96, 316
Grazing, (vs. meals), 81
Graveyard in organization, 270–71
Gripe airing, 285
Gun-to-head technique, 211

Hands-on-approach, 87
Headhunter handling, 294
Higher-up relationships, 71–88
  bad-news trumpeting, 86–87
  befriending higher-up's child, 87–88
  big talk use, 75–76
  business etiquette for, 78–80
  coolness appearance, 74–75
  contacting new office holders, 78
  dirty-hands stunt, 87
  identification with management,
     73–74
  Japanese-style behavior for, 83–84
  laugh at jokes for, 83
  luncheons for, 80–81
  meetings conduct, 71–73
  name recognition for, 81–82

president's pet project and, 85–86
show of interest in firm, 76–77
small talk avoidance, 75–76
social ladder climbing and, 84–85
Hirsch, Paul, 293
Home court technique, 136
Humor on the job, 83, 91

Image projection, 161–62
Imitation of power holders, 6–8
Impression methods, 50–51
Impressive questions, 189–90
Indirect questions, 39
Indispensable worker, 176
Ineffective boss, 234–236
Information gap, 284–285
Information hub technique, 186–87
Information management, 181–94
  advance information and, 185–86
  body language use, 182–83
  buzz-word technique, 189
  confidante role, 194–85
  control of vital information, 183–84
  counsel taking, 192–93
  cultivating sources, 181–82
  good news bearing, 190–92
  impressive questions, 189–90
  information hub technique, 186–87
  initial power technique, 192
  inside information use, 181
  secret keeping, 193–94
  stockpiling ideas, 187–89
  worthwhile information technique,
    185
Information sharing, 91–92
Ingrate job elimination, 201
Initial power technique, 192
Innocent lamb, 31, 106
Innocent-appearing questions, 37
Innovation strategy, 309
Interest in others, 94–95
Internal job campaign, 289
Intolerable boss, 238–41
IOU technique, 132–33

Japanese work ethic, 83
Jekyll and Hyde boss, 236
Job description, 6
Job hunting (internal), 289–90
Job performance consistency, 160
Job slippage, 264–65
Job title and power, 138–39

Kennedy, Marilyn Moats, 40
Key people access, 135–36

Kissinger, Henry, 124, 144
Kravis, Henry, 278

Lateral move advantage, 172
Laughing at boss's jokes, 83
Lean department, 157
Lean and mean organization, 288–89
Lean and mean style, 157–58
Letters of congratulation, 78
Line vs. staff jobs, 127–28
Listening for relationship building, 114
Loose tongue, 220
Loyalty, 66–67
Luck management, 177–78
Lunch politics, 80–81
Lying for gain, 207, 208–209

Machiavelli, Niccolo, 155
Machiavellianism, 11–12, 30
Manipulators, 247–49
Manners and etiquette, 78–80
Marry into power, 139–40
Mass, concentrated offensive, 146–47
Meetings, 71–73
Mentor finding, 167–68
Meyers, Gerald, 278
Mobility in career, 294
Money game, 135
Mood cycles, 46–47
Multiple boss problems, 243–44

Naysayer handling, 221–23, 307–308
Negotiating with difficult people,
  251–52
Nepotism, 48
Networking, 129–30, 163–64, 294,
  303–304
  abuses of, 303–304
  career advancement and, 163–64
  effective use of, 163–64
  for handling takeovers, 294
  lateral type, 304–305
  for power grabbing, 129–30
  suggestions for, 129–31
Nixon, Richard M, 144

Objective performance measures, 4–5,
  313–314
Office party or picnic, 102–104
Office politician categories, 30–32
  company politician, 30–31
  innocent lamb, 31–32
  Machiavellian, 30
  straight arrow, 31
  survivalist, 31

Office Politics (*see also* most topics)
  adversity handling, 255–75
  boss relationships, 53–88
  career boosting, 159–79
  cost-effectiveness of, 34–36
  control of, 313–22
  co-worker relationships, 89–107
  defense against, 295–312
  devious tactics, 195–214
  downward relationship, 109–22
  higher-up relationships, 71–88
  inevitability of, 1–17
  information management, 181–94
  lower-ranking people, and, 109–22
  mergers and acquisition implications,
    277–294
  need for, Preface, 1–2
  planning and goal setting for, 33–52
  political tactic analysis, 19–32
  planning campaign for, 33–52
  power acquisition tactic, 123–158
  reasons for (causes), 1–17
  risk assessment, 35
  test for, 19–32
  upward relationships, 53–88
Oldtimers and information, 38–39
Office romance, 70, 211–12, 230–31
Optimism and healing, 266
Organization charts, 38
Outside expert technique, 153–54


Panic behavior, 258–59
Participative management, 110, 114
Path for success, 170–73
Performance consistency, 160
Personal life of boss, 68–70
Personality quirk, 250–51
Personalization of problems, 258
Personal style, 161
Pest behavior, 219–220
Planning political campaign, 33–52
  boss relationship analysis, 42–47
  cost-effectiveness aspect, 34–36
  dispute avoidance, 562
  goals for, 34
  indirect question technique, 39
  information sources for, 36–42
  need for, 33
  nepotism analysis, 48
  organization chart and, 38
  person-organization fit, 39–40
  political tactics analysis, 47–51
  political war avoidance, 52
  power analysis for, 40–42
  questioning technique, 37, 39
  risk assessment and, 35

  sizing up boss, 42–47
  status symbol analysis, 51–52
Political blunders (or taboos), 215–232
  bridge burning, 228–29
  bypassing the boss, 216
  complaining about former boss, 218
  deviating from custom, 227
  disloyalty to the organization, 217–18
  dumping important person, 227–28
  expense account chiseling, 229–30
  fond belief challenging, 224–27
  indiscreet office romance, 230–232
  loose tongue, 220–21
  naysaying, 221–23
  pestiness, 220
  refusing top management, 223–24
  surprising the boss, 215–16
  yelling at the boss, 230
Political enemies, 43
Political Orientation Questionnaire,
  19–32
Political tactic analysis, 47–48, 49–51
Political wars, 52
Person-organization fit, 39–40
Positive thinking, 265–68
Power, 9–11, 19–32, 36–42, 123, 269–73
  analysis of, 36–42
  climbing back into, 269–73
  craving for, 9–11
  identification of players, 36–42
  nature of, 123
  test for tendencies, 19–32
Power-grabbing tactics, 123–58
  acting and looking powerful, 125–26
  agenda controlling, 156
  alliances with powerholders, 124, 143
  bidding by others, 133
  bit-by-bit approach, 126
  coalitions for, 145–46
  committee assignments and, 137–38
  compliant board of directors for,
    156–57
  constructive chaos for, 148–49
  control of resources, 142–43
  cooptations for, 145–46
  controlling access to key people,
    135–36
  cultivation of superiors, 143–44
  decisive engagement for, 147–48, 231
  expertise development, 124
  feared rather than loved, 155
  future assignment control, 131–32
  groom princes and princesses, 149–50
  home-court advantage, 136–37
  IOU technique, 132–33
  job activities for, 157
  key problems focus, 151

lean department for, 157
line responsibility for, 127–28
maintaining a mystique for, 150–51
mass, concentrated offensive for, 156–57
marrying into power, 139–40
meeting boss's expectations, 158
money game, 135
networking for, 129–31
outside expert technique, 153–54
power game, 154–55
proof of prowess method, 155–56
quick-showing method, 128–29
retention of power, 157–58
rule bending for, 151–52
self-titling technique, 138–39
seniority approach, 137
talent developer, 158
tender power, 133–34
thinking and winning big, 141–42
transfer of competition, 158
Power craving, 121
Power game, 154–55
President's pet project, 85–86
Pressure handling, 74–75
Probing for information, 182
Problem acceptance, 257–58
Promotion refusal, 173
Prowess display, 155–56
Psychological sabotage, 248

Quick showing method, 128–29
Quitting appropriateness, 178–79

Recognition folder, 169
Recognition giving, 112–14, 253
Refreshments for political gain, 120–21
Refusing top management, 223–24
Resource control, 283–85
Results vs. politics, 50
Retaliation against politics, 35
Risk assessment, 38
Risk taking, 169–70
Rival handling, 196, 197–207, 209–10
Robbins, Steven, 8, 35
Rock-bottom feeling, 260

Scarcity of resources, 2–3
Sculley, John, 56
Secretaries and administrative assistants, 36, 120

Secrets in organizations, 193–94
Self-control of emotions, 160
Self-defeating behavior, 52
Self-interest and politics, 15–17
Self-promotion, 168
Self-protective behavior, 61–62
Self-serving advice, 207–208
Seniority for power, 137
Sensitivity to relationships, 115–16
Setup questions, 72
Sham support technique, 208
Skills update, 169
Small talk, 68
Smokescreen, 205
Snipers, 249–50
Social ladder climbing, 84–85
Social life and job, 68–70
Sponsor for career, 166–67
Spying techniques, 199–200
Status symbols, 18
Sticking with best talents, 159–60
Stockpiling ideas, 187–88
Strategie of organizations, 282
Styles of boss, 59–61, 234–36
Supplies handling, 101
Support the boss, 56–57
Support network, 259–60
Surprising the boss, 215–16
Survivalist, 31
Swimming against the tide, 174–75

Tainted organization members, 178–79
Team formation, 317–18
Team play, 90–92
Technofright, 148
Telephone courtesy, 117
Tender power, 133–34
Test for political tendencies, 19–32
"Them vs. us" mentality, 286
Threats, manipulative type, 248
Truth telling, 315–16

Unconventional career path, 174–75
Undesirable assignment, 172
Upstaging boss, 62

Verbal bullies, 245–46
Visibility in career, 164–66
Visualization technique, 268

Win-lose organizational philosophy, 8